Navigating
Materialistic Minefields

BY THE SAME AUTHOR

Finding the Real You
Nurturing a Healthy Human Spirit in the Young

Navigating
Materialistic Minefields

Viv Bartlett

GEORGE RONALD • OXFORD

George Ronald, Publisher
Oxford
www.grbooks.com

A catalogue record for this book is available
from the British Library

ISBN 978-0-85398-653-9

CONTENTS

PART 3: Understanding Spiritual Processes and Systems

This book is dedicated to my three children,

Fleur, Leila and Kalim.

Each, in different ways, have experienced testing times. I hope that through this dedication they will, in some small measure at least, feel my love for them and my admiration for their spiritual accomplishments.

ACKNOWLEDGEMENTS

I was introduced to the teachings of Bahá'u'lláh and His successor, 'Abdu'l-Bahá, as a young man at a time I called myself an atheist. The influence of those followers of Bahá'u'lláh I met, mostly in the Cardiff and surrounding areas of South Wales, had a profound influence upon me when I had no idea of the transforming spiritual force of love, kindness, patience and acceptance they emanated. Over a year I read some of the Bahá'í literature, attended many Bahá'í talks and took part in many discussions in homely 'fireside' meetings. Through these souls I became more and more attracted to the three central figures of the Faith – the Báb, Bahá'u'lláh and 'Abdu'l-Bahá – and their teachings.

My limited atheistic worldview and dislike of what I thought was 'religion', gradually faded in favour of the soul-stirring, beatific vision of love for God they brought, and the goal of global citizenship founded on love for all, harmony and a just system of governance.

From deep within my soul, I want to record that I am eternally grateful to these followers of Bahá'u'lláh and acknowledge that without their love, care and wisdom I would not have been capable of writing this book.

Foremost among them is my mother, Doreen Bartlett, who, after her 14-year-old son, Peter, accidentally electrocuted himself, felt compelled to search for answers to the many questions as to why this would happen to an innocent child. A young girl, Rita Bridge, who later became my wife, joined her in this search. Their yearning for truth, deeper understandings and reality increased over time and drew me into their compulsion. They have both since passed into the spiritual world, where I hope they can now gather the intense feelings of love I have for them.

Upon this platform so many, too many to mention by name, contributed to my understanding of the Bahá'í Writings and have indirectly enabled this book to be written. Special mention must be made of some illustrious Bahá'ís such as Bill Sears, John Robarts, Adib Taherzadeh and Betty Reed along with many members of the United Kingdom National Spiritual Assembly, who moved my heart and soul and set it on fire with a deep and longing desire to forever serve Bahá'u'lláh. Among their many gifts of the spirit, they inspired me to study the authoritative expositions of the Holy Writings by Shoghi Effendi, the appointed Guardian of the Bahá'í Faith, which had a profound effect my intellectual capacities. It enabled me to move from a place of failing to pass the simple school-leaving English examination at the age of 15 to that of gaining an honours degree in design and education as a mature student and to make a little contribution to Bahá'í literature. I mention this to impress upon anyone who defines their rational faculties as 'low' in comparison to those whose natal intelligence is 'high', that a door, wider than earth and heaven, has now been opened to humanity for the exponential growth of all the gifts God has deposited in our souls.

Some chapters include descriptions of scientific endeavours, for which I have received help from experts in their field. In particular, I want to thank Dr Graham Walker, prominent head and neck surgeon, for his assistance in Chapter 5 on the brain, along with Peter Hume (OBE), retired Head of the Herefordshire Psychology Services, for his help in Chapter 18 on the emergence of maturity. I want to stress, however, that any shortcomings in these chapters should be attributed to me rather than these kind souls. The late Brian David, a good friend for over three decades, a well-wisher of humanity and altruistic in temperament but ill-disposed to what he considered 'religion', engaged in many discussions. He represented the manifold views of those who have hearts of gold, but regard 'religion' as a major contribution to world problems. Many thanks to Brian for all our conversations as he provided a significant stimulus for this book. Some time was spent holidaying with family members Riaz and Ulrike Missaghian in their beautiful home in Spain, where I was able to focus for extended periods on writing without the responsibilities back home. Many thanks to them. Also, I am extremely grateful to May Hofman who edited this work and guided me to reconsider some aspects and discard superfluous text only tangentially pertinent to its theme.

Finally, I began writing this book a few years before my beloved wife, Rita, passed away through cancer. When she could, and with great magnanimity, she willingly heard my 'ramblings' of early texts and was unstintingly encouraging. I am eternally grateful for this and hope that through her self-sacrificing nature, her radiant spirit will be felt by all those who engage with this work. Lastly, I want to record my immense gratitude for the help of my daughter, Fleur, whose timely intervention when I had become seriously ill and was tenuously holding on to life led to an operation that saved my life. Consequently I recovered and was able to bring this book to its conclusion.

1

DAYS OF SEARCH

The death of my brother, Peter, smashed into our family like a comet hitting the earth. And the repercussions of that tragic event are still operating over fifty years later. That happened in 1960 and I was 15 years of age; my brother had just turned 14.

Cycling home from work one bright summer's day I saw a crowd of neighbours gathered around our home in Ely, Cardiff. They were not looking happy, a few tried to prepare me for the shock to come. I raced inside the house, my mother was being comforted by friends and my brother, Peter, was on the floor receiving artificial respiration. This was not the modern, mouth to mouth resuscitation, but the arms being pulled over the head and placed back by the side. Peter was breathing, or so it seemed to me, as I heard air coming out of him; but this was just the result of the respiration process. I thought he was joking around again as he often did this, to my annoyance, and I remember getting angry with him. But it was no practical joke this time. The ambulance arrived, and he was taken to hospital to get better, so I thought. So, I broke through the arms of the neighbours who tried to restrain me and cycled like mad, trying to catch the ambulance. Peter was dead even before respiration was applied, which was confirmed at the hospital after I arrived. I don't know how I got back home, everything went black and hazy. I do remember my father arriving home from work and being told the shattering news that his son was dead. He 'lost' it, couldn't process the information; it took four men to hold him down as he started to rip a door off its hinges.

How did Peter die? Well, I had some part in it, although an innocent part. After leaving school at fifteen and a half I started work in preparation to become an apprentice engineer in a firm of manufacturers of pulley blocks and lifting tackle. The factory was situated in Bute Street, Cardiff, more popularly known as 'Tiger Bay'. One of the very first mosques in the UK was in the same street as the factory, but I didn't know anything about diversity in those days, even though a cross-section of the world had gathered in Tiger Bay.

My wages at this time were £1 and 15 shillings a week, a huge increase over the money I had earned as a paper-boy. I gave my mother, Doreen, all my wages, out of which she gave me back the 15 shillings (75 pence in today's money). I was anxious to spend this money, so I bought a reel-to-reel tape recorder and happily spent hours recording songs from the radio. The start of the 1960s exploded with new music, new stars, new freedoms, and I was excited to be part of it. Peter, like many younger brothers, wanted what his older brother had. So, after school one day, he took my tape recorder onto the garden lawn, fixed up his home-made extension lead and happily lay down to listen to the songs. Mother was talking to a neighbour while sitting on the garden wall. Then it happened; one of the two bare wires making up the extension lead disconnected. How this happened is still the subject of speculation. Peter leaned over on the humid grass, caught hold of the live wire and instantly electrocuted himself. Massive internal brain damage, we were told; death by misadventure, the coroner's verdict. The most heart-rending thing is that my mother saw this horrific scene – her son being electrocuted in front of her eyes and she could do nothing to save him! Coincidentally, the song he was listening to on the recorder was 'Halfway to Paradise', a popular song by pop star Billy Fury at the time.

Dad's response to Peter's death was to switch off to enquiry, watch TV and automatically assume there is no God, because if there was how could He let such a terrible thing happen to an innocent child? His heart was broken, his whole world collapsed even though he had four remaining children. Dad (George) eventually carried on in life, but he never did recover, nor did it prompt him to search for answers to the tragedy. Strange indeed, that although our family, working class as it was, had, through Dad and Mam's hard work, many of the material benefits of living, yet these were of little benefit to any of us to be able to cope with the calamity of Peter's sudden and violent death. Black grief descended and enveloped every thought, every hope, every aspiration!

Mam's response to Peter's death was so different to Dad's. She had to find out 'why'! Is there a purpose and meaning to life beyond just physically existing? If we are here today, gone tomorrow, why is life so transient? Why do innocent children die while some adults who commit heinous crimes live long? Perhaps in the back of Mam's mind was the thought that Peter's death should not be in vain. She certainly set about searching for answers with a driven sense of mission. Over years she visited many churches, beliefs and religious societies. From time to time I accompanied her, learned quite a bit, but developed a distinct dislike of clergymen, not necessarily the person, but the 'office' they represented. I remember wanting to ask questions during their sermons, but centuries of passivity by the congregation and a general air of superiority by the clergy rendered the atmosphere impermeable. So, I sat there quiet, but fuming inside. In some cases, I would approach the minister after the sermon and ask questions, particularly where science and religion seemed to clash. Responses ranged from polite snubs to beliefs that deny the existence of a rational human being, never mind an intelligent Creator. Mam, however, was not there to argue, an activity I was beginning to enjoy – she was a seeker and truth was her goal.

The most pressing question after Peter's death, however, was 'is there life after death?' Quite naturally we wanted to know that if there is life after death, could we contact Peter? Together we visited several Spiritualist Churches in the Cardiff area and were spoken to by some clairvoyants who assured us that Peter was alive on the 'other side' and wanted us to know that he was 'doing well'. The sessions we attended were centred on mediums providing personal messages from loved ones in the next life with the aim of proving that life is continuous. Most sessions included hymn singing and a little talk based upon some teachings in the Bible that supported their belief that life does carry on after the physical body dies; teachings such as when Christ disclosed that 'In my Father's house are many mansions: if it were not so, I would have told you. I go to prepare a place for you.'[1] We were approached a few times to train as clairvoyants but never took up their invitations.

Absent healing, or healing by psychic means, was of great interest to us so we visited the Spiritualist Centre in London for a sitting with Harry Edwards, a well-known Spiritualist healer. Edwards, apparently, was told by a medium when he was a young man that he was 'born to heal' but he had no idea as to what was meant by a 'healer', so 'he joined a development circle to see what would happen'. He quickly developed trance mediumship and then attempted absent healing. After years of successfully healing many people, Edwards brought to attention the fact that divine laws are universal and not contained in denominational rituals or performances of the Church of England, Methodists, Congregationalists or for that matter Spiritualists. The power of healing according to this divine law 'is our common heritage,' he pointed out. 'This universal power would fail those who 'try and control it by ritual or set performances of any kind . . .'[2]

I liked the concept of divine laws being universal and not restricted to narrow-minded religious ownership. It reminded me of physical laws discovered by eminent scientists and great thinkers through the centuries. In fact, at about this time I reflected a lot on the first law of thermodynamics which states that energy under normal conditions cannot be created or destroyed, simply transformed from one type of energy to another. And the reason I gave a lot of thought to this was because I felt there could be a link between this law and proof of life after death – a pressing subject since the death of my brother. So, following this law of thermodynamics, I asked that if kinetic energy, for instance, can be transformed into electrical energy which can be transformed into heat energy, and so on, where goes the energy that powers a human being when he dies? Of course, the physical body decomposes becoming incapable of using any energy, but when alive, what makes the body do things like kick a football, play a piano, shake a hand, sing a song, chew and swallow? These activities are done voluntarily – they are thought about and then they are done. This being the case, the mental faculties use thoughts and the thoughts use the body to do what it has thought. I reasoned then, that thought must be an energy – yes, different from physical energy – electrical, mechanical and the like, but nonetheless an energy that moves the body's muscles to perform what it thinks. By applying the first law of thermodynamics to this process I concluded that thought, although non-physical, is an energy which is also capable of transformation when a person dies, and that transformation must be into another form of energy in a non-physical world. I was content to conclude this reasoning by assuming that the non-physical world was the next life, life after physical death, where the thinker would carry on existing. Since these thoughts years ago, it is wonderful to note that science has developed the ability to produce a prosthetic limb and connect it to an electronic chip, which is controlled by thoughts that actually move the artificial limb. Who would have imagined decades ago that thoughts would control inanimate objects?

One of the most exciting discoveries at this stage of search was to come across the works of Robert James Lees (1849–1931), a renowned spiritualist who claimed he knew the identity of 'Jack the Ripper' who was responsible for the murders in Whitechapel in 1888. Our interest as to who was the Whitechapel murderer was only tangential to our absorption in a trilogy of the several books he wrote – *Through the Mists*, *The Life Elysian* and *The Gate of Heaven*, written between 1898 and 1931. He claimed that his books were dictated to him by a soul who had died trying to save a little street urchin from being run over by a horse and carriage, in Victorian England. The books are therefore subtitled *Leaves from the Autobiography of a Soul in Paradise*. And this subtitle sums up the content of the books, as we are taken by this soul in 'paradise' on his journeys of discovery and progress in the world beyond.[3]

Whether or not we accepted the premise on which the books were written was not important to us. What was important is that we were introduced to possibilities of circumstances and laws operating in the next life, that seemed entirely feasible and related to our growing understandings of spiritual truths found in all the sacred scriptures.

Some years earlier, around 1963, my mother had been joined in her search by a young girl my own age – seventeen. This girl came to my house in Cardiff to visit my mother, as they had met a while earlier to speak about 'spiritual things' and wanted to continue their conversation. I asked her name, to which she replied, 'Rita Bridge, and just because I'm a Bridge does not mean you can walk over me!' Then I asked her what her sign of the zodiac was (along with Mam I was heavily involved in astrology at that time). She wanted to know what for, and I replied, 'So as I can know how to handle you!' Not initial comments from either of us to start a healthy relationship, but which led to our marriage seven years later!

Rita's passion for seeking truth matched my mother's and although there was a large age difference, they teamed up to find answers to life's existential questions. As for me, although I was not a seeker, nonetheless I was receptive to new thoughts and enlarged understanding – so I tagged along with them. Rita's story about how she came to team up with my mother is very interesting. She was the eldest of three girls who were all brought up by their mother to be devoted Catholics. Her mother, a strict Roman Catholic from Ireland, had come over from Dublin in the War years and married a worker in a smelting and casting foundry in Cardiff where she obtained work. Surprisingly, he was an ardent Communist, committed to atheism, and you would not think such a union would work. But, as they say, 'love conquers all' and he promised his wife that he would not interfere if she wanted to raise the children as Catholics. He kept his word. So, all three daughters, as well as attending Catholic schools, attended Mass on Sunday, observed all the holy days and church requirements with a passion, prayed ardently and submitted to the authority of the priesthood. She told us that there were never any arguments in her home about religion, as her mother and father respected each other's stance. After entering adolescence, however, some of the teachings of the church began to weigh heavy on her. Rita's atheist father, she was told, was destined for hell, which was described as being in an oven and roasted forever. Rita loved her mother and father dearly but could not understand why her kind, devoted, moral and principled father deserved such an appalling fate. He actively taught his children aspects of social justice, abhorred racial prejudice and felt the only way to raise the suffering poor out of grinding poverty was by the Communist system. To her he was the best father a child could have, and being conflicted about her beliefs she sought relief in asking many questions; perchance someone, anyone, could answer them.

Triggered by concerns about her father destined for 'hell', a host of religious queries invaded her stable Catholic world. Why were there no dinosaurs in the Adam and Eve story? Why did God love only Catholics? Why were many Catholic countries poor while the church was very rich? Are all the other religions false? Her mother was not able to answer these questions and referred her to their local priest. On several occasions she was recommended by the priest to recite two 'Our Fathers' and three 'Hail Mary's'. This didn't work, so she asked her friends and they got fed up with her asking. Then she asked her neighbours, who were equally as perplexed as her. Then she would start the cycle again – mother, priest, friends, neighbours. For years no answers came until eventually she was so confused that she used to visit the Catholic Cathedral in Cardiff and pray, 'Oh God I'm an atheist, please help me.' One of the many profound statements of Christ fortunately kept her going, for she was assured:

> Ask, and it shall be given you; seek, and ye shall find; knock, and it shall be opened unto you: For every one that asketh receiveth; and he that seeketh findeth; and to him that knock-eth it shall be opened.[4]

Then, after many questions unsuccessfully answered by her friend's mother, she was told that her husband's 'dancing partner up the club may be able to help'. This dancing partner was my mother, and so they met. Life was never the same after for this young girl, nor for me, in more ways than one. Not only did my mother answer her questions with efficiency, blunt directness and cutting logic, but this young girl eventually married me and became Mrs Rita Bartlett.

Now we were a team of three, Mam and Rita – ardent seekers, and me – developing an interest in esoteric and religious questions but maintaining a safe distance from any type of commitment. Alongside our quest into Spiritualism and after our excursions into the more established churches including the evangelical ones, we spread out, visiting such beliefs as the Quakers, Unitarians, Rosicrucians, Theosophists; Islam, Sufism, Buddhism, Hinduism and the works of individuals such as Swedenborg, Gurdjieff, Ouspensky, Krishnamurti and Carl Jung. And all of these were interspersed with great interest in astrology, palmistry, native American prophecies, tarot cards, Ouija boards – anything of the occult or the mystical we could get our hands on.

Of particular interest was Sufism centred on the secret, esoteric, symbolism aspects of religion, of which some are related to one's search for a mystical love reunion with Allah (which we learnt was the Arabic name for God). We loved reading some of the poems and works of mystics such as Farid al-Din 'Attar and Jalal ad-Din Rumi. One story, loved by the Sufis from Persian and Arabian lore, was of particular interest – the story of Leili and Majnun. The story centres on Majnun searching for his beloved Leili from whom he was separated. In despair and driven to look anywhere perchance he may find his heart's desire, he was seen: 'Sifting the dusty highway, grain by grain.' Asked why he was searching in the dust, when: 'The dust will not conceal this precious pearl,' Majnun replied; 'I search in every place; Who knows where I may glimpse her lovely face.'

This story was significant to my mother and Rita as they were like Majnun – insatiable, crazy in their search. Later I found out that Majnun means someone who is crazy – but the type of craziness when one is in love. They were like Majnun, looking anywhere to find answers that would satisfy their yearning for truth or pure spirit, which is what Leili represents. As for me, this story only gradually affected me, as the sacred symbolism of yearning to be united with pure spirit (God) took root in my heart. The story of Leili and Majnun has since affected me in such a deep way that one of our daughters is named Leila.

It is difficult to imagine the degree of intensity that went into these explorations. Rita used to visit my mother as often as she could, sometimes every evening of the week. Dad would get frustrated, as this incessant talking interfered with his watching Bonanza, or the like, on TV, so they voluntarily banished themselves to talking in the kitchen. I would join in their conversations, listen to what they were reading at the time and when possible try to find flaws in the teachings under examination. Rita filled exercise books of passages from the scriptures or teachings that particularly caught her eye. Mam would frequently read from the book she was currently studying and often left them lying around the house open on pages she wanted me to read – a cunning way of drawing me into what was her life's passion.

An intense interest in astrology left an indelible impression upon me, although I have long since moved away from it as being a remnant of a superstitious age. Nonetheless, it introduced me to another concept of diversity. Differences of colour, religion, class and the like were quite apparent, but differences in the way people thought, how their views were formed and how they approached life was, to me, challenging. I held the view, quite confidently, that if others thought differently to me then there must be something wrong with their thinking. Perhaps this is a phase all young people pass through if they are to become mature people? Suffice it to say that astrology helped me realize that there are at least eleven different types of people whose thinking could be different from mine but equally valid.

One of the most illuminating books we read throughout the years of relentless search was *In Tune with the Infinite* by Ralph Waldo Trine, first published in 1897. Here was a book bursting with universal understandings and written in a way that was accessible to all. Trine, who passed away in 1958, was an American philosopher, mystic, teacher and author of several books. *In Tune with the Infinite* became a bestseller with over two million sold worldwide. With all our ramblings through various beliefs and teachings we were acquiring the distinct feeling that there were pearls of knowledge and wisdom everywhere. Trine expressed this feeling in tangible words that thrilled us. He wrote:

> There is a golden thread that runs through every religion in the world. There is a golden thread that runs through the lives and the teachings of all the prophets, seers, sages, and saviors in the world's history, through the lives of all men and women of truly great and lasting power. All that they have ever done or attained to has been done in full accordance with law.[5]

Although my mother, Rita and I were appalled at the divisions many so-called religious people had made, thinking themselves as 'saved' and going to heaven and those of a different belief as 'damned' and destined for hell, Trine illumined our awareness that the essence of every religion is the same.

> This is the great fundamental principle of the universal religion upon which all can agree. This is the great fact that is

permanent. There are many things in regard to which all cannot agree. These are the things that are personal, non-essential, and so as time passes they gradually fall away. One who doesn't grasp this great truth, a Christian, for example, asks 'But was not Christ inspired?' Yes, but He was not the only one inspired. Another who is a Buddhist asks, 'Was not Buddha inspired?' Yes, but he was not the only one inspired. A Christian asks, 'But is not our Christian Bible inspired?' Yes, but there are other inspired scriptures. A Brahmin or a Buddhist asks, 'Are not the Vedas inspired?' Yes, but there are other inspired sacred books. Your error is not in believing that your particular scriptures are inspired, but your error is – and you show your absurdly laughable limitations by it – your inability to see that other scriptures are also inspired . . . Let us not be among the number so dwarfed, so limited, so bigoted as to think that the Infinite God has revealed Himself to one little handful of His children, in one little quarter of the globe, and at one particular period of time. This is not the pattern by which God works . . . In reality, however, there is but one religion.[6]

The search became more intense as time went by; but I remained an atheist, although the direction had been set, a yearning had been awakened for the things of the 'spirit'. Over time I became aware that there are two distinctive ways of thinking that lead to differences in how we humans perceive 'reality'. One way is through a 'materialistic' lens, the other is through a 'spiritual' lens. The difference between the two is not small, it is so vast that every aspect of life is affected.

Perhaps at this point it is helpful to make a distinction between the two ways the term 'materialism' is used in this book. Firstly, there is philosophical reductive materialism, which is understood to be

the view that all facts (including facts about the human mind and will and the course of human history) are causally dependent upon physical processes, or even reducible to them.[7]

Secondly, materialism is used in terms of values, as an

> attitude that physical well-being and worldly possessions constitute the greatest good and highest value in life . . . Concern for possessions or material wealth and physical comfort, especially to the exclusion of spiritual or intellectual pursuits.[8]

I would also add that materialistic behaviour can be seen in those seeking a higher position of authority, status or power for selfish ends. Hopefully you will be able to discriminate between the ways I use the word 'materialism' throughout the book – philosophical or lifestyle/attitudes. For instance, atheism proceeds from a materialistic philosophy, as do all the materialistic assumptions described in Part One.

It is now necessary to explain my understanding of the word 'spiritual'. I am aware that this word is a 'turn-off' for many, for a variety of reasons. For me it carried a lot of negative baggage, maybe because it has been hijacked over the ages by many unscrupulous, misinformed, prejudiced, superstitious and ambitious religious leaders, as well as literal interpretations of holy scriptures that are, evidently, symbolic in nature. 'Spiritual' had come to be linked, one could say shackled, to tradition emanating from church, mosque, synagogue and temple.

But since the 1960s a movement away from this has seen more and more people considering themselves as 'spiritual but not religious' (SBNR), mainly as a reaction to 'organized religion'. 'Spiritual', these days, 'has often become associated with the interior <u>life</u> of the individual, placing an emphasis upon the <u>well-being</u> of the mind-body-spirit . . .'[9] Certainly this was the path that my Mother, Rita and I were on; no restraints on our freedom to search for truth and reality were countenanced. This flow into SBNR has been identified as a 'new age' movement with an increasing number trying to find peace of mind, body and spirit in, for instance, neo-paganism, wiccan, shamanic, meditation or mindfulness practices. In hindsight our interest in SBNR concepts were of passing value, even as are stepping-stones to much larger realizations; this will become apparent as you read further.

So, I do not identify 'spiritual' with the rituals, traditions and ceremonies of the historic religions, nor do I link it with SBNR movements. A dictionary definition of 'spiritual' is 'pertaining to the spirit or soul, as distinguished from the physical nature'.[10] Many, however, have not given thought as to whether the soul or human spirit actually exists, although it has become popular to refer to the human spirit as a manner of speech, akin to when someone speaks of 'the spirit of a party', or 'community spirit'. A later chapter examines this question in more detail. Suffice it to say that the human spirit is essentially what makes a human being human. In fact, Professor Viktor Frankl, a survivor of Auschwitz and other Nazi death camps, stressed that 'the "spiritual" is what is human in man', and further points out that he uses the word 'spiritual' 'without any religious connotations'.[11]

Following from this, we need to ask: what is it that pertains to the spirit or soul of a human being that makes it spiritual? We know, for instance, that it is the education of man's intelligence, inherent as latent potential, that develops the intellect. Similarly, for the soul to become spiritual it needs education, but a special type – an educational influence that illumines it to manifest all those gifts inherent in the soul or human spirit, in selfless service to others. This book is about such an influence and how, when welcomed into one's life, it overcomes obstacles for the human spirit, enabling it to function in a way that brings personal and social happiness, well-being and progress.

However, it must be understood from the start, my motive in writing these pages is not to try to convert anyone to a specific belief. My objective is to stimulate a process of independent thinking, unfettered by the materialism of our time. Unfortunately, much of secular, materialistic worldviews and lifestyle choices have penetrated society's thinking about 'reality', as an indoctrination process, and we don't even know it is happening. It is comparable to the worldview and behaviours generated by superstitious religion during medieval times that indoctrinated the masses then. How the pendulum has swung from one extreme to the other!

What follows then, is my thought process, illumined by a spiritual educational influence that can be likened to the influence of sunshine on a seed, necessary for its growth. In another metaphor, it is an internal journey of the spirit, travelled over years, that enabled me to navigate around apparently insurmountable, dangerous obstacles that I have called 'materialistic minefields'. It was not easy, as my root belief was atheistic, and my reasoning was that a major cause of world problems was religion.

2

BECOMING AWARE

It became evident to me that I was living in two worlds and pulled in two different directions. On the one hand a materialistic, hedonistic lifestyle had started and on the other an emerging attraction to spiritual realities and a spiritual lifestyle. Tension between the two had to be resolved by a decision about what path in life I would take. In a sense, I was experiencing what is expressed in a wise story about this conflict, which hails from First Nation American wisdom:

> One evening an old Cherokee told his grandson about a battle that goes on inside people. He said, 'My son, the battle is between two "wolves" inside us all. One is Evil. It is anger, envy, jealousy, sorrow, regret, greed, arrogance, self-pity, guilt, resentment, inferiority, lies, false pride, superiority, and ego.
>
> The other is good. It is joy, peace, love, hope, serenity, humility, kindness, benevolence, empathy, generosity, truth, compassion and faith.'
>
> The grandson thought about it for a minute, and then asked his grandfather: 'Which wolf wins?'
>
> The old Cherokee simply replied, 'The one you feed.'

I was incapable of making such a profound decision, until I had a dream that changed everything. I dreamt I was a child of about seven or eight years old walking around a huge department store. At the level I was on, many people could be seen interested in the furniture, light fittings, carpets and the like, which were on display. My eye caught sight of a small booth in the corner of the store, to which I was attracted. In the booth was a majestic, kindly looking man, with snowy white hair and beard. He was very friendly, so I presented myself in front of him, after which he greeted me and asked whether I would be interested in him showing me something important. With a little child's curiosity, I said, 'yes please'. Then he started manipulating various objects on the counter of the booth and had them all floating around at his will. He said: 'This is what you can do if you believe.' I was very intrigued indeed. At this point the man asked whether I was interested in seeing more, to which I readily assented. Then he changed from one shape to another and very fast – as fast as the flicker in the old black and white movies. He went through many animal shapes and many human shapes, but all the time his eyes stayed the same, very kind, loving and focused on my response. Then he stopped changing, came back to his original form and stated: 'This is what you can do if you love.' I was totally amazed, blown away! And then I woke up.

As we sometimes do upon being wakened by a significant dream, I started reflecting on it. 'Why was nobody else interested in this very unusual man who could do all these astounding things?' I thought. 'Why were they only interested in the furniture and carpets?' 'Why was I a little boy in the dream?' 'What did the dream mean, that is, if it had a meaning?' Among many things I had learnt quite early on was that if a dream is powerful enough to wake me up and is remembered, it is then a significant dream and has meaning. It had the ring of being a 'truthful' dream even though its meaning remained a mystery.

Some things were clear, but it was only later that I became aware of an overall interpretation of the dream. This greatly helped me to make a decision to renounce my hedonistic ways, to make every effort, very faltering for several years, to follow the path of spiritual realities. If you are still with me at the end of this book, I will share with you a meaning of the dream; of course, please feel free to make your own sense of it. What path of spiritual realities to follow became very clear after the dream.

Although I did not realize it at the time, I have since become aware of the great benefits of 'meaning' to one's life that can fill the emptiness of an existential vacuum. Viktor Frankl, author of over thirty books focused on the importance of 'meaning' in life, writes in his book, *Man's Search for Ultimate Meaning*:

> despair over the apparent meaninglessness of life constitutes a human achievement rather than a neurosis. After all, no animal cares whether or not its existence has a meaning. It is the prerogative of man to quest for a meaning to his life, and also to question whether such meaning exists. This quest is a manifestation of intellectual sincerity and honesty. In particular, it is the challenge of youth to question the meaning of life. However, the courage to question should be matched by patience. People should be patient enough to wait until, sooner or later, meaning dawns on them. This is what they should do, rather than taking their lives – or taking refuge in drugs.[1]

Frankl also quotes Einstein in his book as stating; 'The man who regards his life as meaningless is not merely unhappy but hardly fit for life.'[2]

What my Mother, Rita and I learnt in our efforts to find 'meaning' is that there is a lot of truth and reality in many of the paths mentioned previously and in others not so much, but they did tickle the imagination. I also became aware that I was not attracted to 'meaning' in personal salvation beliefs that promised happiness, but were silent, incoherent or outdated regarding specific, realistic understandings for the transformation of the world – a world so totally different from that which gave birth to the ancient religions. Yet another realization was that I was to avoid the sweet shop, 'pick and mix' mentality, in my search for reality. In other words, I had noticed that so desperate had many people become to find a sense of well-being that they mixed together a variety of teachings, spiritual and pseudo-spiritual, to suit their taste, like one would mix different sweets in a sweet shop. In effect some souls, although seemingly seeking 'reality and truth', only accept teachings that conform with their personal views and opinions. Perhaps life had become so painful, confused or mean-ingless for some that any relief in beliefs offering an escape were acceptable. Sadly, but understandably, they were constructing their own version of reality and would flee from anything that challenged their syncretic construct or escapist beliefs. Finally, I decided that the Teachings of Bahá'u'lláh, Founder of the Bahá'í Faith, satisfied not only my own yearning for 'reality', 'truth', and 'meaning' but also the yearnings of my Mother and Rita. That was over fifty years ago, during which time I have not entertained a single regret for becoming a member of the world-wide com-munity of Bahá'ís – many tests but no regrets. I did not know it at the time, but Benjamin Franklin had an insightful word to say on the value system we choose. He wrote:

> We stand at the crossroads, each minute, each hour, each day, making choices. We choose the thoughts we allow ourselves to think, the passions we allow ourselves to feel, and the actions we allow ourselves to perform. Each choice is made in the context of whatever value system we've selected to govern our lives. In selecting that value system, we are in a very real way, making the most important choice we will ever make.[3]

A little while after the dream, I recognized from photographs the majestic figure in the booth to be 'Abdu'l-Bahá, son of Bahá'u'lláh – one of the three centrally important figures of the Bahá'í Faith. I did struggle, however, with an overall interpretation of my dream, but one thing was clear from the start: the people in the department store were not interested in the majestic person in the corner booth. Their attraction was centred on all the material items on display. I later concluded that they were not inclined to the things of the 'spirit', but only had eyes for the things of the material world – sofas, chairs, carpets and the like – they were consumers. Years later I realized that the dream in the department store, with all its items, and the booth with the majestic person, was a symbolism of a testing ground to separate those who were interested in the realities of the spirit from those who were materialistically minded.

To make this differentiation is not to say that those on a spiritual path are good and those who are consumers are bad. All of us are consumers to a greater or lesser degree. What does become evident, eventually, is that consequences are determined, good or bad, upon the choices we make for our belief system. And let us acknowledge from the start that 'consumer culture' is an aspect of 'materialism's gospel of human betterment'[4] even if no conscious decision has been made to follow a materialistic value system. This will happen by default, without any effort. It is as simple as this, metaphorically: if you don't plant flowers in your garden, by default and without any effort, all you'll get are weeds. This materialistic value system shouts very loudly for converts; its method is to beguile unsuspecting individuals that the way to 'happiness', 'fulfilment' and 'success' is attained by acquiring the physical things of life. When we consider that the media and advertising aim at seducing our resistance to the things on sale we can easily recognize that, on all sides, the bells of the 'church of materialism' are constantly peeling. By such means, and a plethora of other ways, have the mass of mankind been indoctrinated into materialistic perspectives of reality. A significant insight on this point reveals:

Fathered by nineteenth century European thought, acquiring enormous influence through the achievements of American capitalist culture, and endowed by Marxism with the counterfeit credibility peculiar to that system, materialism emerged full-blown in the second half of the twentieth century as a kind of universal religion claiming absolute authority in both the personal and social life of humankind.[5]

Materialism's promise of happiness is that it will be achieved by owning a more beautiful house, a better car, wallowing in luxury, becoming wealthy, gaining higher qualifications, acquiring and updating gadgets, devotion to fashion, plastic surgery, Botox and/ or body-building regimes to beautify oneself and keep looking young. Along with seeking a higher position of authority, status and power in society for selfish ends, even gaining a partner and children are viewed as material acquisitions. All this is at a dreadful price: 'Whether as world-view or simple appetite,' we are informed, 'materialism's effect is to leach out of human motivation – and even interest – the spiritual impulses that distinguish the rational soul.'[6]

Materialism's roots have gone deep into the soul of man, creating an insatiable desire to 'acquire' and 'consume'. Consumerism underpins 'individualism', a dangerous atomization of community, enervating most attempts at working together in unity and harmony for the well-being of all.

> No aspect of contemporary civilization is more directly challenged by Bahá'u'lláh's conception of the future than is the prevailing cult of individualism, which has spread to most parts of the world. Nurtured by such cultural forces as political ideology, academic elitism, and a consumer economy, the 'pursuit of happiness' has given rise to an aggressive and almost boundless sense of personal entitlement.[7]

Materialism promotes 'destination addiction', a habit-forming 'drug' with the result that happiness is deferred until the next acquisition is achieved, such as a promotion at work. This 'drug' is peddled by parents and teachers from an early age, deluding the young with a vision of happiness formed around examination success and the like. How many instances have there been of young people worrying to the point of sickness, self-harming and even suicide, because of feelings of worthlessness, especially during stressful times such as when studying for exams? Of course, it is necessary to provide encouragement and a supportive environment for students to do their best in exams, but to what end? Regrettably, however, as a secondary school teacher in times past, I too have counselled adolescents to work and study hard for good exam results as the means to success. And success was spelled out in terms of a high-income job to be able to acquire better and more things – no mention of 'service'.

How many adults have devoted years of their lives to an aspiring ambition for a higher position, only to find that failure to achieve it induces feelings of anger, futility, envy and the like, leading to harmful addictive life-style choices to deaden the torment and anguish? On the other hand, of those who do manage to climb the ladder of so-called 'success', how many are really happy and tranquil, yet forced, by their 'destination addiction' to seek a yet higher position? Hence, such an addict is never content with being in the 'now'. This addiction breeds loneliness, gnawing anxieties, periods of panic, anguish, corruption in high places, a lust for ever more material things and/or status to feel secure and at peace. Alarmingly, those who prioritize the physical over the spiritual are usually ignorant of the detrimental effect of their materialistic beliefs. Where is the peace of the human spirit in these enterprises? What is left of the potential for nobility latent in every person, as regrets, disillusionment and even feelings of shame eat into the vitals of what it means to be truly human? What becomes of the human spirit which has been able, at all times and in all cultures, to serve others with love, humility and sacrifice of personal gain? Those that discern the deadly symptoms of materialism can see the altruistic potential of others eviscerated and eventually atrophied.

I had to learn that walking a spiritual path does not mean there is no place for the physical things in life, nor does it mean that life should be spent by abstracting oneself from the world as some religious orders require. At a basic level we all need the necessities of life – food, warmth, a roof over our heads, good healthcare, wholesome relationships, access to communication with others, and the chance (for most of humanity) to procreate in a loving relationship, thereby ensuring the continuance of the human race. Indeed, there are benefits in the increase of necessities in life provided they enable us to walk the spiritual path more faithfully.

Walking a spiritual path always requires courageous persistence at nurturing and activating those qualities that are distinctly human. Hence a person on this path will put great effort into becoming altruistic, loving to all without prejudice, a well-wisher of humanity, just and fair-minded, honest, trustworthy and reliable, humble, magnanimous and courteous, patient, forbearing and forgiving. The development of all these spiritual qualities is in selfless service to others, starting in the family and broadening out. It is an effort to make the shift from just being an individualistic 'consumer' to a community 'contributor'. A spiritually aware person realizes that no one would want to live in a family or community bereft of these virtuous qualities, even if they had all the wealth in the world!

Reading the Writings of Bahá'u'lláh and 'Abdu'l-Bahá has been for me as necessary as eating and drinking. It has become the 'food' for my soul. Without it there is just an empty 'hungry' feeling, a spiritual 'malnourishment'. Most of their works are edifying, illuminating, uplifting and encouraging in content and tone; however, there are also warnings. I have learnt that if we are to be sincere seekers of 'meaning', 'truth and reality' we are to 'be detached from all that are in heaven and on earth.'[8] We are warned that we will never really understand the meanings and mysteries of life or ourselves, unless we cease 'to regard the words and deeds of mortal men as a standard for the true understanding and recognition of God and His Prophets'.[9] In other words, if we just increase our understanding and knowledge of things in the physical world and are not open to spiritual influences, then those understandings, truths, and insights of the spirit will remain hidden in the heart of man.

An unwillingness to enter the spiritual path leads to wayward behaviour, in effect a contamination of the human spirit. It is a function of the spirit to absorb that which is around it – good, bad or indifferent, whether or not we are conscious of it. A cleansing process must take place, therefore, a cleansing from negative materialistic influences which involves detachment from 'all that is earthly – their ears from idle talk, their minds from vain imaginings, their hearts from worldly affections, their eyes from that which perisheth.'[10] This is required when seeking the path of truth and reality, and also continues when on the path. Much attention is to be given to developing a genuine relationship with the Prophets of God, or, as Bahá'u'lláh terms them, the Manifestations of God. Their guidance He calls the 'wine of certitude'.[11] By this means we discern truth from falsehood, and reality from constructs of our imagination. We are required to empty the cup full of our contaminated views, opinions and beliefs, to be ready for truth and reality to be poured in. If the cup is full of 'self', or, in the words frequently used by Bahá'u'lláh, 'idle fancies and vain imaginations,' how is it possible for a soul to accept anything new or challenging? In another place Bahá'u'lláh warns those who dismiss out of hand the knowledge, understandings and inner significances of the things of the spirit revealed by the Manifestations of God, 'not to reject that which they do not comprehend'.[12] How immature is one who does this!

Bahá'u'lláh also proclaims to all mankind that He has been sent to this age as a Manifestation of all the wondrous names and qualities of God, for the specific task of drawing all peoples together in one united, loving and caring family. To those who have a materialistic mindset this maybe a statement which could evoke immediate revulsion. I can understand this. Being a one-time atheist, I found any mention of special souls called 'Prophets of God' and the like, illogical and particularly off-putting. There are reasons for this, which revolve around the huge damage done to religion by interreligious wars, sectarian violence, cult movements and by ignorant, superstitious and sometimes fanatical, murderous outbreaks of violence on the part of the followers of all the historic religions. The waters of peace, love and wisdom in all the holy scriptures have been seriously muddied! Also, popular irreligious reason seems to hold that in every case when an individual declares himself a Prophet or Messenger of God, such an one is a charlatan. Again, this is understandable, given that during the over 170 years the Bahá'í Faith has been in existence there have, indeed, been many religious charlatans. Inevitably, all these types of reasons have led to an assumption that religion is a bad thing for humanity.

For those who have come to this conclusion, I ask you to retrace your steps and not make a judgement on such a hugely important issue without researching history in an unbiased and informed way. Alongside this, I would appeal to every fair-minded individual to read the works of Bahá'u'lláh and 'Abdu'l-Bahá, which provide an ocean of knowledge as a counter to the uninformed, prejudiced views and opinions floating around religious and secular society. Today, it is these great personages, Bahá'u'lláh and 'Abdu'l-Bahá, that have set out very new ways of reading history whilst providing compelling, new understandings for the existence of a Higher Power. Through their works they have forever disarmed the atheists and materialists of their 'weapons' against God and religion. They have provided for modern understandings that define religion (a Bahá'í definition of 'religion' can be found at the beginning of Chapter 8) and exalt it to its proper place as an indispensable power for the transformation of the individual and society. So, let me be clear as to the challenge in these pages, to those who dismiss 'religion' out of hand, as I did – first look into the lives of Bahá'u'lláh and 'Abdu'l-Bahá, read, at least, some their works, putting aside all prejudice and bias to do so. Then make an assessment of whether it is possible to retain atheistic beliefs and materialistic assumptions. I am sure that any fair-minded person would want to avoid the warning contained in the following statements of Bahá'u'lláh:

> They still reject the truth and have turned towards their own selfish desires.[13]

Nevertheless, if We reveal aught which, even to the extent of a needle's eye, runneth counter to their selfish ways and desires, they will disdainfully reject it.[14]

Much of what you will read in this book is about the difference between two ways of perceiving 'reality'. One way is through a 'materialistic' lens, the other is through a 'spiritual' lens, as mentioned in Chapter 1. Looking through a spiritual lens is not to deny that material reality – everything in the material universe and that which is discovered by science – is unreal or of little importance. It is of huge importance, especially when material reality is used for the betterment of humanity and in harmony with nature; it is, in fact, like one wing of a bird. The other wing is spiritual reality. When both wings work in unison then the bird of humanity can truly soar in the atmosphere of great scientific discoveries and technological innovations with a tranquil heart, and with those virtues, that some call values, such as love for all, justice, forgiveness, magnanimity, and selfless service to others that fit the needs of this age and the exigencies of this time.

Throughout this book I have referred to a variety of significant insights and arguments from the works of Bahá'u'lláh and 'Abdu'l-Bahá to navigate around the materialistic minefields that present themselves while seeking 'meaning', 'truth' and 'reality'. It is my hope that it will stimulate at least a little desire to study, without bias, these works.

To complete this chapter, you may like to reflect on the amazing insights, embodying tremendous hope for the whole of humankind, in the following passage from a work named *Who Is Writing the Future?*

Rejecting the reigning dogmas of materialism, Bahá'u'lláh asserts an opposing interpretation of the historical process. Humanity, the arrowhead of the evolution of consciousness, passes through stages analogous to the periods of infancy, childhood, and adolescence in the lives of its individual members. The journey has brought us to the threshold of our long-awaited coming of age as a unified human race. The wars, exploitation, and prejudice that have marked immature stages in the process should not be a cause of despair but a stimulus to assuming the responsibilities of collective maturity.[15]

PART ONE

NAVIGATING THE MINEFIELD OF MATERIALISTIC ASSUMPTIONS

3

MATERIALISTIC ASSUMPTION 1: THERE IS A BEGINNING OF THE UNIVERSE, WHICH OCCURRED BY CHANCE

A materialistic assumption is made when all facts depend upon and are reduced to physical causes and processes, and explanations of them. However, their veracity must be questioned. This I now attempt to do by providing a perspective, viewed through a spiritual lens, when trying to answer the question: Did the universe have a beginning and did it come into existence through chance circumstances?

Answers to these questions are of intense interest to cosmologists as well as those who are interested in cosmology. Unfortunately, many support materialistic arguments pertaining to this issue. However, these arguments are not based on facts because they are not provable by the scientific method. The scientific method requires a process – in this case, of investigation that allows the investigator to observe the universe at its beginning, or the investigator to have gathered incontrovertible material evidence, to be able to deduce that the universe came into existence by fortuitous occurrences. Even stating this, another assumption is made, that is – the universe had a beginning.

The Big Bang theory is the prevailing cosmological model for the beginning of the universe, time and space. It was first posited by George Lemaitre in 1927, coming quickly on the heels of American astronomer Edwin Hubble's discoveries that there are galaxies apart from our own Milky Way galaxy. It is theorized that the universe is expanding, not exploding, from a super dense point, smaller than an atom (a singularity), of extremely high temperature and density, some 13.8 billion years ago, as galaxies fly away from each other at an immense speed.[1] Interestingly, Bahá'u'lláh, revealing the power of God, stated about 140 years ago: 'It is in Our power, should We wish it, to enable a speck of floating dust to generate, in less than the twinkling of an eye, suns of infinite, of unimaginable splendour . . .'[2]

The Big Bang theory is tremendously sophisticated – indeed, it is supported by extensive evidence. I have no resistance to accepting its veracity and feel humbled when contemplating the painstaking, detailed work of the scientific community in producing such a wonderful cosmological model. The more difficult question to answer, however, is: what is the origin of the Big Bang, what caused it? Answers are invariably speculative, the singularity mentioned above being just one theory. There are computer-generated models that attempt this, resulting in what could be understood as something that 'ignited' or 'seeded' the Big Bang. On the other hand, Dr Alastair Gunn states:

> The Big Bang is the moment that space and time (or 'space-time') came into existence. Before the Big Bang there was no space or time. So, it is actually meaningless to ask what caused the Big Bang to happen – there was no Universe in which that cause could have existed.[3]

Even so, to make the claim that before the Big Bang there was nothing in existence – that, in fact, everything came from nothing, is an assumption that needs to be questioned. Assumptions around this abound in the form of theories but offer no proof. For the moment, they are just suppositions mostly arrived at by materialistic thought processes applied to limited collected data. Conversely, it is possible to arrive at a different conclusion to the same question by looking through the spiritual lens provided by Bahá'u'lláh and 'Abdu'l-Bahá. This is what I have attempted, maintaining the directive of the Bahá'í teachings that science and religion should go hand in hand. It is admitted, however, that this method will not prove, in the scientific sense of the word, the conclusions arrived at. What it does is to give an alternative answer to the questions 'Did the universe have a beginning, and did everything it contains, including human beings, come into existence through chance occurrences?' To be fair, this answer could also be called an assumption by those who have not accepted the authority of Bahá'u'lláh and 'Abdu'l-Bahá to speak on this issue. This does not mean their pronouncements are null and void because they come from the domain of religion, independent of scientific investigation. To counter this objection, one only has to recall that Muhammad, speaking as a mouthpiece for God, indicated the heliocentric system of our solar system centuries before Copernicus did, which was proven later by Galileo.[4]

It is generally accepted that the universe has been, and still is, evolving since its inception from the Big Bang. We can conclude, therefore, that to enable evolution to run its course, it is logical that evolution must begin from something that exists, even if we have no definite proof of the origin of the universe. From then on, the unfoldment inherent in the evolutionary process proceeds. The implication here is that evolution cannot start from non-existence. So, an acorn is the seed starting point of evolution leading to a mature oak tree. The oak tree cannot evolve to be an oak tree if there is no acorn from which it can grow. Prior to the acorn seed, there must have been an oak tree from which acorns were produced and prior to that tree, there must have been innumerable oak trees and acorns for the continuation of oak trees. Yet we know that we cannot regress indefinitely with this process, as there was a time when no oak trees existed on the planet; indeed there was no planet Earth over five billion years ago in which oak trees could grow. Now we take a huge jump back in time, some 13.8 billion years, to the Big Bang, the point that many say the universe began, triggering the evolutionary process. From the acorn seed example, the Big Bang, analogously, is the seed of the entire observable universe from which all the planets, stars and galaxies evolved.

It is now logical to ask, where did the Big Bang come from? Did it just suddenly come from nothing or was there something in existence prior to it? Could it have come from something beyond our imagination or investigation at this time? But to categorically state it came from nothing is a trite answer; it is like saying that the oak tree that came from an acorn is nowhere apparent in the acorn seed because we have no way of observing it. Inherent in the Big Bang that seeded the universe, it is logical, therefore, to assume 'something' caused the Big Bang to happen! And then we regress further with this line of enquiry to ask, what was before this 'something' and then what was before that – and so on ad infinitum. Eventually we are forced, by reasoning, to admit that which is stated above – evolution cannot start from non-existence – there must be something in existence from which evolution can proceed. On this point 'Abdu'l-Bahá states: 'the world of existence, this endless universe – has no beginning,' and that 'absolute non-existence lacks the capacity to attain to existence. If the universe were pure nothingness, existence could not have been realized.'[5]

Also, Bahá'u'lláh writes about this process, stating that there is 'a beginning that hath no beginning' and inevitably proceeds to 'the end that hath no end.'[6] In other words, the universe is 'eternal'.

These are very abstruse points to get a handle on. Even though it cannot be proven, as yet, by scientific processes, our rational faculties may come to rest on the fact that there has never been a time when there was nothing in existence. There has always been 'something', even if we have not known what that 'something' is. Similarly, there will never be a time when existence degenerates into non-existence – when nothing whatever exists.

Within the state of existing, however, we know that things

will come into and go out of being in their particular forms. A tomato, for instance, may be eaten by a man, after which it loses its existence or form as a tomato, but its elements are taken into the body, helping it maintain a different form – that of a human being. Let's take another example, that of a planet. We know that when elements came into existence after the Big Bang they coalesced over billions of years to form planets. Looking way into the future, after billions of years, the earth will be vapourized as the dying sun expands into a red giant. The earth will lose all the elements that make up its form, only to be taken up later in a different form, perhaps a transformation from matter into energy. This process of coming into and going out of being is related to the forms of all physical phenomena – the elements go on existing and are used in other forms. Hence, Bahá'u'lláh declares; 'That which hath been in existence had existed before, but not in the form thou seest today.'[7] You could call this the 'most great recycling process' or the mother of all recycling processes!

Taking this line of reasoning further, we can ask: how did every natural existing thing come into being? We must bear in mind here that every natural existing thing is fashioned after a pattern which is replicated time and time again with inherent little changes. So, for instance, the cell structure in the body of a human being is replicated over a person's life, replacing redundant cells. At first it produces a physically mature body, after which the cells do not replicate themselves exactly – mutations occur, which lead to a gradual degeneration in the body which, over years, become manifest as old age.[8]

This process of coming into existence (having life in a particular form), arriving at a point of maturity and then a gradual decline, then decomposition, leading to disintegration (death in that form), is a pattern for absolutely all existing things, whether great or small. So far science has not discovered any deviation from this, which means that it is a pattern under a universal rule, or law, of existing things. Speaking on this point 'Abdu'l-Bahá states:

As for created things, their life consists in composition, and their death is decomposition. But matter and the universal elements cannot be entirely destroyed and annihilated. No, their annihilation is merely transformation. For instance, when man dies, his body becomes dust, but it does not become absolute non-existence: It retains a mineral existence, but a transformation has taken place, and that composition has been subjected to decomposition. It is the same with the annihilation of all other beings; for existence does not become absolute non-existence, and absolute non-existence does not acquire existence.[9]

I then became interested in the answer to two questions: how did existence come into being; and why is there no deviation in the universal pattern just described? In an attempt to answer the first question, it seemed to me that if there have always been existing things, no matter what they are, then they have either come into existence by themselves through fortuitous circumstances, or there is a power or fashioner that has brought things into being. Similarly, the second question leads to two more questions: if there is an unaltered, universal pattern in all existing things, then the pattern either came into being by itself or there is a pattern-maker that has stamped its authority on existing things.

Now, we can have three possible responses to these questions. We can throw our hands in the air and exclaim, 'I don't have a clue,' or we can assume that existing things can just come into existence by themselves, or we can conclude that there is a power, a fashioner, a pattern-maker behind all existing things. I reasoned that the first response can lead to agnosticism if left alone, the second response leads to a materialistic approach to thinking, and the third response opens the door to spiritual thinking.

For agnostics, there is an urgency to come to some conclusion on matters like this, not to 'sit on the fence', as to continue to do so results in spiritual stagnation. Decide one way or the other. The following biblical injunction reveals the reason for this

– 'So then because thou art lukewarm, and neither cold nor hot, I will spew thee out of my mouth.'[10] This can be understood as a warning whose implications require a deeper analysis. In the interests of not straying from the main theme of this chapter, it will have to wait for another time.

Those who have concluded that existence has come into being by chance must ask some more searching questions. First, to bring anything into existence requires a conscious will to do so. So, we may ask, do the physical things throughout the universe have a conscious will to bring themselves into existence? Does the sun, for instance, if it is to come from non-existence, make a decision to come into existence as a sun? Does a tree make a decision to become a tree or a camel make a decision to become a camel? If the answer to these questions is 'yes' then we attribute to the sun the tree and the camel the power to make decisions before they come into existence – which, of course, is an impossibility. How can any non-existing thing make any decisions at all if it is non-existent? Further, we know that in all nature, in all-natural existing things, there is no power to make decisions. The sun in all its magnificence, the tree with all its benefits to the planet, the camel with all the help it has given to humanity, had no choice other than to be what they are. Therefore, we conclude that they have no conscious will, nor the power of choice to bring themselves into existence, or to be other than what they are. 'Abdu'l-Bahá underlines this point:

> The sun itself with all its majesty is so subservient to nature that it hath no will of its own and cannot deviate a hair's-breadth from the laws thereof. In like manner all other beings, whether of the mineral, the vegetable or the animal world, cannot deviate from the laws of nature, nay, all are the slaves thereof.[11]

Now we investigate the last possibility, that existence came into being through a power, a fashioner, a pattern-maker. Such abilities demand the facilities of conscious will, the power of choice and the power to bring things into existence – and to keep doing so. Let's take this last point first – there must be a power to not only to bring things into existence but to keep doing so. When we observe the universe, it just keeps on going, replicating the pattern outlined above for all existing things. You would think that sometime during this process, it would run out of energy and come to a grinding halt, after which there would be no existence of anything at all. As yet, this has not happened. Such an observation is in line with the scientific principle of entropy, as Craig Loehle explains:

> Entropy is a principle of physics which posits that disorganised states are more likely to exist than are organised states, and that energy must be expended to move from a disorganised to an organised state. Anyone with small children knows the vanishingly small probability that the result of their play will be a neat and well organised house. In a closed system complete disorder is the ultimate, most likely state. Only with constant input of energy can a complex system be maintained. Our bodies require food (energy) constantly, for example, to maintain themselves. The same is true for any complex structure.[12]

An examination of this principle reveals that the supply of energy must be external to the system, to move it from a disorganized state to an organized one and maintain it as such. After all, the complex, organized system of the human body does not produce within the system its own energy (food); no, this energy comes from outside the system. Similarly, the energy needed to maintain the existence of the complex system we call the universe does not come from within the system; if it did, then the 'entropy principle' would not hold. Therefore, we conclude that the energy is supplied by a power which is continually poured into existence by the source of that power. That power, we can further conclude, also enables change to happen within and between all existing things. Change, 'Abdu'l-Bahá states, 'is a necessary quality and an essential attribute of this world, and of time and place'.[13] We normally call this type of change 'evolution'; it is the application of a law in the universe which directs everything to move, usually over great periods of time with innumerable stages of development, to higher levels of perfection or, as noted before, to maturity. In religious terminology the energy or power mentioned is called 'Spirit'.

This fashioner or pattern-maker, must, if existence has no beginning and no end, also have no beginning and no end. All we can say here is that because fashioned things have always existed then there must have always been a fashioner in existence. Also, this fashioner must always have had the power to energize and maintain existence. However, there is a great difference between the fashioner and that which is fashioned. That which is fashioned, we can conclude, is dependent for its existence on its fashioner, just as a chair is dependent on its maker for its existence. Therefore, the fashioner is an 'absolute' existence, whereas that which is fashioned is a dependent existence and therefore termed a 'contingent' existence.

The Buddha explains this concept in these terms:

There is an Unborn, Unoriginated, Uncreated, Unformed. If there were not this Unborn, this Unoriginated, this Uncreated, this Unformed . . . the originated, the created, the formed, would not be possible.[14]

It is quite logical really, if there is an Uncreated, it pre-supposes that which is created, from which all creation is brought into being; if there is an Unoriginated, it presupposes that which is originated, from which all origination is brought into being; if there is an Unborn it presupposes that which is born, from which all birth is brought into being. This a wonderful ontological argument of Buddha for the existence of a fashioner or pattern-maker.

'Abdu'l-Bahá was asked: 'What is the nature of the connection
. . . between the Absolute and the Inaccessible One and all other
beings?' He replied: 'The connection . . . is that of the originator
and the originated . . . of the craftsman and his handiwork.'[15]

Traditionally this source of power, the fashioner, the pattern-
maker has been called 'God', but, unfortunately, this name has
been choked with the thorns and brambles of superstitious religious doctrine and therefore does not appeal to a large section of
society. But why limit ourselves to just one name, 'God' when
there are so many more that can appeal to our many construc-
tions or perspectives of reality?

Nevertheless, let's take this point further by examining the
relationship between the Absolute and the contingent, the Uncreated and the created. Can a painting, for instance, exist without a
painter? And here is another point: has the painting any faculty to
know anything at all about the painter|? Can a book exist without
an author? And again, has the book any faculty to know anything
at all about its author? Can a human being exist without a fashioner? And still yet again, has a human being any faculty to know
anything at all about its fashioner? These points are taken up
more thoroughly in another chapter. But as Julio Savi writes: 'To
maintain that evolution is not just the outcome of chance, but is
moved by an Intelligent Being Who guides it, does not belong
– as the Bahá'í texts explain it – to the realms of tales and myth,
but to the domains of reason.'[16] He quotes a previous author,
Guy Murchie, who relates the following humorous story about
a teleological argument concerning a Fashioner, a Patternmaker:

> Charles Boyle, the fourth Earl of Orrery, who flourished in
> southern Ireland early in the eighteenth century – and of the
> theorem that bears his name. Having heard of Kepler's famous
> discovery of the laws of planetary motion and of Newton's
> recent work on gravitation, Lord Orrery had a working model
> of the solar system built inside his castle. It was an extraordi-
> nary dynamic and up-to-date piece of clockwork with orbital

hoops and a brass sun in the center plus smaller globes representing Mercury, Venus, Earth, Mars, Jupiter and Saturn slowly revolving around it, even a moon circling the Earth and four little ones going around Jupiter.

But it seems that Lord Orrery had an atheist friend who had an utterly materialistic outlook and thought of the universe as just an immense moving system of natural machinery that somehow coasts along, blindly but automatically maintaining itself without benefit of consciousness, mind or intelligence of any kind. So when the friend heard tell of Orrery's new and wonderful machine, he lost no time in going to the castle to see it. Entering the great hall where the model was in operation, the atheist's eyes widened with awe and the first question he asked Lord Orrery was: 'Where did you get this magnificent thing? Who made it?'

But Orrery, remembering previous arguments with the atheist about creation, surprised him by replying, 'Nobody made it. It just happened.'

'How could that be?' retorted the atheist, 'Surely these intricate gears and wheels couldn't create themselves. Who made them?'

Lord Orrery stood his ground, insisting that his model of the solar system had just happened by itself. Meantime, the atheist worked himself into a state of hysterical frustration. Then at last, judging the time was ripe, Orrery let him have it. 'Up to now', he declared, 'I was testing you. Now I am going to offer you a bargain. I will promise to tell you truly who made my little sun and planets down here as soon as you tell me truly Who made the infinitely bigger, more wonderful and more beautiful real sun and planets up there in the heavens.'

The atheist turned a little pale and, for the first time, began to wonder whether the Universe could really have made itself, or possibly be running all this time automatically and unguided by the slightest twinge of intelligence. And this was the origin of the Orrery Theorem which says: 'If the model of any natural system requires intelligence for its creation and its working, the real natural system requires at least as much intelligence for its own creation and working.'[17]

Because the painting, book, the universe and human beings are dependent on that which brings them into existence, we can say, as mentioned earlier, that they are contingent existences. With this in mind 'Abdu'l-Bahá asks: 'How then can the contingent conceive the Reality of the absolute?'[18] Meditation on the following words of Bahá'u'lláh on this theme will help to open the eye of spiritual discernment:

> How puny and insignificant is the evanescent drop when compared with the waves and billows of God's limitless and everlasting Ocean, and how utterly contemptible must every contingent and perishable thing appear when brought face to face with the uncreated, the unspeakable glory of the Eternal! We implore pardon of God, the All-Powerful, for them that entertain such beliefs, and give utterance to such words. Say: O people! How can a fleeting fancy compare with the Self-Subsisting, and how can the Creator be likened unto His creatures, who are but as the script of His Pen? Nay, His script excelleth all things, and is sanctified from, and immeasurably exalted above, all creatures.[19]

With the above considerations in mind we can make some observations about the existence of human beings. We, humans, are a part of existence that has been created by the Uncreated. As existence has always been in existence it is only proper to state that somewhere along the line of fashioning things the Fashioner had in mind (if mind is the right word) to create human beings, as we did not create ourselves. Whether or not human beings exist/ed somewhere else in the universe other than planet Earth since the Big Bang, or even prior to the Big Bang, maybe settled by future discovery/scientific investigation. This is an exciting prospect.

Interestingly, there are, statements in the works of Bahá'u'lláh that there are creatures on other planets. For instance, Bahá'u'lláh writes: 'Know thou that every fixed star hath its own planets, and every planet its own creatures, whose number no man can compute.'[20] It is worth noting that when Bahá'u'lláh revealed this in the late 19th century, there was no proof whatever that any other star, outside our solar system, had planets orbiting it. Proof came in 1995; since then over four thousand planets have been discovered. Long before Star Trek and the Star Wars films triggered our imagination about life on planets apart from earth, Bahá'u'lláh declared, 'Verily I say, the creation of God embraceth worlds besides this world, and creatures apart from these creatures.'[21]

Intuitively we feel that sentient beings with the gift of free will must exist on other planets in the universe, given the vastness of the universe. Whether or not such beings have the same form as human beings on earth is doubtful, as every form of existence develops in its own environment, and other planets, according to the principle of uniqueness for every created thing, will not have exactly the same environment as mother Earth. Surely it is easy to imagine conscious beings on other planets, with intellectual abilities the same as human beings, even if the outer form may be greatly different? Be that as it may, this is another line of enquiry that is beyond the scope of this book.

4

MATERIALISTIC ASSUMPTION 2: MAN IS NO MORE THAN AN INTELLIGENT ANIMAL

Another popular materialistic assumption is that because man has evolved on this planet over millions of years, he is basically an evolved animal. Put another way, man is an intelligent animal. This chapter opens an enquiry into this assumption which continues sporadically as a issue in subsequent chapters.

To state that man has gone through an evolutionary process over millions of years along with other species on the planet, is not to conclude that he is just an evolved or intelligent animal. The human body is part of nature in as much as it is made of natural elements, but a human being is so much more than nature. Similarly, we would not say that an animal, say a squirrel, is an evolved carrot because both share the characteristic of growth. An animal has instinct, the power of the physical senses and it can move around – all of these abilities are entirely absent in the vegetable. That vegetables and animals are distinct categories of existence no one would argue against. However, to assert that because a human being has a physical body with the abilities animals have, and thus conclude that humans are evolved animals, is to disregard all the wonderful characteristics that make a human being a distinct creation of the Fashioner.

'Abdu'l-Bahá offers irrefutable evidence that man is not an evolved or intelligent animal:

All created things except man are captives of nature. The stars and suns swinging through infinite space, all earthly forms of life and existence – whether mineral, vegetable or animal – come under the dominion and control of natural law. Man through scientific knowledge and power rules nature and utilizes her laws to do his bidding . . . For instance, man has brought electricity out of the plane of the invisible into the plane of the visible, harnessed and imprisoned that mysterious natural agent and made it the servant of his needs and wishes . . . Man, as it were, takes the sword out of nature's hand and with it for his sceptre of authority dominates nature itself. Nature is without the crown of human faculties and attributes. Man possesses conscious intelligence and reflection; nature does not . . . Man can seek out the mysteries latent in nature, whereas nature is not conscious of her own hidden phenomena. Man is progressive; nature is stationary, without the power of progression or retrogression. Man is endowed with ideal virtues – for example intellection, volition, faith, confession and acknowledgment of God – while nature is devoid of all these. The ideal faculties of man, including the capacity of scientific acquisition, are beyond nature's ken. These are powers whereby man is differentiated and distinguished from all other forms of life. This is the bestowal of divine idealism, the crown adorning human heads.[1]

'Abdu'l-Bahá states that man has a power above nature. Because this power is above nature it is called a 'supernatural' power. This power is known as his intellect, his rational faculties, and with this power he is able to make choices in life and has the will or volition to carry out his choices. For instance, he sees that a river flows in a certain direction and has no will or volition to change its course. But for a specific reason, say irrigation of the land, he chooses to change the course of the river. Not only does he have the volition to do this, but he also invents the tools to do so. Animals do not have these powers except in a very rudimentary way.

Of course, animals have undergone physical changes over the millions of years of evolution on the planet, the same as humans have, but where is proof that certain animals are potential human beings just waiting to evolve? Darwin's theory of evolution stimulated a search for the link between man and animal, but it was never found – hence it has been left dangling as the 'missing link'. Surely, if some animals evolve into humans, this must be a process that is still ongoing; it must be a continuous process? This being the case, why do we not, with all our scientific apparatus, detect that process in play at this moment? If this process of animal to man has not come to an abrupt end sometime in the past, we should be able to see a whole range of behaviours from animal graded to human. If the process has abruptly ended, why, and where is evidence for it? As this is not so, we are compelled to accept that humans are a distinct species from animals. Animals are the captives of nature, which governs their activities through instinct. Compare their lack of intellectual development with that of man, who has created civilizations and now sends some of his kind into space and is starting to explore the universe. That is why 'Abdu'l-Bahá, in his statement above, writes: 'Man is progressive; nature is stationary, without the power of progression or retrogression.'

Yet another characteristic present in human beings, but entirely absent in nature, is that humans have the ability to act in virtuous ways. A nugget of gold, for instance, has no understanding of the virtue of 'hope'; a potato has no ability to act wisely, a lion will never develop the virtue of 'forgiveness', a crocodile will never choose to sacrifice a meal for other crocodiles. Further, if say, a bacterium causes a severe illness in a human being we do not attribute blame to it, because we know that because it has no choice other than to act according to its nature. Similarly, if a poisonous snake strikes a human being, we do not attribute blame to it. However, if a human being poisons another, we consider it blameworthy. Why is this? Because a human has choice of behaviour. Animals have no choice other than to behave in a predetermined way. How different humans are to animals! And no matter how biologically, metabolically or DNA similar some animals are with man, none have made the step of developing a conscience. Further, no animal at any time has reverenced a higher power with love and gratitude, a higher power that they can't see, hear, feel, taste or smell; a Being for which humans are willing to transform their lives for the better, and even suffer martyrdom rather than recant their faith in such a Being when pressed to do so, as many early Christians, Muslims and Bahá'ís have done.

Part of the problem related to humans being thought of as simply more advanced animals is the ever-present tendency to anthropomorphize life forms that are not human. It is a characteristic observed in children, for instance, when playing with dolls. When a child engages in a conversation with a doll, she might ask it, 'What is making you sad?' Then she may answer for the doll, 'It's because you have not given me a cuddle.' The child in this case has attributed to the doll human characteristics. The same can be observed when adults talk to their pets, attributing to them all manner of human qualities. Further, we may listen to well-known presenters of wildlife and natural history who explain many actions of animals in terms of human behaviour, to appreciate that they have not let go of the childish characteristic of anthropomorphizing. To behave in human ways, say to control anger or act kindly, requires thought processes that activate the will to do so. Animals have no such thought process, they only have instinct. Animals behave in animal ways, humans in human ways – there is a huge difference. When all these points are considered we can conclude, in the words of 'Abdu'l-Bahá:

> Notwithstanding the gift of this supernatural power, it is most amazing that materialists still consider themselves within the bonds and captivity of nature. The truth is that God has endowed man with virtues, powers and ideal faculties of which nature is entirely bereft and by which man is

elevated, distinguished and superior. We must thank God for these bestowals, for these powers He has given us, for this crown He has placed upon our heads.[2]

5

MATERIALISTIC ASSUMPTION 3: MAN'S RATIONAL FACULTIES ARE THE PRODUCT OF HIS BRAIN

The study of the brain is an achievement of the intelligence of man that has far-reaching possibilities. Weighing about 1.3kg, this very complex organ has the potential of functioning way beyond what we now know. But there are differences in understanding the source of man's rational faculties.

Those who view human beings through a materialistic lens have concluded that all rational faculties – thinking, comprehending, imagining and memorizing – are the product of the brain along with free will, the ability to dream and near-death experiences. Neuroscience, a relatively new field of study, has underlined this assumption. The British Neuroscience Association states:

> Neuroscience is the study of the brain and nervous system in both humans and non-human animals, and in both health and disease...
>
> The brain is responsible for our thoughts, mood, emotions and intelligence, as well as our physical movement, breathing, heart rate and sleep. In short, it makes us who we are and facilitates almost every aspect of what it means to be alive.[1]

Thus, *humans* fit into the same category as *animals* because they have similar biological brain functions to animals. The assumption that the brain, *by itself,* however, 'is responsible for our thoughts, moods, emotions and intelligence', needs to be questioned. Trying to navigate this particular materialistic 'minefield', I continued to draw on the insights of Bahá'u'lláh and 'Abdu'l-Bahá, to provide a spiritual lens through which their vision on this issue could be considered alongside science.

In my attempt at doing so I would like to start by offering an analogy. At the beginning of the Industrial Revolution, all the machines in a factory, say a cotton mill, were linked by belt to one central belt drive machine, powered by a waterwheel and later by steam. With the invention and application of electric motors, each machine could be separated from a central drive, to be powered by an individual motor. It seems to me that there is a crude comparison here between the energy source for animals and that of humans. Animals are linked with a central power source whereby each species performs almost identical actions. For instance, we can observe in the cat family the same hunting and general cat behaviour whether in a pet cat or a lion. On the other hand, humans have their own individual power source, which can be likened to the individual electric motor for each machine. This is absolutely necessary if humans are to perform their activities independently of each other and in unique ways that, hopefully, progress society. So, we observe that humans are free to go here and there and to do vastly different things from each other and at any time of the day or night or in any season. Animals, however, have no choice but to behave in a predetermined way; that is why all their comings and goings adhere to the same pattern, even if animals of the same species are continents apart. We could say that their power supply keeps them, just like the central belt drive mentioned above, linked together in behaviour by means of 'instinct'.

Another way of describing the limitations of animals is that they are bound by the world of nature, whereas humans occupy the 'world of reason'.[2] Animals function primarily through their physical senses operating through instinct, metaphorically tied to a power source that drives them all. Humans perform intellectual functions, functions that are not part of nature, powered by their individual power sources that free them from the restrictions of their physical senses and animal instinct. Among the many functions of our intellect is that of choice: we can choose what to think, what to say and how to behave, and we have the individual power source that frees us to do this in unique ways. (More on this later in the chapter on free will.) Of course, there are limits to this, but in comparison with the animals, human abilities are totally 'other worldly'. But let us look at this human ability to choose a little more closely.

Everyone knows that they can choose to think good thoughts or bad thoughts, can choose good words over bad words, can choose good behaviour over bad behaviour. Education should be able to not only develop our latent intellectual potential, but also guide/train us to choose good thoughts, words and behaviour over bad, and to realize that negative thoughts, words and behaviour are really a source of human unhappiness. Through conscious use and reflection on these abilities we realize how vastly different to animals we are. But is this difference just because of the brain?

Before this theme is taken further let us look into some research into the training of animals and their capabilities. Functioning primarily through the brain, animal physical senses – hearing, sight, taste, touch and smell and even their power of memory – can be more developed than man. For instance, racing pigeons are capable of finding their way home from thousands of miles away. They do so because of a collection of cells in their brains

> that respond considerably to magnetic stimulation. Each brain cell in the group responds with a unique signalling pattern to a particular magnetic field intensity, which the pigeon is able to interpret. Pigeons harness this power to detect changes in the Earth's magnetic field dependent on location, decoding the signals to determine their exact geographical position.[3]

The sense of smell in animals can be much greater than in humans because that part of the human brain 'devoted to smell, the olfactory bulb, is comparatively small'. For instance, the 'olfactory bulb of sharks occupies a staggering two-thirds of their brains, the largest of which belongs to the great white shark'. Further, 'two rodents (agouti and capybara) have the largest olfactory bulbs of mammals, with another powerful rodent, rats, employed to sniff out land mines with extraordinary accuracy.'[4]

These two examples indicate that animals are genetically programmed regarding their instinctive behaviour. The pigeon does not devise or use a 'sat-nav' system for geographical guidance. Sharks and rats have not invented a synthetic olfactory system as humans would have to do to acquire the super-smelling sensitivity that they have.

Dog owners will also have experience of the loyalty of their dogs, a certain affection they receive from them and their response to training that are part of their cognitive abilities. The amazing work of John Pilley, psychology researcher, for instance, trained his dog Chaser to 'recognize over a thousand toys, by name . . . Over 90% of the time, Chaser could recognize certain toys when Pilley asked for them.' Chaser had even learned to recognize 'verbs and nouns taught by Pilley' who instructed Chaser to 'put her paw and nose on objects, and even pick them up'.[5]

Over thousands of years humanity has domesticated and trained originally wild animals, to be of use to man. On this point 'Abdu'l-Bahá states: '. . .we observe that animals which have undergone training in their sphere of limitation will progress and advance unmistakably, become more beautiful in appearance and increase in intelligence.'[6]

It is also known that certain behaviours of animals have been learnt in the 'course of their evolution which have become permanent in that species through cultural transference, i.e., not on account of genes. . .'[7] For instance, chimpanzees can make tools and help each other get at termites in their nests by pruning and shaping twigs.

Undoubtedly there is an intelligence possessed by animals that we, through observation and the endeavours of scientific investigation, are becoming more aware of. However, to conclude that training or cultural transference will enable animals to experience thinking, learning and consciousness such that humans do, is to misunderstand demarcations between the categories of existence on planet earth. A demarcation between plants and animals, for instance, enables us to accept the futility of trying to cultivate a parsnip, say, to become a poodle. On the demarcation between animal and human intelligence, 'Abdu'l-Bahá states:

> The power of the intellect is one of God's greatest gifts to men, it is the power that makes him a higher creature than the animal. For whereas, century by century and age by age man's intelligence grows and becomes keener, that of the animal remains the same. They are no more intelligent today than they were a thousand years ago! Is there a greater proof than this needed to show man's dissimilarity to the animal creation? It is surely as clear as day.[8]

This statement by 'Abdu'l-Bahá, however, should not be taken as a directive to curtail training or further scientific investigations into animal intelligence. We still do not know the limitations of animal intelligence. What we do know, taken from 'Abdu'l-Bahá's statement above, is that there is a limitation which is entirely absent in humans.

An assumption about human brains that has fuelled misogynistic tendencies and racial prejudice has been linked with larger brain size being the reason for superior intelligence. The Bahá'í Writings uphold modern scientific knowledge in categorically repudiating this:

> Anthropology, physiology, psychology, recognize only one human species, albeit infinitely varied in the secondary aspects of life. Recognition of this truth requires abandonment of

prejudice – prejudice of every kind – race, class, colour, creed, nation, sex, degree of material civilization, everything which enables people to consider themselves superior to others.[9]

Research into the brain has made great advances through magnetic resonance scanning (MRI), which enables us to 'see a picture of the brain at work – helping . . . to understand how a brain reacts to a particular stimulus or how differences in brain structure can affect a person's health, personality or cognitive functioning.'[10] Scans of the brains of dogs have shown that ' "networks" of interconnected <u>brain regions</u> related to such traits as smell, vision, and navigation . . . were larger or smaller in various animals as a result of breeding . . . It was no surprise to find evidence that humans had shaped dogs' brains . . .'[11]

The neuroscientist Ray Dolan has undertaken much research 'using neuroimaging, (and) has defined anatomical areas of the brain that are involved in controlling human emotion (such as empathy) and decision making.'[12] Interestingly neuroscientists, through neuroimaging mapping brain activity, are considering the possibility of predicting how intelligent you are.[13] At this point, however, it must be re-emphasized that MRI does not prove that the brain is the source of intelligence, human emotions, etc. No, all it shows is a neurological aspect of that part of the brain that is functioning when thinking – for instance making moral judgements, imagining, memorizing and the like.

Interestingly, Dr Graham Walker cites in his article on science and morality an experiment to assess spare brain capacity in humans. Three groups 'of adults matched for age and sex' were formed, of which none were piano players. Two groups were 'shown piano finger exercises', one group of which 'practised three times per day'. The second group were only 'allowed to observe a piano player' playing the exercise three times daily. The 'third group were the controls and were not shown the exercises nor did they play the piano'. He writes:

Functional brain scans were carried out on all three groups once each day for five days. While the scans taken before the experiment began were comparable with regard to the areas of the brain which were to be studied, over the next five days groups one and two showed a gradually enlarging area of activity. By contrast the controls showed no change. The change was evidence of new activity – new synapses rapidly developing over a short period, not only in the motor cortex (brain tissue that controls movement) but also in the social// emotional part of the brain.[14]

Dr Walker concludes from this experiment that the human brain has 'immense spare capacity' which does 'not accord with our accepted understanding of evolution, where functional demand precedes structural modification . . .' He states: 'we seem to have been endowed with a structure far beyond the requirements of the time'. He then asks: 'If the rapid enlargement of the human brain (which occurred relatively recently in evolutionary terms) was not a response to need, why did superfluous brain tissue occur?' The implication here is that evolutionary animal brain development stops at the point of 'functional demand' whereas human brain development is 'endowed with a structure far beyond the requirements of the time'. This excess brain function in humans is yet another characteristic that sets humans apart from animals. Perhaps this is why Dr Walker posits the question: 'Could one argue that this would indicate an interventionist God, Who, knowing what our future would require, equipped humans with the necessary latent capacity?'[15]

Research on the human brain by the Brazilian neuroscientist Suzana Herculano-Houzel has led her to believe that she has found how some primates of ancient times progressed to become human. Her research shows that human brains have 86 billion neurons on average, of which 16 billion are located in the cerebral cortex, which is the seat of functions like awareness and logical abstract reasoning. Because of the energy needed to eat and digest raw foods, primates must spend up to nine hours a day doing so. Consequently, primates must employ many more neurons to this activity, along with all other bodily functions, than humans (known as the Encephalization Quotient – EQ),[16] depriving neurons that could be devoted to rational abilities such as humans have. Hence, fewer neurons in the cerebral cortex keep primates from evolving to human beings. Herculano-Houzel concluded that it was through the invention of 'cooking food' by our ancestors some 1.5 million years ago that more neurons were available to evolve intelligence beyond that experienced by primates. She noted that cooking uses fire to pre-digest food outside the body, enabling food to be easier to chew into mush and thereafter to be completely digested and absorbed into the gut, making it yield much more energy in much less time. So, cooking, she states, frees time for us to do much more interesting things with our day and with our neurons than just thinking about food, looking for food, and eating food all day long. Herculano-Houzel concludes: 'No other animal cooks its own food. Only humans do. And I think that's how we got to become human . . .'[17]

Herculano-Houzel's research and findings on the brain are significant, but the case she makes for the difference between primate and human brains through cooking, although intriguing, is highly suspect. If this is so, then what act of reasoning enabled the brain of a primate to 'invent fire' in the first place? Secondly, by what further act of reasoning did such a primate think it was advantageous to throw raw food, such as meat, onto the fire? Even if we accept that serendipity played a large part in inventing fire, why do we not observe today's primates lighting fires to cook their food? And let us not overlook the obvious – many of today's primates, in the wild or in captivity, have had ample time to observe humans lighting fires and cooking food, yet they remain fixed in a raw-food diet.

'Abdu'l-Bahá differentiated between animal and man. However, He does stress that the variety of elements of all different life forms are 'brought together in countless combinations, each of which gives rise to a different being'. He further notes that:

> Among these are sentient beings possessed of certain powers and senses. The more complete the combination, the nobler the being. The combination of the elements in the body of man is more complete than in any other being, and its elements have been combined in perfect equilibrium, and thus is more noble and more perfect.[18]

Man is a more complete being, with the outstanding feature of an intellect way beyond that of primates. And at the centre of intellect is the brain. So, although humans and primates share many common characteristics, humans have not become humans through 'cooking' but are created, in the first place, as 'more noble and more perfect' beings than primates. But this nobility and perfection, the Bahá'í texts point out, appeared gradually over millions of years in an evolutionary process, similar to that which occurs from the conception of a child through its embryonic development, birth, babyhood up to its mature phases.

Now we come to questions of the mind – where does it reside and what is its relationship with the brain? That mind and brain exist in a relationship is rarely doubted. However, materialistic reductionism posits that the mind is produced by the brain. To those who view this relationship through the lens of the Bahá'í Writings, this is unacceptable. In fact, the relationship between the body/brain and mind is only clearly understandable when linked with the soul of man. So, let's look into this relationship.

It seems to me that what we should be looking at here is not the difference or similarity between animal and human brains, but the brain's power source and how it is connected to the brain. To help us do so, let's return to the connection of the power source that operates multiple machines through a single belt drive and that of a power source that is specific to each machine, allowing each machine to fully function independently of any other machine.

Spiritually minded people will conclude that animals function directly from a power source flowing from the Power Supplier. And, as stated before, another name for the Power Supplier is 'God', enabling animals to be directed and function through the power called 'Spirit' operating at an animal level. Spiritually minded people may also conclude that the same power or Spirit flowing from the Power Supplier does not flow directly to the human body or the brain, but indirectly through a non-physical reality called the 'soul', which operates the body and intellectual functions in all ways. Animals are the captive of nature; human beings are free from this captivity. Basically, what makes a human being a human being is the soul or the human spirit. It is the soul, when linked with the body, that is conscious of its physical existence. 'Man – the true man', 'Abdu'l-Bahá says, ' – is soul, not body; though physically man belongs to the animal kingdom, yet his soul lifts him above the rest of creation.'[19]

It is admittedly very difficult to prove the existence of the soul, because the soul is not perceived by the senses. Materialistic reductionist philosophy argues, 'you cannot see, feel, hear, touch or taste the soul, therefore it does not exist'. Animals are not in the least exercised about whether they have a soul, because they have no rational capability to do so. None of the multitudinous species of animals, throughout the millions of years of existence on planet earth, have ever taken time out from its instinctual preoccupations to ponder on whether it has a soul or not. But humans have debated this over millennia, admittedly with conflicting results. 'Abdu'l-Bahá, however, cuts through this confusion, stating:

> One of the strangest things witnessed is that the materialists of today are proud of their natural instincts and bondage. They state that nothing is entitled to belief and acceptance except that which is sensible or tangible. By their own statements they are captives of nature, unconscious of the spiritual world, uninformed of the divine Kingdom and unaware of

heavenly bestowals. If this be a virtue the animal has attained it to a superlative degree, for the animal is absolutely ignorant of the realm of spirit and out of touch with the inner world of conscious realization. The animal would agree with the materialist in denying the existence of that which transcends the senses. If we admit that being limited to the plane of the senses is a virtue the animal is indeed more virtuous than man, for it is entirely bereft of that which lies beyond, absolutely oblivious of the kingdom of God and its traces whereas God has deposited within the human creature an illimitable power by which he can rule the world of nature.[20]

'Abdu'l-Bahá states that when materialists question, 'Where is the soul? What is it? We cannot see it, neither can we touch it', this is how we must answer them: 'However much the mineral may progress, it cannot comprehend the vegetable world. Now, that lack of comprehension does not prove the non-existence of the plant.'[21]

It is explained in the Bahá'í Writings that the soul, or human spirit, 'like the intellect, is an abstraction. Intelligence does not partake of the quality of space, though it is related to man's brain. The intellect resides there, but not materially. Search in the brain, you will not find the intellect.'[22] The Writings further explain that the soul is like the sun which shines upon the body, causing everything to perform its various functions.[23] When the soul 'shines', or the 'rays' of the soul are associated with the brain, it is called 'mind'. The mind is the power that enables us, through the brain, to think – but it is not that the brain is thinking. 'Abdu'l-Bahá states that 'the mind . . . has no place, although it is connected with the brain'.[24] Elsewhere He writes:

Now regarding the question whether the faculties of the mind and the human soul are one and the same. These faculties are but the inherent properties of the soul, such as the power of imagination, of thought, of understanding; powers that are the essential requisites of the reality of man, even as the solar ray is the inherent property of the sun. The temple of man (his body and brain) is like unto a mirror, his soul is as the sun, and his mental faculties even as the rays that emanate from that source of light. The ray may cease to fall upon the mirror, but it can in no wise be dissociated from the sun.[25]

In another analogy 'Abdu'l-Bahá explains that the mind

is the power of the human spirit. The spirit is as the lamp, and the mind as the light that shines from it. The spirit is as the tree, and the mind as the fruit. The mind is the perfection of the spirit and a necessary attribute thereof, even as the rays of the sun are an essential requirement of the sun itself.[26]

So, the body of man exists because of the connection with the soul. The intelligence of man exists through the brain receiving 'light'(mind) from the soul. Here is another insight from the Writings of 'Abdu'l-Bahá about the soul of man and our mental faculties:

It is through the power of the soul that the mind comprehendeth, imagineth and exerteth its influence, whilst the soul is a power that is free. The mind comprehendeth the abstract by the aid of the concrete, but the soul hath limitless manifestations of its own. The mind is circumscribed, the soul limitless. It is by the aid of such senses as those of sight, hearing, taste, smell and touch that the mind comprehendeth, whereas the soul is free from all agencies.[27]

When the body is not connected with the soul at the time of death, all intellectual and bodily functions cease. The soul, however, keeps on 'shining' when the body dies, just like the sun keeps on shining, even if a mirror, that has reflected its light, ceases to exist. After the body dies, the soul continues to manifest itself in the unseen world, but in a different form, a form that is not in any way physical. Recall the words of 'Abdu'l-Bahá above, 'the soul hath limitless manifestations of its own'. Bahá'u'lláh states that after death: 'When the soul attaineth the presence of God, it will assume the form that best befitteth its immortality and is worthy of its celestial habitation.'[28]

Further consideration on evidence for the existence of the soul can be found in Chapter 9.

6

MATERIALISTIC ASSUMPTION 4: IT IS IMPOSSIBLE TO CHANGE HUMAN NATURE BECAUSE HUMANS ARE SELFISH AND AGGRESSIVE

How often it is stated that it is impossible to change human nature because humans are essentially animals. Sadly, 'uncritical assent is given to the proposition that human beings are incorrigibly selfish and aggressive . . .'[1]

This materialistic assumption about human nature is very damaging indeed, it is at the core of much disempowerment, disaffection and anti-social behaviour and has a most debilitating effect on young people. 'True loss', Bahá'u'lláh writes, 'is for him whose days have been spent in utter ignorance of his self.'[2] 'Abdu'l-Bahá adds, 'The root cause of wrongdoing is ignorance . . .'[3] Yet the call for man to 'know himself' is not new, it has been at the heart of all sacred teachings of the great Prophets of old and has been echoed in the pronouncements of illustrious philosophers throughout history. How could we, in this day and age, when there is an explosion of scientific and technological knowledge, get it so absolutely wrong? Evidently, we are out of touch with spiritual realities, those deep inner significances, out of touch with that knowledge which inspires us to transform from 'base metal into gold'.

Perhaps the origin of this disastrous assumption about human nature is the pseudo-religious teaching, taught only in Christianity, that man is essentially sinful and is born in sin. Known as the concept of original sin, it proclaims that every newborn baby inherits the guilt of Adam and Eve, the first human sinners,[4] for disobeying the instruction of God, when in the Garden of Eden, forbidding them to eat of the 'tree of knowledge of good and evil'.[5] Immature minds over the centuries have elaborated this assumption, which is at the foundation of church doctrine. It provides a rationale for a necessary intermediary function of ministers of the Christian religion, between the people and God. It also provides a spurious rationale that only through Christ can sins be forgiven and absolved, as he suffered martyrdom on the cross as a ransom for these sins. Effectively, the doctrine provides, for Christians who accept it, an argument for the superiority and exclusivity of Christ and His Revelation over other Prophets. If this were the case, acknowledging that a 'just' God exists, who forgave the inherited sins of millions of souls prior to the coming of His Holiness Christ? Jesus, Himself, would not recognize this doctrine – why then, should we?

Be that as it may, one can understand that because 'aggression and conflict [have] come to characterize our social, economic and religious systems . . . many have succumbed to the view that such behaviour is intrinsic to human nature and therefore ineradicable.'[6] Hence the common expression 'you can't change human nature'. Unfortunately, many, including those from scholarly circles, never challenge this. 'On the one hand, people of all nations proclaim not only their readiness but their longing for peace and harmony, for an end to the harrowing apprehensions tormenting their daily lives.'[7] Then, on the other, without giving much thought, the same people introduce the assumption that you can't change human nature. Thus human beings are considered to be 'incapable of erecting a social system at once progressive and peaceful, dynamic and harmonious'.[8] What this does is to produce 'a paralyzing contradiction . . . in human affairs'.[9] And to be paralyzed is a condition sane people would not wish for themselves or others, it is a condition where there is no movement at all.

In an attempt to overcome this paralysis of will, to effect movement towards a tranquil heart and harmony between nations, let us look through a spiritual lens at what is human nature. 'Abdu'l-Bahá declares that 'every individual is born holy and pure, and only thereafter may he become defiled'.[10] No matter what condition the body may be in at birth, the soul is a perfect entity made out of love by a perfect Creator. It is an indictment on the state of the human race that every pure and untarnished newborn child has to enter a world that is more descriptive of 'hell' rather than 'heaven'. What chance does any soul have in such an environment, to avoid becoming 'defiled'? Yet the possibility exists, when, from the earliest moments of their lives, children are nurtured and trained both materially and spiritually in ways that bring out the best of what it is to be human.

The Writings of Bahá'u'lláh are replete with insights about what it means to be human. He declares that man has been created 'rich' and God has 'bountifully shed My [His] favour upon thee';[11] man is made with the 'hands of power . . . and with the fingers of strength'; and within him has God 'placed the essence of My [His] light';[12] man is created noble, and moulded out of the clay of God's love.[13]

Another key pronouncement from Bahá'u'lláh states: 'Regard man as a mine rich in gems of inestimable value.'[14] Evidently these 'gems' must be those wonderful gifts deposited within the 'mine' of our true selves and known as our 'potential'. Every human being has the gems of their rational faculties, creative abilities, particular talents, etc. Above all, humans are endowed with the potential to develop the 'gems' of virtuous characteristics, such as selflessness, knowledge, love, justice, wisdom, hope, compassion, trustworthiness, humility and self-effacement. But, as the above words of Bahá'u'lláh indicate, all this potential is hidden, even as are gems prior to excavation, in the mine of our true selves.

At the root of our predicament is that humanity rarely receives the type of education necessary for the discovery and release of all those virtuous 'gems' in the 'mine' of self. Hence Bahá'u'lláh declares that: 'Lack of a proper education hath, however, deprived him of that which he doth inherently possess.'[15] This 'proper education' is three-fold – material, human and spiritual. 'Abdu'l-Bahá states:

> Material education aims at the growth and development of the body, and consists in securing its sustenance and obtaining the means of its ease and comfort. This education is common to both man and animal.
>
> Human education, however, consists in civilization and progress, that is, sound governance, social order, human welfare, commerce and industry, arts and sciences, momentous discoveries, and great undertakings, which are the central features distinguishing man from animal.
>
> As to divine education, it is the education of the Kingdom and consists in acquiring divine perfections. This is indeed true education, for by its virtue man becomes the focus of divine blessings, and the embodiment of the verse, 'Let Us make man in Our image, and after Our likeness' (Gen. 1:26) This is the ultimate goal of the world of humanity.[16]

When education focuses on material and human education alone, essential as it is, the recipients of such education are immersed in the sea of materialism. Of course, there are necessary great material benefits here, but for humanity to truly progress it is in need of spiritual or divine education. 'The spirit of man', 'Abdu'l-Bahá states:

> is not illumined and quickened through material sources. It is not resuscitated by investigating phenomena of the world of matter. The spirit of man is in need of the protection of the Holy Spirit. Just as he advances by progressive stages from the mere physical world of being into the intellectual realm,

so must he develop upward in moral attributes and spiritual graces.[17]

Generally, it seems that the trend in education is becoming more secular, being focused on material and human education only. Consequently, divine or spiritual education has been seriously neglected. In the home also, there is diminishing responsibility of parents to nurture their children in spiritual ways. Of course, it is no easy thing to identify what is 'divine' or 'spiritual' to be able to focus on it. Sadly, many people have lost confidence in moral and ethical religious teachings for a variety of reasons, no matter from what religion they proceed. The original source of material, human and divine education is, 'Abdu'l-Bahá declares, the Founders of the world's great religions; these are the perfect Educators of mankind. Even so, huge numbers of people these days can see no benefit in following the teachings of the great Prophets, and have decided to 'go it alone', without God. (This issue will be examined in more detail in the next chapter.) In a sense they have, even as I did, 'thrown the baby out with the bath water'. 'Abdu'l-Bahá adds that such an attitude is the product of immature thinking. He states that if anyone should say:

> 'I am endowed with perfect reason and comprehension, and I have no need for such an educator', he would be denying the obvious. It is as though a child were to say, 'I have no need of education, but will act and seek the perfections of existence according to my own thinking and intelligence', or as though a blind man were to claim, 'I have no need of sight, for there are many blind people who get by.'[18]

In relation to spiritual education the Bahá'í teachings direct us to focus on identifying those 'gems of inestimable value', in particular those virtues or values that are the glory of being human, and put them to service for the welfare and well-being of others. 'The Purpose of the one true God,' Bahá'u'lláh declares, '. . . in revealing Himself unto men is to lay bare those gems that lie hidden within the mine of their true and inmost selves.'[19] Another insight reveals that 'man is a reality which stands between light and darkness'.[20] 'Every child', states 'Abdu'l-Bahá, 'is potentially the light of the world – and at the same time its darkness; where-fore must the question of education be accounted as of primary importance.'[21]

Imagine then, that it is possible for a child to become aware that it has a high, light nature and, conversely, a low, dark nature. With the right nurturing and training, which in reality is 'spir-itual' or 'divine' education, the child can develop an attraction to its high nature, through the influence of the Manifestations of God, and repulsed by negative behaviours driven by the demands of its low nature. In effect, everyone can form the habit of making daily choices as to what direction to take – towards one's high or towards one's low nature. The choice is, metaphorically, between 'light' or 'darkness'. Every adult recognizes that they can be very, very good or very, very bad. 'Man has the power both to do good and to do evil . . .'[22] says 'Abdu'l-Bahá. It is in his higher, light nature that all the jewels of inestimable value lie hidden. 'Abdu'l-Bahá states:

> The attributes of his Divine nature are shown forth in love, mercy, kindness, truth and justice, one and all being expres-sions of his higher nature. Every good habit, every noble quality belongs to man's spiritual nature, whereas all his imperfections and sinful actions are born of his material nature.[23]

Man's material lower, dark nature has also been called his 'animal' nature. What is meant here is not that animals are evil or bad. As mentioned before, all their activities are governed without free will, being the product of instinct. In other words, they have no choice than to behave in the ways ordained for them, and in com-parison to some human beings, their behaviour is to be preferred, for when humans exhibit base, dark-nature tendencies they can sink lower than the animals. We humans are fashioned to behave in human ways, not animal ways, using our virtues to do so. But if we do not make a move towards our higher spiritual nature, it is for sure that the darkness of our lower nature will enslave us. Imperfections such as ignorance, cruelty, savagery, selfishness, despair, injustice, vengeance, arrogance, laziness, like weeds and brambles will spring up threatening to choke our spiritual nature. The Manifestations of God are indispensable for educating and motivating the human race to move from their lower, dark animal nature to their higher, light, spiritual nature. 'Abdu'l-Bahá declares:

> The holy Manifestations of God [the Founders of the world's great religions] come into the world to dispel the darkness of the animal, or physical, nature of man, to purify him from his imperfections in order that his heavenly and spiritual nature may become quickened, his divine qualities awakened, his perfections visible, his potential powers revealed and all the virtues of the world of humanity latent within him may come to life. These holy Manifestations of God are the Educators and Trainers of the world of existence, the Teachers of the world of humanity. They liberate man from the darkness of the world of nature, deliver him from despair, error, ignorance, imperfections and all evil qualities. They clothe him in the garment of perfections and exalted virtues.[24]

So far then, we have explored the possibility that man's potential is rich in 'gems of inestimable value.' In particular, these gems are wondrous virtues and characteristics the value of which we cannot estimate. It is also proposed that man has a high, light, spiritual nature and, conversely, a nature which is low, dark and animal. The high nature is associated with the soul of man whilst his low nature is connected with the pulls and tugs of his body which is animal in construction. The Manifestations of God, through their example and teachings, attract those who are receptive to divine precepts. Their attraction is like that of a magnet on anything with an iron content – iron here can be likened to souls who are receptive to their teachings. On the other hand, the pull of the lower nature can be likened to a 'bungee rope', fixed to the extremity of one's lower nature. The more one is attracted to the Manifestations of God, efforts are made to develop inherent virtuous qualities – wisdom, patience, forgiveness, etc. When this happens, one is naturally moving towards one's higher nature, but the consequence of this is that the tension of the bungee rope becomes greater. When this process is set in motion one naturally feels a discomfort, a conflict resulting from two opposing forces acting upon the soul. One force is the ever-present demands of the animal nature, for instance to gratify one's carnal desires, and the other force is a compelling attraction to the things of the 'spirit' which gradually appear as an irresistible beatific vision. If one persists in a process of moving toward this vision, then the habit of using spiritual qualities is developed while the character is strengthened. The result of so doing on character development is stupendous, beyond any earthly, materialistic conception; hence Bahá'u'lláh writes:

> The light of a good character surpasseth the light of the sun and the radiance thereof. Whoso attaineth unto it is accounted as a jewel among men. The glory and the upliftment of the world must needs depend upon it.[25]

By reconfiguring our understanding of human beings in this way, the paralysis of will, mentioned earlier, is overcome. To continue to hold the view that humanity's low, dark nature as impossible to educate, is to prolong the ignorance of a distorted view of human nature indeed. Yet another great danger of materialism's 'gospel' is to completely distort everything that is viewed.

After discovering these wonderful insights in the Bahá'í teachings, I became very interested in finding out more about the process of 'spiritual' or 'divine' education and its benefits. Continuing my search, I found that Bahá'u'lláh stated: 'Man is the supreme Talisman.'[26] This suggested to me that Bahá'u'lláh used the word 'talisman' not in the superstitious sense of being a good luck charm in the form of a pendant or item of jewellery which has magical properties. The meaning of 'talisman', in the way it is related to a human being, is better understood in reading the words of Bahá'u'lláh in the round. From His statements above, and also those of 'Abdu'l-Bahá, we can form the view that when man is attracted by the spiritual forces emanating from the Manifestation of God and makes every effort to live in accordance with those spiritual powers, he naturally becomes a conduit through which these powers can flow. The individual becomes 'as a reed, through which the spirit may descend, and quicken souls'.[27]

When this happens, the individual is essentially happy because his soul is imbued with transcendent knowledge which helps him face the tests and trials of life in profoundly new ways. He will radiate a life force, like a light emanating from a lamp, which has an uplifting effect on others. He has life, but in the words of Christ, he has it 'more abundantly', [28] becoming as a spiritual talisman attracting powers from a heavenly source. Metaphorically he transforms from a 'gnat into an eagle',[29] soaring high above the world of materialism, and becomes a complete enigma to those who hold to a materialistic perspective of life. But Bahá'u'lláh does not say that man is just a talisman, He states he is the 'supreme Talisman', indicating that although certain powers are allotted to everything in creation, nevertheless, man is way above these powers, as they only find expression in the natural world. Man's powers are above nature, they are 'supernatural', hence out of all creation he is supreme.

It may be encouraging to know that a few of these understandings have been incorporated in courses run in many primary and secondary schools in Swindon in the United Kingdom. The course, known as the Swindon Young People's Empowerment Programme (SYEP)[30] is specifically designed to help disaffected youngsters overcome disengagement in education and/or anti-social behaviour. Beginning in 1999, the most difficult, vulnerable and challenging youngsters were given access to the course run by teachers or learning mentors who were trained as course facilitators. SYEP is run in ways that youngsters become agents in their own learning about their own reality, through involvement in two environments – the 'Tranquillity Zone' and the 'Discovery Zone'. The course focuses on two concepts; that everyone is a 'mine rich in gems of inestimable value'[31] and that: 'Every child is potentially the light of the world – and at the same time its darkness.'[32]

The course helps young people to develop a sense of self-worth and overcome challenges. It requires facilitators to clear up debilitating, commonly held misconceptions about human reality, and encourage, support, motivate and inspire them to become attracted to their higher nature.

The results have been staggering. Hundreds of disaffected youngsters, once aware of their true nature, have voluntarily taken the first faltering steps to change by giving up unrewarding behaviour. Indeed, they have begun to turn their lives around, becoming willing to engage in contributing positively to their families, in school and in the community. Along with the empowering insights of their 'gems of inestimable value' they inevitably, almost without exception, state that they did not know they had a high, light nature. Stuck with the disempowering thought that they were essentially 'bad kids', it came as an inspiration to change for the better when they learnt they had a high, light nature towards which they could grow.[33]

The course was evaluated in 2008 by Dr Stephen Bigger of the Education department of Worcester University, who stated in his executive summary:

> This report discusses a range of factors contributing to this success [of SYEP], primarily relating to trusting and empowering the young people so that they value themselves and their

abilities, build positive and caring relationships with others, and work towards creating a better world. It shows that young people can transcend their limited world view, learning to see themselves differently as people with energy, potential, compassion and the ability to affect positive change. In this they can reach out to others and with others, building moral understanding and cascading positive attitudes and energies to those around them.

It has had rapid and lasting results with needy and disengaged children aged nine to thirteen. The processes involved should therefore be taken very seriously by government, schools, and youth services as a powerful intervention that has shown it is able to turn youngsters from actual and potential delinquency to becoming committed to contributing to society as good citizens. The report looks forward to ways of enabling whole classes of children to benefit. It shows how SYEP approaches can become a central strand in citizenship, personal, social and moral education, spiritual education, creative thinking skills, and social and emotional aspects of learning. Inspired by the teachings of the Bahá'í Faith, it is non-partisan and works openly and transparently with all faiths and none. It looks forward to expanding its work to other schools.[34]

7

MATERIALISTIC ASSUMPTION 5: AN INNATE SENSE OF HUMAN DIGNITY WILL PREVENT MAN FROM COMMITTING EVIL ACTIONS

In contrast to those who believe that human nature is so bad that it cannot be changed for the better are those who maintain 'that an innate sense of human dignity will prevent man from committing evil actions and insure his spiritual and material perfection'.[1] Perhaps this thought was seeded as far back as the Enlightenment period of history. We find, for instance, in '1765 the author of an anonymous article in a French Enlightenment periodical spoke of "The general love of humanity".'[2] That was when the word 'humanism' was coined and has since grown to be a popular concept in a secular society. Indeed, humanists are keen to point out that humans 'can live ethical and fulfilling lives without religious beliefs', believing that one's moral code is derived 'from the lessons of history, personal experience, and thought'.[3]

Reflecting on those Bahá'í teachings that could be taken as a counter to this materialistic assumption, I realized that this view, apparently benign, is, in fact, insidious and pernicious. At the heart of it is that human faculties such as the ability to think, comprehend, imagine and memorize will produce an instinct that will 'refrain from inflicting harm on his fellow men and will hunger and thirst to do good.'[4] In other words, left without any moral and ethical education derived from guidance and teachings from a higher moral authority, man will naturally aspire to develop good qualities and do good works. This assumption insidiously slides into a belief that a higher power is not necessary in man's education and training. Further down the slide it follows that if God is not necessary, then there is no need for Prophets or Manifestations of God Who speak in His name. It seems that throughout the ages, humanity has sought, by all means possible, to find excuses or reasons for not believing in the existence of the one, compassionate, all-knowing God. Paganism and idolatry have been history's preoccupations of denial. Today, however, this has been replaced by exalting the intellectual faculties of man to that of 'deity'. One could say that in a godless society, man's rational faculties have been placed upon the altar of worship by an ever-increasing number of materialistic thinkers. 'God is dead', as declared by Friedrich Nietzsche, is now a common expression of belief. As one who once held this belief, I 'get' it. Who can reject such an expression when humanity has terribly suffered from ingrained religious superstition and prejudice, misused priestly authority, church opposition to scientific investigation and their results, along with justifications for so many injustices in society such as apartheid and colonialism? No wonder Nietzsche wrote his oft-quoted statement on the death of God. But if we read more than this 'sound bite', it becomes clear that he was very concerned about its consequences:

> God is dead. God remains dead. And we have killed him. How shall we comfort ourselves, the murderers of all murderers? What was holiest and mightiest of all that the world has yet owned has bled to death under our knives: who will wipe this blood off us? What water is there for us to clean ourselves? What festivals of atonement, what sacred games shall we have to invent? Is not the greatness of this deed too great for us? Must we ourselves not become gods simply to appear worthy of it?[5]

Nietzsche was clearly concerned about the rejection of religion and moral principles:

> Nietzsche's works express a fear that the decline of religion, the rise of atheism, and the absence of a higher moral authority would plunge the world into chaos. The western world had depended on the rule of God for thousands of years – it gave order to society and meaning to life. Without it, Nietzsche writes, society will move into an age of nihilism. Although Nietzsche may have been considered a nihilist by definition, he was critical of it and warned that accepting nihilism would be dangerous.[6]

So let us look at this assumption, that without any higher moral authority it is possible for a human being to become a morally developed person who will instinctively do good. It does not take much imagination to conclude that if a newborn baby were to be left on its own, without any love, care, guidance or training, its ability to develop morally would be seriously compromised. In fact, even its mental faculties, without stimulation and education, would atrophy, presenting a very sorry condition of a human being indeed.

We only have to recall the horrific neglect of children in orphanages set up in the late 1980s by the Communist dictator Nicolae Ceausescu to realize that no one can develop even the most rudimentary human behaviour without caring nurturing. Reports made at that time shocked the world. We learnt that Ceausescu banned contraception and abortion and demanded that women under the age of 45 must have at least five children. Increasing numbers entering the military was a major objective of his policies. And when poor parents could not afford to raise large families it became accepted that children were taken into large orphanages, with the aim of making them 'compliant subjects for the Romanian military'. Hence, when Ceausescu was over-thrown and executed in 1989, more than 150,000 children were found in the orphanages – their condition was heart-renderingly diabolical:

> No consideration was ever given to the developmental needs of the children . . . most under the age of three, many covered in bedsores, lying on urine-soaked cots in steel cribs. Most had not learned how to walk or talk, and significant numbers were dying of infectious diseases. Studies showed that the orphans, sometimes lying quietly and unattended for 18 to 20 hours a day, were severely socially, emotionally, and developmentally delayed.[7]

Another report stated:

> There are no toys in Romania's orphanages; instead the children play with dirty needles in old hospital dumping grounds. The playgrounds are a classic display of violence cycles. The older children bully the young, and the young in turn attack those that are sick or weak . . . reporters found the orphans left alone for long periods of time, tied to their beds, with bottles of gruel propped into their mouths. The orphans were so neglected that they failed to show any emotions at all. They didn't cry or show anger or even respond to people coming in and out of the rooms.[8]

Surely the evidence of the heart-breaking plight of thousands of orphans proves the point, giving ample support to the words of 'Abdu'l-Bahá below, that our moral development is dependent on education and training?

> We also observe in infants the signs of aggression and lawlessness, and that if a child is deprived of a teacher's instructions his undesirable qualities increase from one moment to the next. It is therefore clear that the emergence of this natural sense of human dignity and honor is the result of education.

Secondly, even if we grant for the sake of the argument that instinctive intelligence and an innate moral quality would prevent wrongdoing, it is obvious that individuals so characterized are as rare as the philosopher's stone. An assumption of this sort cannot be validated by mere words, it must be supported by the facts. Let us see what power in creation impels the masses toward righteous aims and deeds![9]

A further example of the need for an educator in the nurturing and training of human beings is the case of so-called 'feral children'. Throughout the years there have been 'over one hundred reported cases of feral children'.[10] A feral child is described as one 'who has lived away from human contact from a very young age, and has little or no experience of human care, loving or social behavior, and, crucially, of human language. Feral children are confined by humans (often parents), brought up by animals, or live in the wild in isolation.'[11] Here is one story of a feral child called 'Shamdeo':

> In May 1972, a boy aged about four was discovered in the forest of Musafirkhana, about 20 miles from Sultanpur. The boy was playing with wolf cubs. He had very dark skin, long hooked fingernails, matted hair and calluses on his palms, elbows and knees. He shared several characteristics with [other similar cases]: sharpened teeth, craving for blood, earth-eating, chicken-hunting, love of darkness and friendship with dogs and jackals. He was named Shamdeo and taken to the village of Narayanpur. Although weaned off raw meat, he never talked, but learnt some sign language . . . He died in February 1985.[12]

Another story concerns a five-year-old girl called, Natasha, who suffered severe neglect by her father, and was raised by feral cats and dogs:

In 2009, welfare workers were led to an unheated flat in a Siberian town where they found a 5-year-old girl they called 'Natasha'."While technically living with her father and other relatives, Natasha was treated like one of the many dogs and feral cats that shared the space. Like her furry companions, Natasha lapped up food from bowls left on the floor. She didn't know any human words and only communicated with hisses and barks. The father was nowhere to be found when authorities rescued the girl, and Natasha has since been placed in an orphanage.[13]

Evidently, as the cases of Shamdeo and Natasha show, these children had intelligence but were unable to develop it in a way that would make their behaviour human. Their unstimulated rational faculties atrophied when left to copy the ways of animals around them and, it must be said, were successful enough to guarantee their physical survival. However, there was no higher intelligence from a mature human to take their behaviour above that of the animals around them. With these examples in mind the following words of 'Abdu'l-Bahá strike home:

> If a man is left alone in a wilderness where he sees none of his own kind, he will undoubtedly become a mere animal. It is therefore clear that an educator is needed.[14]

The first environment experienced by every newborn baby is that created by the mother, the first educator of the infant. Over the thousands of years of man's evolution humanity has developed using the handed-down guidance, instruction and training of previous generations, which has secured the survival and progress of the human race. But to think that there has been no intervention from a higher being in this process is to give encouragement to the assumption that 'an innate sense of human dignity will prevent man from committing evil actions and insure his spiritual and material perfection'.[15] This flies in the face of the evidence of the Romanian orphans and the feral children.

It is a principal teaching of the Bahá'í Faith that humanity has always been in need of and received education from a higher authority. Although Bahá'ís name a number of these great Teachers such as Abraham, Krishna, Moses, Zoroaster, Buddha, Christ, Muhammad, the Báb and Bahá'u'lláh, sacred scriptures posit that these Educators have appeared constantly, in all parts of the world over the millions of years of humanity's evolution. For instance, Muhammad stated, 'And to every people have we sent an apostle.'[16] (An Apostle, in Quranic terms, is a Manifestation of God.) They 'have been sent down from time immemorial,' writes Bahá'u'lláh, 'and been commissioned to summon mankind to the one true God.'[17] He further adds: 'That no records concerning them [pre-Adamic Manifestations of God] are now available, should be attributed to their extreme remoteness, as well as to the vast changes which the earth hath undergone since their time.'[18] A statement by Bahá'u'lláh concerning the ubiquitous visitations of these Divine Educators is truly mind-blowing. He writes:

> Through His potency the Trees of Divine Revelation have yielded their fruits, every one of which hath been sent down in the form of a Prophet, bearing a Message to God's creatures in each of the worlds whose number God, alone, in His all-encompassing knowledge, can reckon.[19]

In the light of what has just been written, the guidance and training handed down over countless generations must have originated from a source, which may be divided into two parts. One part is our ancestors' own discoveries, the other through the teachings of Manifestations of God suited to humanity's stage of development. As a possible example of this we can imagine a time in mankind's evolution that cave-dweller ancestors might have discovered how to climb a tree for the fruit in its branches, while a Manifestation of God taught them rudimentary insights into how to become more united as a family or tribe, in their competition with wild animals and the environment. Bahá'u'lláh states: 'From the beginning of time the light of unity hath shed its divine radiance upon the world . . .'[20] The intervention of Manifestations at this stage would have continued from previous ones who helped humans develop through many different forms and through many stages prior to the cave-dweller stage. We are informed that:

> Though we cannot imagine exactly what the Manifestations of the remote past were like, we can be sure of two things, They have been able to reach their fellow-men in a normal manner – as Bahá'u'lláh reached His generation, and They were sent from God and thus Divine Beings.[21]

This process of education by the Manifestations of God, the higher authority, takes place over millions of years, usually with long intervals between their coming, and a time lapse before the guidance given by a specific Manifestation finds its way to those living further away from the Source. Losing track of the original Source, it is reasonable to suppose that the guidance came only from human discovery and thinking – the Source of that knowledge coming from the Manifestations of God being entirely forgotten, perverted to the point of repulsion or ascribed to some mythical entity. Perhaps it is partly for these reasons that humanism has become increasingly popular. Be that as it may, the assumption that 'an innate sense of human dignity will prevent man from committing evil actions and insure his spiritual and material perfection'[22] is negated by 'Abdu'l-Bahá: 'if we ponder the lessons of history it will become evident that this very sense of honor and dignity is itself one of the bounties deriving from the instructions of the Prophets of God.'[23] Clearly, those who think our virtuous ways of being are but a product of man's own making have either entirely forgotten that they originated from the guidance of previous Manifestations of God, or are incapable of tracing the link of this intervention back to its Source.

Of course, they just deny without giving any consideration of this point. So widespread and fundamental have been the Manifestations' influence on educating humanity that Bahá'u'lláh has written, 'were it not for those effulgent Lights [Manifestations of God] that shine above the horizon of His Essence, the people would know not their left hand from their right, how much less could they scale the heights of the inner realities . . .'[24] In a soul-stirring overview of the influence of the Manifestations of God throughout history 'Abdu'l-Bahá writes:

Men are ignorant; the Manifestations of God make them wise. They are animalistic; the Manifestations make them human. They are savage and cruel; the Manifestations lead them into kingdoms of light and love. They are unjust; the Manifestations cause them to become just. Man is selfish; They sever him from self and desire. Man is haughty; They make him meek, humble and friendly. He is earthly; They make him heavenly. Men are material; the Manifestations transform them into divine semblance. They are immature children; the Manifestations develop them into maturity. Man is poor; They endow him with wealth. Man is base, treacherous and mean; the Manifestations of God uplift him into dignity, nobility and loftiness.

These holy Manifestations liberate the world of humanity from the imperfections which beset it and cause men to appear in the beauty of heavenly perfections. Were it not for the coming of these holy Manifestations of God, all mankind would be found on the plane of the animal. They would remain darkened and ignorant like those who have been denied schooling and who never had a teacher or trainer. Undoubtedly, such unfortunates will continue in their condition of need and deprivation.[25]

Yet another consideration that would incline hearts and souls as to the central position of the Manifestations of God in moral and spiritual education is that They open 'new doors' that are nowhere in the purview of human thought. For instance, consider the words of Christ when He stated, 'Love your enemies, do good to them which hate you, bless them that curse you, and pray for them which despitefully use you.'[26] It is only those who have a heart and ear open to spiritual realities that can accept this teaching, for Christ Himself stated he was addressing such people: 'But I say unto you which hear.'[27] Many things said by the Manifestations of God are counterintuitive to us. It is counterintuitive to return good for evil – yet They know that the transformation of base, low, 'dark nature' characteristics comes only through high, 'light nature' qualities. Darkness cannot be dispelled by darkness. Here is another such statement, this time from Buddha:

> Even, O monks, should robbers and murderers saw through your limbs and joints, whoso gave way to anger thereat, would not be following my advice. For thus ought you to train yourselves: 'undisturbed shall our mind remain, no evil words shall escape our lips; friendly and full of sympathy shall we remain, with heart full of love, and free from any hidden malice; and that person shall we penetrate with loving thoughts, wide, deep, boundless, freed from anger and hatred.'[28]

And who else, even if we take into account the entire range of philosophers or moral writers, has guided humanity in these ways without the influence of the Manifestations? On this point we are informed by 'Abdu'l-Bahá that from the civilizing teachings of Moses, and the Prophets that followed, the Israelites became most advanced in education, scholastic works and industries and their philosophy became renowned. 'In the splendour of the reign of Solomon', 'Abdu'l-Bahá states, 'their sciences and arts advanced to such a degree that even the Greek philosophers journeyed to Jerusalem to sit at the feet of the Hebrew sages and acquire the basis of Israelitish law.'[29] Further:

Even Socrates visited the Jewish doctors in the Holy Land, consorting with them and discussing the principles and basis of their religious belief. After his return to Greece he formulated his philosophical teaching of divine unity and advanced his belief in the immortality of the spirit beyond the dissolution of the body. Without doubt, Socrates absorbed these verities from the wise men of the Jews with whom he came in contact. Hippocrates and other philosophers of the Greeks likewise visited Palestine and acquired wisdom from the Jewish prophets, studying the basis of ethics and morality, returning to their country with contributions which have made Greece famous.[30]

In light of the above evidence and observations, it proved untenable for me to hold the view that mankind can 'go it alone', can make progress in all aspects of life without the aid of a divine educator, a higher moral authority. However, the difficulty of trying to induce materialistic thinkers to rethink their assumptions is comparable to trying to persuade fanatical religious followers to re-read their scriptures in such a way as to become well-wishers of humankind. Unfortunately, both materialistic assumptions and fanatical ways of reading scripture originate from an uninformed base and conclude with damaging consequences. The word commonly known for this state of being is 'prejudice':

If it is true, in general, that 'ideas have consequences', then man's ideas about man have the most far reaching consequences of all. Upon them may depend the structure of government, the patterns of culture, the purpose of education, the design of the future and the human or inhuman uses of human beings.[31]

8

MATERIALISTIC ASSUMPTION 6: THERE SHOULD BE NO LIMIT TO PERSONAL LIBERTY PROVIDING ONE'S FREEDOM DOES NO HARM TO OTHERS

Because man is thought by many to be only a material being, materialist ideals have so permeated society that they appear to be accepted as 'human rights'. The basic proposition of such thinking is that there should be no limits to personal liberty providing one's freedom does no harm to others.

My main concern, while we look at the subject of personal liberty and freedom, is not that of a legalistic outline of 'human rights and responsibilities'. Thankfully this has been well taken care of since the adoption of the Universal Declaration of Human Rights by the United Nations in 1948 and has since effloresced by its acceptance in most nations on earth. My concern is related to the assumption that religion has no part to play in defining human rights and responsibilities. Also, there is an assumption that religion has no part to play in outlining what liberty is for the well-being, happiness and progress of the individual and society. My logic underpinning this concern is that inherent in the sacred scriptures of the world's great religions, is the teaching that God created humanity and therefore knows how we should behave and relate to each other.

Before we go further it may be useful to bring forward a

definition of what religion is, so that inaccurate assumptions about it, which abound these days, can be dispelled. 'Religion" declares 'Abdu'l-Bahá,

> consists in the necessary relationships deriving from the reality of things. The universal Manifestations of God, being aware of the mysteries of creation, are fully informed of these necessary relationships and establish them as the religion of God.[1]

This is an astounding statement by 'Abdu'l-Bahá on the reality of religion, which has never been previously defined with such clarity. However, it does require reflection. In my attempt to understand this statement I separated its elements to have a closer look at them. I take it that when 'Abdu'l-Bahá mentions 'things' this is everything created by God because God is not a 'thing'. The reality of God is above all creation as its Creator, but, as previously mentioned, is an unknowable Essence. So let us consider some of the things God has created. Human beings may top our list, followed by the environment in which we live – essentially planet earth, which includes all the minerals, the vegetables, the insects, bacteria, animals and so on. If we expand out, this will include all the galaxies containing their stars, planets, moons, asteroids, black holes and the like, that populate the universe. We should also include the possibility of all the creatures on other planets. Also, we should give some thought to the possibility of all the non-physical worlds of God that, like the physical universe, could be infinite in number. At the top of my list, however, would be the Messengers or Manifestations of God Whose distinction from human beings will be discussed later. So, referring to the quotation above – every 'thing' created by God has a 'reality' which emanates from it or 'derives' from it; and everything has a connection or 'relationship' with every other thing which is a 'necessary' or essential connection.

Now we must look into what 'necessary' or 'essential' means in this context. 'Abdu'l-Bahá explains that 'essential requirements cannot be separated from the reality of things. Thus it is impossible to separate heat from fire, or wetness from water, or the rays from the sun, for they are essential requirements.'²

If it were possible to separate the rays from the sun it would immediately cease to be the sun; similarly, if heat were separated from fire it would cease to be fire. An essential reality of human beings is that we have mental faculties and free will (free will be studied more extensively later on). If we did not possess mental faculties and free will, we would cease to be human beings. Animals have the power of their senses and instinct – if they did not possess these functions, they would cease to be animals. Vegetables have the power of growth, if they did not have this power they would cease to be vegetables. Minerals have the power of mutual attraction with other minerals to make compounds, and if this attractive power is non-existent then minerals cease to be minerals.

In mentioning God, we know He is not a 'thing', but, 'Abdu'l-Bahá states, He has an essential reality: 'the essential reality of God is revealed in His perfections'.³ So, without perfections God would cease to be God. Some of God's perfections are His love, justice, forgiveness and knowledge. Now, when we consider what is the essential reality of the Manifestations of God, we learn that They reflect or manifest the perfections of God to humanity. If They do not manifest these perfections, then they are not Manifestations of God. An over-riding attribute, or perfection of God is that He is infallible, that is, He is infallibly perfect in every sense. He never makes mistakes, nor does He change the way He goes about things. If God is not infallible, He would cease to be God. Therefore, because the Manifestations reflect His perfections, one of which is 'infallibility', they are essentially infallible. Their knowledge, wisdom, love, compassion, etc, are all perfections that are infallible reflections of the qualities of God. 'Abdu'l-Bahá puts it thus: 'Infallibility in essence is confined to the universal Manifestations of God; for infallibility is an essential requirement of Their reality, and the essential requirement of a thing is inseparable from the thing itself.'⁴

Let's recall the statement above that 'the supreme Manifestations of God are aware of the mysteries of creation', therefore
They understand the essential connections or relationships, and
by this knowledge establish the religion of God. In other words,
because the Manifestations know 'mysteries of creation', They
are able to state what the connection or relationship should be
with everything in existence. Hence, they give guidance, insights,
exhortations, laws and examples showing what the essential connections are. They explain how God connects with mankind
through His Manifestations, what the behaviour of human beings
should be in relation to God and His Manifestations. They give
laws, exhortations and guidance to govern relationships between
human beings, and between human beings and nature. They give
directives as to how to behave in preparation for the next life. All
essential relationships are considered by the Manifestations – this
is religion!

In a materialistic society there is utter confusion as to how
humanity should relate to everything. So, where do we go to find
the essential connection between all created things? The answer
has always been there – we find it in the sacred scriptures of all the
world's great religions. Although it may not seem obvious, whenever there is a decline in religion, man – when he is disconnected
from a 'Higher Source' of guidance and training, then looks elsewhere for what he feels is appropriate regarding relationships and
to satisfy his needs. Unfortunately, instead of looking up to the
'heaven of understanding', he looks down to the material world
with its materialistic ideologies, thinking that all his needs will
thus be satisfied. With the rejection or ignorance of guidance as
to how man should relate to others and to the material world, the
first thing he demands is freedom to live a materialistic lifestyle.
Any restraints on his decision are immediately rejected. One can
actually hear time and time again the 'materialistic' mantra of
modern times, chanted by an increasing number of people – 'give
me the freedom to do exactly what I want'. The more discerning add 'as long as I do no harm to others'. Perhaps beyond its

connection with art, literature and architecture, this is what is meant by 'postmodernism'.

But how is man to discern what will be of no harm to himself and others, from that which is harmful? Parents who educate and train their children properly are constantly protecting their children from that which can harm them. Why? because they know the things necessary to do so, whereas the child does not. To do this they use knowledge handed down, mentioned earlier, much of which has come from past Manifestations of God, even if they don't know it. However, even for adults, there is always ongoing guidance necessary from a Higher Authority in a world that is rapidly changing, as change throws up new problems that are not answered through the handed down knowledge of old. A part of a prayer from Bahá'u'lláh acknowledges this:

> Ordain Thou for me, O my God, the good of this world and the world to come, and grant me what will profit me in every world of Thy worlds, for I know not what will help or harm me. Thou, in truth, art the All-Knowing, the All-Wise.[5]

There were many things that I was ignorant about as to what would help or harm me. For our protection against such ignorance, the directive from our Maker has always been the same – turn to the teachings of the Manifestations of God, particularly the one sent for the day and age in which we live. And because materialistic man chooses not to turn for guidance to the Manifestation, he remains unaware of the dangers inherent in purely materialistic lifestyles. As such, he is unable to discern that which is helpful from that which is harmful. Here now follows a brief mention of some Bahá'í teachings that challenge the assumption that materialistic ideals will satisfy human needs. The first to be considered is on materialism itself.

'Abdu'l-Bahá states, 'The world for the most part is sunk in materialism . . .'[6] Such a statement does not imply that material/physical things are evil or harmful to mankind, but that attraction to these things has passed the point of moderation and created a disabling imbalance in the way life is lived and governed. In another place 'Abdu'l-Bahá states:

> Consider to what a remarkable extent the spirituality of people has been overcome by materialism so that spiritual susceptibility seems to have vanished, divine civilization become decadent, and guidance and knowledge of God no longer remain.[7]

Although one often hears people speaking about the benefits of moderation, it is usually in ignorance of spiritual principles that would moderate materialistic attitudes, lifestyles and even governance. Materialistic perspectives are, in fact, short-sighted, as that which is seen is only that which is immediately ahead. Of course, some have longer vision than others, but in comparison to the vision of the Manifestations of God they are as blind. At a time when humanity, like lemmings, was approaching a cliff-edge, Bahá'u'lláh made several pronouncements on what He could see as a disastrous rush to doom. Materialism is at the heart of all the evils in the world, hence Bahá'u'lláh, writing in the late 19th century, clearly advised:

> It is incumbent upon them who are in authority to exercise moderation in all things. Whatsoever passeth beyond the limits of moderation will cease to exert a beneficial influence. Consider for instance such things as liberty, civilization and the like. However much men of understanding may favourably regard them, they will, if carried to excess, exercise a pernicious influence upon men . . .[8]

Bahá'u'lláh's insights into that which is harmful included the systems of governance at the end of the 19th century through to this time, well over one hundred years later. We have only to recall all the horrors of this time period, horrors that were not prevented by existing systems of governance, to realize how far-seeing was Bahá'u'lláh when He wrote:

> The winds of despair are, alas, blowing from every direction, and the strife that divideth and afflicteth the human race is daily increasing. The signs of impending convulsions and chaos can now be discerned, inasmuch as the prevailing order appeareth to be lamentably defective.[9]

In another place and on a different topic, Bahá'u'lláh warned that 'in earthly riches fear is hidden, and peril is concealed'.[10] Conversely, for many, riches are considered as the means to a more joyful and happy life. When we recall the scenes we see on TV of rejoicing by lottery winners, it is easy to realize that mankind is far removed from its awareness of what causes happiness. In reality, wealth is one of the greatest impediments to happiness, hence Bahá'u'lláh states:

> O Son of Man! Thou dost wish for gold and I desire thy freedom from it. Thou thinkest thyself rich in its possession, and I recognize thy wealth in thy sanctity therefrom. By My life! This is My knowledge, and that is thy fancy; how can My way accord with thine?[11]

And 'Abdu'l-Bahá writes that 'human happiness is founded upon spiritual behaviour'.[12] Of course, everyone needs the necessities of life to be able to function as human beings; from a Bahá'í perspective, the future of humanity is material as well as spiritual well-being. But who is aware that behaving in a spiritual way is the base upon which all happiness is built? Even if there is some inkling of this truth, we are still left with the great question: how to behave in a spiritual way? Yet again it is not left to the limitations of man›s knowledge and experience as to what is spiritual behaviour; it is determined by the Manifestations of God, Who are aware in every age of 'the necessary relationships deriving from the reality of things'.[13]

A major aspect of behaving spiritually in this day, declares Bahá'u'lláh, is to become conscious of the oneness of mankind and then relate to all peoples as members of one family. As a corollary of this consciousness, a just system of governance for all humanity is essential. A significant way of behaving spiritually in this age is to acquire 'universal' aspirations whereby nationalistic phrases such as, 'my country, right or wrong', will not beguile an electorate.

> O ye beloved of the Lord! In this sacred Dispensation, conflict and contention are in no wise permitted. Every aggressor deprives himself of God's grace. It is incumbent upon everyone to show the utmost love, rectitude of conduct, straightforwardness and sincere kindliness unto all the peoples and kindreds of the world, be they friends or strangers. So intense must be the spirit of love and loving kindness, that the stranger may find himself a friend, the enemy a true brother, no difference whatsoever existing between them. For universality is of God and all limitations earthly.[14]

Although the people of the earth are moving in this direction, nonetheless there is a great distance to travel. A thought may come to those who have acquired such a universal outlook, that if a win on the lottery came their way they would spend their gains not on themselves and immediate family, but on helping the poor, downtrodden and destitute. And here's another thought. Consider those souls who live in grinding poverty through unjust or corrupt systems of governance, who offer their prayers to God for the relief of their suffering. Perhaps God decides, at least in part, to answer their prayers by giving in abundance to lottery winners, and the wealthy, out of their fellow-feeling for the suffering of 'family members' in other countries, give abundantly and with love from their wealth. God always answers prayers – sometimes in ways that require very different thinking from those of materialistic man!

Here are some statements by Bahá'u'lláh that highlight the inadequacy of human intellect to discern, without the guidance of the Manifestation of God, that which is helpful from that which is harmful. These statements are focused on raising awareness of the parameters of 'liberty':

> Consider the pettiness of men's minds. They ask for that which injureth them, and cast away the thing that profiteth them. They are, indeed, of those that are far astray. We find some men desiring liberty, and priding themselves therein. Such men are in the depths of ignorance.
>
> Liberty must, in the end, lead to sedition, whose flames none can quench. Thus warneth you He Who is the Reckoner, the All-Knowing. Know ye that the embodiment of liberty and its symbol is the animal. That which beseemeth man is submission unto such restraints as will protect him from his own ignorance, and guard him against the harm of the mischief-maker. Liberty causeth man to overstep the bounds of propriety, and to infringe on the dignity of his station. It debaseth him to the level of extreme depravity and wickedness.
>
> . . . We approve of liberty in certain circumstances, and refuse to sanction it in others. We, verily, are the All-Knowing.
>
> Say: True liberty consisteth in man's submission unto My commandments, little as ye know it. Were men to observe that which We have sent down unto them from the Heaven of Revelation, they would, of a certainty, attain unto perfect liberty. Happy is the man that hath apprehended the Purpose of God in whatever He hath revealed from the Heaven of His Will that pervadeth all created things. Say: The liberty that profiteth you is to be found nowhere except in complete servitude unto God, the Eternal Truth. Whoso hath tasted of its sweetness will refuse to barter it for all the dominion of earth and heaven.[15]

Hopefully, after a brief examination of the assumptions that man is basically a material being so that materialist ideals will satisfy his needs, and that there should be no limits to personal liberty providing one's freedom does no harm to others, it becomes clear that this view is short-sighted and not held by those who view life through a spiritual lens. To their detriment, materialists can only see what is in front of their physical eyes, because physical eyesight is all that is functioning at this stage of their development; it is all they believe in. Insight, which enables a much longer vision, is provided by the Manifestations of God Who are knowledgeable of that which will help us, as opposed to that which is harmful. This help is because the Manifestations know the 'necessary relationships deriving from the reality of things',[16] and therefore provide guidance from our Maker, called 'religion', to guide us away from short-sighted behaviours to that which is personally rewarding and of benefit to humanity. Spiritual and materialistic perspectives are diametrically opposed. We need to judge fairly of the efficacy of these differing perspectives by their 'fruits', in other words, what they actually contribute to individual happiness and the well-being of society.

PART TWO

NAVIGATING THE MINEFIELD OF EXISTENTIAL QUESTIONS

For me, the most difficult minefield to navigate was around questions of the apparent contradictions humans face. For instance, there is so much suffering and evil in the world that the existence of a loving, caring God almost defies a rational explanation. Curt answers to this, such as 'This is a mystery and we must have faith,' do not satisfy any enquiring mind. And then there are questions of whether human beings carry on existing in some way or another after their physical death. If so, are there any implications for this that need to be considered, such that human existence is viewed in a way more profitable materially, socially, creatively, emotionally, intellectually and spiritually?

As in many things in life, a platform or base must first be established upon which to build something that is safe and enduring. What materials to select to build a base, from the large range available, is extremely important. Analogously, I have chosen two 'materials' to build a foundation upon which to answer questions as to why there is so much evil and suffering in the world. The first is the nature of human beings, which, I have concluded after consideration of the teachings of Bahá'u'lláh and 'Abdu'l-Bahá, is essentially 'spiritual'. This has been discussed previously. We are spiritual beings having an experience of life through the instruments and organs of the body. The second 'material' is the existence of a non-physical entity called the 'soul' or 'human spirit' which continues its life after the physical body dies. When these two 'materials', the spiritual nature of human beings and its continuity, are mixed, it provides the cement that enables a strong, safe and an enduring foundation upon which many existential questions or problems can be answered in a coherent way.

9

EVIDENCE OF THE HUMAN SPIRIT AND A SPIRITUAL WORLD

For those sceptical about the existence of the soul and its continuity, it is necessary to provide some evidence. I have tried to do this, gathering insights and information from various sources to share with you in this chapter.

It must be stated that it is very difficult to prove the existence of the human spirit or the soul of man, and perhaps even more difficult to prove that it continues to exist after the body dies. But 'difficult' is not the same as 'impossible'. It helps to give thought to two categories of existence – material and intelligible. Material things exist and are provable by our senses; non-physical things also exist but are provable by our intellect. Just because we cannot, say, bury a thought or incinerate virtues does not mean that thoughts and virtues do not exist. Similarly, it is possible to understand that we cannot bury or cremate the spirit of a human being, because the spirit is not a physical reality but a spiritual one. To get a handle on this requires the use of our intellect, or rational faculties, over and above our physical senses.

The assertion that the soul continues to exist after physical death in worlds that transcend the material universe, I believed to be true even before coming into contact with the Bahá'í teachings. But this contact greatly deepened and expanded my understanding. However, those who only view life through a material lens deny the existence of the human spirit, claiming that because it is not physical and therefore not tangible to the senses, there is no proof that it exists. Historically, this question of whether man is more than just his physical body has vexed philosophers and thinkers throughout the ages. One such great soul was Ibn Sina (980–1027 CE) a Muslim, whose Latinized name was Avicenna, one of the greatest polymaths the world has ever known. Jim Al-Khalili, in his book *The Golden Age of Arabic Science*, quotes the 'floating man' thought experiment of Ibn Sina:

> Suppose that a man is created all at once, fully developed and perfectly formed but with his vision shrouded from perceiving all external objects – created floating in the air or in space, not buffeted by any perceptible currents of the air that supports him, his limbs separated and kept out of contact with each other. Then let the subject consider whether he would affirm the existence of himself. There is no doubt he would affirm his own existence, although not affirming the reality of any of his limbs or inner organs.
>
> Hence the one who affirms has a means to be alerted to the existence of his soul as something other than the body and to his being directly acquainted with their existence and aware of it. [1]

A spiritual understanding of the existence of the human spirit is that it is connected with the body, but not in a physical sense. The human spirit or soul is not a physical entity, so it does not reside in the body or any place in the material world. We need to revert to metaphor to get a handle on the association of the soul with the human body. Hence, as explained in the Bahá'í Writings, the human spirit is connected with the body as the sun is connected with a mirror. Here, 'sun' is analogous to the human spirit and 'mirror' is analogous to the body. The implication is that just as the sun can be seen shining in a mirror or, indeed, can be seen shining even if the mirror is damaged or ceases to exist, so too does the spirit of a human being function in association with a physical body or even if the body is disabled, damaged or ceases to exist.

Looking more closely in the Bahá'í Writings I found that the association of the spirit with the human body is just one way that humans function. By 'function' is meant the way we can acquire knowledge, develop understandings and decide on a course of action that the body carries out. On this point 'Abdu'l-Bahá states that it is the spirit of man, through the instruments and organs of the body, that is doing this:

> . . . it sees with the eye, hears with the ear, speaks with the tongue. These are actions of the spirit and operations of the human reality, but they occur through the mediation of bodily instruments. Thus, it is the spirit that sees, but by means of the eye; it is the spirit that hears, but by means of the ear; it is the spirit that speaks, but by means of the tongue.[2]

There is another way that the spirit can know, understand and act, and that is without instruments and organs of the body. 'Abdu'l-Bahá gives an example of this, stating that:

> in the state of sleep, it sees without eyes, it hears without ears, it speaks without a tongue, it runs without feet – in brief, all these powers are exerted without the mediation of instruments and organs...
>
> While asleep, this physical body is as dead: It neither sees, nor hears, nor feels, and it has neither consciousness nor perception – its powers are suspended. Yet the spirit is not only alive and enduring but also exerts a greater influence, soars to loftier heights, and possesses a deeper understanding.[3]

In both instances, however, whether asleep or awake it is the human spirit that can know, understand and act; these functions are not the product of bio-chemical processes in the brain. During wakefulness, of course, the instruments of the human senses, the organ of the brain coupled with the intellectual abilities, are necessary connections with the human spirit. But the human spirit exists independently of these agencies just as the sun exists independently of a mirror.

So far, a few statements about the human spirit indicate its existence, but it would be right to point out that these statements are not proof of the continuance of the human spirit after death. Building on what has been mentioned above, then, what follows are some points to be considered as to its existence and continuity, the first being a consideration of the functioning of the human spirit while awake. 'Abdu'l-Bahá points to an internal process every person undertakes daily, as a proof of the existence of the human spirit. He states:

> When you wish to reflect upon or consider a matter, you consult something within you. You say, shall I do it, or shall I not do it? Is it better to make this journey or abandon it? Whom do you consult? Who is within you deciding this question? Surely there is a distinct power, an intelligent ego. Were it not distinct from your ego, you would not be consulting it. It is greater than the faculty of thought. It is your spirit which teaches you, which advises and decides upon matters. Who is it that interrogates? Who is it that answers? There is no doubt that it is the spirit . . .[4]

In another place 'Abdu'l-Bahá calls this 'conversation with the higher self'.[5] But let us underline the point 'Abdu'l-Bahá is making here. Everyone asks himself questions regularly and frequently and a reply is received. This is not one thought consulting another thought, it is the human spirit that is consulted, and this spirit is not the same as thought; it is 'greater than the faculty of thought'. Although the mental faculties have a part to play in this process by forming the questions and receiving the answers, it is the 'I' of a person, his soul or spirit, that is the instructor and advisor. Now, if there were no human spirit to consult, then there would be no guidance or instructions forthcoming; but because guidance and instructions are received this is one proof of the existence of the human spirit. I must admit, it took some time for the 'penny to drop' on this explanation. To grasp hold of it I needed an analogy, which now follows.

Just as thought has a non-physical existence, along with imagination and memory, the spirit, as stated, also has a non-physical existence. Although different parts of the brain are linked with thought processes, imagination and memory, this is no proof of it being the producer of thoughts, imagination and memory. A TV, for example, receives signals in the form of electrical impulses of moving images and sound from a transmitter and changes them back into moving images and sound. In a rough analogy, the brain is like the TV receiver and the spirit is analogous to the transmitter. Although everyone knows that the TV exists because it is a physical thing, just as the brain exists because it is a physical thing, yet it takes an act of reasoning to accept that the TV is only able to produce images and sound if its parts are in good working order and the transmitter is transmitting. It does not produce images and sound without the transmitter; clearly the TV is useless without the transmitted signals. It takes another act of reasoning to understand that if the TV is damaged or is even non-existent, it in no way means the transmitter is damaged or non-existent. Similarly, if the brain is damaged and cannot perform its functions properly this does not imply that the soul is damaged or non-existent.

In the following passage 'Abdu'l-Bahá gives insights into what is mentioned above, regarding the existence of the human spirit which, this time, He calls man's 'reality':

> It is manifest that beyond this material body, man is endowed with another reality, which is the world of exemplars constituting the heavenly body of man. In speaking, man says, 'I saw,' 'I spoke,' 'I went.' Who is this *I*? It is obvious that this *I* is different from this body. It is clear that when man is thinking, it is as though he were consulting with some other person. With whom is he consulting? It is evident that it is

another reality, or one aside from this body, with whom he enters into consultation when he thinks, 'Shall I do this work or not?' 'What will be the result of my doing this?' Or when he questions the other reality, 'What is the objection to this work if I do it?' And then that reality in man communicates its opinion to him concerning the point at issue. Therefore, that reality in man is clearly and obviously other than his body – an ego with which man enters into consultation and whose opinion man seeks.[6]

The quality and degree of accuracy of answers received from the soul, after it has received an existential question, depend upon the degree to which the soul has been illumined with the insights of the heavenly world. Of course, no one has to be on any spiritual path to get answers to questions of a material nature, such as what the speed of light is or how to bake a cake. However, 'Abdu'l-Bahá makes it clear that for the human spirit to emit answers that are spiritual, the spirit or human consciousness must become 'divine', 'sanctified' and 'holy'.[7] What is meant by divine, sanctified and holy, and how this is done, is a subject of great interest but will have to be left at this point because, if taken further, it will take us too far away from the main aim of this chapter. Suffice it to say, as an example of the importance of the condition of the human spirit, if when consulted it requires a wise answer, this will only be forthcoming if the human spirit is illumined with the divine quality of wisdom.

Now let us focus on proofs of the existence of the human spirit and its ability to know and understand, without instruments and organs of the body, primarily during the sleep state. In this condition every part of the human body is as dead, yet in the sleep state an amazing amount of life is going on. Sleep is defined in an article published by the Rand Organization 'as a suspension of normal waking consciousness that involves a diminished capacity for interaction with one's environment.'[8] This is an interesting definition as it clearly underlines part of the point above made by 'Abdu'l-Bahá. Yet it only explains what is not happening when asleep, while everyone knows what does happen – we experience another world, the world of dreams.

Approximately one third of our life is spent asleep, which seems a waste of time if its only purpose is to replenish the body's energy and health ready for the next day. Yet many think this is its only purpose. But sleep is not just essential for recuperation of the body, it's necessary for the human spirit to experience another world – a non-physical world. Usually this is experienced during the rapid eye movement phases of sleep when we dream.[9]

There are indeed many things to learn about this dream-world. 'Abdu'l-Bahá comments on 'how often it happens that in the world of dreams the spirit solves a problem that it could not solve in the realm of wakefulness.'[10] There is enough evidence to demonstrate this point. The idea for Google, for instance, came to Larry Page during a dream which showed that he could download the entire web onto computers. He 'spent the middle of that night scribbling out the details and convincing myself it would work'.[11] In a dream, the 19th-century chemist Dimitri Mendeleyev 'understood . . . that the basic chemical elements are all related to each other in a manner similar to the themes and phrases in music'. When awake, 'he was able to write out for the first time the entire periodic table, which forms the basis of modern chemistry'.[12] Fredrick Banting won a Nobel Prize in 1921 for discovering how to treat diabetes with insulin. The idea came to him in a dream: 'With the help of Charles Best, he finally isolated the compound that has changed the lives of millions of diabetics ever since.'[13]

Srinivasa Ramanujan (1887–1920), living in the slums of Madras, was a great, self-taught, Indian mathematical genius. He was invited to Cambridge University in 1914 by English mathematician G. H. Hardy who recognized his unconventional genius. He worked there for five years producing startling results and was elected a Fellow of the Royal Society, a major honour.[14]

Ramanujan made substantial contributions 'to analytical

theory of numbers, elliptical functions, continued fractions, and infinite series, and proved more than 3,000 mathematical theorems in his lifetime. Ramanujan stated that the insight for his work came to him in his dreams on many occasions.'[15] Ramanujan developed formulas and theories 'that nobody needed – until they needed them. For example [some work on black holes] . . . Nobody even knew that black holes were something to study when Ramanujan was alive . . . What's astonishing is that Ramanujan has done this for us several dozen times.'[16]

One such dream giving a mathematical solution to a problem is described by Ramanujan:

> While asleep I had an unusual experience. There was a red screen formed by flowing blood as it were. I was observing it. Suddenly a hand began to write on the screen. I became all attention. That hand wrote a number of results in elliptic integrals. They stuck to my mind. As soon as I woke up, I committed them to writing . . .[17]

Apart from problem solving during the dream state, there are also many documented accounts of dreams being an artistic reservoir of creativity. In 1999, 'Yesterday', a song from the Beatles *Help* album, was voted by BBC Radio 2 listeners as the best song of the 20th century. The *Guinness Book of Records* holds that it is 'the most covered song ever, with over 3,000 versions recorded, and Broadcast Music Incorporated asserts the song was performed over seven million times in the 20th century alone . . .' It was composed by Paul McCartney who woke after a dream with the melody in his head.[18] The South African group Ladysmith Black Mambazo began in 1964 after Shabalala 'dreamed of pure vocal harmonies in the style known as isicathamiya, originated by black workers in the South African mines'.[19]

Scenes of the *The Strange Case of Dr Jekyll and Mr Hyde* came to Robert Louis Stevenson in a dream. Some believe that this story is about schizophrenia before this condition was medically understood. Other writers such as Samuel Taylor Coleridge, Edgar Allan Poe, Stephen King and Stephanie Meyer, author of the popular *Twilight* series, have all been inspired by dreams to write about characters and plots.

It must be emphasized that those who have found answers to problems while asleep and those who have been creatively inspired have indicated that the answers or creative inspiration were given as a gift. They claim they did not think of it themselves nor did they work things out in their dream. No, they were the receivers, but, of course, they had to work on that gift while awake to bring it into the physical world.

The sceptic, perhaps, may consider problem solving and creativity flowing from the dream state as no clear proof of the existence of the human spirit, yet alone that it can be detached from the body to function in another, non-physical world when asleep. They may conclude that because the brain has moved from alpha and beta wave patterns while awake to theta and delta wave patterns while asleep, it is still active in a more relaxed mode, allowing the imagination to work around the solution of problems or to enhance creativity. But those who have had these experiences, (and I know several people who have, making it a fairly common occurrence) who are not famous people, and have solved more mundane problems or have been creatively inspired when asleep, need no persuading of the existence of the human spirit and of a spiritual world. For them their experience is significant, real and is all that is needed, even if the sceptic objects to it being only anecdotal evidence.

More compelling as proof of the existence of the human spirit and a world transcending the material world occurs when a glimpse of the future is experienced during the dream state. Whether we call this insight 'precognition' or 'premonition', this phenomenon, which is in no way a rare happening, occurs so frequently that we could say it is a feature of being human.

One example of a premonition dream was experienced by Eryl Mai Jones, a ten-year-old girl who attended Pantglas Junior

School at Aberfan. On 21 October 1966 a mountain of coal slag and waste, towering over the Welsh mining village, was destabilized by recent rains, releasing a deadly flow of black coal sludge and rocks which engulfed Pantglas Junior School, obliterating a cottage and 20 houses on its path of destruction. Actually, my father was one of the men at the scene shortly after, as part of the BBC news crew covering the tragedy. He, along with scores of others, tried to rescue the children and adults – but to little avail. Little Eryl was one among 116 children and 28 adults who were crushed or suffocated to death that day, in what has been recognized as one of Britain's most horrific peacetime tragedies. Eryl, uncannily, had told her mother days before the catastrophe that she was 'not afraid to die', and added, 'I shall be with Peter and June.' The day before it happened Eryl said to her Mum, 'Let me tell you about my dream last night. I dreamt I went to school and there was no school there. Something black had come down all over it!' We all understand that children have great imagination and can sympathize with Eryl's Mum and feel her soul-crushing suffering for not understanding or taking her child's dream premonition seriously. Peter and June were Eryl's school friends who also died and were buried side-by-side in a mass grave, as predicted in the dream.[20]

Another premonition dream was linked with 11 September 2001, a day remembered as a day of horror. Hijacked planes were flown by terrorists, with all the crew and passengers aboard, into the Twin Towers in New York and the Pentagon, while another crashed in a field in Pennsylvania. Mayhem ensued, resulting in 2,830, at the time, confirmed deaths. Several people had premonitions of aspects of this terror, but not the full picture. A week before the attack, a North Carolina mother, for instance, dreamt that she heard a voice repeating 2,830 while she was spinning about in darkness. She also heard a name that she couldn't identify which sounded like 'Rooks' or 'Horook'. The woman had family tickets to fly to Disneyland on that fateful day but cancelled them, 'despite protestations from her husband that she was over-reacting'. It turned out that first officer of United Airlines flight 175, which crashed into the South Tower, was called Michael Horrocks.[21]

A more personal premonition dream comes from a mother living in Washington State. Waking at 2.30 a.m. she recalled a disturbing nightmare. Above her baby's cot hung a large chandelier which had fallen and crushed the baby. A violent storm also raged, and she remembered the time on the clock reading 4.35 a.m. Alarmed by this nightmare when she awoke, she rushed to her baby's room and took the baby back to her own bed. 'Two hours later, the couple were woken by a loud crash. They dashed into their child's room to find the crib demolished by the chandelier, which had fallen directly onto it. In a further twist, a storm was raging – and the time on the clock read 4.35 a.m.'[22]

'How often it happens', stated 'Abdu'l-Bahá, 'that the spirit has a dream in the realm of sleep whose purport comes to be exactly materialized two years hence!'[23]

It's quite natural that dreams of some pending future disaster catch our attention. In fact, dreams of future events have now become the subject of research. One such study, undertaken by M. S. Stowell for her doctoral dissertation, involved investigating the claims of 51 presumed precognitive dreams. She proved that 31 such dreams had indeed come true.[24] Many people, however, have had precognitive dreams of a future mundane event and as such they do not rise to the surface as something exceptional to be noted. A little chat with friends and family will reveal at least one person, if not several, who have had precognition type dreams.

Bahá'u'lláh, in evincing proofs of the human spirit and a spiritual world transcending this physical world, writes:

> Behold how many secrets are deposited therein [in dreams], how many wisdoms treasured up, how many worlds concealed. Observe how thou art asleep in a dwelling, and its doors are shut; on a sudden thou findest thyself in a far-off

city, which thou enterest without moving thy feet or weary-
ing thy body. Without taxing thine eyes, thou seest; without
troubling thine ears, thou hearest; without a tongue, thou
speakest. And perchance when ten years have passed, thou
wilt witness in this temporal world the very things thou hast
dreamt tonight.[25]

Note Bahá'u'lláh's mention of the many 'secrets' and 'wisdoms'
that are stored within the dream world. Bahá'u'lláh wants us to
consider one secret and wisdom at least, which is that two worlds
are involved when we dream of future events. One is the physical
world where the body is asleep and therefore is non-functioning,
a condition similar to death. The other is a world where a future
event is seen in the dream. He then concludes that because there
is a time difference between dreaming of the event and its actual
occurrence in the physical world, the world entered in the dream
is different from the physical world. If this were not the case,
then the future event should occur at exactly the same time it is
dreamt. Here is what Bahá'u'lláh writes about this:

Behold how the thing which thou hast seen in thy dream
is, after a considerable lapse of time, fully realized. Had the
world in which thou didst find thyself in thy dream been
identical with the world in which thou livest, it would have
been necessary for the event occurring in that dream to have
transpired in this world at the very moment of its occurrence.
Were it so, you yourself would have borne witness unto it.
This being not the case, however, it must necessarily follow
that the world in which thou livest is different and apart from
that which thou hast experienced in thy dream. This latter
world hath neither beginning nor end.[26]

To me, this is conclusive proof that human beings, apart from
having a physical body through which the human spirit works,
also have access to a non-physical world, a spiritual world, when

asleep, where the soul has a life without a body. Bahá'u'lláh asks us to 'Consider the difference between these two worlds, and the mysteries they conceal'; and the purpose of this, He states, is that, 'attended by divine confirmations, thou mayest attain unto heavenly discoveries and enter the realms of holiness.'[27] It is of great comfort to know that the proof of something as important as the existence of the human spirit and of a spiritual world beyond this physical universe is available within each human being. Everyone sleeps, everyone dreams, everyone can, by reflecting on the differences between the awake world and the dream world, 'attain unto heavenly discoveries and enter the realms of holiness'. Bahá'u'lláh takes this point even further, specifying that proof of such an important issue as the existence of the spiritual world spoken about by the Prophets of God is within everyone, so that materialistic philosophers will not be able to convince us otherwise. Here are Bahá'u'lláh's words:

> God, the Most High, hath placed these signs in men so that veiled minds might not deny the mysteries of the life beyond, nor belittle that which hath been promised them. For some hold fast to reason and deny whatever reason comprehendeth not, and yet feeble minds can never grasp the reality of the stages that we have related: The universal divine Intellect alone can comprehend them.[28]

Yet another aspect of proof for the existence of the human spirit and the spiritual world has surfaced during the second half of the 20th century. Dr Raymond Moody's ground-breaking studies of hundreds of people who claimed they had out of the body experiences when they were categorized as 'clinically dead' has since stimulated serious research, resulting in 1978 in the International Association for Near Death Studies (IANDS). This was the first organization in the world devoted to the scientific study of Near Death Experiences (NDEs) and their relationship to mind and consciousness. Generally, those who have had an NDE came within a fraction of death through such traumas as a heart attack, severe illness, or accidents, but were later restored to consciousness. They lived to tell their story of what happened to them when classed as virtually dead.

The neuroscientist Mario Beauregard, at the Departments of Psychology and Radiology and the Neuroscience Research Center at the University of Montreal, writes:

> NDEs are the vivid, realistic, and often deeply life-changing experiences of men, women, and children who have been physiologically or psychologically close to death. They can be evoked by cardiac arrest and coma caused by brain damage, intoxication, or asphyxia. They can also happen following such events as electrocution, complications from surgery, or severe blood loss during or after a delivery. They can even occur as the result of accidents or illnesses in which individuals genuinely fear they might die. Surveys conducted in the United States and Germany suggest that approximately 4.2 percent of the population has reported an NDE. It has also been estimated that more than 25 million individuals worldwide have had an NDE in the past 50 years.[29]

Those interested in reading more about the research into near death experiences, may like to explore the best-selling book *Evidence of the Afterlife.* by radiation oncologist and NDE experience expert Dr Jeffrey Long and his colleagues Paul Perry and Bob Dunsworth, gathering findings from the Near Death Experience Research Foundation (NDERF) which gives strong scientific evidence for life after death. In Long and Perry's recent book, *God and the Afterlife*, which is the result of the largest NDE study in history, the findings are staggeringly in favour of the existence of an afterlife.

Why these experiences have only surfaced now, considering the longevity of the human race, may be due to the development of modern science and technology that is capable of rescuing from the clutches of death those who would have surely died in more primitive times. In rare cases in the past, however, it is safe to assume that some would recover after being clinically dead and an even smaller number would have had a NDE. As Helen Thomson writes in the *New Scientist*, 'Near-death experiences have been passed down through folklore, myth and storytelling since ancient civilisations.'[30] However, I'm sure many would have kept such an experience to themselves, given the ignorance and superstition of those times. Who would dare share their experience with others?

Those who have undergone an NDE state that they experience a similar series of events such as floating or being outside their body and looking at it, being aware of what is happening, being drawn to a light at the end of a tunnel, meeting members of the family or friends who have passed on, being drawn by great attraction to a Being of Light and reviewing their life with the Being of Light. Most do not want to return to their bodies; only a few volunteered to return for a specific responsibility or purpose, for instance, caring for their small children. Although most NDEs are recorded as positive, heavenly experiences, nonetheless, accounts are now being recorded of 'hellish' encounters. For the purpose of this book, however, even though all experiences are of great interest, I am more focused on whether being out of the body is verifiable, as this would go a long way to validate the existence of the human spirit or soul.

Unfortunately, most of what people who have had an NDE state is not verifiable. How can it be proved, for example, that they have passed through a tunnel or met a Being of Light? It is of interest, though, that so many experiences are similar, having been gathered from thousands across the world. This may be analogous to the similar experiences of childbirth, but under so many different circumstances. But similarity, although far-reaching and from a diversity of cultural backgrounds, is not proof of consciousness outside of that experienced by the body when awake, although it may point in that direction. Interestingly, researchers of NDEs have documented evidence of a range of verifiable 'out of the body' incidents. One of the original researchers in the field of near-death studies, P. M. H. Atwater, writes:

> Messages of various types, revelations, family secrets laid bare, information the experiencer absolutely could not have known before – pop up during the phenomenon, perhaps during that part where the individual is met by loved ones who have died before, maybe while he or she is talking with an angel (a Being of Light), often as part of the past-life review or during 'meetings' with otherworldly beings.[31]

A typical NDE is related in Mario Beauregard's book Brain Wars. Singer-songwriter Pam Reynolds, based in Atlanta in 1991, experienced feeling extremely dizzy, losing her ability to speak, and difficulty moving her body. 'A CAT scan showed that she had a giant artery aneurysm – a grossly swollen blood vessel in the wall of her basilar artery, close to the brain stem. If it burst, which could happen at any moment, it would kill her. But the standard surgery to drain and repair it might kill her too.' To perform surgery on the aneurysm, neurosurgeon Robert Spetzler and his surgical team at the Barrow Neurological Institute in Phoenix, Arizona, induced a cardiac arrest hypothermically, that is, Pam's body temperature had to drop so low that she was essentially dead, and her brain would not function. 'The low temperature would also soften the swollen blood vessels, allowing them to be operated on with less risk of bursting. When the procedure was complete, the surgical team would bring her back to a normal temperature before irreversible damage set in.' During this very complicated procedure Pam, who was classed as clinically dead, came out of her body and witnessed many details of the operation which she reported later. These were 'especially important because cardiologist Michael Sabom was able to obtain verification from medical personnel regarding crucial details of the surgical intervention that Pam reported'. There was no way Pam could have known through the usual brain and sense activities of awareness, as the brain, heart and bodily functions had closed down; beside this she was heavily anaesthetized.[32]

It is interesting to recall Pam's out-of-the-body experience (OBE) which developed into a NDE during the course of the operation. She found herself:

> floating out of the operating room and traveling down a tunnel with a light. She saw deceased relatives and friends, including her long-dead Grandmother, waiting at the end of this tunnel. She entered the presence of a brilliant, wonderfully warm and loving light, and sensed that her soul was part of God and that everything in existence was created from the light (the breathing of God). But this extraordinary experience ended abruptly, as Reynolds's deceased uncle led her back to her body – a feeling she described as 'plunging into a pool of ice'.[33]

In the same book we also read of Maria, who had a severe heart attack and whose case was documented by her critical care social worker, Kimberly Clark:

> Maria was a migrant worker who had a severe heart attack while visiting friends in Seattle. She was rushed to Harborview Hospital and placed in the coronary care unit. A few days later, she had a cardiac arrest but was rapidly resuscitated. The following day, Clark visited her. Maria told Clark that during her cardiac arrest she was able to look down from the ceiling and watch the medical team at work on her body. At one point in this experience, said Maria, she found herself outside the hospital and spotted a tennis shoe on the ledge of the north side of the third floor of the building. She was able to provide several details regarding its appearance, including the observations that one of its laces was stuck underneath the heel and that the little toe area was worn. Maria wanted

to know for sure whether she had 'really' seen that shoe, and she begged Clark to try to locate it.

Quite skeptical, Clark went to the location described by Maria – and found the tennis shoe. From the window of her hospital room, the details that Maria had recounted could not be discerned. But upon retrieval of the shoe, Clark confirmed Maria's observations. 'The only way she could have had such a perspective,' said Clark, 'was if she had been floating right outside and at very close range to the tennis shoe. I retrieved the shoe and brought it back to Maria; it was very concrete evidence for me.'[34]

Another story of an OBE was related to me by my wife several years ago. She heard it on a BBC Radio 2 programme, but didn't remember the references that could be checked to validate it. Luckily my daughter did some sleuthing on her computer and found the story. It can be found in the book *Facing Death and Finding Hope*, by Christine Longaker. The story is told of a 'massive car accident on a major highway':

A man in the accident sustained multiple fractures and major damage to internal organs, and clinically died. He felt his consciousness rise above his body and was able to survey the accident scene below . . .

Unable to see the accident, but surmising that it must have been quite serious, a woman whose car was now at a standstill down the freeway began to pray. The consciousness of the man who had clinically died was immediately attracted to her prayer, and found it gave him strength. Eventually, the emergency crew were able to resuscitate him; upon reentering his body he experienced unimaginable pain. After many months of surgery and rehabilitation, he was finally able to leave the hospital.

Soon after, grateful for her prayers and thankful that he was still alive, he went to the woman's home to thank her. She was surprised, as she didn't remember doing anything special. Besides, how did he know she had prayed for him? And how did he find her again? Feeling the love and positive power of her prayer when his consciousness was above the accident scene, he was so grateful for her compassion that in order to thank her later, he had noticed and remembered her licence plate number![35]

In trying to prove the existence of the human spirit, and that it functions without the physical body in another condition that is the world of the spirit, I have referred to several facets of human experience that indicate its existence. It has been stated that when holding an internal conversation, it is the human spirit that is consulted, and it is the human spirit that makes the decisions as to what to say and do. When we are awake and when any of the physical senses are used, they become vehicles through which the human spirit functions, so when the eye sees and the ear hears, it is the human spirit or the soul that is seeing and hearing. Also, when the arms or the legs move or when there is any other voluntary movement of the body, it is the human spirit directing those movements – so if it kicks or embraces someone, it is doing so through the instrumentality of organs and instruments of the body. During the sleep stage, the human spirit functions independently of the body, because the body is asleep, but in the dream world it functions without the body's instruments and organs. In that state the human spirit walks, runs, talks, meets others and can even fly. During the dream state, many people are given answers to problems they have not solved when awake. Some have increased their creativity when asleep. They have heard music, been inspired to write creatively; in fact, the dream state has been a reservoir of creativity from which artistic developments have been drawn and used when awake. Further, many people have dreamt of future events, whether called premonitions or precognition, and have experienced or validated these events while awake, sometime in the future. Finally, there is a ground swell of evidence of out-of-the-body experiences that are verifiable from those who have had a NDE when classed as clinically dead. In other words, their out-of-the-body experience is evidence that it is the human spirit that has functioned independently of the body in a non-physical world.

Bearing all these phenomena in mind, it is not unreasonable to accept that their aggregate points in the direction of the existence of the human spirit and a spiritual world. At the very least, this direction should not be dismissed because it does not fit with a materialistic interpretation of reality. Perceptions and understandings of reality can grow and develop over time and room should be made for this, otherwise we could find ourselves blinkered and 'out of sync' with spiritual and material progress. This lesson came home to me when one day I reflected on how much vegetarianism has taken root in our society so as to be a normal, everyday life-style choice. This was not always the case. In the 1960s vegetarians were considered somewhat 'weird people', on the fringe of society. How would they get their protein if they didn't eat meat, was commonly asked? And I was one of the majority who used to think this way.

Inevitably, in a society where materialism is the prevailing 'religion', there are those who will not let go of their hardened opinions on this subject, even if irrefutable proof of the existence of the soul of man were to be laid before them. A conversation between philosopher Neal Grossman and an academic colleague underlines this point. Bernard Haisch, in his book *The God Theory*, writes about this conversation:

> . . . the academic cavalierly dismisses accurately reported details of near-death experiences that could only have been perceived from a vantage point outside the body as coincidences and lucky guesses. An exasperated Grossman finally asks: 'what will it take, short of having a near-death experience yourself, to convince you that they are real?' Rising to the occasion . . . the academic responds: 'If I had a near-death

experience myself, I would conclude that I was hallucinating, rather than believe my mind can exist independent of my brain.' Then, to dispose of the annoying evidence once and for all, the champion of enquiry confidently states that the concept of mind existing independent of matter has been shown to be a false theory, and there can be no evidence for something that is false. Grossman observes: 'This was a momentous experience for me, because here was an educated, intelligent man telling me that he will not give up materialism, no matter what.'[36]

Now, I would like to put to you a question. If only one person in the entire world experiences only one, never mind a number, of the above phenomena and it is verifiable, does this not point to the possibility of the existence of the human spirit (some may call it consciousness, or mind) that can function without the human body, as well as the existence of a spiritual world transcending the material universe? For if it can be experienced by one person, it surely proves, because we are all human beings and share certain common characteristics, that it is possible for it to be experienced by any other human being. To appreciate this point, suppose (in another analogy) you came across only one person who whistled. Would you conclude no one else in the world could whistle or would you rationalize that whistling is possible for all humans, given that they belong to the same species with common, shared characteristics of the species? This has huge implications for our understanding of the scientific method, when it is rigidly based on accepting some phenomena as verifiable only when it conforms to large-scale surveys, which is the main method used to test hypotheses in the study of the humanities, as opposed to the physical sciences, that prove a hypothesis only when an experiment is replicable under defined conditions.

To hold the view that the human spirit does not exist is gradually becoming untenable as more is observed about human phenomena. Similarly, the existence of a non-physical world, wherein the human spirit can function without the use of the body's instruments and organs, is increasingly the subject of research and study.

Because the human spirit is not physical, it cannot die but continues to function in the spiritual world after the body is discarded. In a sense, it is like the discarding of the placenta after a baby is physically born into this world. While in the womb the placenta is essential for the growth of the baby, but after birth it is no longer needed. When reflection on this subject is freed from the undertow of materialistic assumptions, more and more people will readily accept that we are indeed spiritual beings, undergoing a physical experience. Hence 'Abdu'l-Bahá stated that man 'is, in reality, a spiritual being, and only when he lives in the spirit is he truly happy.'[37]

This is a profound statement. Put in a negative way, 'Abdu'l-Bahá is saying, unless we realize that our reality is spiritual and not physical and if we live our life focused only on the material world, we will never be happy. And not to be happy, for whatever the reason, is to experience suffering. With these thoughts in mind, we now have a platform to build on, in an attempt to understand why human beings experience suffering, without undermining in the slightest, belief in the existence of God, Who is Compassionate and Merciful. This attempt will follow in the next chapters.

10

THE EXTENT OF SUFFERING

How are human beings to develop their potential for consciousness without the means to do so? Surely, in the process of becoming aware of ourselves, our treasury of latent abilities will require trying times in order to develop, sometimes with prolonged periods of pain and suffering. For instance, how are we to develop empathy if we have not felt suffering? How are we to become courageous if there is no fear to overcome? How are we to become wise if there are no painful consequences for foolishness? How can we desire to sacrifice if we have not felt the flame of love consume us?

The faculties we have for spiritual consciousness and growth require thought processes that can analyse, reflect, modify behaviour, and try new ways of responding to life's events. That the same rational faculties can be used to better our physical condition through scientific and technological progress is an indication that physical and spiritual well-being should go hand in hand. Unfortunately, so much suffering has been visited upon humanity, that it can overwhelm our abilities to make sense of it all. From this feeling of inadequacy there is a short step to dismissing the existence of God, as many have concluded that if He exists, He is guilty of the most heinous crime of unmitigated callousness. But is this not the reasoning of children – to look for blame in others rather than in our own unawareness, weakness and wickedness? When immature reasoning has masqueraded as the best that our rational faculties can produce, no wonder that

belief in God slips into the quagmire of futility, where materialism engulfs the human spirit and spawns its fruit of hopelessness,
gnawing anxieties, moral laxity and self-serving motives.

This chapter, then, is written as a beginning to help understand why human beings experience suffering if there is a God
who is supposed to be compassionate and merciful. It builds
on the previous chapter, which attempted to produce evidence
that the human spirit exists as an entity distinct from the human
body, and that this entity or spirit functions not only through
the human body, but also in a spiritual world apart from material existence. The logic for taking this course, instead of rushing
headlong into reasoned arguments for the prevalence of suffering, is to first establish that human reality is essentially spiritual
in nature and that the material world is something we are just
passing through on our journey of progress through all the worlds
of God. We are informed that 'Man is destined by God to undergo
a spiritual development that extends throughout eternity. His life
upon this earth is only the first stage of that development.'[1] It is
incomprehensible to me that anyone can make an argument for
the existence of suffering, if human life is confined to just the
time spent with a physical body. This would imply that there
really is no purpose in suffering if life ends at physical death, and
if there is no purpose it is logical to believe that God cannot exist.
Conversely, the spiritually minded person believes that because
God exists and life for human beings is eternal, there is a purpose
to suffering. The materially minded person, however, may have
difficulties accepting this.

Having examined some evidence for existence of the human
spirit as a reality distinct from the human body, it may be possible
to conclude that if it continues to exist after the body has died,
it also has awareness, consciousness. Thus, the human spirit is
capable of gaining more and more understandings as it progresses
in a world beyond this physical world. For what would be the
purpose of continuity and consciousness if it were impossible to
become more aware, more conscious? If the human spirit lives

on, the reason for and purpose of suffering, as taught by all the great Prophets of God, is a factor in spiritual development and growth; whether in this world or in the world to come, it is not an obstacle to it.

In this regard it is instructive to reflect on the process of growth of awareness in children. How many times as adults do we look back at our undeveloped understanding as children and are thankful for the processes we have gone through from birth in this world to arrive at maturity? Every child experiences freedoms and restrictions when growing up, and as adults we still do. When a parent keeps a child safe by restricting its movements it can be quite upsetting for the child. The fact that the child does not understand why it cannot play near the edge of a precipice or eat a sweet that has been dropped on a toilet floor, is no reason to assume that there is no rationale behind the restrictions. Similarly, it may take more than the duration of physical life for a person to mature spiritually, to understand that for every single incident of suffering there has been a reason, or perhaps a wisdom which may be impossible to understand at the time. Admittedly it is hard to accept this assertion, but is it not just as hard for a child to accept that it will only really understand the processes it is going through when it reaches maturity many years later? In relation to this point, when Winston Churchill was experiencing grave setbacks in the Second World War, it was suggested to him that these were all blessings in disguise. To which he humorously replied that if they were blessings, they were indeed well disguised! Shoghi Effendi, Guardian of the Bahá'í Faith, takes this positive view of the reason for suffering:

As long as there will be life on earth, there will be also suffering, in various forms and degrees. But suffering, although an inescapable reality, can nevertheless be utilized as a means for the attainment of happiness. This is the interpretation given to it by all the prophets and saints, who, in the midst of severe tests and trials, felt happy and joyous and experienced what is best and holiest in life. Suffering is both a reminder and a guide. It stimulates us better to adapt ourselves to our environmental conditions, and thus leads the way to self improvement. In every suffering one can find a meaning and a wisdom. But it is not always easy to find the secret of that wisdom. It is sometimes only when all our suffering has passed that we become aware of its usefulness. What man considers to be evil turns often to be a cause of infinite blessings. And this is due to his desire to know more than he can. God's wisdom is, indeed, inscrutable to us all, and it is no use pushing too far trying to discover that which shall always remain a mystery to our mind.[2]

Some will not accept that it is only after a long period of suffering that reasons for the experience become clear, and for them the last comment in the passage above may be 'a bridge too far'. Also, there is the indication that our 'mind', with its limitations primarily stuck in the material world, may never discover the reason for suffering. This may be because the intellect of man needs to be lifted to a higher level, to the spiritual level, to make sense of what has happened, and if this does not occur, then suffering will always remain a mystery. However, according to the insights given by Bahá'u'lláh and 'Abdu'l-Bahá, the mind does not continue into the next life; consciousness and awareness of the human spirit is achieved through other means that are not clear to us in this life. It will be through these new powers that the soul will become aware of the mystery of suffering.

But let us not get too far ahead of ourselves. At this point I want to express heartfelt sympathy for anyone who is suffering for whatever reason. Certainly, during this time we have a taste, to a greater or lesser degree, of 'hell' and I would not wish this condition on anyone. When those who love us, long to help and have our best interests at heart, suggest that there is 'light at the end of the tunnel', it does little to assuage the anguish, sorrow or misery of suffering at that time, even if the statement is true. It seems that each portion of suffering we experience is felt in a distinct way by every individual, which implies that it must be handled in a way that is unique to each person. I recall that when my father-in-law suddenly died through a heart attack while playing chess for a club against a rival club, years later we could joke about it by recalling that he made his 'last move' and 'check-mated' himself. At the time, however, my wife was racked with grief. Her love for her father was so strong that she never thought she would recover from the shock of his dying so suddenly. We both believed in the next life and also prayers for dear departed ones. This was helpful, but perhaps we needed to be at a more advanced stage of consciousness to detach from the grief that drains one's life-force. Then a few weeks after the passing of my father-in-law, my wife had a significant dream. She dreamt that she was paddling in the sea, feeling safe, when suddenly a huge tidal wave could be seen developing on the horizon. She knew there was no time to run for safety – the wave was coming her way and she would be drowned. All she could do was to invoke God's help through a special short invocation that Bahá'ís offer in many circumstances. 'Ya-Bahá'u'l-Abhá'– O Thou the Glory of Glories – she cried out loud, several times. Immediately the huge tidal wave reduced to several small waves that lapped over her ankles, leaving her feeling greatly relieved. She woke me in the early hours of the morning to relate her dream, seeking some form of interpretation of it. As if out of nowhere there suddenly appeared an explanation that was of great help. The tidal wave represented the huge misery of grief my wife was suffering, a grief that threated to entirely drown her inner condition of well-being and composure. It was suggested that the help of God had come by reducing the size of the deadly wave when she called out for His protection; the tidal wave which represented an uncontrollable grief being reduced to that of small waves representing a grief that could be managed. At no point was it felt she should not grieve for her father's passing, but that she should not yield to it. Yielding to grief was, in fact, the tidal wave. Many years later after I had nursed my wife through cancer that eventually claimed her life, I recalled this dream. It was of great comfort to me also in trying to handle my own grief. I had also learned, in the intervening years, a passage from the Bahá'í Writings that confirmed this approach as to how to handle such potentially life-sapping despair: 'Yield not to grief or sorrow, they cause the greatest misery.'[3]

In the hope that I do not sound callous, I now want to take a different tack. Hopefully, you will stay with me, as I believe that the points that are raised will be of significance while travelling through the 'tunnel', towards the 'light' at its end. At the same time, I'm attempting to make the case for the existence of a Higher Being, no matter what name it is called.

So, I now want to make an incursion into the huge range and depth of suffering that has been the experience of the human race, for this has to be acknowledged. What follows will be depressing reading indeed, as the magnitude of suffering experienced by the human race is explored. As a means to categorize what many would regard as major sources of suffering, I have placed them under the headings of a contemporary interpretation of the Four Horsemen of the Apocalypse: pestilence (infectious diseases), war, famine and death.

Let us take a brief look at pestilence, the first of the Four Horsemen. Over the centuries, virulent diseases have wiped out whole swathes of humankind and have left many people crippled or maimed for life. In the 1300s the Black Death is estimated to have killed between a third and two-thirds of Europe's population, while in the 20th century, the 'Spanish flu' of 1918–19 killed 50 to 100 million people in less than two years, while smallpox was responsible for the deaths of more than 300 million people worldwide until its recent eradication. Today, malaria still causes one to three million deaths annually – one death every 30 seconds, and attacks the particularly vulnerable such as young children and pregnant women. AIDS and its related diseases have led to the deaths of more than 25 million people since it was first recognized in 1981, making it one of the most destructive epidemics in recorded history.[4] And let us not overlook the toll on human life cancer takes, even though most cancers are not considered an infectious disease. According to the World Health Organization (WHO), cancer is a leading cause of death worldwide (1 in 6 deaths), with 9.6 million deaths in 2018.[5]

I cannot complete this section on pestilence (infectious diseases), without reference to the pandemic still raging in 2022. Covid-19, the name given to the coronavirus which was first identified in Wuhan, China has swept around the world with deadly effect. Its death toll, some 7.5 million to date, with its severity mitigated through a vaccination programme, albeit inequitably and inadequately administered worldwide, is causing global havoc. No one can forecast its devastating effect on the economy, food and fuel supply, employment, education, and global structures of interconnectedness that have emerged in recent centuries!

The second Horseman of the Apocalypse is war. Violence and warfare have been a ubiquitous characteristic of humanity throughout history. Axes, spears, arrows, bayonets, bullets, bombs, killing machines on land, sea and air, gas and chemicals – apart from killing countless millions, have left their mark on an even greater number of the wounded and maimed, making life for them virtually unbearable. An estimated 3,023 wars have been recorded during human history; only five with the largest death tolls are mentioned here. Over 60 million were killed in World War II (1939–1945), over 30 million during the Mongol conquests (1206–1324), 25 million during the Qing dynasty conquest of the Ming dynasty (1616–1662), 20 million during the Taiping Rebellion in Southern China (1850–1864) and over 16 million in World War I, the Great War (1914–1918).[6] Interestingly, out of these five, only the Taiping Rebellion could be classed as a religious war. It was led by Hong Xiuquan who believed, after a number of visions, that he was the younger brother of Jesus. He set up the Taiping Heavenly Kingdom with its capital at Nanjing with his army controlling large parts of southern China and ruling about 30 million people. Seeking to establish his form of Christianity led to a huge civil war against the ruling Manchu-led Qing Dynasty.[7]

Famine, the third of the Four Horsemen, still stalks the planet in the 21st century, decimating populations and leaving those who survive precariously balanced between life and death. Thousands of famines have occurred throughout history, some on a small scale and others of huge severity. 'Between 108 BC and 1911 AD there were no fewer than 1,828 major famines in China, or one nearly every year in one or another province.'[8] The Great Chinese Famine came to an end in 1962 after a disastrous attempt by Communist leaders to force their policies on an unwilling population, leaving 43 million dead. Still in China, the famine of 1907 came as a result of 'poor harvests and massive storms which flooded 40,000 square miles of lush agricultural territory destroying 100% of the crops in the region.' Food riots took place and were often quelled with deadly force. This left 25 million dead. The Chalisa famine of 1877 in Northern India left 11 million dead. Under the brutal collectivization programme of Joseph Stalin, the Soviet Union eventually lost 10 million people to famine between 1932 and 1933. The Bengal famine of 1770 took the lives of 10 million souls: at that time Bengal was largely ruled by the British-owned East India Company. Ignoring severe drought and crop shortages, taxes were increased by the Company and the farmers were forced to grow indigo and opium, as they were more profitable than cheap rice. With no stockpiles of rice or food reserves, the famine swept away a third of the Bengali population. And in 1943, British policies during the Second World War led to the deaths of seven million during the Bengal famine of 1943.[9]

The last Horseman of the Apocalypse, death, seems a strange category to register part of the enormous suffering of humanity. Death already plays a prominent role in the first three Horsemen: pestilence, war and famine. So here, I take the liberty of naming some causes of death not contained within the three categories already mentioned. I start with death by murder which would include the whole range of homicides from maternal filicide to gang knifings to robbery shootings to those tortured to death to the murder of the aged. Suicide would encompass child suicides to suicide bombers and those killed as a result. Those who die of drug overdose, alcoholism, obesity and other bad lifestyle choices are to be included here; for instance, the World Health Organization estimated that the harmful use of alcohol resulted in three million deaths in 2016.[10] Also considered are those that have been worked to death as slaves or as peasant populations, or suffered martyrdom, or were subject to racial attacks, or those who have melted away because of poverty, tyranny or corruption. A common occurrence of death is through accident, miscarriage, and, often undiscovered on a global basis, euthanasia. Also to be considered are those that die through some natural disaster such as a tsunami, earthquake, flooding, volcanic eruption and the like. The list of causes of death is almost endless, leaving indelible marks upon those who remain. And we should acknowledge that no one ever in the history of mankind dies of 'death', but does so through some cause.

Yet even if we consider all the suffering that has overtaken the victims of pestilence, war, famine and death and couple it with the suffering of those who, through association or close contact, have been brought within the cruel embrace of these afflictions, we would only be making a beginning on cataloguing human suffering. We all know that circumstances that lead to death are only one form of suffering. Other causes include poverty, injustice, crime, vice, divorce, mental illness, loneliness, toxic relationships, managing dysfunctional children, child abuse or neglect, money and future anxieties, constant depressive negative news; distress caused by animal cruelty, climate change, ecological mismanagement and political and academic hubris. Perhaps here we should stop, as to go further in listing the different sufferings of humanity would be to take us down a spiral of misery away from the main theme of considering whether or not there are reasons or wisdom behind suffering. You, however, may want to add to the list, even if it is to make obvious several categories that I have left out.

Those with a spiritual view on life can be just as aware of the immense suffering humanity has experienced as those holding a materialistic view – but their conclusions about why there is suffering in the world are often diametrically opposed. Suppose, for instance, that two parties holding their respective views are looking at a piece of coal. Each would agree that it is black, incapable of reflecting light in this condition. Both would also agree that given the right conditions, that piece of coal can change into a diamond capable of reflecting light in a scintillating way. The right condition for the coal to change into a diamond is that it undergoes pressure in a mine over a huge amount of time. It is the pressure that causes transformation. If this is true of the lowest degree of existence, the coal being a mineral, the spiritually inclined person would conclude that the highest degree of existence on the planet, humanity, can also transform, through the pressure of suffering, from a base nature, incapable in that condition of reflecting the qualities of God, into a creation that reflects all the qualities of the Creator. After all, how is it possible to develop the noble qualities of courage, determination, perseverance, patience, resignation and the like without experiencing some very challenging, painful and, at times, despairing moments? This is not a justification for the continuance or repetition of the horrors causing suffering that humanity has experienced. The next chapter will clarify this.

11

SUFFERING: RESPONSIBILITY AND DETACHMENT

Every person born on planet Earth is introduced to a world that has existed for over 4.5 billion years. According to NASA, our planet's life span will come to an end, destroyed by the Sun expanding, before becoming a white dwarf, and engulfing our solar system's 'inner planets, toasting Mercury and Venus, and potentially Earth too'.[1] Another five billion years is estimated for this, but human life will cease to exist long before the planet heats up, in about a billion years when the oceans will have evaporated.[2] About 500 million years is left for humans when 'temperatures on Earth will rise to the point that most of the world will be a desert'.[3]

The physical body of every human being comes from the materials of the universe. This is why Imám 'Alí, the son-in-law of the Prophet Muhammad, could write over 1,500 years ago:

Dost thou deem thyself a small and puny form,
When thou foldest within thyself the greater world?[4]

Whether we look at our planet or our physical body, it is axiomatic that they are not everlasting. It has been humorously stated that 'none of us are going to get out of this alive'. Yet we find that as society sinks deeper into the quagmire of materialism, there is an insatiable yearning for physical life to last forever. Material things become more and more addictive, while spiritual, moral and ethical development takes a back seat. Make-up, hairstyling, Botox, plastic surgery and the like are applied in an attempt to hold back or disguise old age, while cryogenics is seriously considered as a means to outwit death itself. Hanging onto physical life is an overarching desire of materialists who believe that their life ends when the body dies. Conversely, some would prefer to end their lives rather than face the suffering of a serious disease. Take, for instance, the case of the Hungarian-born Arthur Koestler, a renowned intellectual, well respected for his thirty books, who rose to fame and critical acclaim. He and his wife Cynthia were found dead in their London home on 3 March 1983. Apparently, Koestler suffered from Parkinson's disease, although his wife was not known to have any ailments. They had committed suicide from an overdose of barbiturates.

Of course, all people, whether absorbed in materialism or led by spiritual values, will hold on to life as long as possible. But there is a big motivational difference between the two – the materialists want to take as much out of physical living as possible, as they believe we only have life in the physical body. The spiritually led person will want to continue life to contribute to the betterment of society as much as possible.

Everything in the material world is an indication that for human beings it is not our real home. Water that quenches thirst can also drown us; fire that warms when cold can burn us; food that sustains can cause diabetes or heart problems; the air we breathe can carry deadly gases; moderate sunshine can give a tan, but too much can bring on cancer; bacteria and viruses can cause pandemics; volcanoes can bury a town in ash; tsunamis can wipe out coastal populations; droughts can destroy acres of crops. The list of things that can be of harm is virtually endless. Yet materialists cling to this world, with no faith in the spiritual worlds of God that are completely immune from the deadly dangers of the physical world.

The fact that we are not promised the next moment should alert us to consider that the material world is not our home but our grave. After a lifetime of placing importance in acquiring things – money, cars, house, comforts, holidays, entertainment, sexual encounters, etc., the only physical thing we will call our own is a grave, six foot under, or a vase of our ashes. Those who have not yet developed spiritual intelligence may find it hard to believe that the spiritual world of God is our real home. Yet Christ made this clear when, over 2,000 years ago, He said:

> Lay not up for yourselves treasures upon earth, where moth and rust doth corrupt, and where thieves break through and steal: But lay up for yourselves treasures in heaven, where neither moth nor rust doth corrupt, and where thieves do not break through nor steal: For where your treasure is, there will your heart be also.[5]

'Abdu'l-Bahá underlines this point when He states that 'all the sorrow and the grief that exist come from the world of matter – the spiritual world bestows only the joy! If we suffer it is the outcome of material things, and all the trials and troubles come from this world of illusion.'[6]

Detachment from the physical world has been a constant theme of all the great Messengers of God, but man's natural inclination is to form attachments. This is the source of our suffering; this is the cause of all the misery in the world. Detachment, of course, does not mean we have nothing to do with the physical world. We all need the things of the earth for our bodies to live, to thrive, and to be healthy. Everyone recognizes that our material existence and well-being depend upon the mineral, vegetable and animal kingdoms. Yet the wise person is aware that his spirit, his internal reality, is independent of material things. Virtues of the human spirit, such as wisdom, justice, hope and harmony, for instance, are not dependent on gold, sumptuous meals or fine clothes. Wisdom cannot increase by feeding it caviar, neither can you clothe justice in wealthy attire, and hope is not born through dependence on palaces and pageantry – no, rather fear and anxiety are its children.

Drawing on our understanding of the existence of the human spirit before and after the body dies, 'Abdu'l-Bahá states:

> In the spiritual world the divine bestowals are infinite, for in that realm there is neither separation nor disintegration, which characterize the world of material existence. Spiritual existence is absolute immortality, completeness and unchangeable being. Therefore, we must thank God that He has created for us both material blessings and spiritual bestowals.[7]

Throughout the entire Bahá'í Writings runs the theme of the spiritual worlds of God, to which we can form a healthy connection while in this life and eventually experience in full when we leave behind the physical body. Nothing from that world can be of harm to the human spirit; it bestows only joy, love, insights, sacredness, inspiration – in fact it holds everything that is prepared by an all-wise, all-loving Creator for our becoming more in tune and aligned with the wonders of reality. Of course, this material world offers material blessings that both spiritually inclined and materialistic people can appreciate. Who can fail to be moved by a beautiful sunset, or be satisfied after a delicious meal, or feel the heart dilated by a moving melody, or be filled with wonder after a new scientific or technological breakthrough? It is, however, only the spiritually inclined person who will thank God for these blessings, as they will be understood as gifts of a benevolent Creator.

Ingratitude on the part of the materialistically minded, even if they are unaware of being ungrateful, is a grave source of suffering, for it closes the door on the gifts that the generous Lord wishes to bestow. These gifts can be multi-faceted. They can take the form of material relief in times of austerity, or a kind and gracious ear when overtaken by depression or grief, or a helping hand when tasks become overwhelming. But gifts are not just relief while undergoing dire tests and trials, as welcome as they are; mostly they are in the form of new and creative ways of thinking about things and solving problems; insights into reasons for this or that happening; upliftment to persevere in the face of dire tests and calamities; joy and tranquillity as one seeks to be of selfless service to others. 'Abdu'l-Bahá points out:

> All that has been created is for man who is at the apex of creation and who must be thankful for the divine bestowals, so that through his gratitude he may learn to understand life as a divine benefit.[8]

Referring to this kind of happiness, 'Abdu'l-Bahá states:

> When man in response to the favours of God manifests susceptibilities of conscience, the heart is happy, the spirit is exhilarated. These spiritual susceptibilities are ideal thanksgiving.[9]

Now, if man were in tune with the blessings and bestowals of God and truly thankful for them, how could he wage war against his fellow human beings, how could he disdainfully look down upon the poor and allow disease to multiply and overtake great swathes of humanity, how could he not take the greatest precautions to prevent famine, and how could the multiple causes of premature death and affliction be not reduced to the lowest possible level? Surely, when the love of God is enthroned in every heart and His guidance understood; when humanity is disconnected from prejudice, self-serving priorities, and ignorance of his spiritual reality; and when the human race is motivated by an desire to create spiritual environments for the development of human potential to contribute to material and spiritual progress – then, the Four Horses of the Apocalypse will be well and truly bolted in their stables.

A main point about suffering is that most of it is created by humanity itself – inflicted either by others or oneself. And this happens when the advice, guidance, exhortations and insights of the Messengers of God are misunderstood, violently opposed, ignored, given lip-service or fanatically spread. A huge amount of human-inflicted suffering could easily cease if humanity took hold of just one of the great teachings of the Manifestations of God – a teaching that should be well known to the followers of all religions as a central tenet of their belief. It has been described as the 'Golden Rule' – 'Do unto others as you would have them do unto you.' On this theme Bahá'u'lláh writes, 'Wish not for others what ye wish not for yourselves . . .'[10] In fact, He takes this teaching further, maybe with the expectation that as humanity is entering its long-awaited mature phase, it would be able to aspire to the possibility of a much higher relationship with others: 'Blessed is he who preferreth his brother before himself.'[11]

The Golden Rule is not a 'bolt-on' teaching, it is not a teaching found at the periphery, it is at the heart of all religious teachings. As a concept of the ethic of reciprocity, it has its roots in a wide range of world cultures, and is a standard way that different cultures use to resolve conflicts.[12] In the Judaic Talmud a wise story highlights this point:

> A certain heathen came to Shammai and said to him, 'Make me a proselyte, on condition that you teach me the whole Torah while I stand on one foot.' Thereupon he repulsed him with the rod which was in his hand. When he went to Hillel, he said to him, 'What is hateful to you, do not do to your neighbor: that is the whole Torah; all the rest of it is commentary; go and learn.'[13]

Christ's directive when reiterating the Golden Rule was: 'Whatever you wish that men would do to you, do so to them.'[14] He also added, 'You shall love your neighbour as yourself.'[15] An Islamic tradition records Muhammad as saying, 'Not one of you is a believer until he loves for his brother what he loves for himself.'[16] A Hindu teaching found in the Mahabharata states, 'One should not behave towards others in a way which is disagreeable to oneself. This is the essence of morality. All other activities are due to selfish desire.'[17] In Buddhism, 'One should seek for others the happiness one desires for oneself,'[18] and Zoroaster taught, 'Do as you would be done by.'[19] Even in the traditional African religions we find this same theme; 'One going to take a pointed stick to pinch a baby bird should first try it on himself to feel how it hurts.'[20] This great teaching has gradually permeated the planet; it is time now to live by it if the human race is to experience a radical decrease in suffering.

Those who believe in God would declare that He has not failed in teaching humanity about how to relate to each other. Just like a kind and wise parent, He has said the same thing in different words many times. The failure lies within the hearts of people, who have not listened and have preferred to follow the dictates of their own selfish ways and materialistic desires. Is it possible, we should ask ourselves, that if we were to 'Do as you would be done by', we could hate others to the point of destroying them, or to follow an ideology that seeks to impose the concept of a 'master race', or to engage in terrorist activities, or wish for the downfall of other nations, or to gain an economic advantage over a section of humanity that precipitates ruin or even starvation? These are the activities of those who have cast aside the Golden Rule to pursue their own opinions as to what is right or wrong, or their own selfish desire – in fact to design their own moral compass where the 'true north' is oneself!

One of the most dangerous mistakes anyone can make is to close the door on God, to conclude that as misery, pain, suffering and the like have been the lot of humanity to date, then it is not possible for a kind, loving God to exist. Hopefully the above insights will remove some irrational thinking about the existence of suffering as a reason to discard belief in the existence of God.

Of course, this does not entirely satisfy most people who do not believe in God; in fact, it may not even satisfy those who do. Both will point out that even if we remove all the misery and distress that humanity has brought upon itself through turning a deaf ear to or misunderstanding the teachings of the Messengers of God, there is still a lot of suffering going on. We need to take a look at this. But let's be clear: a scrupulous rationale must first be made for every case of suffering to prove it is not human inflicted, before we can move on to suffering that is independent of human activity. It seems to me that those who cannot believe in God because there is so much suffering in the world have failed to distinguish between man-made suffering and unavoidable suffering. As mentioned earlier, it may be that there are valid and crucial reasons, unbeknown at the time, as to why no human being can escape some type of suffering. Tracing the cause of any suffering should be undertaken before blaming God for it! An attempt at this will now be made, focusing on a few current issues.

At this time of the universal application of science and technology, the masses of humanity are becoming more aware of the consequences of their actions. Young people in particular, are very concerned about climate change, for instance, and are making their protests heard. They realize, along with others, that if not effectively addressed now, climate change will cause even greater environmental degradation, loss of species and a future of disasters such as the world is just beginning to see.

For instance, the thousands of melting glaciers around the planet are already having effects. According to the UK's Royal Geographical Society:

> the melting of glaciers in the Himalayas will affect the drinking supplies of the millions of people who rely on meltwater rivers. In addition, when sea levels rise, people living close to sea level will have their homes flooded. This will have a major impact on the hundreds of millions of people living on low-lying land (for example) in Bangladesh. Out of the four places suggested: Asia, Africa, the Arctic and the Amazon, the impact of climate change and melting glaciers is likely to be felt most in Asia, because this is the region that has the highest population.[21]

Bangladesh, cited in this example, is one of the most densely populated countries in the world and one of the most susceptible to flooding. It has over 800 rivers, including three of the most powerful passing through it – the Ganges, Meghna and Brahmaputra. Its population of over 140 million people is crowded into low-lying land. Bangladesh has been on the flooding 'danger list' for decades: 'About one half of the land area in Bangladesh is at an elevation of less than 8 meters above sea level. Up to 30% of the country has been covered with flood waters. In 1991 more (than) 200,000 deaths resulted from flooding and associated tropical cyclones.'[22]

Many other countries are now at risk from the now exponential melting of the glaciers. The development of glaciers over a long period of time has been and still is providential, even though it has taken until recently for the scientific community to understand it. Those who believe in God may conclude that glaciers are a God-given providence; those who do not may believe that glaciers are just a chance occurrence – but both would agree that up until the time of rapid increase in the population of the planet and the massive increase in use of fossil fuels since the Industrial Revolution, the relatively low-level production of carbon dioxide and soot from fires created by humans was not sufficient to precipitate the ecological catastrophe we are now experiencing. The movement from rural to urban communities during the industrialization period was not humanity's finest hour. Millions of people became virtual slaves of their industrial masters, making them wealthy, some beyond the dreams of wealth owned by monarchs. There was virtually no regard for the integrity of human life and certainly no regard for the environment. Grinding poverty was the lot of the masses. Everything was sacrificed for the profit of the few. Social injustice was rife.

The consequence was that ideological revolutions, such as Communism, promised a better future for the downtrodden masses. It failed miserably! It was a godless attempt to poison the wells of the love of God and one's fellow man. Yet another manifestation of materialism's doctrine has now surfaced – consumerism, and with it the enormous waste that accompanies it, such as plastics. Interestingly, it is the environment itself which is now in revolt against this ungodly behaviour. The natural world does not like what we are doing to it and is making its complaint known. Nature exists and flourishes because it is subject to laws which are a guarantee of its survival. Humanity has broken these laws, and having discarded the central ethical law of religion, the Golden Rule, must now live with the consequences of its actions. For it is certain that had the Golden Rule taken hold of human thought, word and deed, the vast majority of suffering over this period of time would not have happened, and humanity's relationship with the environment would have been more harmonious.

In this particular source of suffering, God is not guilty. Historically it has been man's ignorance about, for example, the necessity of glaciers in ecological balance, coupled with the callousness with which wealthy members of society, and now prosperous multinationals and countries, take advantage of the poor and ignore their plight for greater profit. Ignorance and greed have combined to produce global warming, an ecological planetary calamity that threatens the very survival of the human race.

Having advanced the claim that most of humanity's suffering is human-inflicted and after discussing just one particular issue pertaining to it, I do not mean to imply that this type of suffering is purposeless. That there is something of great value being learnt from these terrible afflictions is an indication that they have a purpose. One of the main factors that distinguishes the human spirit is its ability to learn and make progress, not only in the physical environment but also in the domain of abstract thought, creativity and relationships. For many, if we have not learnt much after the experience of an ocean of man-made afflictions, the conclusion is that human nature cannot be changed. But as we have argued in a previous chapter, this is tantamount to saying that we cannot learn from our mistakes and paralyses any attempt to do so. For sure, it is the dark side of human nature, the lower, self-oriented side of man, that has caused this suffering, but every human being has a light nature, a higher, divine self also. If this were not so, man's actions would be predetermined, even as animal actions are predetermined by their instinct. In other words, man would be condemned to lead the life of a mere animal and be incapable of learning in a way that rights wrongs and enables progress.

What then, can be learned from the huge amount of human-inflicted suffering the race has experienced? If we take the example of the melting glaciers, it becomes obvious that man has either not been aware of natural laws governing physical safety and well-being or has chosen to ignore them; worse still – has chosen to oppress a mass of people, rendering them powerless to improve their condition. What is not so obvious is that humanity thrives when it is aware of and applies moral and spiritual laws. These laws are, for the most part, not discovered by human beings, as in the case of natural laws, but are revealed by the Manifestations of God, Who have been commissioned by God to make them known to us.

Two knowledge systems have been the source of humanity's progress and upliftment: science and religion. What, we may ask, is the use of every child in school learning about the laws of nature that science has discovered, such as that ice begins to melt at temperatures above 0 degrees centigrade and that a dark surface absorbs more heat than a white surface, only to flaunt these laws for a seeming personal advantage? On the other hand, are ethical imperatives such as the Golden Rule to be ignored or discarded by a godless society because they hail from religion? Similarly, are moral laws, such as not to commit adultery or to refrain from promiscuity, to be traduced because a secular society regards them as impingements on personal freedom and are inclined to make a person feel guilty or ashamed if they are broken? Unfortunately, many people have decided that the directives that come from reli-gion should play no further part in society. Yet such moral and spiritual laws are common to all religions, a factor that should help humanity become united. When unimpeded by superstition and fanaticism, religion has been the power to illumine the conscience of masses of human beings, inspiring them to leave behind lower, dark-nature behaviour and advance towards their higher, spiritual nature out of love for God and fellow humans.

In this age, however, what emerges as the great lesson to learn is the imperative that science and religion must become integrated as the only means for human survival. This is a principal teaching of Bahá'u'lláh. He has removed from religion two major elements that prevent it from being in harmony with science. The first is superstitious interpretations of the world's scriptures that are figurative as distinct from those that are perspicuous. The second is that He has abrogated scriptural laws and ordinances that have served their purpose in ancient societies but are no longer relevant and has revealed new laws that meet the needs of today. If we don't learn how to integrate science and religion when there is such a compelling need to do so, then, in the simplest of terms, humanity will have to 'touch the stove many more times to register it is hot' until it does.

It is as uncomplicated as this, that the overarching reason for suffering is to 'learn lessons' that need to be learnt. For it is common to all, whether living in the past or the present, that when we have drunk from a cup of suffering, we no longer desire a second draught. Therefore, suffering can be the greatest motivator to change for the better. Bahá'u'lláh wrote:

> My calamity is My providence, outwardly it is fire and vengeance, but inwardly it is light and mercy. Hasten thereunto that thou mayest become an eternal light and an immortal spirit. This is My command unto thee, do thou observe it.[23]

However, for those who hold a materialistic perspective of reality, this type of reasoning will not be satisfying. Rather, it may cause such souls to dig their heels in and make further objections regarding the existence of God. 'Where is the working out of justice in all this suffering if God exists?' they may ask, 'for He certainly lets a lot of guilty people get away with their cruel or selfish behaviour.'

Regarding the 'justice' aspect of suffering, I would like to leave this until a later chapter, where more time can be given to it. What I want to do here is to reintroduce the point made in an earlier chapter, that the soul continues to exist in the spiritual world when the body dies. 'What is the reason for so much misery and pain,' I ask myself, 'if at the end we just die, and there is no more life for us – conscious beings that we are?' I am persuaded, however, that 'lessons learnt' not only have value here but hold even greater value in the hereafter as a means for the increase of personal and collective understanding and happiness. 'Abdu'l-Bahá states:

> Man passes through different phases and when in a lower consciousness he cannot comprehend the consciousness above. When we were in the state of the unborn child we had no knowledge of the world of man. If the vegetable kingdom could speak it would cry out, 'Where is the world of man?' We cry out, 'Where is the kingdom of the spirit?'[24]

Somewhere along the line of earnest inquiry into spiritual matters one becomes aware that this physical stage of existence is a preparation for the next stage in the world beyond. However, preparation is not achieved by placing all our hopes on some personal future heavenly reward in the next life. Bahá'u'lláh states that it is prepared by making our unique contribution in carrying 'forward an ever-advancing civilization' here on earth.[25] Preparation requires effort, the learning of lessons and the sacrifice of our lower nature for our higher nature, according to the guidance from the Messengers of God as to how to do this. In effect, it requires the sacrifice of our will for the will of God Who encourages the development of virtues, such as compassion, love, justice, reverence, selflessness, trustworthiness, and the like. For civilization to be ever advancing, each individual must take responsibility for his own transformation so that one's own lower nature can, in terms of a metaphor, be changed from base metal into gold.

Imagine, if you will, a just economic system serving the needs of all humanity based upon the foundational quality of 'trustworthiness'. Take time to ponder on how much suffering would be eliminated if this were so. Essential as is the need for individuals to transform themselves for 'an ever-advancing civilization', a parallel effort is also needed to transform the present-day order of governance. (This will be further discussed in a later chapter.) The role of the individual in this process, Bahá'u'lláh states, is to be, 'anxiously concerned with the needs of the age ye live in, and centre your deliberations on its exigencies and requirements'.[26] To be so involved is, in this age, to lead a 'spiritual life'. All are summoned to be protagonists in this mighty endeavour, not to abandon society to those who, either consciously or unconsciously, would make life a misery for others. To be fully engaged in the movement to eradicate suffering on a scale undreamt of in past ages requires the abilities, skills and talents of everyone in service to the needs of this time. By so doing, the essential characteristics of preparation are developed for the hereafter, as a by-product of living such a life of service here. In effect, not only are we to be responsible for our own spiritual transformation, but we must accept that we have personal responsibility for making our contribution to the transformation of society. As Victor Frankl points out: 'being human is not being driven (by instincts) but by "deciding what one is going to be", to quote Jaspers . . . I would say that being human is being responsible, responsible for one's own existence.'[27]

Now we have to look at another aspect of suffering. Having excluded all human-inflicted suffering as avoidable in this age, there is a need to look at unavoidable suffering. Again, we need to draw on the two knowledge systems available to humanity, science and the revelations of religion, to be able to get clarity on this issue. To identify what is avoidable from unavoidable suffering, however, is no easy task. If we take, for instance, the many diseases the human body is prone to, it is very difficult to ascertain in all cases whether a certain affliction is self-inflicted, has a social cause, or is caused by hereditary factors which could have been avoidable, or are unavoidable. So, let's spend some moments looking at each of these categories.

An example of that which is self-inflicted could be suffering as a result of wrong lifestyle choices. An unhealthy diet, such as foods that are rich in refined carbohydrates, trans fats or alcohol coupled with lack of exercise have seriously increased disease in the wealthier parts of the world.

Social causes of suffering include severe health problems caused by conditions such as air pollution to squalid housing conditions, among others, or from malnutrition to sexually transmitted infections (STIs). Many of these circumstantial causes of disease are traceable to ignorance, to uncaring selfish human beings as noted when the English-owned East India Company ignored the plight of farmers who worked for them, resulting in the Bengal famine of 1770 which took the lives of 10 million people, as mentioned previously. Although the suffering resulting from these types of causes is not self-inflicted, nonetheless they are visited upon others by the actions and attitudes of fellow human beings and must, therefore, fall under the category of avoidable suffering.

There is still very much to learn about hereditary factors that cause tremendous suffering. Take the distressing condition of cystic fibrosis (CF), for instance, where '10 million Americans are carriers of a faulty CF gene', although 'many of them don't know they are CF carriers'. Men who have CF are infertile because they're born without a vas deferens. A person with CF, however, must inherit two defective CF genes – one from each parent.[28] Research on this subject reveals the clinical causes of CF, but not why or when the defective mutations in the human body presented in the first place.

When all is said and done, what we are now left with is

suffering which is unavoidable by those who inherit a disease or malfunction from their ancestors, an inheritance that can have life-changing consequences.

In one sense accidents, by definition, are avoidable, but they do happen and will continue to happen just as long as man has a physical body. An accident, however, although man-made, is not a deliberate act to harm someone, which puts it outside intentional harming. Every human being will experience an array of accidents in their life, caused either by themselves or others, whether it be spilling coffee or stubbing one's toe to being involved in a more serious accident, such as falling off a ladder or a car crash. World-wide there are millions of people who suffer daily because of a serious accident.

Perhaps the most common causes of unavoidable suffering involve those who die or are maimed during an earthquake, flood, drought, tsunami, volcanic eruption and the like. Natural disasters are mainly considered disasters when human beings are involved. In the world of nature, they are the natural events of a planet that is alive, as, for instance, the movements of the earth's tectonic plates causing earthquakes. With the progress of science and technology we can look forward to a time when these natural happenings are anticipated, and warnings given to populations in those areas. Even now there are some early warning systems in place. Be that as it may, we will never be able to prevent the movement of the earth's crust, nor should we try to do so, as this would destabilize the natural system of life on the planet.

I'm sure you can think of other ways in which suffering is unavoidable but let us not forget that every human being will experience some form of suffering, whether avoidable or not. And sooner or later everyone will die, an occurrence which causes anguish and grief for loved ones left behind. With this in mind, surely we should ask where all suffering comes from, to which we may answer from the above examples and those mentioned in the previous chapter. But this answer only identifies the 'branches' of the problem, which materially minded man can see. Spiritually minded souls can identify the 'root' of suffering, that part of the 'tree' which is not seen. 'Abdu'l-Bahá answers the question by quite simply stating: 'If we suffer it is the outcome of material things, and all the trials and troubles come from this world of illusion.'[29] He then elaborates this by stating:

> For instance, a merchant may lose his trade and depression ensues. A workman is dismissed and starvation stares him in the face. A farmer has a bad harvest, anxiety fills his mind. A man builds a house which is burnt to the ground and he is straightway homeless, ruined, and in despair.[30]

'Abdu'l-Bahá then takes us further, identifying not only the root of suffering, but indicating where suffering no longer exists:

> All these examples are to show you that the trials which beset our every step, all our sorrow, pain, shame and grief, are born in the world of matter; whereas the spiritual Kingdom never causes sadness. The ills all flesh is heir to do not pass him by, but they only touch the surface of his life, the depths are calm and serene.[31]

'Abdu'l-Bahá was no stranger to intense and prolonged suffering. He spent over 60 years of His life in either exile or prison, when He served in the most humble and self-sacrificing way His beloved Father, Bahá'u'lláh, Who brought teachings of hope, love and peace for all peoples. He, along with His saintly wife, Munírih Khánum, experienced the death of four sons, all in their infancy. An examination of 'Abdu'l-Bahá's life is recommended as an example of how to face the most testing of times, the direst vicissitudes, the most soul-crushing anxieties and responsibilities. When all of life's calamities fell upon Him, He showed us how rise above them with radiant acquiescence. 'Today, humanity is bowed down with trouble, sorrow and grief, no one escapes,' He said:

the world is wet with tears; but, thank God, the remedy is at our doors. Let us turn our hearts away from the world of matter and live in the spiritual world! It alone can give us freedom! If we are hemmed in by difficulties we have only to call upon God, and by His great Mercy we shall be helped.

If sorrow and adversity visit us, let us turn our faces to the Kingdom and heavenly consolation will be outpoured.[32]

So, the root of suffering is that we are not yet detached from the things of the material world; we are still ignorant of, hesitate or refuse to take a step into, the Kingdom, which 'Abdu'l-Bahá states is the spiritual world. And stepping into the spiritual world requires not only a belief in God, which could be considered the first step, but also a recognition of our powerlessness, without the aid of God, to affect any spiritual growth. Just as a seed with all its potential is powerless to grow without the sunshine, we humans cannot transform ourselves from low-level, materially based thoughts, words and actions without the sunshine of the power of God shining on us through His guidance. When these conditions are fulfilled, the soul of man – slowly by degrees for some, others at a quicker pace – find that they have risen above the cares and trappings of this world and entered a condition of 'perpetual joy'.[33] Such a soul lives in the spiritual world of understanding and is patient, even thankful, with what God has prepared for his development. Metaphorically speaking he is in the pure state of freedom, or in religious terminology 'heaven' or 'nirvana. In some measure, when considering suffering, we have covered the same ground spoken of by Buddha centuries ago. He advocated becoming conscious of the Four Noble Truths:

They are the Noble Truth of Suffering, the Noble Truth of the Origin of Suffering, the Noble Truth of the Extinction of Suffering, the Noble Truth of the Path that leads to the Extinction of Suffering.[34]

Although material man may think that such a heavenly condition does not exist, this is no proof of its non-existence. There have been innumerable souls throughout history who have attained to this condition of spiritual progress, but suffice it to say that today, 'Abdu'l-Bahá serves as the master exemplar of this station. Let us recall some of His words, spoken shortly after His release in 1908, after 40 years imprisonment in the penal colony of 'Akká, formerly of Palestine:

> 'Will you tell us how you felt while in prison and how you regard your freedom?' I asked. 'We are glad that you are free.'
>
> 'Thank you,' he said graciously, and continuing –
>
> 'Freedom is not a matter of place. It is a condition. I was thankful for the prison, and the lack of liberty was very pleasing to me, for those days were passed in the path of service, under the utmost difficulties and trials, bearing fruits and results.
>
> 'Unless one accepts dire vicissitudes, he will not attain. To me prison is freedom, troubles rest me, death is life, and to be despised is honour. Therefore, I was happy all that time in prison. When one is released from the prison of self, that is indeed release, for that is the greater prison. When this release takes place, then one cannot be outwardly imprisoned. When they put my feet in stocks, I would say to the guard, "You cannot imprison me, for here I have light and air and bread and water. There will come a time when my body will be in the ground, and I shall have neither light nor air nor food nor water, but even then I shall not be imprisoned." The afflictions which come to humanity sometimes tend to centre the consciousness upon the limitations, and this is a veritable prison. Release comes by making of the will a Door through which the confirmations of the Spirit come.'[35]

'Abdu'l-Bahá continued:

The confirmations of the Spirit are all those powers and gifts which some are born with (and which men sometimes call genius), but for which others have to strive with infinite pains. They come to that man or woman who accepts his life with radiant acquiescence.[36]

A consideration of the purpose of suffering, however, cannot be complete without emphasizing that 'attachment' is not a bad thing of itself. Its ability has been installed within the human soul to enable it to become attached to our Creator. However, the pull of our lower, dark nature is always present, demanding that it be given priority over our higher, light nature. Its physical characteristic, essentially not harmful, has been needed for the survival of the human species. But when the ability to form attachments is misdirected through 'wants', passions and base appetites for material acquisitions, status and power, it lowers the vision of man to the things of the earth. In effect, when this occurs, man's behaviour degenerates and his noble abilities become atrophied. 'To act like the beasts of the field is unworthy of man,' declares Bahá'u'lláh, and He adds: 'Those virtues that befit his dignity are forbearance, mercy, compassion and loving-kindness towards all the peoples and kindreds of the earth.'[37]

The Writings of Bahá'u'lláh emphasize that attachment to our Creator can only be achieved through being attracted to the source of love and power emanating from the Manifestations of God, in particular, Bahá'u'lláh as the Manifestation of God for this age. It is all a question of what we attach our heart to, for it is a fact, in the words of 'Abdu'l-Bahá, that 'God has given man a heart and the heart must have some attachment.'[38] 'Abdu'l-Bahá, taking this thought further, states:

We have proved that nothing is completely worthy of our heart's devotion save reality, for all else is destined to perish. Therefore the heart is never at rest and never finds real joy and happiness until it attaches itself to the eternal. How foolish the bird that builds its nest in a tree that may perish when it could build its nest in an ever-verdant garden of paradise.

Man must attach himself to an infinite reality, so that his glory, his joy, and his progress may be infinite. Only the spirit is real; everything else is as shadow. All bodies are disintegrated in the end; only reality subsists. All physical perfections come to an end; but the divine virtues are infinite.[39]

So, if we attach our hearts to perishable material things, vain fancies and idle imaginings, this will be the source of great unhappiness and suffering in this world and the next, where only spiritual realities exist. By what means, then, can materialistic man be full of joy and gladness in the world beyond if all his attention, desires and yearnings are for the continuation of physical things? Such a person will arrive in that world utterly confused, totally disorientated, longing for a return to his earthly life, ignorant that his powers of physical existence have passed.

I'm reminded of a story here, about a high-ranking, wealthy clergyman who passed into the next world. While entering into his new life without all the trappings, rituals and status of his material existence, he inquired from a guide who accompanied him as to where he would live. He was told to have patience while being taken to his new home. As they proceeded down a spacious avenue the clergyman, catching a glimpse of a magnificent-looking palace, automatically assumed this would be his new abode. His guide said that this was not to be his, but it was further on. After a while, another magnificent building appeared, not quite as grandiose as the first, evoking from the clergyman the question as to whether this would be his residence. Again, he was told to be patient as they carried on. The religious leader took with him into the next world his understanding that because he had great religious authority and standing in his earthly life, his heavenly reward would be a home fit for a great soul. They next passed a mansion. Again, the clergyman was disappointed. Several buildings appeared along the avenue, each one less magnificent than the previous one. At this stage, the clergyman was convinced that his new home would be an extra special building such as a 'palace' fit for a king, and certainly not the small, demeaning buildings he had just passed. He made his thoughts known to his guide, after which they came upon a few bricks and planks of wood. 'There is your new home,' said the guide. The clergyman was dumb-founded and began to complain. 'There must be some mistake,' he said in anger, 'I gave thousands of sermons on earth urging others to do good; I headed all the great religious festivals and ceremonies; I counselled an abundance of people and made them realize they had to change their ways because they were sinners; I taught them that if they followed the creeds and dogmas of the Faith then they would go to heaven.' The clergyman carried on in this vein, getting angrier and angrier, while the guide waited patiently with much compassion, for his tirade to end. 'My dear one,' returned the guide, 'but we could not build you anything better because this is all you sent us from your earthly life!'

We can imagine the clergyman grudgingly realizing, perhaps over a long duration, that his earthly life had not prepared him for the spiritual world. What, we may ask, could be the reason for this? Perhaps the over-riding characteristic of the clergyman who carried no fruit into the future was hypocrisy! He had lived a life of opulence, wallowing in his 'exalted station' and power over people, teaching dogmas and creeds that strangled the spiritual development of others. How lamentable indeed is such a demise. It would have been better for him not to be born, or to have suffered the loss of all his wealth, rather that carry on with his hellish influence. Having passed to the world of the spirit, the clergyman had no means to re-enter the physical world to make good that which was harmful. And what would be the point of returning, as the reincarnationists believe, if a person cannot remember his wrongdoing in a previous incarnation, so as to be able to put it right?

There are many stories of those who sacrificed their ignoble lifestyles, indeed their very lives, as martyrs in the Faith of

Bahá'u'lláh when given a vision of heavenly behaviour by the Báb, Bahá'u'lláh or 'Abdu'l-Bahá. Recorded circumstantially in many of the histories of the Bahá'í Faith, these souls, and countless others since then, have willingly let go of their attachment to the things of the world, realizing that fear, regret, disillusionment, shame, and the like are materialism's fruit. They became aware, through Bahá'u'lláh's teachings, that they had been ignorant of, or misunderstood the purpose of their lives. Prejudice, fame, power, influence, luxury, hedonism, indolence, and a host of other aberrant behaviours that had seduced them, gave way to compassion and service to others and a willingness to bring souls together in an expanding circle of unity. By so doing they avoided a great personal catastrophe in their lives, spoken of by Bahá'u'lláh in these words: 'O ye that are bereft of understanding! A severe trial pursueth you, and will suddenly overtake you. Bestir yourselves, that haply it may pass and inflict no harm upon you.'[40]

The degree of effort man must make to transfer attachment from ignoble thoughts, words and deeds to that of a loving attachment to Bahá'u'lláh cannot be overestimated. A divine wisdom has decreed that for those who do not heed the exhortations of God's Manifestations, the only way forward to personal and societal spiritual progress is to experience the consequent suffering of breaking spiritual laws. In effect this is a 'prizing loose' process (imagine the effort it takes to try to prize limpets loose from shoreline rocks). It is a kind act of God, motivating us to move away from suffering to become attracted to the spiritual worlds with true joy and ecstasy. Progress from attachment to detachment is always held (helled) 'back by reason of what their hands have wrought,' states Bahá'u'lláh.[41] It is worth repeating His words: 'My calamity is My providence, outwardly it is fire and vengeance, but inwardly it is light and mercy.'[42]

To end this brief look at the purpose of suffering, the following passage from 'Abdu'l-Bahá sums up what has been written on this subject:

O thou servant of God! Do not grieve at the afflictions and calamities that have befallen thee. All calamities and afflictions have been created for man so that he may spurn this mortal world – a world to which he is much attached. When he experienceth severe trials and hardships, then his nature will recoil and he will desire the eternal realm – a realm which is sanctified from all afflictions and calamities. Such is the case with the man who is wise. He shall never drink from a cup which is at the end distasteful, but, on the contrary, he will seek the cup of pure and limpid water. He will not taste of the honey that is mixed with poison.[43]

12

OPPRESSORS AND THE SUFFERING OF THE INNOCENT

Many of those who hold a materialistic perspective of reality as opposed to a spiritual one have concluded that belief in God and religion is a major reason why suffering continues. I would like to offer an inverse way of looking at this. Wars, conflicts, corruption, upheavals and the like are the indirect result of not understanding what religion is. This is important to consider because it is fair to assume that all suffering, including that of children and the innocent, does not occur in a vacuum. All things that grow require an environment to do so, whether this is a plant or the good and evil in society. In this light, the statement below is included to raise awareness that humanity has yet more suffering in store because the environment that true religion creates is virtually non-existent. A thoroughly negative, injurious environment, worldwide, is now the experience of all who dwell on planet Earth. From a Bahá'í perspective, this is the consequence of several generations' inability to consider, without prejudice or bias, the teachings of Bahá'u'lláh revealed over a 40-year period between 1852 and 1892. These teachings identify principles needed to create a global civilization embodying the will of an all-wise Creator. These principles are viewed by Bahá'u'lláh's followers as essential ingredients for a healthy planet, just as we accept a prescription of various elements prescribed by a doctor for our healing. In a book containing a series of letters published in 1938, Shoghi Effendi, the Guardian of the

Bahá'í Faith, anticipated the disastrous spread of this spiritual 'pandemic' of heedlessness; he wrote:

> The process of disintegration must inexorably continue, and its corrosive influence must penetrate deeper and deeper into the very core of a crumbling age. Much suffering will still be required ere the contending nations, creeds, classes and races of mankind are fused in the crucible of universal affliction, and are forged by the fires of a fierce ordeal into one organic commonwealth, one vast, unified, and harmoniously functioning system. Adversities unimaginably appalling, undreamed of crises and upheavals, war, famine, and pestilence, might well combine to engrave in the soul of an unheeding generation those truths and principles which it has disdained to recognize and follow. A paralysis more painful than any it has yet experienced must creep over and further afflict the fabric of a broken society ere it can be rebuilt and regenerated.[1]

Humanity is being called to maturity, to leave behind childish behaviour, but it refuses to do so. (This subject will be considered in a later chapter.) To behave childishly when mature capacities have been granted is at the root of prodigality. This is not a rhetorical statement on my part; irresponsibility, when there is mature capacity, is very dangerous indeed. The childish age of humanity, for instance, had the ability to invent and use sword, spear and bow and arrow as weapons of war. The mature capacities of man produce sophisticated, infernal weapons of mass destruction, to the extent that the whole human race can be wiped out. Yet we still think that we can continue our childish, irresponsible behaviour with impunity!

Of greatest sadness, however, is that innocent people, especially children, suffer along with the guilty, while humanity learns the lessons of 'responsibility'. It is a child's way to blame others for his own immature, irresponsible actions; in this case the 'other' is God, Who, ironically, they don't believe exists! Surely humanity should be humble enough to accept the possibility that there are lessons to be learnt, parochial attachments and attitudes to be challenged, and enlarged understandings to grasp? One of these understandings is that when wrongdoing is activated, events or occurrences are out of control of the wrongdoer. In a sense a domino effect is started, the harmful results of which cannot be foreseen at the beginning of the wrongdoing. Consider the case of Arch-Duke Ferdinand of Austria who was assassinated in Sarajevo. This event is considered to be the immediate trigger for World War I, and the 'falling of dominoes' did not stop there. World War II followed quickly as a result of totally inadequate means of preventing further conflict. How many millions of innocent people, men, women and children were crushed, slaughtered, swept aside as death machines and death plans, unheard of in past conflicts, ripped the world apart.

In reality, the wrongdoer puts himself outside the guidance and protection of God because he is either not aware of God's guidance for this modern age or, if so, ignores or rejects it. To the degree of wrongdoing is the degree to which the wrongdoer harms himself, all those he loves and others, even if these include innocent souls. This is a huge lesson to learn and we are learning it now, as a foundational truth, in preparation for the building of a world civilization. 'Know thou, of a truth,' Bahá'u'lláh writes, 'these great oppressions that have befallen the world are preparing it for the advent of the Most Great Justice.'[2] A world civilization based upon justice will include, over the coming millions of years of mankind's life on earth, generations of people whose numbers will be so huge that it would be difficult to estimate. These future populations will look back at this time of lesson learning with such love and tender heartedness for all those souls who, although innocent, suffered indescribably tortured lives and painful deaths for this lesson to take root in the consciousness of all peoples. May God recompense them for their sacrifices in the spiritual world to which they have fled, in such wise that their life there is a hundred times better than their lives would have been here in the physical world.

It is admittedly difficult to accept that the innocent suffer along with the guilty in this life, and sometimes in place of the guilty. However, it is a fact that cannot be ignored, and strenuous efforts must be made to build a just society that relegates this happening to the dustbin of history. 'Bestir yourselves, O people, in anticipation of the days of Divine justice,' Bahá'u'lláh writes, 'for the promised hour is now come. Beware lest ye fail to apprehend its import and be accounted among the erring.'[3] We must always bear in mind that those abhorrent and terrifying deeds perpetrated by oppressors and tyrants are not unnoticed by God, Who is All-Perceiving. Even if they escape the justice of man in this world there is no way of escaping the justice of God in the next. Addressing any person who is an oppressor, Bahá'u'lláh, speaking on behalf of God, commands them to 'Withdraw your hands from tyranny, for I have pledged Myself not to forgive any man's injustice.'[4] And in another place, He writes: 'Say: God hath pledged in His Book to lay hold upon every oppressor for his tyranny, and to uproot the stirrers of mischief.'[5] Writing to a specific tyrant He elaborates on what awaits him because of his oppression of the innocent:

> Erelong shall your days pass away, as shall pass away the days of those who now, with flagrant pride, vaunt themselves over their neighbour. Soon shall ye be gathered together in the presence of God, and shall be asked of your doings, and shall be repaid for what your hands have wrought, and wretched is the abode of the wicked doers![6]

How heartrending are the sacrifices of the innocent to those who perceive with spiritual eyes, how crushing a weight upon their souls. How they long to rush to their aid and recompense them with loving-kindness, wrap them in a mantle of compassion that dissolves every pain and confusion, and wash away their fears with tears of loving empathy. When souls feel anguish at the plight of the innocent, particularly babies and children who suffer at the hands of depraved individuals or systems, they long for a way to prevent such oppression. The Bahá'í way to do so is to ardently support the Cause of Bahá'u'lláh to bring His healing remedy to all humanity. In relation to this, the international governing body of the Bahá'í community, the Universal House of Justice, writes:

> As to your own torment and suffering arising from your perception of the fate of children and their oppressors, the way to peace and security for you and for humanity as a whole, is through service to the Cause to which you have so earnestly committed yourself.[7]

It must also be borne in mind that just as the concept and actual practice of compensation is known and applied in many cases here, in this physical life, it will also have its application in the next world. But it will be God's compensation and therefore perfectly fitted to repair and uplift the souls of all who have innocently suffered. Writing about this, the Universal House of Justice states:

> In addition, we know from the Bahá'í Writings that man's soul 'is independent of all infirmities of body or mind', and not only continues to exist 'after departing from this mortal world', but progresses 'through the bounty and grace of the Lord'. Therefore, an evaluation of man's material existence and achievements cannot ignore the potential spiritual development stimulated by the individual's desire to manifest the attributes of God and his response to the exigencies of his life, nor can it exclude the possibility of the operation of God's mercy in terms of compensation for earthly suffering, in the next life.[8]

'Abdu'l-Bahá has a special word to say about God's compensation in the next world for infants, children and defenceless souls who are treated in cruel and horrific ways:

As to the subject of babes and infants and weak ones who are afflicted by the hands of oppressors: This contains great wisdom and this subject is of paramount importance. In brief, for those souls there is a recompense in another world and many details are connected with this matter. For those souls that suffering is the greatest mercy of God. Verily that mercy of the Lord is far better and preferable to all the comfort of this world and the growth and development of this place of mortality.[9]

How God compensates an innocent soul in the next life for the horrors it has experienced here, we do not know. But when it is considered that God is all-merciful, all-loving, and the most compassionate, we can rest assured that His justice will not allow even the slightest trace of affliction to encumber the soul of an innocent. Just as physical chains can be removed from the necks of people here, so can the 'chains' of immense trauma be removed from an oppressed soul in the next world. There a soul will receive, as just quoted, 'the greatest mercy of God' for its suffering and such that this will be 'far better and preferable to all the comfort of this world and the growth and development of this place of mortality.'

Of course, one who accepts this will believe in God and life after physical death. It is mentioned, therefore, not so much to convince someone of the existence of God and life after death, but as an exposition of a system of justice which extends past our physical lives into our life in the world to come. How otherwise would it be possible to believe God is a just God? If all life for humans ended upon one's physical death there would be no guarantee that tyrants would receive their punishment, nor would those innocent souls oppressed by them be compensated for their sufferings. Viewed through a spiritual lens this is a perfect system of justice in operation; it tends to encourage responsible behaviour.

If there is no belief in a world beyond, where none can escape justice for their actions in this world, then many evils flow from such a belief. 'Abdu'l-Bahá explains that there are extremely bad consequences here in this world, for individuals and society that do not accept that there is a next life. This He calls 'the conception of annihilation'. He declares:

> The conception of annihilation is a factor in human degradation, a cause of human debasement and lowliness, a source of human fear and abjection. It has been conducive to the dispersion and weakening of human thought, whereas the realization of existence and continuity has upraised man to sublimity of ideals, established the foundations of human progress and stimulated the development of heavenly virtues; therefore, it behooves man to abandon thoughts of nonexistence and death, which are absolutely imaginary, and see himself ever-living, everlasting in the divine purpose of his creation.[10]

Anyone who gives time and attention to reflect on this statement of 'Abdu'l-Bahá will discover a powerful antidote for the prevention of much suffering. So let us dwell on this astounding insight, but relate it to a shameful act perpetrated against children, namely sexual abuse. First, it is obvious that such abuse is degrading and debased – an ignoble act that is diametrically opposed to the purpose of God in creating every human being 'noble'. As a counter to all wayward thoughts, words and acts, great or small, we are exhorted by Bahá'u'lláh to: 'Bring thyself to account ere thou art summoned to a reckoning, on the Day when no man shall have strength to stand for fear of God, the Day when the hearts of the heedless ones shall be made to tremble.'[11] And in another place Bahá'u'lláh states: 'Bring thyself to account each day ere thou art summoned to a reckoning; for death, unheralded, shall come upon thee and thou shalt be called to give account for thy deeds.'[12]

Every paedophile started life as an innocent baby. What disposes that child, when grown up, to perpetrate such ignoble acts may be due to multiple factors. One main factor, as 'Abdu'l-Bahá states above, is ignorance about the continuity of life and that we shall be called to account for our life in this physical world when we die. Another main factor is ignorance about our own human nature. If children were taught from their earliest days about the continuity of life and encouraged to review each day as to whether they have exhibited dark, low-nature characteristics, or light, spiritual qualities, then a pattern is set to become a 'noble' being. Of course, this should be done with the utmost patience and wisdom, bearing in mind that children are tender plants that need knowledgeable, wise, loving nurturing to grow to spiritual maturity. If such a pattern of spiritual education existed it would tend to create a wholesome person who, living in the freedom and joy of their higher nature, would keep the promptings of their lower nature well and truly under control. If society could be populated by these souls, they would create such a positive environment, thereby reducing the incidents of depraved behaviour to almost non-existence. We must take note, as stated previously, that the growth of anything, such as weeds, or flowers, needs an environment to do so.

Another point mentioned by 'Abdu'l-Bahá above is that anyone who holds that there is no life after death contributes to the pool of 'human fear and abjection', a source of much suffering. Reflection on this point reveals that materialistic man is prone to an array of many desires, worries, anxieties and wayward thoughts that dictate how he approaches life. A secular society, which utterly refutes that there is a life beyond, increases fear – fear of dying, fear of the future, fear and suspicion of others, fear of losing 'position', fear of getting old, fear of being alone, fear of what others think of them, fear of losing economic control – the list is almost endless. Bahá'u'lláh, in His book *The Four Valleys* refers to an Arabic quotation on fear: 'And he that feareth not God, God shall make him to fear all things; whereas all things fear him who feareth God.'[13] Mental ill-health, if not caused by a physical malady, can be one of the first symptoms of out-of-control thoughts, but the way of handling this by many focuses mainly on the physical and is rarely spiritual. Instead of using mental disturbances as a prompt to arrive at inner peace, all manner of escapist behaviours are engaged in – alcohol and drug abuse, self-harming, over-eating, running up debt, pornography and gambling addictions and the like.

Of course, if the natural tendency of anxiety and worry can be used to advantage, to develop a way of thinking and acting whereby to navigate trials and adversities with spiritual under-standings and behaviours, then they are blessings in disguise. In other words, there is a healthy way of considering these things. What checks these fears is a consideration of what is required to live in tranquillity in this world and in preparation for the life to come, and for this to happen we need the aid of God. Consider, for instance the promise of Bahá'u'lláh that God 'will aid everyone that aideth Him, and will remember everyone that remembereth Him'.[14] We are not left to work out how to aid God as, in several other places, Bahá'u'lláh makes it clear, it is to aid His Cause. This is another significant factor for reducing per-sonal and collective suffering as it focuses attention on where to apply one's thoughts, words and activities. And to aid the Cause of Bahá'u'lláh, amongst many things, is to share with others His insights on life after death. This is a major factor, as mentioned, to counter not only anxiety and worry but also wretched, con-temptible and humiliating behaviour, all words synonymous with 'abjection'. Bahá'u'lláh also adds that should a soul aid His Cause, he is promised that God has 'destined' for him that which 'excel-leth the treasures of the earth.'[15]

To end this chapter on a cheerful note it is necessary to recall the words of 'Abdu'l-Bahá related to some of the positive conse-quences of belief in the next life. He states, as we have read: 'the realization of existence and continuity has upraised man to sub-limity of ideals, established the foundations of human progress and stimulated the development of heavenly virtues.'[16] To lift vision above the cares, concerns and physicality of the material world, to ideals that are sublime, is one of the greatest gifts that can be given to humanity. In effect, to do so is to attract the human spirit to purity and altruism by a vision of the potential that lies hidden in the soul of man. (More will be said about this subject in a later chapter.) How, we may ask, can humanity progress without a vision of something higher, more enthralling than that which presently exists? With just a material vision of humanity's potential, we would gradually regress to animal behaviour. Becoming aware, however, that every human being can be stimulated to develop heavenly virtues, enables those qualities of love, justice, forgiveness, honour, selfless service to others, wisdom, humility and the like, to provide an environment in which humanity can progress spiritually, morally, intellectually and socially. An awareness of the continuity of life is a powerful motivator to rectify conduct that cause suffering, by growing qualities of the spirit in this world. In fact, Bahá'u'lláh declares that the underlying purpose of every Messenger of God is to enable everyone to enter the life to come with essential spiritual qualities:

The Prophets and Messengers of God have been sent down for the sole purpose of guiding mankind to the straight Path of Truth. The purpose underlying their revelation hath been to educate all men, that they may, at the hour of death, ascend, in the utmost purity and sanctity and with absolute detachment, to the throne of the Most High.[17]

13

FREE WILL

'Abdu'l-Bahá was asked: 'Is man free and unconstrained in all his actions, or is he compelled and constrained?' Before answering, He replied, 'This is one of the most important questions of divinity, and it is most abstruse.'[1] Perhaps all inquiring human beings will ask the question sometime in their life, in a reflection on what they are responsible for, what praise or blame can be attributed to them for their actions. It has certainly exercised me over the years. We can be sure, then, that it is not easy to answer this question in a definitive way. In fact, many philosophers over millennia have made their contributions to this question and they are not all in agreement. Having said this, it should be possible, by taking the lead from 'Abdu'l-Bahá's answer, to arrive at some conclusions that will satisfy our intellect even if we admit that there are many questions that remain unanswered. So here goes.

First, it is obvious that there are many things that are not subject to man's freedom of will and action. Let's look at a handful of these. None of us has a choice as to whether we are born. We do not choose our parents, consequently the colour of our skin, hair, eyes or anything to do with hereditary factors whether healthy or unhealthy. We do not choose our siblings or the lack of them, nor our extended family. We do not choose the country we are born into, nor the general population of that country. We do not choose the historical context at the time of birth, whether there is peace or war, whether the region is progressive or archaic. These are all predetermined, all out of our control. All of this has an extensive effect upon our development and may determine many things we will do for the rest of our life. Take for instance the constraints imposed upon one who is born blind, or, on the other hand, what many would regard as the life-enhancing factor of someone who is born into wealth. 'Abdu'l-Bahá particularly mentions that 'there are certain matters where man is forced and compelled, such as sleep, death, sickness, failing powers, misfortune, and material loss: These are not subject to the will of man and he is not accountable for them, for he is compelled to endure them.'[2]

Some hold the view that because so many things have happened outside an individual's control, then every action taken is predetermined. They argue that individuals do not have any real power of freedom of will or action. To them thoughts and volition, character and external actions, are all merely the inevitable outcome of circumstances, they are 'all inexorably predetermined in every detail along rigid lines by events of the past, over which he himself has had no sort of control'.[3]

Conversely, most people feel they have some control of their lives and although they admit some aspects are predetermined, nonetheless they have freedom of will and action in many important things. For instance, they can choose to be responsible parents or reprobate, be polite or discourteous, waste time gambling or use it industriously, be mean or generous, smile or frown. They believe that 'man possess[es] genuine moral freedom, power of real choice, true ability to determine the course of his thoughts and volitions, to decide which motives shall prevail within his mind, to modify and mould his own character.'[4] 'Abdu'l-Bahá clearly underlines this understanding of human agency, stating that some things 'are subject to the free will of man, such as acting with justice and fairness, or injustice and iniquity – in other words, the choice of good or evil actions; It is clear and evident that the will of man figures greatly in these actions.'[5]

With this view, man is morally accountable for his actions in life. It is therefore on this basis that all exhortations, advice, encouragement, admonitions, warnings and the like, issue from the Manifestations of God to humanity. If man is not morally accountable, what would be the logic in summoning human beings to use their freedom of will and action in the correct way? And it is not only in the religious domain that man is considered to be accountable. The whole legal system related to judgements against perpetrators of illegal acts is based on the fact that they used their freedom in an incorrect way. Of course, there are in some cases reasons why a person is not truly accountable, as when an offender is judged to be mentally ill. Taken even further, the whole of society functions freely, within identified constraints, when its citizens have been trained and educated to be responsible. If all is determined and man is not morally accountable, why put so much effort into this education and training?

However, there could be a grey area between these two positions of hard determinism and free will, which needs to be examined. It could be that if someone is summoned for national conscription in one of the armed forces of a country then he has no freedom of action. That is, if he wants to avoid imprisonment (a curtailment of his freedom), then he must obey the authorities; in this he has no real freedom of action. In several places in the world children are still subject to arranged marriages by their parents. Putting aside whether or not these marriages work, many feel that if they are to continue as a member of their family (and usually the community) they have to accept the fate decided for them by their parents. So entrenched has this mode of functioning become in some communities that to question it may put the young person's life in danger.

I'm sure that lots of other examples of this kind can be given, but these will do to serve the point to be made, that these examples, national conscription and arranged marriages, are not of the natural predetermined type. The natural type consists of those things which God has determined, such as life, death, sleep, decline of powers when one gets older, and so on. National conscription and arranged marriages are the decisions not of God but of man, perhaps the ruling elite or the governing body in regard to national conscription, and the family and community in the case of arranged marriages. They are man-made 'social constructs'. Even if we consider a person who is born blind, this is not predetermined by God as are life and death, but may be a result of wrong moral choices of one's forebears causing a genetic mutation through, say, a sexually transmitted infection. It is the result of human agency using free will and action wrongly. Similarly, if a child is born into a war zone, the war zone is not the result of predeterminism by God, as He forbids war, but is the result of the wrongdoing by those who came before the child was born. We are to be careful not to attribute to God those choices and decisions that He has allowed to human agency, and call them predeterminism.

Sadly, some who have suffered because human agency has taken away their freedom of action may feel a terrible anger, resentment or bitterness, which can bias them to the point where they feel there is really no free will at all. Imagine someone, for instance, who although a peaceful soul and a well-wisher of mankind, when conscripted into the army kills someone his government has identified as an enemy. What agonies of grief and deep regret could haunt that soul for the remainder of his life? Also, imagine the anguish of a young girl pressed into a marriage that demands she relinquish all thoughts of developing her potential abilities and talents, to raise a large family from which she will have to arrange the marriages of her children, thereby repeating the cycle of oppression.

Loss of hope is one of the devastating consequences of oppression. Fundamentally this means that whether one feels they have moral freedom of will and action, they are so overshadowed by the cruelty of their oppressors that they have given up hope of the possibility of justice working in their lives. It is obvious that the oppressed are not responsible for their affliction; they have not freely chosen their condition, it has been imposed on them by other humans, but not by God! Even in this condition they have the choice of good or bad actions, although it must be much more difficult for oppressed souls to choose good actions. One can imagine that they have to valiantly struggle with themselves to let go of bitterness or anger and, as appropriate, choose resignation, look for the good in others and renounce enmity, be cheerful and radiant in place of bitterness and complaining. It is possible, however; Nelson Mandela and Mahatma Gandhi stand out as shining examples of this possibility.

History also records other soul-stirring examples of radiant acquiescence in the face of the most horrific of oppressive circumstances. One such story concerns a man named Mullá 'Alí-Ján who was born in Persia in 1846. As a young man he studied the Qur'án and the traditions of Islam and became aware that God had promised a new Messenger or Manifestation of God, whom he eventually identified, after much searching, as Bahá'u'lláh. With great courage and devotion, he taught many others about Bahá'u'lláh, which incited a lot of opposition, especially from the Islamic clergy. He knew that these activities would put his life in danger, yet the enthusiasm generated by his love for Bahá'u'lláh and His teachings spurred him on. As a moth sacrifices itself to the flame, Mullá 'Alí-Ján used his free will and freedom of action as a sacrifice for Bahá'u'lláh. No inducement could get him to change his mind and convert back to Islam. To recant his newfound faith, even if offered all the treasures of the earth, would be a betrayal of conscience and love so great that death was preferred. He would not recant, and he would not stop teaching the people, so the death sentence was pronounced against him. He was sent to Tehran where he was imprisoned, in June 1883, with the approval of the king of Persia he was executed and disposed of in the 'vilest' of circumstances: 'his neck was wounded and his body swollen from the waist to the feet. On the day of his martyrdom he asked for water, performed his ablutions, recited his prayers, bestowed a considerable gift of money on his executioner, and was still in the act of prayer when his throat was slit by a dagger, after which his corpse was spat upon, covered with mud, left exposed for three days, and finally hewn to pieces.'[6]

Dr. J. E. Esslemont writes, 'There is nothing to keep men from forsaking religion if they wish to do so. 'Abdu'l-Bahá says: "God

Himself does not compel the soul to become spiritual. The exercise of the free human will is necessary.""[7]

It would be misleading to assume that man is capable of faultlessly discerning predetermined action from that which is the product of free will. When a law of the land is broken it is for the judiciary to determine guilt and what sentence to pass on the criminal. This process is not infallible, but is the best system we have if justice and due diligence are exercised in the process. At an individual level, we are exhorted by all the Manifestations of God to overlook the shortcomings of others and even forgive perpetrators of the most heinous of crimes. This is a seemingly impossible task, but one that we can aspire to with the aid of God. Generally, we do not know the circumstances of a person's life that may predispose someone to certain actions. The song sung by Elvis Presley, 'In the Ghetto', comes to mind:

As the snow flies
On a cold and grey Chicago morning
A poor little baby child is born
In the ghetto
And his mama cries
Cause if there's one thing that she don't need
It's another hungry mouth to feed
In the ghetto.

People, don't you understand
The child needs a helping hand
Or he'll grow to be an angry young man some day
Take a look at you and me,
Are we too blind to see?
Do we simply turn our heads
And look the other way?

Well the world turns
And a hungry little boy with a runny nose

Plays in the street as the cold wind blows
In the ghetto.

And his hunger burns
So he starts to roam the streets at night
And he learns how to steal
And he learns how to fight
In the ghetto.

Then one night in desperation
A young man breaks away
He buys a gun, steals a car,
Tries to run, but he don't get far
And his mama cries.

As a crowd gathers round an angry young man
Face down on the street with a gun in his hand
In the ghetto.

As her young man dies,
On a cold and grey Chicago morning,
Another little baby child is born
In the ghetto.[8]

On the other hand, part of being a human being is that we have a conscience, though it will be more pronounced in some in comparison to others. Even the most depraved individuals, such as the serial killer and necrophiliac Denis Nilsen, after a deprived and unstable childhood 'saw himself as having a good and evil side'. He 'wrestled with himself when thinking whether or not to commit murder'.[9] This struggle between one's good and bad nature is exemplified by the Gollum character in the famous *Lord of the Rings* story by Tolkien. Seduced by 'the power of the ring', Gollum holds conversations with himself as to whether he should let his good side be completely overwhelmed by his evil side to gain this power. As in the case of Nilsen, the lower side of his nature won the battle.

No human being can assess another as to exactly what they are responsible for throughout their lifetime, or what rewards or sanctions, according to the principle of justice, they should receive. Although the general rule is that we are all morally accountable for our actions, as 'Abdu'l-Bahá indicates, how much is mitigated in the case of blameworthy actions is a judgement that only the omniscient, almighty God can make. Perhaps it is in this light that Christ admonished: 'Judge not, that ye be not judged. For with what judgment ye judge, ye shall be judged: and with what measure ye mete, it shall be measured to you again.'[10]

The teachings of Bahá'u'lláh declare that although man has free will and freedom of action, nonetheless if he is a captive of the world of nature, he is not really free at all. In a succinct aphorism He states: 'O My Servant! Free thyself from the fetters of this world, and loose thy soul from the prison of self. Seize thy chance, for it will come to thee no more.'[11] As an example of 'the fetters of this world', take for instance the heroin addict or the alcoholic. In these conditions of addiction, one has used freedom of will only to be enslaved by chemicals. Perhaps not so obvious are the daily routines and lifestyles chosen by millions enmeshed in materialistic pursuits, completely heedless of the spiritual world, which alone can release the 'soul from the prison of self'. At the lower end of attachment to the material world, man uses his free will to become completely chained to his selfish desires and gratifications. 'Abdu'l-Bahá gives clear insight into this condition:

And among the teachings of His Holiness Bahá'u'lláh is man's freedom, that through the ideal Power he should be free and emancipated from the captivity of the world of nature; for as long as man is captive to nature he is a ferocious animal, as the struggle for existence is one of the exigencies of the world of nature. This matter of the struggle for existence is the fountain-head of all calamities and is the supreme affliction.[12]

14

FREE WILL AND THE POWER OF THE MANIFESTATIONS OF GOD

Further reading and reflection on free will uncovered another aspect of it, which may come as a surprise to some, as it did to me: It is this – we are allowed to keep our free will by the permission of the Manifestations of God. This needs to be explained.

In some of His works, Bahá'u'lláh states that one of the names of God is the All-Compelling. As an example, He writes: 'Say: If it be our pleasure We shall render the Cause victorious through the power of a single word from Our presence. He is in truth the Omnipotent, the All-Compelling.'¹ It has to be remembered what the Manifestations of God are commissioned by the Almighty to manifest. Shoghi Effendi writes, that the 'divinity attributed to so great a Being and the complete incarnation of the names and attributes of God in so exalted a Person' clarifies Bahá'u'lláh's exalted nature.

As one of the attributes of God is the All-Compelling, I have concluded that Bahá'u'lláh also possessed this attribute. By applying this attribute to that which He could compel, it becomes obvious that if Bahá'u'lláh wanted to use this power He could make everyone to turn to God. Free will could not survive under this power. He comments, however, that He prevents Himself from such a command issuing from His mouth. These are His words: 'Within the throat of this Youth . . . there lie prisoned accents which, if revealed to mankind to an extent smaller than a needle's eye . . . would compel every head to bow down in worship and every face to turn in adoration towards this omnipotent Ruler . . .'²

Prior to the Revelation of Bahá'u'lláh, the Báb expressed this same powerful ability:

> Should it be Our wish, it is in Our power to compel, through the agency of but one letter of Our Revelation, the world and all that is therein to recognize, in less than the twinkling of an eye, the truth of Our Cause . . .³

It may be difficult to believe that the Manifestations of God, Who outwardly seem as other men and only appear occasionally throughout history, could be invested with the power to remove man's free will. Even so, man himself has the ability, in relation to the animal kingdom, to dominate it in such a way as to completely remove all their senses and freedom of movement, even to the point of destroying them if he wishes. Further, through the power of his intellect working through science and technology, man has harnessed energies that could completely wipe out all life on the planet. Plant and animal life have not the faintest idea that this is so; but their ignorance is not a proof against the powers that humanity possess. The creation story in Genesis reveals that this powerful potential was latent in man from the beginning of his appearance on earth. It was intended by God that humanity would be 'fruitful, and multiply, and replenish the earth, and subdue it: and have dominion over the fish of the sea, and over the fowl of the air, and over every living thing that moveth upon the earth.'⁴

It is similar with the Manifestations of God in relation to humanity. Our ignorance of the powers they possess is not a proof that they do not possess them. To outward seeming the Manifestations of God are ordinary, mortal human beings who eat, sleep, breath and bleed like any other human, yet they have all the powers and characteristics of God. According to the will of God, to which they are absolutely submissive, they conceal their reality behind a thousand veils. This concealment is the means whereby everyone who comes into contact with the Manifestation is left with their free will intact; for who in the presence of such awesome power and glory would dare to challenge their authority? On this point Bahá'u'lláh states:

> Know verily that the veil hiding Our countenance hath not been completely lifted. We have revealed Our Self to a degree corresponding to the capacity of the people of Our age. Should the Ancient Beauty be unveiled in the fullness of His glory mortal eyes would be blinded by the dazzling intensity of His revelation.[5]

In a further statement on this point Bahá'u'lláh declares:

> Were we to divest Ourself of the mortal raiment which We have worn in consideration of your weakness, all that are in heaven and on earth would offer up their souls for my sake. To this thy Lord Himself doth testify. None, however, can perceive it save those who have detached themselves from all things for the love of their Lord, the Almighty, the Most Powerful.[6]

Our usual response to the removal of something that belongs to us, against our will, is to resist it happening. So, for instance, if someone tries to rob us of our possessions, we will either try to personally prevent this happening or appeal to the law enforcement agency to protect our rights as citizens. In relation to the Manifestations of God, however, we are obliged to consider the removal of something which inherently makes us human beings, namely our free will and freedom of action, in a different way. Firstly, if it were seized from humanity we would not, from that point on, have any means, abilities or powers to make any objections whatsoever. Because the Manifestations of God have the power of compulsion, given to them by the All-Compelling, they can remove humanity's free will in the blink of an eye and mankind would have no idea, no awareness that such a thing had happened. In relation to this, consider the case when someone becomes the subject of a hypnotist during an entertainment. In this state people are at a higher level of suggestibility, during which some free will is separated from that which is maintained. Here they perform all manner of strange acts dictated by the hypnotist. Evidently the free will that would normally restrain such behaviour has been compromised to some degree, even if they retain the 'will' to resist actions that are morally repulsive to them. Often, when the subject is released from this state, the 'victim' may have no memory of the strange and silly ways which have been used to amuse the audience.

A second way in which we can understand the removal of free will is not by it being taken against one's will, but voluntarily given. In other words, it is possible that the heart and soul can be so entranced, so consumed by the power of love and beauty that emanates from the person of the Manifestation of God, that one immediately relinquishes all control over oneself and gives the gift of free will into the hands and safekeeping of the Manifestation. An indication of this power is recorded in the memoirs of Áqá Riḍá, who attained the presence of Bahá'u'lláh in 'Akká:

> In the gatherings of the friends, if the Blessed Beauty [Bahá'u'lláh] turned his face to a person, that individual was unable to gaze upon His countenance and see the effulgent rays of the Sun of Truth. It was therefore Bahá'u'lláh's practice to look to the right side as He spoke, so that the friends might find it easier to look at His face. And if He ever turned His face towards the friends, He would close His eyes and speak.[7]

One may ask why the friends, as related in the above experience, found it easier to look at the face of Bahá'u'lláh when He closed His eyes to speak to them? Evidently those in His presence found it very difficult, if not impossible, to look directly into the eyes of the Manifestation. It may be surmised that if Bahá'u'lláh granted someone to look into His eyes, it is possible that so powerful would be the 'effulgent rays' pouring from Him that the individual's free will would be entirely compromised. Another of the believers who attained the presence of Bahá'u'lláh recounted:

> Know with absolute certainty that if anyone, whether friend or foe, claims that he was able to look directly into the blessed face of Bahá'u'lláh he is a liar. I tested this repeatedly and tried time and again to gaze upon His blessed countenance, but was unable to do so. Sometimes, when a person attains the presence of Bahá'u'lláh, he is so enamoured and carried away that in fact he becomes dumbfounded, awe-struck, oblivious of himself and forgetful of the world. And whenever he is not carried away, should he try to look into His blessed face with concentration, it would be like looking into the sun. In the same way that the eye is blinded by the effulgent rays of the sun, causing tears to flow, should one persist in gazing upon the countenance of the Blessed Beauty, tears will fill the eyes making it impossible to gain any impression of Him.[8]

In fact, it is recorded that those who were humble and submissive in His presence could not carry out the simplest of actions such as holding a cup of tea without spilling it, so magnetized were they by the majestic power that flowed from Him. Many there were who determined to ask Bahá'u'lláh a series of questions but found in His company that they had become so spellbound by His being and the flow of words of consummate love, wisdom and authority, that they had entirely forgotten what they were going to ask. Then, to their utter amazement, they found in His presence that, one by one, their unasked questions were being answered by Bahá'u'lláh.

The accounts of Bahá'u'lláh's association with the believers and also with those who had not, as yet, received the gift of faith, tell us that even the minutest indication of the glory of His reality, if revealed by Him, would propel the observer into another world. That world is the world of resplendent majesty, of union with God as manifest in His divine representative. It is a relationship of such love and acceptance that overwhelms and instantly burns away any worldly desire. In this condition one becomes like a moth to a flame, where sacrifice to its all-consuming heat and light becomes the only objective. Nothing else but sacrifice is possible for such a soul caught within this ravishing conflagration. All reason is lost, all restraint is burnt away; nor is there the slightest wish to return to one's previous limited condition of free will, for the soul has entirely replaced its will with the will of God. This condition of ecstasy has been explained by Bahá'u'lláh in the following words:

> For when the true lover and devoted friend reacheth the presence of the Beloved, the radiant beauty of the Loved One and the fire of the lover's heart will kindle a blaze and burn away all veils and wrappings. Yea, all he hath, from marrow to skin, will be set aflame, so that nothing will remain save the Friend.[9]

Bahá'u'lláh did concede to the wishes of a few believers to lift the veil to an extent not normally done, to reveal a greater indication of His glory. One such account of this experience is that of a rich and influential man who undertook an arduous six-month journey to visit Bahá'u'lláh in 'Akká as a pilgrim. After two occasions in the presence of Bahá'u'lláh, he initially felt disappointed:

> I [had] accepted the hardships and burdens of a six month journey hither to 'Akká perhaps I might witness some extraordinary and divine happening . . . but Baha'u'llah speaks like other men and He gives instructions and teachings similar to other men. There is perhaps nothing extra-ordinary or miraculous here.
>
> I was immersed in these thoughts when on the third day

one of the servants there said to me that Bahá'u'lláh wants to see you alone and unaccompanied. I went to the presence of the Blessed Beauty (Bahá'u'lláh) immediately and I lifted aside the curtain of the room where He was, to be close in His presence. I bowed and instantly I saw the Blessed Beauty as an incredibly bright and dazzling Light, and so intense was my experience of this Light that I fell and lost consciousness. All I recall is that He said: 'fee Amani'lláh', which means go with God's safety.

The servants were able to drag me to the corridor and subsequently to the pilgrim house. I could not eat or sleep for two days after. What happened is as if I beheld His overwhelming Presence everywhere I went and I constantly was telling the other pilgrims that He is here.

My other fellow pilgrims got tired of me and asked 'Abdu'l-Bahá to help me. After another two days again the servant came back and took me to Bahá'u'lláh's presence. When I attained His presence, He poured forth loving kindness and gracious utterance. He bade me be seated.

Then Bahá'u'lláh said: '. . . The Manifestations of the Divine Essence are forced to appear in human attire and clothes. If Their true Being, that which is behind the veil of concealment, if that were to appear then all humanity, like your good self will lose consciousness and swoon to the unconscious realm.' Then Bahá'u'lláh went on: 'Do you know how parrots are taught to speak?' I bowed and said: 'I do not know.'

Bahá'u'lláh explained: 'The parrot owners have a parrot within a cage. Then they bring a big mirror in front of the cage. And then a man hides behind the mirror and starts repeating phrases and talking . . . The parrot sees that there is another parrot identical to itself talking in the cage in front (reflected in the mirror) and imagining that it is the reflected parrot that is doing the talking it too starts mimicking and learns to speak. Now if the person who is actually behind the mirror should reveal himself from the start, then the parrot will never learn to speak. It is thus that the Manifestations of the Divine should come into the world in human attire and human clothes so that They will not frighten mankind with Their awesome Being . . .'[10]

Another moving story about the immense power and glory of Bahá'u'lláh concerns Siyyid Ismá'íl of Zavárih, who willingly gave up his free will for Bahá'u'lláh. Siyyid Ismá'íl, described by Shoghi Effendi as 'one of His ardent lovers . . . formerly a noted divine, taciturn, meditative and wholly severed from every earthly tie',[11] attained the presence of Bahá'u'lláh in Baghdad. When Bahá'u'lláh served Siyyid Ismá'íl some light refreshments he, with the utmost humility and lowliness, pleaded with Bahá'u'lláh to 'receive instead . . . a portion of spiritual food from the unseen treasury of His divine knowledge'.[12] His wish was granted. Words of such 'incomparable power and awe' flowed from Bahá'u'lláh, words 'which were filled with spiritual significance and which, according to Bahá'u'lláh's testimony, no one is capable of describing'.[13]

The effect of being instantly plunged into the spiritual world completely overwhelmed Siyyid Ismá'íl. Intoxicated with the wine of the love of God he was no longer able to carry on with day to day living. A world spiritually glorious was opened to his inner eyes, severing all attachment to this physical world. His innermost being was set on fire by the love of Bahá'u'lláh. Unable to live even for a moment outside the spiritual reality unveiled by Bahá'u'lláh, he longed to sacrifice his life for his Beloved. Shoghi Effendi relates that Siyyid Ismá'íl took upon himself the task of sweeping the approaches to Bahá'u'lláh's house: 'he would, at the hour of dawn, gather up, with infinite patience, the rubble which the footsteps of his Beloved had trodden, would blow the dust from the crannies of the wall adjacent to the door of that house, would collect the sweepings in the folds of his own cloak'. Not wanting any other to walk upon such precious rubble on which his Beloved had walked, he carried the contents of his cloak to the river and threw it in. For forty days he denied himself both sleep and food; his whole being was already in another world. Then, by the banks of the river Tigris one day, he 'performed his ablutions, lay down on his back, with his face turned towards Baghdád, severed his throat with a razor, laid the razor upon his breast, and expired.'[14]

Apart from a heart-rending statement of Bahá'u'lláh that: 'No blood has, till now, been poured upon the earth as pure as the blood he shed,'[15] this is an account of a believer taking his own life out of a soul-consuming love for the Manifestation of God. Through this, we are given a glimpse of a reality that mature contemplation will come to understand. We should not think that when Bahá'u'lláh gave to Siyyid Ismá'íl a portion of 'spiritual food' that He was ignorant of the consequences of doing so. Responding positively to the pleadings of this devoted follower, Bahá'u'lláh knew his love for Him would become inflamed to the point that he could no longer live in this world. Yet, Bahá'u'lláh still responded to Siyyid Ismá'íl's request. In a sense the link between body and soul had been rendered tenuous when Bahá'u'lláh revealed those words to him. Indeed, Siyyid Ismá'íl felt compelled to sever himself from life in this world.

When out walking sometime after this event, Bahá'u'lláh was approached by a government officer who reported that 'one of His followers had been killed and his body thrown on the riverbank'. '"No one has killed him," replied Bahá'u'lláh. "Through seventy thousand veils of light We showed him the glory of God to an extent smaller than a needle's eye; therefore, he could no more bear the burden of his life and has offered himself as a sacrifice."'[16] It is clear from Bahá'u'lláh's eulogy of Siyyid Ismá'íl that his death was not a suicide but a sacrifice. In fact, Bahá'u'lláh gave him the title 'Dhábih', which means 'sacrifice'.

To those who are immersed in the things of the world, who think that success is linked to material acquisition, status and influence over others, this concealment of the power and glory of the Manifestation may be interpreted as weakness. In reality, however, the Manifestations of God are endowed with tremendous love and power, majesty and sovereignty. Their influence is over the hearts and minds of men, and the general direction that humanity should take for its spiritual and material progress. To think, then, that the Manifestations of God did not have or could not use this power to compel people to believe and follow them is to completely misunderstand and underestimate the powers every Manifestation of God had at their disposal. The injustices each experienced, the cruelty, tyranny, oppression and betrayal they suffered with such meekness and submission, has left a paradox that mystifies the worldly wise. They argue that if they had such awe-inspiring power, why did they not use it to accomplish their ends?

A heart-melting account of the restraint and absolute submission to the will of God to use only heavenly power can be read in the Gospels. The disciple John tells us that the Governor of Judea, Pilate, when interrogating Christ, was afraid because of the insistence of the Jews that He should be crucified. Pilate tried many times to get a confession from Christ that He was claiming to be the Son of God, as this would render Him guilty of blasphemy in the eyes of the Jews, making it easy for the death sentence to be pronounced against Him. Before Caiaphas, the head of the Sanhedrin Council, the chief priests and a multitude of people who came to witness Christ's sufferings intent on deriding and injuring Him, Pilate continued with his interrogation. Jesus held His peace and made no reply. Relating this story to explain that Christ's power was not earthly but heavenly Bahá'u'lláh writes:

Finally, an accursed of God arose and, approaching Jesus, adjured Him saying: 'Didst thou not claim to be the Divine Messiah? Didst thou not say, "I am the King of Kings, My word is the Word of God, and I am the breaker of the Sabbath day?"' Thereupon Jesus lifted up His head and said: 'Beholdest thou not the Son of Man sitting on the right hand of power and might?' These were His words, and yet consider how to outward seeming He was devoid of all power except that inner power which was of God and which had encompassed all that is in heaven and on earth. How can I relate all that befell Him after He spoke these words? How shall I describe their heinous behaviour towards Him? They at last heaped on His blessed Person such woes that He took His flight unto the fourth Heaven.[17]

The challenge to Pilate, Caiaphas and all present was to see, not with physical eyes, eyes laden with earthly arrogant and ignorant impediments, but with spiritual eyes. Jesus was apparently a helpless captive in the hands of a despotic power and an ignorant people. Yet He proclaimed that He was 'sitting on the right hand of power and might'. None on earth at that time, including His disciples, were aware of His tremendous power. To His tormentors he was more helpless than a kitten. At least a kitten scratches back when cornered. In reality the unbounded power of God surrounded Christ and worked through Him. Submission to God's will is not weakness but the essence of might and majesty. Pilate became more frustrated at what he perceived to be His indolence. 'Speakest thou not unto me? knowest thou not that I have power to crucify thee, and have power to release thee?', he asked. The answer Jesus gave is quite perplexing, He said, 'Thou couldest have no power at all against me, except it were given thee from above' – that is, from God.[18]

In other words, Christ was saying that it was God who had given power to Pilate to take his life. It is clear from this event and others that God has given the power to everyone to do both good and bad. But this does not mean that God is colluding with the evildoers. The choice of good or bad is included in the make-up of human beings, as discussed before, it is a product of free will. If Christ were suddenly to change this law of creation for His own ends, as He certainly had the power to do, what effect would this have on all who hold His life as a perfect example of how to live? Instead of trust in God and a life of reliance on Him and steadfast faith, especially in the most testing of circumstances, we would be left to the promptings of our lower nature, a nature that would stop at nothing to get its own selfish way. If Christ gave in to the allurement of selfishness, when pushed to the limits, what chance, it could be argued, do we mere mortals have?

But how can we make sense of a perfect God assisting everyone, without exception, to do good or bad? This is how 'Abdu'l-Bahá explains it:

> . . . man's stillness or motion itself is conditioned upon the aid of God. Should this assistance fail to reach him, he can do neither good nor evil. But when the assistance of the all-bounteous Lord confers existence upon man, he is capable of both good and evil. And should that existence be cut off, he would become absolutely powerless. That is why the aid and assistance of God are mentioned in the Sacred Scriptures.[19]

At the heart of the above passage, 'Abdu'l-Bahá states what the assistance of God is that enables someone to do either good or evil, and that is 'existence'. In other words, if someone exists, he has life, because the bounty of God allows him to exist – to carry on living. Christ, being perfectly aware of this reality, did not rail against His oppressors. Rather did He acquiesce to the will of God that allowed His oppressors to put Him to death. Sooner or later, everyone will die, and with it the power to do evil also. The help of 'existence' in the physical world is sooner or later 'cut off', but until this happens each person maintains his free will to do good or evil. 'Abdu'l-Bahá uses a wonderful analogy to explain this:

> This condition can be likened to that of a ship that moves by the power of wind or steam. Should this power be cut off, the ship would become entirely unable to move. Nevertheless, in whatever direction the rudder is turned, the power of the steam propels the ship in that direction. If the rudder is turned to the east, the ship moves eastward, and if it is

directed to the west, the ship moves west. This motion does
not arise from the ship itself, but from the wind or steam.[20]

This explanation fully answers the question why, if God exists
and no one can do anything without His assistance, does He not
prevent people doing terrible things? Well, He does prevent them
– according to His decree they die (the power of physical existence is removed) sooner or later and they are called to account
for their ways. If you want that evildoer to die sooner rather than
later, then you are removing the time given by God, for reasons
that He is knowledgeable about and which may be understood
only at a later stage in spiritual development. Only God can make
this type of decision. One speculative reason for not removing
the decree of 'existence' may be that evil just does not exist in
a vacuum and pop up here and there in the form of Jack the
Ripper or Vlad the Impaler. No, it is mostly a product of society,
of an environment, for example, of great moral laxity or terrifying social subjugation. Humanity, according to the wisdom and
guidance of God, has to learn these hard lessons, and one way of
doing so is to experience what happens when the ship's rudder is
directed towards the rocks!

Each soul, therefore, had their choice in past ages as to how
to respond to the Manifestations of God. No power from God
forced them in either direction. It is still the same today – one
responds to Bahá'u'lláh and His claims entirely through one's
own free will.

Such are the lessons of free will!

15

EVIL AND HOW TO COUNTER IT

One of the most difficult minefields to navigate is that of the prevalence of evil in the world and how to counter it. When 'Abdu'l-Bahá was asked, 'What is evil?' he replied, 'Evil is imperfection.'[1] In another place, He stated:

> . . . the praiseworthy attributes and perfections of man are purely good and have a positive existence. Evil is simply their non-existence. So ignorance is the want of knowledge, error is the want of guidance, forgetfulness is the want of remembrance, foolishness is the want of understanding: All these are nothing in themselves and have no positive existence.
> . . . Whatsoever God has created, He has created good. Evil consists merely in non-existence. For example, death is the absence of life: When man is no longer sustained by the power of life, he dies. Darkness is the absence of light: When light is no more, darkness reigns. Light is a positively existing thing, but darkness has no positive existence; it is merely its absence. Likewise, wealth is a positively existing thing but poverty is merely its absence.
> It is thus evident that all evil is mere non-existence. Good has a positive existence; evil is merely its absence.[2]

The first point I note from the above passage is that what 'God has created, He has created good.' In other words, He did not create any evil thing. Next is the point that evil is the absence of something which exists. For example, knowledge, guidance, under-standing, wealth and light all exist. We have to switch the light on, we cannot turn the darkness off; we have to make effort to acquire knowledge, we don't have to make any effort to be ignorant; we have to work hard to acquire wealth, we don't have to make any effort to be poor; to be able to see requires so many functioning parts in the body, it requires nothing to be blind. So, let us examine one of these analogies, namely the concept of 'darkness' for a fuller understanding that God did not create anything evil.

It must be understood that when 'Abdu'l-Bahá uses the word 'darkness' in this context it is really only a metaphor; in the physical world darkness is not an evil thing. I'm sure we can all think of examples where physical darkness is beneficial, such as when one wants to sleep or has a migraine. Interestingly, there is some discussion in the scientific community as to what darkness actually is. Is there something that can be called absolute darkness, a place where it cannot get even darker, the complete absence of light, or are there only varying degrees of darkness?

Visible light is only part of a range of the <u>electromagnetic radiation</u> (EMR) spectrum that is detected by the human eye. EMR propagates waves, of which 'the absorbed energy of the electromagnetic waves' (a photon) is 'absorbed at single locations the way particles are absorbed . . . This dual wave-like and particle-like nature of light is known as the <u>wave–particle duality</u>.'[3] Also, 'photons are waves of electromagnetic energy that come in different wavelengths, or colours'.[4]

So, darkness for a human being is when the electromagnetic energy wavelength is reduced to a level that is outside visible detection. This does not imply that wavelength energy is not present just because the eye cannot see a particular colour. It may be that the frequency of energy wavelengths occurring in the darkest recesses of space become less and less but are never actually not present. This point has a parallel in human beings, for it may be that someone who is considered absolutely evil contains some goodness (such as a love for their dog), even if it is not visible to others. Be that as it may, even though darkness exists in the physical world, it should not be viewed as something evil because as such it is a creation of God and God did not create any evil thing. Let us now return to the statement of 'Abdu'l-Bahá that good has 'a positive existence. Evil is simply . . . its . . . non-existence. So ignorance is the want of knowledge, error is the want of guidance, forgetfulness is the want of remembrance, foolishness is the want of understanding: All these are nothing in themselves and have no positive existence . . .'[5]

It is clear that ignorance, error, forgetfulness, foolishness, death, darkness, and poverty are only analogies or metaphors for something missing. It seems that 'Abdu'l-Bahá has given these analogies for us to get a handle on the concept of something that is lacking in human beings, so as we can become conscious of it and then take the step of remedying the situation. Out of all existing things on the planet, it is only human beings that have the ability to become conscious of what they were previously unaware. Nature itself is not conscious of its state and never can be. Hence a rock or a courgette or a hedgehog does not think of itself as being ignorant or foolish, because they do not have the faculties, as humans have, to rationalize their condition in this way. So, if someone is, say, ignorant, that condition in relation to being knowledgeable is considered in the same way as evil is in relation to good. It is not that a human being has been made ignorant by God, because God does not make non-existing things. In fact, it is outside logical thinking to believe that anybody, God included, can make a non-existing thing. It may be that 'Abdu'l-Bahá said it in this way to help us understand why we do not have to make any effort at all to be ignorant or foolish, so as we can understand that an effort is needed to be knowledgeable or understanding. After all, a garden of weeds and brambles requires no effort to produce it; it exists in the absence of a garden of flowers trees and shrubs which, through the gardener's effort are grown.

In pre-scientific times many thought that death was synonymous with evil; many believed that if one was afflicted with blindness, deafness or disease it was a result of evil forces. Virtually all 'bad' happenings were interpreted as evil visitations. Such was the sway of superstitious reasoning during humanity's immature phases of development. Today we know that blindness, deafness, disease and the like are part of afflictions that are present in human and animals and have physical causes.

However, if God creates blindness and deafness, along with all the other conditions that afflict humans and animals, then we could say that God is a creator of imperfections – which would invalidate Him being God in the first place. But let's return to the point mentioned earlier, that neither God nor anybody else can make non-existing things. How can anyone make the condition of blindness or deafness?

This is different from asking whether a sighted or deaf person can be made blind or deaf. Of course they can, and there are many causes for these conditions. Similarly, nobody can create ignorance, but you can enable someone to be in the condition of ignorance by simply not educating them. If the All-Knowing is then accused of not educating humanity and therefore is guilty of enabling ignorance to flourish, then we could say He is complicit in 'allowing' ignorance and all the horrors that stem from it. This may seem a reasonable argument for those who have difficulty believing in God.

But there is another aspect to be considered; that is, the All-Knowing and All-Wise Creator has educated humanity, throughout its long history, by two methods, one through the teachings of the Prophets or Messengers of God, and the other through the result of man's rational faculties (provided by God) whereby he discovers knowledge, which we now call the result of scientific investigation. Both knowledge systems require the ability to reflect on the knowledge supplied by these two systems and then to either accept or reject that knowledge. In other words, man has the power of choice when doing so. As this power of 'choice' is innate in humans, we must ask; what would be the reason for this if there is nothing to make a choice about?

It seems to me that what is meant when we examine the

concept of evil is that it is non-existent in anything in nature because the system God has created is absolutely perfect. (This point will be discussed more fully later.) But out of all created things we find it is only human beings that are guilty of evil actions. This is because man has the power of choice, a requisite of being human. That man quite often chooses bad actions over good ones is seriously complicated. So, let's dwell on some reasons for this. It has been posited previously that every newborn child has the potential to choose light, high nature qualities or slip into dark, low-nature characteristics. How a child is educated to enable it to incline itself to its higher, noble nature is of great importance here. 'Abdu'l-Bahá therefore writes:

> From his infancy, the child must be nursed at the breast of God's love, and nurtured in the embrace of His knowledge, that he may radiate light, grow in spirituality, be filled with wisdom and learning, and take on the characteristics of the angelic host.[6]

So, if a parent puts effort into nursing her child 'at the breast of God's love, and nurtured in the embrace of His knowledge, that he may radiate light, grow in spirituality, be filled with wisdom and learning, and take on the characteristics of the angelic host,' then it is a powerful influence for producing a 'good' person. Conversely, if a parent does not make this nurturing effort with their child, then the absence of this effort allows a host of negative characteristics (like weeds) to multiply. These negative characteristics can accumulate on the 'path of ignominy and abasement',[7] a path which Bahá'u'lláh warns us to beware of choosing, because it can be harmful to ourselves and others. It is negative characteristics Bahá'ís regard as evil, not the individual. Evil then, is only a consideration in the human kingdom and is a result of wrong choices, leading us away from becoming 'the light of the world,' to that of 'its darkness'. It is perhaps for this reason that Shoghi Effendi explained the following:

We know absence of light is darkness, but no one would assert darkness was not a fact. It exists even though it is only the absence of something else. So evil exists too, and we cannot close our eyes to it, even though it is a negative existence. We must seek to supplant it by good, and if we see an evil person is not influenceable by us, then we should shun his company for it is unhealthy.[8]

Some may be concerned about the continuous use of the word 'evil'. It is a word that carries a lot of baggage. We live in a vastly different world from that in which this word originated. Over millennia the fear of evil, for the most part, was linked with ignorance and superstition. If the crops failed, the community felt they had to appease an angry deity; herbal treatments in medieval times were considered to be evil concoctions administered by witches; ministers of religion demonized the advance of science – the investigation into the material world. Virtually one's whole life was dominated by the fear of attracting the Devil, and many evil actions were prevented, not out of love for God but for fear of going to hell. So, 'evil' is really a word that has to be reconfigured in this phase of approaching maturity. This has been done in the Bahá'í Writings, hence 'Bahá'ís do not attribute to the phenomenon the objective existence it was assumed at earlier stages of religious history to possess.'[9] Put another way, Bahá'ís do not believe in an entity called the Devil or Satan from which all evil flows.

The Bahá'í understanding of an 'evil' person is more in tune with the scientific times we live in – evil is considered a 'spiritual disease',[10] a disease of the human spirit. And, as with disease in general, there are varying degrees of it. So, for instance, two of the most infected, malignant spirits of the twentieth century were Hitler and Stalin, who 'systematically tortured, degraded and exterminated millions of their fellow human beings' and whose motives were 'obsessions fuelling an apparently bottomless hatred of humankind'.[11] The cause of this spiritual disease is what 'Abdu'l-Bahá often called 'the insistent self'. That is why Shoghi Effendi stated that just as we could become infected by someone with a physically contagious disease 'then we should shun his company for it is unhealthy'; similarly, we should also shun people who are spiritually diseased until such a time as we are spiritually strong enough to help heal (influence) them. Even then we should be careful, as we could hold an over-estimation of our spiritual well-being, thereby running the risk of becoming 'infected'. Be that as it may, 'Abdu'l-Bahá mentions that amongst mankind there are only three categories of people that need special help, of which one of these are those who are spiritually sick. Perhaps in this way He was guiding us away from the ancient way of naming some people as evil. This is what He said:

> Among the sons of men some souls are suffering through ignorance, let us hasten to teach them; others are like children needing care and education until they are grown, and some are sick – to these we must carry Divine healing.[12]

A most difficult question to answer is; if God exists and He doesn't actually create evil, why does He knowingly permit it? Humanity has experienced so much of it throughout the ages that many would think surely God could have prevented at least some of it. How do we know He hasn't? Our difficulty is that we rarely consider things that **have not** happened! Part of an answer to this is contained above, but to understand it is helpful to dismiss the use of the word 'evil' and replace it with one or another of the three categories just mentioned: there are spiritually ignorant people, spiritually immature people and spiritually sick people. In each case there is a remedy – the ignorant must be enlightened, childish behaviour must be overcome with care and training, and spiritually sick people must be healed.

How this is to be done, however, needs to be discovered in the light of science and true religion working in harmony. A more detailed answer to this question follows in the next chapter.

16

DOES GOD ALLOW EVIL? A MORE INVOLVED ANSWER

A more involved answer to the question whether or not God allows evil will now be considered. It is an abstruse question to try to answer, which requires patience so that a spiritual interpretation or perspective of a process can be laid out. 'Soundbite' answers can be very frustrating. My purpose is to present a rational argument that, although it may not induce someone to believe in God, will demonstrate that a Bahá'í, who does, has not built his belief on an unscientific or superstitious platform. So here goes.

Bahá'u'lláh explains that in the whole creation of God there is a plan, a reason, a purpose for creating it. This concept is logical because anyone who decides to make something does so with a purpose in mind. Hence, for example, a chair is made with the plan of someone sitting on it, and a car is made for the purpose of transporting people to various destinations. Most of the time, when we look at a chair or a car, we are not conscious of the creative process that has gone into it. With a little thought, we know that the chair and the car started as an idea in someone's mind which later was expressed in design and working drawings. But to make the chair or car, materials had to be acquired along with the tools and machinery to make them. Then skilled craftspeople could take the next step and actually make the chair or car. It is a similar process that God employs when He creates.

Bahá'u'lláh tells us that the plan or idea of God in making everything is to produce human beings, or more correctly, conscious beings with 'the unique distinction and capacity to know Him and to love Him – a capacity that must needs be regarded as the generating impulse and the primary purpose underlying the whole of creation.'[1]

This requires various stages in the process of creation. First of all, the mineral kingdom has to be brought into being. Science is supplying us with lots of information about this process which it is believed started the observable universe, with the 'Big Bang' some 13.8 billion years ago. Over an extended period of time mineral matter came into existence and coalesced to form stars and planets, during which planet Earth came into existence. Upon this platform of minerals in planet Earth and with the play of other forces, the vegetable kingdom came into being. Next came the animal kingdom and then much later the human kingdom. Each stage was essential for the emergence of the next stage, much like each stage, when creating a chair or a car to arrive at the conclusion of the plan. The human body could not exist without the previous stages of the process of creation. Hence to arrive at the conclusion of God's plan, each stage is essential. This does not mean that the mineral, vegetable and animal kingdoms are of little value in the process. The fact that mineral existence is ubiquitous throughout the universe, is an indication of how important it is in the stages of creation. Similarly, each stage of the process of making a chair or a car is essential and has immense value of its own as without it the objective of the plan cannot be achieved. That God infuses varying degrees of 'life' in each stage, from the lower to the higher, each with its own ability to express existence in a unique way, betokens the creative genius, grace and bounty of the Creator. Also, our wonder at God's creative genius is increased when it is considered that the earth, which is virtually a closed system, is capable of recycling virtually everything it needs from itself. Within this system, for instance, a flower decomposes, breaking down into minerals which are absorbed in another plant which is then eaten by an animal, after which the animal dies and is eaten by other animals or decomposes into minerals again. The form changes but the elements are recycled. Regarding this, Bahá'u'lláh writes, 'That which hath been in existence had existed before, but not in the form thou seest today.'[2]

If there is no decay, no decomposition in the physical world, it would be impossible for new compositions to come about using elements previously used in other forms. If no decay is possible, then every first composition would be eternal, meaning for example, that the very first tree would last forever. Even if it did bear fruit, it would not propagate itself as the fruit around the seed would not decompose allowing the seed to germinate. And the very first animals, with the ability to propagate themselves, would never die, but increase in number over eons of time to the point that the whole system of life on the planet would collapse because of overcrowding and the depletion of resources to keep them alive. So, death itself in the physical world is just another name for the beginning of decay or decomposition and is an essential part of enabling new life to come about. Moreover, through the continuous process of new life brought into being, it provides a way for the evolution of every created thing, a point that has been taken up in a previous chapter. To be honest, I cannot think of a more perfect system – can you?

But let us look a little deeper as to what is implied by knowing and loving God. If we take God out of the picture for a moment, we all acknowledge that human beings have the ability to 'know' and to 'love'. On the other hand, we do not detect this ability in say a lump of iron ore in the mineral kingdom, or rhubarb in the vegetable kingdom. It seems that some animals can 'know' and 'love' to a limited degree. But even if we admit there is some intelligence here, it is only related to what their senses can inform them of the physical world. The capacity to know and love in the human kingdom is vastly different from that of the animal kingdom. Consider what 'Abdu'l-Bahá says on this point:

> The power of the intellect is one of God's greatest gifts to men, it is the power that makes him a higher creature than

the animal. For whereas, century by century and age by age man's intelligence grows and becomes keener, that of the animal remains the same. They are no more intelligent today than they were a thousand years ago! Is there a greater proof than this needed to show man's dissimilarity to the animal creation? It is surely as clear as day.[3]

Man is endowed with so many gifts that underpin his capacity to know and to love. We are informed by 'Abdu'l-Bahá that 'The greatest bestowal of God to man is the capacity to attain human virtues.'[4] Knowledge, love, humility, justice, kindness and compassion are just a few of the virtues man is capable of developing. 'The Heavenly Father', 'Abdu'l-Bahá further states, 'gave the priceless gift of intelligence to man so that he might become a spiritual light, piercing the darkness of materiality, and bringing goodness and truth into the world.'[5] Under the umbrella of 'intelligence' man has consciousness, the ability to think, comprehend, memorize and imagine, from which all the sciences, arts, technology, commerce, government, legal systems and so on have been developed. But man's intellect has also developed machine guns, anti-personnel mines, weapons of mass destruction, torture chambers, the sex industry, unrestrained consumerism, and a host of other evils. Unlike the animals that are 'savage and ferocious', simply as 'means for their subsistence and preservation',[6] man can use the divine purpose of his creation for selfish, egotistical and materialistic ends. We must not forget that 'the generating impulse and the primary purpose underlying the whole of creation'[7] is for man to know and love God. Unfortunately, however, man can fall seriously short of this purpose and instead use his capacity to know and to love everything other than God.

Now, if a chair is used to tie someone up to ready him for interrogation, or if a car is used as a status symbol or a means to purposely run over a pedestrian, can we blame the maker of the chair or the car? Of course not, because the chair and the car were not made with the idea or plan in mind to be of harm. Similarly, if human beings use their God-given gift to know and to love those things not of God, with all their horrific consequences, can we blame the Maker of human beings? Yet again, the answer is no, because the idea or plan of God endowed humans with the capacity to know and to love only for the purpose of those things that are sanctified by God, things that cause no harm, keep humanity safe and lead to happiness and progress. Therefore, Bahá'u'lláh declares that 'Every good thing is of God, and every evil thing is from yourselves. Will ye not comprehend?'[8]

With the above in mind, the question as to whether or not God permits evil by allowing it to happen, can now be answered, having ascertained that the plan of God, when creating all things, is to bring into existence conscious beings that can know and love Him.

Through His Manifestations, whom 'Abdu'l-Bahá calls the 'divine intelligence', humanity is informed about what they should do to comply with the creative plan of God. Nowhere in this plan is man allowed or permitted to do evil; it is strictly censured. For instance, the Manifestations of God have not allowed man to steal, all have been exhorted to be honest. So, if someone steals or is dishonest this has not been permitted by God, it is against the will of God for man. What is permitted by the Creator is the choice to comply with the will of God or not. As indicated before, man has this ability because God has endowed him freedom, with intelligence, to make decisions on all manner of things. All the lower kingdoms, the mineral, vegetable and animal kingdoms, comply with the will of God because they have no choice but to do so and therefore are not responsible for the way in which they function. It is silly to think for instance, that sand on a beach, or tree or a lion could be appealed to be just or honest. But you can appeal to a human being to be just or honest – to voluntarily comply.

One of the major ways God uses to encourage humans to voluntarily comply with His will, is to inform them, through His Manifestations, the higher intelligence, that there are good consequences for doing so, and bad consequences for not doing so. When we think about it, this is the way that all good parents train their children. To encourage them to be honest and not tell lies, for instance, we may relate the story of the 'boy who cried wolf'. The law of God, then, for all human beings, is that all good actions that are related, consciously or not, to the primary purpose of our Maker, bring rewards sooner or later; and that all bad actions bring negative consequences that can be viewed as punishments, sooner or later. Some rewards and punishments may be very small and may not even be regarded as such. Others could be abundant or severe. Of course, rewards and punishments are very different for children in comparison to adults. Even with adults the severity of the consequences will vary according to the degree of wrongdoing. Another factor in this process is that God can forgive, pardon or overlook faults and wrongdoings if He wishes.

The point here is that man must be taught to take responsibility for his actions and to realize they have an effect, good or bad, on others and even future generations. And just as a parent rewards and sanctions a child in the training process to become responsible, mature adults, capable of enjoying their life and of making their unique contribution to the betterment of society, so too does God educate and train humanity. We should ask, in what other way could humanity be trained to be responsible for its actions? In what other way can it be made abundantly clear that this responsibility goes way past that of individual concern to that of the whole of mankind, indeed to the whole of the planet? The fact that there are very severe consequences indeed for some wrong actions should be understood in the light that the wrong action that caused the severe consequences is not acceptable by God at all. If man does not learn from the guidance of the Manifestations of God, He will learn by testing the wisdom of their commands, that is, by making the mistakes he was warned about or exhorted to avoid – but learn he will!

Let us take as an example of this focused on the concept of

'holy war', universally known now as 'jihad'. At the beginning of the mission of Bahá'u'lláh in 1863, He recorded 'that in this Revelation the law of the sword hath been annulled'.[9] This decree was reinforced later when he wrote: 'O people of the earth! The first Glad-Tidings . . . is that the law of holy war hath been blotted out from the Book.'[10] In its place He advocated that they should use understanding and wise utterance if they are to 'conquer the citadels of men's hearts.'[11] Bahá'u'lláh expresses the hope that 'the weapons of war throughout the world may be converted into instruments of reconstruction and that strife and conflict may be removed from the midst of men'.[12]

A dictionary definition of a 'holy war' is that it is a 'war declared or fought for a religious or high moral purpose, as to extend or defend a religion'.[13] Throughout history many such wars have been fought, justifiable or not, with terrible suffering and loss of life. We are informed that 'there are numerous examples of Buddhists engaging in violence and even war', an example being that 'in the 14th century Buddhist fighters led the uprising that evicted the Mongols from China'.[14] Christians have engaged in many religious wars; the 200 years of Crusades between 1095 and 1291 against the Muslims and the Thirty Years War between Catholics and Protestants between 1618 and 1648, to cite just two. The Old Testament is replete with the wars fought by the Jews against nations that threatened their belief and worship of the One God and to absorb them back into polytheism. Muhammad allowed the 'ummah', the Muslim community, to defend itself if attacked but not to instigate conflict. One meaning of the word 'jihad' is 'to strive or struggle' in the way of God, and so the early Muslims were forced into defensive battles against the polytheists, the Battle of Badr (CE 624) and Uhud (CE 625) being the first attempts of the polytheists on the battlefield to wipe out the ummah.

Unfortunately, the original concept of jihad has now mutated into religious terrorism, which would shock Muhammad and call forth from Him the wrath of God on all who perpetrated such terror. As God's latest Manifestation, Bahá'u'lláh abrogated the law of jihad. He called the leaders of mankind in particular and humanity in general to abolish fighting religious wars, whether in defence of a community for a high moral purpose or to expand their religion. Sadly, the leaders of mankind completely ignored Him, and, although His message over the next several decades reached more and more people, only a few took it to heart. Not only did Middle Eastern rulers ignore Bahá'u'lláh's instructions, but Western rulers also. European rulers had, for the most part, the power in those times to enforce whatever they wanted. History records that they were neglectful of or oblivious to Bahá'u'lláh's summons. Christian rulers, for the most part, were anxious to expand their territories, colonize and 'Christianize' other parts of the world. Putting aside the terrifying wars into which they plunged humanity, they have left a cancerous inheritance – the global war against terror. This is the consequence of not listening to God's latest Messenger. It is not just the Eastern world that did not take heed – it is the West also! We are now in a war against religious fanaticism and hatred, a condition that Bahá'u'lláh warned is 'a world-devouring fire, whose violence none can quench. The Hand of Divine power can, alone, deliver mankind from this desolating affliction.'[15]

In one sense we can think of terrorism as retribution, punishment from God for not heeding the message of the latest Manifestation of God, in much the same way as a child who disobeys his parents warning not to put his hand in the fire. In another sense we could think of the terror of religious fanaticism as consequences instigated by man himself. In reality, they are different sides of one coin. It is man who, through ignorance and prejudice of other religions, created the environments for terrorism to grow; it is man who developed the permissive, immoral society of the West giving the terrorists what they regard as justification for their hate activities. Why do we blame God for these atrocities when He has done everything within the structure of His wise, creative genius to prevent this happening? We must ask ourselves who is going to change, man or God? Are we expecting Him to conform to our will or our idea as to what He should do?

It would help our understanding of this topic, at a deeper level, if we ponder on the reality of this great characteristic of God, namely that He is unchangeable; He is now what He has always been. If we think God is going to change His plan, mentioned above, to fit into our limited, finite, imperfect understandings we really do have to think again. If God is changeable it implies He can get better, improve, and evolve to be more perfect. It also implies that He can get worse. In both cases He would be no more than man, whom he created, a creation destined to change, develop, improve, and evolve. A wise man once said, 'If you don't feel as close to God as you used to, who moved?'

God is ever and always the same – close to us, even though we change as we move closer to Him or at other times drift away. It is quite funny to think that some would like a relationship with God but only in an advisory capacity! Such a person would feel that he has the right to advise God to take away the process by which heedless, irresponsible man becomes responsible – that is, by knowing the consequences of His actions. If God were to oblige this request and remove man's responsibility for his actions, then everything we know about what makes a human being would vanish in an instant. We would no longer be able to think, use our intelligence, comprehend and attain virtues, as by these means man is capable of becoming responsible and without them, he would be no more developed than an animal. With a little thought, it becomes obvious that we humans should get used to leaving God to do what He has always done and get working on ourselves to change for the better. And this is done by aligning ourselves with His will! The more this is done by an increasing number of people, the 'curse' of evil will melt away even as snow when the temperature rises.

PART THREE

UNDERSTANDING SPIRITUAL PROCESSES AND SYSTEMS

17

NO IMPERFECTIONS IN CREATION

People have become more aware in recent decades of the incidents of violence and abuse that man has inflicted upon other human beings, for instance the virtual annihilation and subjugation of the indigenous populations of South and North America. Many would argue that God should have employed some plan at the creation of humanity that would not even allow the thought of exterminating millions of people to be considered. The perception of human nature held by many is that it is entirely imperfect, as there is nothing inherent in the psychology of humans to prevent them from committing such atrocities, or even thinking of doing so (the first step to doing so). With this thought, it is a short step to disbelieving in a perfect Creator, Who, if He exists, has miserably failed where humans are considered.

Let's examine this point – that if God exists, He should employ in His creation of human beings something that would prevent them from doing harm to others. Not only that, but God should make man incapable of thinking harmful thoughts.

Now, let's suppose that God does exist, and that He has decreed the power of choice in His creation of humanity, which includes terribly harmful thoughts and actions against others on the one hand and heavenly, angelic thoughts and actions on the other. Instead of condemning a God that one does not believe exists (an illogical belief), it is important to start by asking the right question, which, in this case is something like, 'If God exists why has He allowed this in His creation of man?' At the back of our minds there may be the thought that God should be all-loving, merciful and compassionate, enabling humanity to live in peace and harmony, and if He wants this to come about then He certainly is not going about it the right way!

Let's question the appropriateness of this thought. Those who see imperfections everywhere have developed what could be called 'arguments from imperfection'. Yet another argument from imperfection is that if God exists, He must be omniscient, and therefore, because He knows everything, past, present and future, He somehow or other defines the actions of humans and is therefore responsible for them. In other words, because God knows everything, all our actions are predestined by Him and are not the result of our choice or free will. This rationale is used to disbelieve in God, because it makes Him guilty of all the wrongdoing in the world. Therefore because, according to this reasoning, He does not live up to expectations of a kind, loving, just and perfect God, then He does not exist. The argument initially sounds plausible, but there is a huge flaw in this type of reasoning. Although God is more than capable of predetermining all man's actions, this would surely make a mockery of allowing man free will to be responsible for his good or bad choices? Such a betrayal on the part of God as to His plan – to endow humans with the ability to know and love in order to be able to make choices freely, would amount to God being disingenuous, not a characteristic one associates with a perfect God. Also, this argument commits God to predetermining some people to be good and others bad. If this were so, then God would be guilty of creating evil.

The flaw in this argument has been pointed out by Bahá'u'lláh. Before revealing it, He explains that not only is God aware of every action before we make it, He is also aware of the thought preceding the act. He writes: 'Every act ye meditate is as clear to Him as is that act when already accomplished . . . All stands revealed before Him; all is recorded in His holy and hidden Tablets.' He then explains that:

This fore-knowledge of God, however, should not be regarded as having caused the actions of men, just as your own previous knowledge that a certain event is to occur, or your desire that it should happen, is not and can never be the reason for its occurrence.[1]

There are many examples that can be brought to make this point clear. For instance, we all know that the sun will rise at dawn tomorrow, but our fore-knowledge is not the cause of the sun rising. Similarly, train timetables show what time a train is due, but the timetable is not the cause of it arriving. Yet again, a doctor can predict the date of the birth of a baby, but this is not the cause of the birth of the baby on that date.

In a sense, everyone who thinks that God, if He exists, has done a bad job, has attributed omniscience to himself, that is, the ability to know everything, which would include the reason for everything. Such a person who, perhaps unconsciously, slips into 'omniscient mode', is really questioning the order of everything that has been in existence, that is in existence and, by implication, everything that will be in existence. Such a person is prone to finding defects everywhere, not just in human beings. Some are fond of articulating a litany of imperfections in creation, such as the sudden extinction of the dinosaurs millions of years ago to the savagery of animals that kill other animals to survive; from naturally caused forest fires that decimate the animal population, to mothers who carry a child for nine months in the womb only to produce a still-born infant. Because these persons have not discovered, during their extremely short time of being alive, any benevolent reason for all these happenings, they are persuaded that there is no God.

What would a person be inclined to do to the existing order of creation if they not only thought they were omniscient, but also were deluded into thinking that they were 'omnipotent', that is, having absolute power to do whatever they wanted? I suspect that they would want to change things to fit into their idea of what is perfect. If this were to happen, there would be a myriad differences between human beings as to what they regard as perfection or the ways to achieve it, not to mention the power struggles these differences of thought would engender. Such profoundly different visions would have far-reaching consequences: they would never evoke love and unity, but lead to increasing argumentation and conflict as each opinion was fought over. However, as perfection is a characteristic of God, what such people are suggesting is that they could do a better job at creating than God. In effect, by questioning the existing order and arrangement in creation and finding it, to their way of thinking, defective, they have, in their minds, occupied the position of God, even if they do not believe in Him. Perhaps, quite unconsciously, they have placed themselves in that position occupied by an All-Wise, All-Knowing Creator.

It has been stated that: 'The imperfect eye beholds imperfections.'[2] Of course, no sane person would consider himself perfect, but the point is that those who see imperfections everywhere are really making a statement about themselves: their own vision and understanding are imperfect. On the other hand, those who believe in a Prophet or Messenger of God as a perfect representative of all the powers and perfections of God are happy to accept that His knowledge embraces a perfect understanding of the perfection of God's creation. Muhammad, for instance, stated; 'No defect canst thou see in the creation of the God of Mercy: Repeat the gaze: seest thou a single flaw?'[3] And 'Abdu'l-Bahá states:

> For all existing things, whether on earth or in the heavens, even this limitless firmament and all that is contains, have been most befittingly created, arranged, composed, ordered and completed, and suffer no imperfection. To such an extent is this true that if all beings were to become pure intelligence and to reflect until the end that has no end, they could not possibly imagine anything better than that which already exists.[4]

When we carefully investigate the kingdoms of existence and observe the phenomena of the universe about us, we discover the absolute order and perfection of creation.[5]

So, to be able to make sense of all the apparent contradictions in the existing order or arrangement of creation, 'perfection' is a requirement – perfect understanding and knowledge. To help humanity along this track, the Messengers of God have, as one voice, claimed that that is what God has commissioned them to do. You will notice that those who believe or follow a Messenger of God do not say that they themselves are perfect, but point to the Messenger of God as perfect, holding a perfect knowledge of the perfection of creation. Because these Messengers are endowed with the characteristic of perfection, they have all insisted that we move from seeing all that is created just through physical eyes (a materialistic perspective). If we don't, we will always see apparent imperfections everywhere. Conversely, the more a person develops 'spiritual eyes' (a spiritual perspective) the more he will realize that there is no fault in the existing order and arrangement of the Creation of God.

Of course, even a person who sees the creation of God from a spiritual perspective is bound to see imperfections in himself and in other people. But his yardstick for this is the teachings of the Messengers of God. This does not mean God has created evil, which would be like saying God has created ignorance. This point has been dealt with previously. So, it is accepted that if someone is cruel or unjust, cruelty and injustice are imperfections and cruelty and injustice are considered evil. However, at the time of birth no child is born predetermined to be evil. If this were so then it would indeed be difficult to believe in God, as that would make God a creator of imperfection, (a nasty thing to do – to create a soul with the plan of setting him up to fail) and an imperfect Creator would not be God. Every child is born pure, a perfect creation of God but, according to a wise plan of God that may be obscure to us, He has given the potential to every child to move towards perfection and, at the same time, the potential to sink into the characteristics of imperfection. As stated before, the Bahá'í Writings declare that 'Every child is potentially the light of the world – and at the same time its darkness.'[6]

Each child, as it develops, will experience many things from within her/his self, from other human beings and from the environment. All these factors influence one's choices in life. By allowing each human being the freedom to make these choices highlights the fact that there is an over-riding perfection in the creation of human beings by God, which is that He has given this freedom to choose. If you take this freedom away from human beings then, essentially, you seriously alter what a human being is. If you take away the ability to make choices between light or darkness, good or bad, you change what is meant to be human. This is so because man's intellect, whether more influenced to be good or bad, is the faculty that is used to make these choices. So, if you remove a human being's intellect, you are left only with an animal body governed, like the animal, by its senses and animal instincts. This would be like removing instincts and senses from an animal, which would essentially reduce it to a vegetative state, a condition no more alive than a vegetable.

We may not agree with the Creator that every child should have the potential to become, metaphorically, light or darkness, but the reality of the situation is that this is a fact. If you want to take up this disagreement with the Creator, you are free to do so. You will, of course, have to believe a Creator exists to do this. However, if you don't believe the Creator exists, then the point that human beings have free will to choose whether to become good or bad must be seen as an imperfection in the order or system of existence, as most evil is perceived to come from the 'dark side' choices of human nature and not from a non-existent God. To take this view, as stated before, is to look at creation with an imperfect eye.

Let us examine a statement of 'Abdu'l-Bahá that helps us move along this track towards perfection. He was asked: 'What is the purpose of our lives?' He replied:

To acquire virtues. We come from the earth; why were we transferred from the mineral to the vegetable kingdom – from the plant to the animal kingdom? So that we may attain perfection in each of these kingdoms, that we may possess the best qualities of the mineral, that we may acquire the power of growing as in the plant, that we may be adorned with the instincts of the animal and possess the faculties of sight, hearing, smell, touch and taste, until from the animal kingdom we step into the world of humanity and are gifted with reason, the power of invention, and the forces of the spirit.[7]

According to 'Abdu'l-Bahá there is a purpose to the existing order and arrangement of creation. It may not be the only purpose, but, from a human point of view, if the earth with all its variety of minerals did not exist then we human beings could not develop to the stage we are at now. For the earth to exist there must have been something that caused it to come into existence and that is able to foster all the grades of being through the vegetable, to the animal, to the human. Now, we find that the planet itself is not a static, dead entity. It is alive; tectonic plates are in continual movement as a result of the generation of convection currents caused by earth cooling. A by-product of this movement is that mountains and valleys are created. Also, along with the flow of water, with the energies of the sun radiating on it and the gravitational pull of the moon, the planet has a weather system which is essential for all life. The fact that a devastating volcanic eruption or tsunami occasionally happens is an indication of a perfect system working perfectly, not a reason for changing it. Also, as science shows, this is a process through which the continents as we know them today have been formed. So, it would indeed be irrational to believe that this is an evil or imperfect process. It would be tantamount to saying, for example, that Australia has come into existence through the evil forces of an imperfect system. Usually, however, the imperfection seen in this case, is not 'Gaia' itself but that a volcano or a tsunami can wipe out entire populations. Now, instead of thinking 'I can find no reason for this, therefore this proves the system is imperfect,' our thinking should change to allow the possibility of an unbiased answer. Hence it is better to ask, 'Does the existence of volcanoes and tsunamis prove, if God exists, that He has created an imperfect system?'

Those who hold a spiritual perspective of reality believe that when a human being dies, his soul lives on, because it is indestructible by any physical means. Those who hold a materialistic perception of reality believe that we do not have an immortal soul, so, when the body dies that's the end of that individual. Both agree that death, for a human being, means the end of the physical body, which from the time of death starts to disintegrate or decompose. Both also agree that death is eventually inevitable for the human body, whether one lives a long or a short life. It is quite logical therefore, for those holding a materialistic perception of reality, to believe that volcanoes and tsunamis are part of an imperfect system, as they can cause their death and there is no more existence for them. However, those who interpret reality as spiritual in essence acknowledge that we are all going to die sooner or later anyhow, but death is only the end of the physical body and a volcano or tsunami cannot kill the soul. Although this argument does not prove that God is a perfect Creator, nonetheless it provides a logical reason to exclude volcanoes and tsunamis as especially part of an imperfect system, just waiting to consume unsuspecting people in the areas where they are active. For without the perfect system of planet Earth being alive and all the other forces acting upon it, man would not be able to exist upon the planet in the first place. And the point still remains that volcanoes and tsunamis, for those who hold a spiritual interpretation of reality, have not been created by God for the purpose of annihilating human beings.

Another point comes into view when considering this issue: even in the absence of volcanoes and tsunamis, human life is precarious at the best of times. In fact, even the next moment is not promised to us. Instead of seeing some defect in this, could we not understand that here is a lesson – the lesson of dependence? For are we not always dependent beings – dependent on light to see, food to eat, air to breathe, and, above all, dependent upon God for our very life and continued existence? Every single entity of creation betokens that it belongs to a contingent existence, whereas for God, His is an absolute existence – independent of everything. This understanding is at the heart of a wonderful virtue in human beings – humility! And it is primarily through humility that man can live in peace and harmony with nature and his fellow humans. Humility, when it is understood, has always been a perfection of human beings, whereas hubris has always been viewed as an imperfection. A truly spiritual person always aspires to be humble; a person immersed in materialism rarely gives it any thought and has a tendency to be arrogant.

This now leads us to a consideration of 'Abdu'l-Bahá's words mentioned above, that for a human to be more than just a member of the animal kingdom, he has to link with 'the forces of the spirit'.[8] When he connects with these spiritual powers or forces, he acquires virtues. He does not acquire virtues from lower levels of existence, i.e. the animal, vegetable or mineral degrees, or, in other words, nature. If a soul turns only to the world of nature for the development of virtues, as pagans do, then, just like seeds that are deprived of sunlight, they will not grow. No matter how much you may turn to a cabbage for guidance in right living, for instance, as it is a member of the vegetable kingdom, a lower kingdom than man's, it will be incapable of giving such guidance. Similarly, if one turns to the world's expert on cabbages for guidance in right living, why should we expect that expert to supply wise answers? A purpose of being 'gifted with reason',[9] which sets man apart from and higher than the animal kingdom, is that it enables him, amongst a host of other activities, to discover, invent, and to become aware of a higher reality. This higher reality in religious terminology is the 'kingdom'; it is the world of the spirit from which a human being can attract to himself the forces of that reality. Hence, when a person turns to that kingdom, the potential to become virtuous is empowered to develop, much as a seed can grow when the sun shines on it. Let us look a little closer to demonstrate this point. Wisdom is a virtuous quality of human beings. We never think of animals being wise, as they are governed by their physical senses and instincts; nor do we think that a carrot, for instance, has made wise decisions for its growth. Similarly, a carbon atom in the mineral kingdom does not have the faculty to make wise choices for its amalgam with other atoms. So, if the animal, vegetable and mineral kingdoms are incapable of wisdom, is it wise to turn to these kingdoms for the power necessary to develop wisdom? Evidently the virtue of wisdom does not exist in these lower kingdoms. We may even ask, is it appropriate to defer to experts on these kingdoms, experts, that is, who may lack any understanding of the higher reality, for their pronouncements on the world of the spirit? Man, however, has the ability to make wise choices but, and here is the point, he does not have the ability to make them disconnected from the forces of the spirit, even if he is a renowned expert on anything in the natural world.

These points should be pondered, for they require detachment from the views, opinions and attitudes of a society that has disconnected its thinking from higher realities. In a sense, huge swathes of humanity are metaphorically acting like frogs at the bottom of a well who, while looking up, convince themselves that there is 'no life up there'. Satisfied with their limited, darkened environment, they share with each other all their understandings of what surrounds them. Surely the lives of those frogs that live at the bottom of a well in comparison with those that live in the light of a higher world is, indeed, pathetic? Weak are their thoughts and insignificant their accomplishments in comparison to what they could be!

18

GRADUAL EMERGENCE OF MATURITY

Many people despair of any hope of a better future for mankind. They look at the past, when so many horrifying things have happened, with the effect that holding a pessimistic view seems to be the only realistic way of handling thoughts of the future. They may argue that what is to come will just be an extension of the past. The two world wars of the 20th century, along with other wars, have certainly had an enervating effect. These dark shadows of a deranged past along with more recent horrors continue to obscure a brighter vision of humanity's future. Not only has the authority of moral values been brutalized through these destructive offences against humanity but, perhaps more damagingly, hope or belief that humanity can rise to a higher level of civilization has receded. The adoption of such a negative outlook/worldview, I would suggest, is not only built upon knowledge of terrifying and devastating historical events but has been reinforced by materialistic ways of writing and presenting history. It is this latter point I want to address, as I feel that hope for a positive future for the human race is a necessity if humanity is to rise above the present condition of futility and pessimism. Hope, however, has to be based on other than a naïve wish for something better; it has to be based upon an interpretation of facts that perhaps have not yet been considered, plus solid reasoning. This I will now attempt to do.

The way history is now processed in the West, led by experts in the field, tends to predispose oncoming generations to scepticism, pessimism and hopelessness. Historical events are viewed and taught in a way that has no relation to God. In fact, there is compelling evidence that many scholars, driven by materialistic assumptions of reality, have relegated the Almighty to the limbo of obsolescence. Instead of interpreting history in terms of an evolutionary process when individuals and huge swathes of humanity have sometimes been in compliance with the will of God, and at others at variance with it, we find that history is interpreted in terms of economic and/or social and political forces. For instance: the movement of peoples around the globe; the settlement of populations; the influence of cultural, technological and scientific developments; the details and consequences of battles, wars and pogroms; experimentation with systems of governance such as plutocracy, aristocracy, oligarchy, democracy; the rise of tyrants and the oppression of subject peoples – all have been viewed primarily as the result of economic and/or social and political power struggles. How to interpret history correctly is a task all historians face. In the words of Nietzsche: 'All things are subject to interpretation; whichever interpretation prevails at a given time is a function of power and not truth.' The result has been disastrous for humanity. What, we may ask, led so many people to accept Hitler's interpretation of history in terms of a form of 'social Darwinism' – the survival and superiority of the fittest in a people he declared to be the 'master race'?

A materialistic interpretation of history has now so consolidated itself that as soon as words like 'spirituality' or phrases such as 'the will of God' are introduced into the process, the mind just switches off. It is here, then, I ask for patience from the reader to outline a spiritual interpretation of history that, far from dismissing historical and scientific evidence, incorporates it as fundamental to its understanding.

The first point is the historical process of human evolution. Stimulated by such eminent scientists as Darwin and Wallace in the mid-19th century, it is now generally accepted that mankind has physically evolved over the millennia to its present form.

This created a huge shock to the religious worldview that had taken literally the Bible creation and Adam and Eve stories. The shock needed to occur, as literal interpretations of Holy Scripture had led humanity, century after century, down the path of superstition. Unfortunately, the scientific method, although well developed by the mid-19th century, was still marginalized by many ministers of religion who influenced their congregations to oppose any suggestion that humanity had evolved over an extensive period of time.

Through the discovery of fossils of our ancient ancestors and the artifacts associated with them, anthropologists have now advanced our understanding that human evolution has been occurring over millions of years. The earliest documented members of the genus Homo are Homo habilis, who, we are informed, 'evolved around 2.3 million years ago; the earliest species for which there is positive evidence of use of stone tools.'[1] Encephalization (brain growth) developed over the next million years with the arrival of Homo erectus, to the extent that human brain size increased in 'every generation having an additional 125,000 neurons more than their parents'.[2] It is believed that 'Homo erectus and Homo ergaster were the first hominine to leave Africa, spreading throughout other continents and the first to use fire and complex tools'.[3] The evolutionary process, of course, has carried on since then up to the present and, by extrapolation, we may assume it will carry on into the unborn reaches of time. It is interesting to note that the name we humans are known by is Homo sapien sapiens, and sapien is Latin for 'wise' or 'intelligent'.

Along with biological, outward changes in the human form, we can detect that amongst many important aspects of the long process of evolution, inner intellectual development has also occurred. This is very interesting, because this is exactly what happens in the evolution of a baby in the womb of its mother; but, of course, the nine-month period of gestation is a much smaller time period than the evolution of humankind. The two processes of growth, however, can be viewed as a microcosmic system in the former and a macrocosmic system in the latter. Both, according to 'Abdu'l-Bahá, are comparable in principle. Speaking about this general principle 'Abdu'l-Bahá states:

> Man is the microcosm; and the infinite universe, the macrocosm. The mysteries of the greater world, or macrocosm, are expressed or revealed in the lesser world, the microcosm. The tree, so to speak, is the greater world, and the seed in its relation to the tree is the lesser world. But the whole of the great tree is potentially latent and hidden in the little seed. When this seed is planted and cultivated, the tree is revealed. Likewise, the greater world, the macrocosm, is latent and miniatured in the lesser world, or microcosm, of man.[4]

So, by focusing on the development of a child in the womb of its mother and after it is born, it is possible to detect aspects of the 'mysteries of the greater world' that occur in the human race as it evolves in the matrix of the world. From the first appearance of the zygote in the mother's womb, to the eventual maturity of that individual, physical stages of development appear in a way that is common to all members of the human race. Consonant with physical development has been the gradual appearance of mental, intellectual capacities, until a state of maturity as an adult is reached, when the signs of reason appear. Although the signs of the mind appear in infancy, compared to the stage of maturity it is imperfect, its reasoning abilities are not developed and as such are inadequate. Only when maturity is reached does it become evident that the mind has attained its greatest power. On this point 'Abdu'l-Bahá states:

> All created things have their degree or stage of maturity. The period of maturity in the life of a tree is the time of its fruit-bearing . . . The animal attains a stage of full growth and completeness, and in the human kingdom man reaches his

maturity when the light of his intelligence attains its greatest power and development . . .[5]

Similarly, anthropologists have discovered that not only has humanity evolved physically, but it has also developed its intellectual capacities in a such way as to be distinctly different from animals. This can be seen from increasing signs of mental activity that have at very primitive stages produced such instruments as stone and bone tools and weapons, and now is capable of sending man into space to explore the universe.

If the concept of the microcosm and the macrocosm is applied to the evolution of the human race, we could say that there must be a stage of its development that mirrors the individual's stage of maturity. In other words, it is reasonable to hold a view on the evolution of humanity, underpinned by scientific discoveries and observations, which maintains that history can be read, in part, in terms of the evolving capacities of humankind, leading to a stage of maturity that is comparable to the stage of maturity of the individual. This is one of the foundational teachings of Bahá'u'lláh. Writing about this, Shoghi Effendi, the Guardian of the Bahá'í Faith, states:

That mystic, all-pervasive, yet indefinable change, which we associate with the stage of maturity inevitable in the life of the individual and the development of the fruit must, if we would correctly apprehend the utterances of Bahá'u'lláh, have its counterpart in the evolution of the organization of human society. A similar stage must sooner or later be attained in the collective life of mankind, producing an even more striking phenomenon in world relations, and endowing the whole human race with such potentialities of well-being as shall provide, throughout the succeeding ages, the chief incentive required for the eventual fulfilment of its high destiny. Such a stage of maturity in the process of human government must, for all time, if we would faithfully recognize the tremendous claim advanced by Bahá'u'lláh, remain identified with the Revelation of which He was the Bearer.[6]

The passage above may well prompt us to ask: when mankind reaches its stage of maturity, what will 'world relations' look like such that previous relations will appear immature, perhaps even as the caprice of children? Many of our answers must revolve around a just process of governance that will be entirely different from today's immature, defective, competitive, nationalistic, unjust and danger-ridden systems, notwithstanding that a few elements in these systems are developed enough, even now, to be subsumed in that which is to come. We may further ask, that when mankind reaches its collective mature stage of evolution, what are the 'potentialities of well-being' providing such an incentive for humanity that it will be propelled to reach, over the ages, its stupendous destiny? It is worth pondering on these questions, for we may conclude that humanity is living in a time when a sense of 'well-being' very much eludes us.

Of course, we have some time to go before the maturity of the human race can be achieved, and the Bahá'í Writings declare that there is a lot more suffering in store to engrave on our consciousness that lessons have to be learnt before we behave in a mature, responsible manner. In a sense we can appreciate that the stage humanity is now experiencing in its long evolutionary process is that of turbulent adolescence. The adolescent period of growth has been identified as a phase of storm and stress, of emotional volcanoes just waiting to explode, with a particular emphasis on conflict with parents, mood disruptions and risky behaviour.[7] Undoubtedly adolescence is a phase we all have to experience if we are to arrive at maturity, but I question whether it is a development that requires all adolescents to be aggressive, self-absorbed, inclined to disregard all values and follow the path of prodigality. Surely it is reasonable to assume that good, wise and loving parenting will enable most youngsters to handle the increase of hormones surging through their body and their physical changes in preparation for reproduction, along with their ability to think independently, in a way that avoids the negative behaviours that are now associated with this phase?

Be that as it may, no one can doubt that the horrors that have afflicted the human race during its adolescent phase of growth have increased scepticism, cynicism and misanthropy. It is very sad indeed that the new burgeoning powers of humanity in the 18th, 19th and 20th centuries, instead of being channelled into that which would create planetary harmony and prosperity, were siphoned off by individuals, conglomerates and nations for their own selfish ends and in complete disregard of any of the holy scriptures that unanimously exhort us to, 'do as you would be done by'.

Is there any way of preventing this maturing process, we may further ask, apart from interfering with an individual's genetic structure or curtailing its life? The answer is 'no'; the zygote is destined to evolve through various stages until it becomes a mature human being and nothing, all things being equal, can prevent this from happening. It is inevitable! Similarly, because it is a principle of evolution in the microcosm, it must apply on a grander scale to the macrocosm. Therefore, as we cannot prevent the eventual maturity in the microcosm, we are unable to prevent the eventual maturity in the macrocosm – the collective life of humanity. Its inevitability is assured!

As a teacher of adolescents over many years, I experienced this movement from immaturity to maturity many times. On several occasions, youngsters whom I had taught and who had left school returned to meet with teachers who had had a beneficial influence on them to thank them for their care and assistance. Some of these youngsters, when in school, were mischievous, others were troublemakers; some were so badly behaved that you would never expect them to mature. Yet this is what they did. While shaking hands one would notice their more assured demeanour, their more responsible talk, the fact that their eyes looked different from when they were immature and that they could look you in the eye. Something had changed and, all quite unconsciously, they had slipped into maturity.

Interestingly, when we reflect on the process of biological growth from one stage to another, we find that it is not subject to our free will. As stated above, growth is something we experience without any effort and planning, and there are reasons for this in the perfect system our Creator has set up for our learning and understanding. On this point 'Abdu'l-Bahá states:

> Man must walk in many paths and be subjected to various processes in his evolution upward. Physically he is not born in full stature but passes through consecutive stages of foetus, infant, childhood, youth, maturity and old age. Suppose he had the power to remain young throughout his life. He then would not understand the meaning of old age and could not believe it existed. If he could not realize the condition of old age he would not know that he was young. He would not know the difference between young and old without experiencing the old. Unless you have passed through the state of infancy, how would you know this was an infant beside you?[8]

This is a truly wonderful principle underlining the fact that mature people will have outgrown their childish/adolescent attitudes, unruliness and impetuosity, if they are balanced individuals. Consequently, they are not doomed to repeat the selfishness, aggressiveness, errors and mistakes they have committed during immature phases of growth – they have moved on. For those who are near to giving up hope that the human race will ever progress out of its self-centredness, its aggressive behaviour, militancy and competitiveness, the above understanding can offer a positive view of the future. As humanity evolves it is not destined to repeat its past horrific ways of behaving – rather, it will grow towards its mature stage of progress when all problems, individual, local, national and international, will be solved by applying mature ways of thinking and acting, of problem solving and conflict resolution, to arrive at peace and harmony. There are many indications, even now, that we are heading with some speed towards this time. Take for instance the millions of people who now spurn war and are troubled by unbridled nationalism and materialism; those who see the human race as one entity and want it to function as one integrated harmonious family. And the number is increasing generation by generation. It is these souls who advocate a spiritual solution to mankind's problems, who realize that we need 'golden' people for a 'golden' age, a trans-formed society. In addition, they realize the need for 'golden' institutions, internationally, nationally and locally, that are con-cerned with the well-being of the whole human race. Looking beyond this turbulent adolescent stage of development, however, the Bahá'í texts, expressed in the words of its Guardian, Shoghi Effendi, foretell a wonderful future for humanity.

> The long ages of infancy and childhood, through which the human race had to pass, have receded into the background. Humanity is now experiencing the commotions invariably associated with the most turbulent stage of its evolution, the stage of adolescence, when the impetuosity of youth and its vehemence reach their climax, and must gradually be super-seded by the calmness, the wisdom, and the maturity that characterize the stage of manhood. Then will the human rac-ereach that stature of ripeness which will enable it to acquire all the powers and capacities upon which its ultimate devel-opment must depend.[9]

But let us look at 'maturity' a little closer and align it, not this time with the findings of anthropology, but with developmental psychology. In particular, we shall look at the stages of cognitive development in children to maturity. The first psychologist to make an investigation into whether children think in the same way as adults was Jean Piaget (1896–1980). Before his investiga-tions into the cognitive development of children it was thought that 'children are merely less competent thinkers than adults'. Piaget changed how people viewed the minds of children by stating that there are important differences in the thinking of adults and children. He put forward his developmental stage theory of four stages experienced by all children – sensorimotor stage, preoperational stage, concrete operational stage and formal operational stage. Since the 1920s, when Piaget developed his ideas, there has been some criticism of them. For instance, some psychologists would rather see development as continuous and not in stages; the age ranges of each stage have also been queried, and some maintain that the influence of culture and social setting was ignored.[10] Bearing these and other criticisms in mind, there is no doubt that there is an ongoing development from the way infants think to that of a mature person's thinking.

Piaget's and other psychologists' insights into the progress of thinking in children could be applied to the development of cognition in the human race as a necessary condition of evolution. The principle of the microcosm operating in the macrocosm still applies here. If we divorce the evolution of cognitive development of our ancestors from their biological evolution, then we deny what is essentially the major human characteristic (our rational faculties) that define us as different from the animal kingdom.

We can imagine then that the sensorimotor stage of evolution, mirroring the individual child's stage of growth from about 0–2 years of age, is centred on infant humanity 'trying to make sense of the world . . . knowledge of the world is limited to his or her sensory perceptions and motor activities. Behaviours are limited to simple motor responses caused by sensory stimuli.'[11] It is not difficult to imagine that the infant behaviour of mankind, at this stage, would be hard to distinguish from animal behaviour. How many millennia were given to this stage of humanity's development falls into the anthropologist's domain of investigation. Just like an infant, humanity's first encounter with the world is predominantly physical, although able to survive in competition with the animal world and able to take advantage of the physical environment, for instance by food gathering.

Somehow, and quite mysteriously, enough of humanity survived to progress to its next stage of evolution, again analogous to that of a child – the 'preoperational stage', which occurs approximately between the ages of 2 and 7. Although language development is a major activity at this stage, Piaget noted that children 'do not yet understand concrete logic, cannot mentally manipulate information, and are unable to take the point of view of other people, which he termed "egocentrism".' They do become 'increasingly adept at using symbols, as evidenced by the increase in playing and pretending. For example, a child is able to use an object to represent something else, such as pretending a broom is a horse.'[12] Interestingly, at this stage of evolution the development of language becomes essential for the progress of the human race. How much conflict there must have been amongst our ancestors who, although quite able at this stage to play, pretend and use symbols, were still essentially unable to consider the point of view of others? Added to this, they must have believed that the whole of creation, in egocentric terms, revolved around them. Putting 'self' first, during this stage of evolution, could have been a necessary aspect of the survival of the human race. It is no wonder that aggression, violence and domination have been characteristics of humanity's development. But, yet again, there must have been enough cooperation and loyalty to family or group to ensure the survival of the human species.

The third stage that could be considered as mirroring childhood development in the evolution of humanity is that of the 'concrete operational stage'. Typical ages for this stage are between 7 to 11 when 'thinking is more organized and rational. They can solve problems in a logical fashion but are typically not able to think abstractly or hypothetically.'[13] At this stage the child moves from being 'egocentric' to 'sociocentric', one 'who is aware that others have their own perspectives on the world and that those perspectives are different' from his own. However, the child at this stage 'may not be aware . . . of the content of others' perspectives'.[14]

Perhaps humanity, at this stage of its evolution, begins to be aware of diversity and therefore is able to allow or welcome some aspects of it rather than opposing or reacting against it.

One can imagine that at this stage of cognitive development our prehistoric ancestors were only able to understand abstract or conceptual realities by relating them to concrete things. Without the concrete, physical things to relate a concept to, it is extremely difficult, if not impossible, to learn to think in abstract terms. So, for instance, when learning to add, children are shown a ball in one hand and a ball in the other and asked, 'how many balls are there'? Because the ball is a physical (concrete) object it is easier for them to answer 'two'. The exercise is repeated many times; 'there are three chairs in one corner of the room and two in another – how many chairs altogether'? They answer by counting all the chairs to arrive at the sum of five. Now, because numbers are concepts or abstractions, it is very difficult to get a child in this 'concrete operational stage' to arrive at answers without the props of physical objects. Surely this is an indication of the need and purpose of the physical world in humanity's educating process – and therein lies its great, overarching value?

The last stage of cognitive development in children – the formal operational stage – begins at about 12 years of age and continues into adulthood. At earlier stages children use trial and error to solve problems, but in this stage of cognitive development, 'the ability to systematically solve a problem in a logical and methodical way emerges . . . [children] are often able to quickly plan an organized approach to solving a problem.'[15] Objects are no longer required and mental operations can be undertaken 'in the "head" using abstract terms . . . The Formal Operational person considers past experiences, present demands, and future consequences in attempting to maximize the success of his or her adaptation to the world.'[16] At this stage of development, we can assume that the individual has the equipment to think in a mature way and therefore can become a responsible person. The goal of human cognitive development has been reached – individuals who can reason and think conceptually and who are able to make hypotheses. With these intellectual tools, individuals should be able to face the future in a manner that we would regard as mature.

It is this formal operational stage the human race is now experiencing, even though the spread of it may not be uniform. One can imagine various sections of humanity still struggling to think conceptually and needing all manner of 'concrete' props to help them do so. The traditions of the ancient religions do not help here, as they require their adherents to respond to rites and rituals frozen in time and prescribed for a less mature phase of human cognitive development. As examples of this we can think of the ritual of circumcision still practised by the Jews, or the ordinance of baptizing children in Christianity. When a mature stage of thinking has been reached, we do not need the concrete props through which a historically cognitively immature people understood vital spiritual truths. These rites and rituals have served their purpose, and now must be left behind if humanity is to progress to higher levels of spiritual development. The following statement sheds light on the consequence of mankind's failure to move with the flow of revelation through successive Manifestations of God:

> The concept of progressive revelation places the ultimate emphasis on recognition of the revelation of God at its appearance. The failure of the generality of humankind in this respect has, time and again, condemned entire populations to a ritualistic repetition of ordinances and practices long after these latter have fulfilled their purpose and now merely stultify moral advance.[17]

We now come to a large 'anti-personnel mine' I had to navigate around – that the ability to reason, conceptualize, and hypothesize is no guarantee that the individual or humanity will automatically arrive at using these powers responsibly. I reflected on the fact that many minds, despite being exercised in solving all manner of problems, their intellects fully capable of reasoning in the abstract and able to consider 'past experiences, present demands, and future consequences in attempting to maximize the success of his or her adaptation to the world', [18] have just added to the world's woes. Although there are an increasing number of human beings equipped to make mature, responsible choices and decisions, we find that many, in all walks of life, do not make responsible decisions at all. At the individual level we find souls enmeshed in immature materialistic pursuits that on the surface promise happiness but at a deeper level only evoke disillusionment, frustration, bitterness, regret or anger. Lifestyle choices, assumptions about reality and a confused moral code have resulted in alcohol-related problems, addiction to drugs or gambling, the spurning of marriage, increased divorce and the breakdown of family life, and disaffected youths, as well as a host of other dangers that betoken a future riddled with problems almost impossible to extricate oneself from. Governance in the last century alone, and at a time when burgeoning mature reasoning capacities should have taken humanity down the road to unity, well-being and prosperity, had, in spite of wonderful advances flowing from science and technology, brought it to the brink of total annihilation through world-wide conflicts and war machines of unimaginable destruction.

I began to understand, after reading more of the Writings of Bahá'u'lláh and 'Abdu'l-Bahá, that mature intellectual capacities needed something else, something outside themselves, to arrive at responsibility and universal benefits. The eye, as an analogy of this fact, needs light to see. Although it has the capacity to see, nonetheless it needs something external to itself to be able to do so. The digestive system, to cite another analogy, needs food to digest for it to be of benefit to the body – the digestive system does not create its own food but is dependent on nourishment outside itself to work properly. There are many other analogies in the same vein that could be mentioned – we have lungs but require air to breathe; we have hearing which requires air to carry vibrations to it; and so on. It became obvious to me that our rational faculty needs something different to itself to function in a way that attracts well-being and universal benefits. If we say that other people's reasoning powers, such as those of the intellectuals in society or of those we elect to govern, are all we need to arrive at these benefits, is this not like saying that all we need are other people's eyes to see or other people's ears to hear?

'Abdu'l-Bahá said that to use our mature capabilities correctly, we are in need of help from outside ourselves, if humanity is to safely progress:

> Just as he advances by progressive stages from the mere physical world of being into the intellectual realm, so must he develop upward in moral attributes and spiritual graces. In the process of this attainment he is ever in need of the bestowals of the Holy Spirit.[19]

Phrases such as 'Holy Spirit' were difficult for me to digest, loaded as it is with all manner of objections formed through a reaction to Christian dogma, ritual and priestcraft. To help disconnect from such distortions of religion I simplified the phrase 'Holy Spirit' by calling it a special power that comes from a Higher Power, analogous to the rays which emanate from the sun. It is the rays of the sun that cause all physical life to grow in nature, but, of course, it does not cause the growth of moral attributes and spirituality in the hearts of people.

Unfortunately, many people who believe their Prophet of God to be the only one with the power of the Holy Spirit, to the exclusion of others, have brought shame on the noble process of religion, to the extent that today religion itself is a major factor causing atheism. In fact, analogously, such people are like those who believe there is only one day of the week on which the sun shines, say a Wednesday, and if confronted with the possibility of other days on which the earth is illumined, they deny it. This analogy seems more than a little apt, as it suggests what is meant by religion being progressively revealed. Just as it is scientifically proven that humanity has evolved physically and cognitively, it is a central tenet of religion, if one examines with an unbiased mind its scriptures, that the 'Supreme Intelligence' (yet another name for God) has always shed light upon the hearts and minds of humanity over its long evolution. It would be very callous of God if having brought into existence the body and mind of human beings, now at the stage of burgeoning maturity, He just left it to trial and error as to how to survive and eventually make progress, physically, intellectually, socially and spiritually. Even though we notice that trial and error are a vital and necessary part in human experience in the young, it nevertheless takes place under the care and training of significant adults. To believe that humanity has progressed only by trial and error does not make sense. If we are to be impartial, it is more difficult to prove that humanity has progressed only through trial and error than to demonstrate that we have been progressively aided and guided by God in the process of cognitive human evolution.

Let us take this point further by examining a principle that can be seen functioning in the microcosm and then look at the possibility of it being active in the macrocosm. All of us who have been reared in caring, loving families have experienced parents who have protected us from our own ignorance, guarded us against dangers that are outside our perception, and trained us to be responsible members of society. Hence, we find good parents admonishing us not to eat certain foods as they are poisonous, not to talk to strangers who may present a danger, to be courteous, clean, concerned about the welfare of others and to leave behind selfish motives in favour of altruistic values, and so on. The nurturing of well-balanced children physically, emotionally, intellectually, morally and spiritually is a tremendous task every good parent will engage in. It is obvious to them that just leaving a child to physically grow and go through the stages of the development of their rational faculties without any guidance, correction, encouragement, love and wisdom is a dereliction of duty that will leave a child no whit better than an animal. Imagine a child, even in today's society, having to rear itself without any nurturing, training or education whatever, and, left to its own devices, having to discover how to survive by only trial and error. Could we say with any confidence that such a child will grow up in such a way as to become mature in the sense of being a responsible citizen? If the answer is 'yes', then why do we put so much effort into good parenting and education? If 'no', then we would subscribe to the principle that children need to be well parented and educated to ensure the release of their potential. Upon this contribution to a child's development will depend its progress, materially, intellectually and spiritually.

The same reasoning applies to the evolution of humanity, but this time it is at a macrocosmic level. Evolving humanity needs the guidance, training and nurturing of special souls, ordained by a wise and caring Creator Who, similar to parents, will guide and train humanity through every stage of its development. Of the necessity of these special souls 'Abdu'l-Bahá states, 'Mankind needs a universal motive power to quicken it. The inspired messenger who is directly assisted by the power of God brings about universal results.'[20] These souls have come to be known by different names in the different parts of the world in which they appeared. They appear as ordinary human beings with a physical body which has to perform all the functions of such a body – eating, sleeping, working, keeping healthy, etc. They have the rational faculties that are common to all human beings such as thinking, comprehending, imagining, memorizing, etc. In addition, they have a special power endowed by the Creator which sets them apart from ordinary mortals. Just as humans are not just progressed animals, these special souls, the Manifestations of God who have appeared throughout history and are the founders of the great religions, are not just progressed human beings. Such a realization is comparable to the realization of the impossibility of an animal being trained to such a degree by a human being that it essentially reaches a stage of becoming human. Followers of the Manifestations of God admit that no matter how hard they try, they can never become one of these special souls. The very best that can be achieved by humans is to reflect the light or illumination that the Manifestations bring in all aspects of their lives.

These souls are known by various names: Great Educators of Mankind, Messengers of God, Apostles of God, Prophets, Avatars, Enlightened Ones, Manifestations of God and the like. For the majority of these Messengers we have no record at all, as they have been lost in antiquity. Emphasizing this point Bahá'u'lláh states:

> Know thou that the absence of any reference to them is no proof that they did not actually exist. That no records concerning them are now available, should be attributed to their extreme remoteness, as well as to the vast changes which the earth hath undergone since their time.[21]

It is the claim of Bahá'ís that humanity's education and enlightenment throughout the eons of time is dependent on these Illumined Ones – not forgetting that in the microcosmic system a child's development is dependent on its parents' training and nurturing. There must, then, always have been these Great Educators (we could also call them 'nurturers of the human race'), assisting humanity throughout the entire period of human evolution on this planet. Just as human beings have existed for millions of years, so must these great nurturers have been present amongst humanity, assisting its development in various parts of the world and at various crucial stages. In fact, it is a basic teaching of the Bahá'í Faith that 'there always have been Manifestations of God, but we do not have any record of their names'.[22] 'Abdu'l-Bahá elaborates this point, stating:

> Thus there have been many holy Manifestations of God. One thousand years ago, two hundred thousand years ago, one million years ago, the bounty of God was flowing, the radiance of God was shining, the dominion of God was existing.[23]

And in the same vein, Shoghi Effendi, quoting Bahá'u'lláh, writes:

> From the 'beginning that hath no beginning', these Exponents of the Unity of God and Channels of His incessant utterance have shed the light of the invisible Beauty upon mankind, and will continue, to the 'end that hath no end', to vouchsafe fresh revelations of His might and additional experiences of His inconceivable glory.[24]

So far-reaching is the teaching that there have always been Manifestations of God, lifting humanity up to ever higher levels of development, that Bahá'u'lláh states, 'were it not for those effulgent Lights [Manifestations of God] that shine above the horizon of His Essence, the people would know not their left hand from their right . . .'.[25]

Although it is difficult to prove that Manifestations of God have always played their part in the development of the human race, those who wish to dwell on its possibility may imagine those times when humanity, during all its stages of development mentioned above, could have been helped along by them. Perhaps these great Educators/Nurturers guided our prehistoric ancestors as to how to be clean, or were the first to make fire for warmth and cooking food. Perhaps, at another stage of development, they helped in the construction of language as a means of communication for greater chances of survival and to start a process of closer relationships with each other. At this time humanity could have been developed enough to start using symbols as a means to represent a power that they would call God. Perhaps at this stage of human development, humanity may only have understood the existence of a Higher Power by relating it to something physical/tangible such as the sun, moon, stars, thunder and lightning and so on. Then, as ages passed, they lost understanding of these symbols of God and started worshipping them. However, it was the work of the Great Teachers to keep directing humanity to worship the One, Invisible, All-Powerful Creator of the universe. One can imagine many setbacks in this process, indeed, even up to relatively modern times, religious texts record the huge struggle these Great Educators such as Noah, Hud, Saleh, Abraham, Moses and Muhammad experienced in trying to draw the people away from idolatry or multiple physical representations of the Almighty, to that which is truly worthy of worship and devotion. It is certain that humanity must have found it very difficult, at another stage of development, to understand abstract concepts pertaining to healthy and harmonious relationships with each other, with God and with the environment. Many of the teachings of Christ, for example, are given in parables and not in direct teachings. The parable of the talents, for instance, is replete with warnings that if one does not use the gifts God has given us in a way intended, then the ability to do so, over time, will become atrophied; atrophy of these gifts is, according to the words of Christ, equivalent to being cast into 'outer darkness'.[26]

Now, as the human race is reaching its long-awaited mature beginnings of cognitive development, it seems to me that Bahá'u'lláh has additionally addressed it in direct language full of concepts and abstractions because humanity is developing the mature capacity to also understand aspects of the new teachings of the latest Divine Educator without always needing to refer to parables and metaphor, though there are some truths that cannot be fully conveyed by any other means.

Take, for instance, the concept of 'heaven' or 'paradise'. In the Gospel according to Matthew there are seven parables which start with 'The kingdom of Heaven is like unto . . .' Then if we look into the teachings of the Prophet Muhammad, six hundred years later, He describes paradise in a 'similitude':

A similitude of the Garden which those who keep their duty (to Allah) are promised: Therein are rivers of water unpolluted, and rivers of milk whereof the flavour changeth not, and rivers of wine delicious to the drinkers, and rivers of clear-run honey; therein for them is every kind of fruit, with pardon from their Lord.[27]

Both Christ and Muhammad taught people according to their stage of development or capacity, which could be considered as being the concrete operational stage of cognitive development. As stated above, the formal operational stage enables those who have reached this mature capacity to understand concepts and abstractions without the need to relate them to parables, similitude, metaphor and the like. Hence, among many statements made by Bahá'u'lláh about heaven and paradise is this:

> Blessed is the soul which, at the hour of its separation from the body, is sanctified from the vain imaginings of the peoples of the world. Such a soul liveth and moveth in accordance with the Will of its Creator, and entereth the all-highest Paradise.[28]

These 'Representatives of God', the Divine Educators, have progressively unfolded the will of God, over millions of years, to a biologically and cognitively evolving humanity. Just as parents and educators have nurtured, trained and educated children in accordance with their growing capacities, with-holding important, vital information and expectations until the child is ready to receive them, the Educators of humanity have similarly nurtured the human race. But this process is not pain-free, nor is it without severe setbacks. Just as children, and particularly adolescents, can resist the will of wise and loving parents, so too have many throughout history resisted and capriciously worked against the divine will as given by its Educators. Who is to be blamed, for instance, if the will of God prohibits murder, a law that when flouted has caused unimaginable sorrow and suffering? Who is to be held responsible, if the will of God forbids conflict and contention but is ignored to such an extent that marriages, peoples and nations become polarized with consequent breakdown in health, stability, harmony and economy? Who is guilty, if the will of God forbids the use of power and authority for personal gain and when ignored has led to millions being held in serfdom, slavery and poverty?

On the other hand, what marvels have been achieved by those who have aligned themselves with the will of God to create schools and universities, hospitals and centres of relief for the poor! How many beneficent rulers, anxious to abide by the will of God, have done all in their power to uplift the downtrodden and the ignorant within their domains! How many valiant souls, following in the footsteps of their Lord, have sacrificed their all in an attempt to succour the dispossessed, bring humane conditions to the prisoner and homes to the orphaned!

The answers to these types of questions are within the depositories of history, but who will read it aright?

19

INTERPRETING HISTORY IN TERMS OF AN EVOLUTIONARY PROCESS

Let us take further the idea of history as an evolutionary process when individuals and huge swathes of humanity have sometimes been in compliance with the will of God and, at other times, at variance with it. For the materialistically minded, what follows here could prove challenging indeed, as it centres on there being a God who has a will. For such people the challenge can be immediately ignored by stating there is no God, therefore there is no 'will'. However, can I appeal to those souls not to be dismissive of the general theme of this chapter, at least until an ear has been given to the following argument?

If there is no will of God because there is no God, then we are left with the world operating on the will of man. If this is the case, then all the problems in the world flow from the wrongdoing of human beings, who exercise their will according to their opinions and worldview. In a secular society, these are guided only by their own lights in relation to the challenges of the world. Differences of opinion, views, world outlook, moral directions and the like are so diverse these days that to obtain a unified, shared vision of how the human race can progress is as complicated as trying to herd a score of cats into a sheep pen.

History has demonstrated that there have been only three major ways of getting masses of people to work together on a common goal. One way has been through the authority and usually oppression of a ruling elite or regime, such as in Roman times. These regimes hold in their hands the power of life or death over their subject peoples. A second way has involved the adoption of an ideology that unites the masses in a revolution against the tyranny of the time, such as the French and Communist Revolutions. The third way has been through the uniting power of the Manifestations of God, such as Buddha, Christ and Muhammad, who energized the souls of their followers with a united larger vision of love, service to others and self-sacrifice for the good of fellow human beings.

The fact that the will of man in the West has, for the most part, overcome oppressive regimes and in its place has developed liberal democracy, yet another ideology, has not been a safeguard against terrible wars and upheavals even to the present day. Unsuccessful efforts to find remedies prevail universally. Even as I write, disunity, malcontent and bitterness of a growing mass of people whether in the have or have-not countries, like a cancerous outbreak in the body of mankind, is eating into the vitals of the best-laid plans of those who believe liberal democracy will save them. Lamenting over the obduracy of peoples who refuse to turn to God through His latest Manifestation for wise guidance, Bahá'u'lláh writes:

> Gracious God! So great is the folly and perversity of the people, that they have turned their face toward their own thoughts and desires, and have turned their back upon the knowledge and will of God . . .[1]

If the will of man is insufficient to guarantee unity, love and harmony amongst the disparate and contending peoples that make up the human race, then why not look at the possibility of the Manifestations of God being able to do so, as the bearers of a will superior and more informed than the limited understanding of human intellect? This is a consideration that is taken up in a later chapter. It is a fact, however, that none of the Manifestations of God has ever said that their teachings and guidance are the product of their own rational faculties. All have refuted this; instead, they have stressed that they are the recipients of an inflow of divine guidance, from God, for humankind, and have acted as a conduit for this flow. Without question, all have been self-effacing and self-sacrificing, and have suffered terribly to bring us guidance. We should not so readily dismiss their life and work just because we have fallen in with the present anti-religion herd mentality.

Why, we may ask, do so many refuse to examine afresh the soul-stirring contributions of the Manifestations of God for the progress and safeguarding of the human race? Those who hold a spiritual perspective of history are aware that the will of God has come through these Manifestations as an act of love and compassion from our Maker. He has not left us to our own deficient devices, but in every age has sent His representative to humanity with necessary instructions as to what is required for that day. Civilizations are borne anew from humanity's response to each new Manifestation of God, and they wither away and die when the spirit they bring does not find its home in the heart of man.

For today, Bahá'u'lláh expresses the will of God and it is this – that all humanity should unite in 'one universal cause, one common faith'.[2] Underpinning this is the insight that 'The Earth is but one country, and mankind its citizens,'[3] and we are to 'Glory not in love for your country, but in love for all mankind.'[4] These are teachings of the one progressively revealed religion for this age. Unfortunately, since these words were spoken by Bahá'u'lláh at the end of the 19th century, the masses of humanity have given scant attention to them or have flatly chosen to ignore them.

Bearing this in mind we may ask: Has humanity been in compliance with the directive of the unity of the human race, which is the will of God in this day? Has it regarded, as Bahá'u'lláh stated, all peoples as citizens of one planet and realized that, for its own well-being, peace and security, it needs to be united? Or, on the other hand, has it been dismissive of this general directive from God and supplanted it with the 'will of man'? Far-reaching consequences flowed from this choice. All hell has broken out for all manner of reasons, and the suffering of humanity continues because we have not chosen the path of uniting, as one people, in one common Faith. Instead, we have chosen the well-trod path of deifying our own mental faculties and insisted that our own will is the way to peace and prosperity.

History is repeating itself. Past Manifestations of God had to contend with the problems of their age and gave remedies for their ills. Moses focused on giving laws to a previously enslaved people that had no civil structure to keep its peoples safe. Christ concentrated on love for all peoples, even one's enemies, thereby giving a new direction to the hearts of men and drawing together peoples who had previously hated each other. Muhammad came to a barbarous, idolatrous people and united them around the worship of the One God, releasing a power so effective that for seven hundred and fifty years Islam was the primary impulse for the progress of humanity. Imagine then, that there had been no response to the past Manifestations of God – from where would come the chief impulse for advancing civilization?

Perhaps it would be instructive to state at this point an example of the tremendous benefits that have come from one of the major religions, to underpin the fact that much unbiased study of the benefits of each of these religions has to be made as a counter to dismissing God and religion as negative influences in humanity's history. For this example we focus on Islam. Those who study Islam are aware that Muhammad

> imbued them [the Arabs] with morals and ethics that were the light of the age, raised aloft the standard of community care and set them on the path in an insatiable thirst for knowledge. The results of raising the bar of civilization were stunning. Nearly a thousand years ago, for example, in an age 'when there was not a single doctor to be found along the entire middle reaches of the Rhine', there were '860 doctors living in Baghdad alone'.[5]

Islam had a very strong influence on Europe, to the extent that:

> Europe was overshadowed by Islam for 750 years, nearly as long as the whole period of Graeco-Roman civilization. It was only through Arabic numerals that modern arithmetic became possible. In medicine, astronomy, and experimental science, in architecture and philosophy, the Muslims were the teachers of the West. The first European universities and colleges, hospitals, dispensaries and libraries were founded on Islamic models.[6]

When other studies are made, without bias or prejudice, into the wonderful, civilizing benefits of religion, then the ignorance of those who decry religion and dismiss it as a problem in the world rather than its answer will be exposed. Of course, those who are anti-religion will draw on their knowledge of the many horrors that have masqueraded themselves in the name of religion, such as the Inquisition, two centuries of the Crusades, present-day terrorism and so on. But surely it becomes clear, on investigation, that these terrible occurrences have nothing whatever to do with religion. If Moses stated 'Thou shalt not kill',[7] how can anyone be a follower of Moses if he murders? If Jesus said, 'Love your enemies,'[8] forgive 'seventy times seven',[9] how can anyone, including a Pope, make a case for the nations of Christianity crusading against the Muslims for two centuries? If Muhammad said: 'There is no compulsion in religion,'[10] how can the terrorists justify their murderous attacks on those who do not believe in the fanatical way they do?

Put simply, if a skilled and knowledgeable doctor prescribes a remedy for a sick patient and the patient complies with the prescription, he will get better. On the other hand, if he does not comply with the doctor's directives, who is to blame if health deteriorates even to the point of death? As said before, the doctors for the ills of mankind are the great Manifestations of God; their remedy is their teachings, which constitute the will of God to remedy the disease of the age. Through this awareness, materialistic interpretations of history can now be seen as positively harmful and a factor in the spread of nihilism, secularism, materialism, paganism, irreligion and hedonism – all symptoms of irreligion. In effect, they play a major role in leaching 'out of human motivation – and even interest – the spiritual impulses that distinguish the rational soul'.[11] If the soul is not motivated by spiritual forces and attracted to higher propensities such as service, unconditional love, sacrifice for the well-being of others, holiness, sanctity, among other qualities, then all we are left with is a 'body without a soul' – a 'dead, materialistic entity'. This, for the most part, is the state of the world right now.

Surely it is plain to see that history could be written in terms of those who, through their own volition, were committed to living by the will of God, and of those who, out of ignorance, obduracy or disobedience, chose to abide not by the will of God but by their own desires and personal inclinations? To chart the activities of these peoples and the consequences of their actions would shed great illumination on the major theme history should teach us: a basic, fundamental theme of all religious teachings – 'You reap what you sow'!

There is a choice then, as to how to interpret historical events. Those who hold to a materialistic interpretation of reality cannot place God at the centre of events because to them, He does not exist; therefore, there is no other way to interpret history. Such an historian – although forced to acknowledge that a large part of history is full of events and happenings directly related to peoples who believed in God, or some form of Higher Power, and those who opposed such belief – will be incapable of reading such events and happenings in terms of compliance or non-compliance with the will of God. To them, when Moses took his people out of bondage and taught them the laws of God upon which a great civilization was built, being the envy of the world at that time, He was not a special soul representing God, He was not a Divine Educator revealing the will of God for that age. Similarly, when

Muhammad, through the power of the One true God, raised up the barbarous and ignorant tribes of Arabia and transformed them into the most educated and progressive force on earth, culminating in an Islamic golden age, He was not seen as the chosen Apostle of God sent to instruct humanity as to how to live in that era. No, to them Moses and Muhammad were, at best, only reformers, great charismatic leaders who syncretized from various cultural thoughts and teachings around them to establish a new religion with its own laws and teachings. Because materialistic historians deny the existence of God, they deny the main, essential truth of every great religion: that is, that God chooses special souls through which He makes known His will. By their very state of mind, such historians spend their lives describing and interpreting what has happened to humanity as if it is a body without a soul, as if there is no heavenly meaning, purpose or reason for the existence of the human race – only 'things that happen'!

George Townshend, sometime Canon of St Patrick's Cathedral, Dublin and Archdeacon of Clonfert, after recognizing Bahá'u'lláh as the Divine Physician, the Manifestation of God for this age, wrote the following. It sums up much of what is written above:

Any enquiry after truth which begins by separating man from God is wrong from the first, is the essence of falsity. The notion that man is independent, that he has the prerogative of laying out the paths of history and of civilisation, the privilege of doing whatever seems best to his own will and his own desire is born of arrogance and is utter illusion.[12]

20

DIVINE INTERVENTION OR NOT?

Another point to be considered, as I navigated around the mine-fields that are prevalent on the path of reality, is the question as to the intervention in human affairs of a Higher Power. Many in a secular society feel that if God exists, He should 'step in' to stop the terrible suffering in the world. Because this is not seen to be happening it throws up all manner of doubts as to the existence of a caring, loving God. So, is there proof of divine intervention in human affairs?

There are various ways that divine intervention, if it exists, has been viewed. At a basic level, the intervention of a Higher Power can be hoped or prayed for in one's daily life. Many souls do this and interpret some events in their lives as important proof of divine intervention. Some may believe God intervened by a serendipitous meeting of a marriage partner, or someone being healed after prayers have been offered, or being the sole survivor of a fatal accident. I would want to stay clear of interpreting intervention in this way, as the conclusions tend to be entirely subjective. This is not to say such occurrences do not happen, but proving that it is divine intervention would be extremely difficult if not impossible. So, I concluded, there is no objective proof of divine intervention through individual experiences of this type.

Let us now consider miracles as possible proof of divine intervention. Even though for Christians the reported miracles of Jesus are one of the foundational beliefs of their faith, they also are impossible to prove as acts of divine intervention. A brief look at all religions reveals that miracles have been reported, usually associated with the Founder of their Faith. We may question why the miracles of Moses, such as the ten plagues of Egypt and the parting of the Red Sea, seemed to have no effect whatsoever on the Egyptians who, if such miracles physically happened, experienced them first-hand. One would expect that their belief in Pharaoh as a god would be severely shaken after such occurrences. But no such challenges to Pharaoh's power are recorded. Even the apparent massive miracle of the parting of the Red Sea is not recorded by the Egyptians – a people who were known to document most important events. It is also recorded that among Buddha's many abilities 'were the power to levitate, to multiply his body, to read the minds of others, to pass through solid rock . . .'[1]

Some basic questioning that would be applied by any person using an unbiased scientific approach would include this: by what criteria can we accept the miracles of one religion and deny the others? Further, as an individual living in the 21st century I have no means to validate the reports of miracles occurring thousands of years ago. We may, in addition, ask: if miracles are so important as proof of God's intervention, why are they not happening on a regular basis now so that all peoples everywhere can be left in no doubt as to the existence of God?

It is educative, on the other hand, to recall the interdiction of the Founders of the great religions regarding whether or not miracles are to be incontrovertible proof of the intervention of God in human affairs. Buddha, for instance, placed no credence in miracles, as the following story reveals:

One day the Buddha met an ascetic who sat by the bank of a river. This ascetic had practised austerities for 25 years. The Buddha asked him what he had received for all his labour. The ascetic proudly replied that, finally, he could cross the river by walking on the water. The Buddha pointed out that this gain was insignificant for all the years of labour, since he could cross the river using a ferry for one penny![2]

Many miracles are associated with Muhammad, but Muhammad Himself explained that the only miracle (or 'ayah', meaning 'sign' in Arabic) is the Qur'án, the depository of the Word of God. By this Muhammad did not mean that the Qur'án, as a book, suddenly descended from heaven in a miraculous way, for it was revealed by Him over a 23-year period. No, He must have meant that the power inherent in the Word of God revealed through a Prophet or Manifestation of God is able to transform a people from a degraded condition to a relatively nobler state. Under its influence it brings former enemies, strangers and the downtrodden into enlarging bonds of friendship and brotherhood and thereby society progresses. This indeed is a miracle, and it has taken place not only in Islam but also in every other major religion, efflorescing in a golden age in comparison to what humanity had experienced before.

Even Christ, 600 years before Muhammad, forcefully made the point that mankind should not look for God's intervention in terms of miracles. The following passage from the Gospel of Matthew highlights this: 'Then certain of the scribes and of the Pharisees answered, saying, Master, we would see a sign from thee.' In this context by asking for a 'sign' they were asking for a miracle . . . 'But he answered and said unto them, An evil and adulterous generation seeketh after a sign . . .'[3]

The phrase, 'adulterous generation', does not mean that the mass of married people were engaged in sexual relationships outside marriage. No, it makes more sense to consider that they had adulterated the Covenant of God by looking for something outside the will or the law of God (an act of infidelity) as a means to prove the validity of a Prophet, in this case Christ. Followers of any Prophet or Messenger of God who look for miracles indicate, in the judgement of Christ, that they are faithless, that they have focused their attention on the physical over and above the spiritual. In fact, they have become materialistic, forsaken the guidance of Christ to 'seek ye first the kingdom of God, and his righteousness',[4] and replaced it by, amongst other things, a desire for miracles. So, it becomes clear that the door is closed by all the Messengers of God to seek God's intervention in miracles. However, we should not discard looking for the possibility of divine intervention in human affairs elsewhere – to be unbiased we should be open to other possibilities!

Those who do not believe in the existence of God will conclude that there is no intervention in human affairs to stop human beings from doing terrible things. The irrational beliefs of many religionists in miracles as a proof of God's intervention does little to persuade them otherwise. The majority know from their knowledge of history, right up to the present time, that atrocities have piled one on another to such an extent that the evidence seems to support the unbeliever's findings that there has never been any intervention to prevent these happenings.

I can understand this assumption as, along with many others, I too have felt this way. All thinking, caring people feel there is a great need for a change in behaviour for the better from many of our fellow human beings, and interventions would be a great way of changing behaviour. It could be acknowledged, however, that those who are not aware of any interventions in human affairs by a Higher Power are perhaps pleading that interventions would be welcome, as they can see no other way out of the terrible mess mankind has got itself into. Perhaps there is an unconscious expectation that for every case of injustice, cruelty or terror, God, if He exists, should intervene in a way that would make it impossible to commit such atrocities. Maybe some would expect a ball of fire to descend on the perpetrators of evil deeds, or the earth to open and swallow them up, or a bolt of lightning to strike them dead? Some may expect that God should instantly change the evil doer's malignant way of thinking to something benign, or that a knight in shining armour would suddenly appear and strike a death blow to the tyrant, or an alien abduction should coincide with the time just before a terrible deed is done? When 'intervention' is considered in these ways, it becomes obvious to every intelligent person that it is ridiculous. And these thoughts may convince someone that because they cannot imagine intervention in any other way then there is no God.

But there is another way of intervention that needs to be given some thought. Those who follow a Messenger of God feel that God *has* intervened in human affairs by sending them their particular Messenger to give guidance, teachings and encouragement to people so that they would use their free will, their power of choice, correctly. That is, to choose high, light-nature behaviour over their low, dark nature, and to make every effort to leave this world a little better than before they were born. There is a logic behind this way of thinking which has been highlighted by Bahá'u'lláh. As mentioned before, He likens the Messengers of God to doctors or physicians whose work it is to intervene in human affairs, even as a doctor intervenes when a person is unwell to diagnose the complaint and prescribe the remedy. Bahá'u'lláh states:

> The Prophets of God should be regarded as physicians whose task is to foster the well-being of the world and its peoples, that, through the spirit of oneness, they may heal the sickness of a divided humanity.[5]

And in another place, He writes:

> The All-Knowing Physician hath His finger on the pulse of mankind. He perceiveth the disease, and prescribeth, in His unerring wisdom, the remedy. Every age hath its own problem, and every soul its particular aspiration. The remedy the world needeth in its present-day afflictions can never be the same as that which a subsequent age may require. Be anxiously concerned with the needs of the age ye live in, and centre your deliberations on its exigencies and requirements.[6]

I discovered early on in my investigation into the Bahá'í Faith that throughout the ages God has sent many Messengers or

Divine Physicians, and for this day and age, for humanity's particular disease, Bahá'u'lláh. It is they who convey the will of God to humanity, and for those who accept them as God's representatives, His interventions, there is every confidence that our Creator has not left humanity comfortless or without guidance as to the best way to peace, harmony, and the reduction of suffering. And this process, Bahá'u'lláh assures us, will continue way into the future, just so long as there is a human race. Intervention in this way allows for an ever-expanding group of people to become aware of the guidance of the Divine Physicians, while not interfering with the over-riding principle of freedom to listen and follow, or not, their teachings.

Bahá'u'lláh diagnoses the disease today as being disunity and specifies that God wants the whole human race to become as one and see the whole planet as one country. Underlining this point Bahá'u'lláh writes:

> The well-being of mankind, its peace and security, are unattainable unless and until its unity is firmly established. This unity can never be achieved so long as the counsels which the Pen of the Most High hath revealed are suffered to pass unheeded.[7]

Of course, there are many ingredients in this remedy for an afflicted humanity, but the point here is that we have a perfectly logical system of intervention advocating a perfectly reasonable remedy. Whether this is the type of intervention envisaged or desired by peoples is not the point. What is obvious is that a logical and coherent system of intervention exists, a system that does not conflict with scientific laws nor, indeed, common sense, neither does it compromise human free will.

But there is more to be explored on this subject which may, indirectly, come under the heading of 'intervention by God'. In a sense, just leaving God to intervene at specific vital points in humanity's development or evolution, by sending His Messenger, may not completely satisfy a feeling that, if there is a God, He should be involved all the time with helping humanity. A reasoned objection to this may be that God is like a person who winds up a clock, lets it run by itself and then comes back to rewind it when necessary. Part of an answer to this objection can be obtained through a little research into the history of the world's religions. This will reveal that the followers of the Messengers of God continue to transmit the Message, or the remedy for the ills of the age, to more and more people after the passing of their Founder. In a sense, these souls could be considered as nurses to the sick body of humankind, who faithfully apply the remedy from the Divine Physician in their own lives, while administering to those who choose to be healed by it. For faithful souls engaged in this work, the promise of divine assistance is given by the Messenger. By divine assistance is meant that a special power or spirit, mostly called the Holy Spirit, flows from God to sustain them, uplift and encourage them to carry on the work in the face of dire vicissitudes or even death. Therefore, each person who takes up the new teachings revealed by the new Messenger of God could be viewed, to some degree, as an extension of the primary intervention through which the remedy of the Divine Physician is offered to others. By this means, God is always involved in intervention through guiding humanity, even after the passing of the Messenger of God.

Usually the response to the intervention/remedy/message is very slow in the beginning, Islam being an exception to this. Over the centuries, love for the Divine Physician and the remedy gathers momentum, attracting an increasing number of souls and thereby providing divinely directed healing, an impulse to the progress of society. This impulse reaches a culmination in a golden age in comparison to what existed before. The fruits of that age are harvested, but thereafter, because of the changed conditions in society, progress stagnates. A veritable 'wintertime' is experienced in human affairs, which prepares it for the next intervention from God in the form of a new Messenger.

Reflection on this perfect system of divine intervention, known as 'progressive revelation', brings to light that we are at present in the slow stage of growth, after the coming of Bahá'u'lláh as God's latest intervention in the affairs of humanity. Those who have accepted Bahá'u'lláh and His remedy as necessary for the progress of society, and an antidote to those 'wintertime' ideologies that would take us back to barbarism, feel a close kinship with the early followers and faithful adherents of previous religions. In the slow growth stage of those religions, their followers experienced the reticence, resistance or oppression of the generality of the community around them to respond positively to the new Message. This is exactly what Bahá'ís are experiencing today; but looking beyond this stage, and following the pattern set by the previous religions, one can expect rapid and universal acceptance of the divine remedy.

Now, if the remedy for this age – the unification of humanity – is not accepted, then to blame God for not intervening is manifestly unjust. Sadly, those souls who for whatever reason (and there are multiple reasons) do not take up the new Message/remedy become as 'obstacles' preventing it from flowing out into the community. They become, by their negative response, a blockage obstructing the divine remedy that can cure the ills of the age. We must be fair in our judgement: is it God Who is to blame or those people who ignore, reject and in some cases persecute those who offer the divine remedy to others? Shoghi Effendi, the Guardian of the Bahá'í Faith, wrote that if the religious leaders of Persia had not prevented the spread of Bahá'u'lláh's prescription through their pogroms against His followers, 'Persia would have been subdued by the power of God in hardly more than two years.'[8] This is very serious stuff indeed, as the patient's health, that is, humanity's health, can deteriorate to the point that terrible afflictions increase daily. The simple fact is that if the prescription from the doctor, the divine intervention, is ignored, rejected or despised, what hope is there for the patient's recovery?

Perhaps an example will clarify this point. It is also relevant to reading history in relation to people being aligned with or against the will of God, as discussed in the last chapter. So, let's go back to the time when the Romans occupied Judaea 63 years before the birth of Christ, when the Jews began to feel the weight of the Roman oppression. At least three major Roman impositions severely tested the Jews. They were taxed and the revenue sent to Rome; the Romans decided who would be the High Priest, effectively robbing the Jews of their own selection process; and when 'the Roman Emperor Caligula came to power in 39 C.E. he declared himself a god and ordered that statues in his image be placed in every house of worship within his realm – including the Temple.'⁹ With this last imposition the Jews were extremely annoyed, as idolatry is strictly forbidden in the Jewish Faith and so they refused to conform. Caligula threatened to destroy the Temple in Jerusalem in retaliation but, providentially for the Jews, he was assassinated before his threat could be carried out. Prior to this and more so after, the spirit of revolt spread amongst the Jews. A faction of the Jews, the 'Zealots', were actively engaged in resisting the increasing oppression of the Romans, then under the orders of the Emperor Titus. In 66 CE the Great Revolt began, culminating in 70 CE with the siege of Jerusalem during which a trench was dug around the city to keep its occupants in. Over 1,000,000 Jews were killed by the Romans, nearly 100,000 were captured and enslaved and Jerusalem was razed to the ground.¹⁰ Although over 100,000 Jews were killed or sold into slavery after an uprising in Galilee before the siege of Jerusalem:

> The slaughter within was even more dreadful than the spectacle from without. Men and women, old and young, insurgents and priests, those who fought and those who entreated mercy, were hewn down in indiscriminate carnage. The number of the slain exceeded that of the slayers. The legionaries had to clamber over heaps of dead to carry on the work of extermination.¹¹

Forty years before the destruction of Jerusalem, Christ was teaching the Jews, amongst many things, how to relate to the Roman occupation. Three specific admonitions, which follow, were given as a means to at least co-exist with the Romans. The Pharisees, trying to entrap Jesus, asked: 'Is it lawful to give tribute unto Caesar, or not?' Then it is recorded that:

> Jesus perceived their wickedness, and said, Why tempt ye me, ye hypocrites? Shew me the tribute money. And they brought unto him a penny. And he saith unto them, Whose is this image and superscription? They say unto him, Caesar's. Then saith he unto them, Render therefore unto Caesar the things which are Caesar's; and unto God the things that are God's.[12]

A second admonition occurred at the time of Christ's betrayal by Judas Iscariot when a crowd came to lay hold of Jesus. Thinking to protect Him, Peter 'drew his sword, and struck a servant of the high priest's, and smote off his ear'. In response to this display of violence by one of His own Disciples, Jesus said to Peter, 'Put up again thy sword into his place: for all they that take the sword shall perish with the sword.'[13]

A third admonition is associated with the well-known words of Christ to 'Love your enemies, do good to them which hate you . . .'[14] From the Jewish point of view, they were inundated with enemies, the Romans at that time. But Christ takes this exhortation much further and even gives a rational explanation of why they should love their enemies:

> Bless them that curse you, and pray for them which despitefully use you. And unto him that smiteth thee on the one cheek offer also the other; and him that taketh away thy cloak forbid not to take thy coat also. Give to every man that asketh of thee; and of him that taketh away thy goods ask them not again. And as ye would that men should do to you, do ye also

to them likewise. For if ye love them which love you, what thanks have ye? for sinners also love those that love them.[15]

These three teachings of Christ alone – to give what is due to Caesar, to refrain from violence, and to love one's enemies – if taken seriously as essential ingredients of the divine remedy, the divine intervention, would have been enough to prevent the massive bloodshed the Jews experienced prior to and during the sack of Jerusalem. The words of Christ, spread further by His followers, was the divine intervention extending past the crucifixion of Christ for 40 years before the dreadful destruction. We can be sure that during these harrowing years, the Jews would have prayed ardently for God's intervention against their Roman oppressors, not realizing that it had already happened. The Bible assures us that before we ask, God has answered.

The events of the destruction of Jerusalem were even predicted by Christ, for He could foresee the consequences of not taking the remedy:

> If thou hadst known, even thou, at least in this thy day, the things which belong unto thy peace! but now they are hid from thine eyes. For the days shall come upon thee, that thine enemies shall cast a trench about thee, and compass thee round, and keep thee in on every side, and shall lay thee even with the ground, and thy children within thee; and they shall not leave in thee one stone upon another; because thou knewest not the time of thy visitation.[16]

To appreciate why Christ's Message of love and tolerance went unheeded we must reflect on the mindset of the people around Him. There is much to be said about this, but what it all boils down to is that the Jews, along with the Romans, could see their circumstances and the way to a better life only through materialistic eyes. The 'intervenor' ('thy visitation') was rejected or ignored because He did not bring what they expected of a Messiah – a revolt against their oppressors, or at least a political solution to their problems. The Jews suffered tremendously because of this, and for two millennia continued to do so as a dispersed and stateless people. (This must not be taken as an argument to justify the persecutions of the Jews by the Christians over the centuries. It is obvious, in this respect, that those Christian persecutors strayed so far from the guidance of Christ as to exclude themselves from the community of faithful Christians.)

For us today, the intervention from God, Bahá'ís believe, is Bahá'u'lláh and His teachings which, when coupled those with the Báb, the Prophet-Herald of Bahá'u'lláh, constitute nearly fifty years of divine revelation to mankind. These teachings have now been taken to people around the planet and offered as the divine remedy for the present age. Signs are that there is a little acceleration in the number of people responding 125 years after the passing of the Founder of the Bahá'í Faith, but this has not been enough to avoid the terrible suffering humankind experienced because of its negative response to the divine remedy for this age of globalization. Writing nearly fifty years after the passing of Bahá'u'lláh, during the onslaught of the Second World War Shoghi Effendi reviewed the mournful response to Bahá'u'lláh as God's latest Manifestation:

Unmitigated indifference on the part of men of eminence and rank; unrelenting hatred shown by the ecclesiastical dignitaries of the Faith from which it had sprung; the scornful derision of the people among whom it was born; the utter contempt which most of those kings and rulers who had been addressed by its Author manifested towards it; the condemnations pronounced, the threats hurled, and the banishments decreed by those under whose sway it arose and first spread; the distortion to which its principles and laws were subjected by the envious and the malicious, in lands and among peoples far beyond the country of its origin – all these are but the evidences of the treatment meted out by a generation sunk in self-content, careless of its God, and oblivious of the omens, prophecies, warnings and admonitions revealed by His Messengers.[17]

Just as the religious leaders rejected Christ over 2,000 years ago and turned the people away from the divine remedy for that time, so too did the religious and ruling authorities reject Bahá'u'lláh. In their minds Bahá'u'lláh did not conform to their expectations of their promised Messenger of God, and so they persecuted him for forty years. As in the days of Christ, they rejected the Messenger and along with this they also rejected the divine remedy.

What was the divine remedy they so easily discarded? The following is an outline, touched on previously, of the 'truths', Shoghi Effendi stated, 'which should be regarded as the animating force and the hallmark of His Revelation'.[18] Judge for yourself whether these teachings deserve to be ignored or disparaged, or whether they are a mighty healing agency for the ills of the human race:

'The world is but one country, and mankind its citizens.' 'Let not a man glory in that he loves his country; let him rather glory in this, that he loves his kind.' And again: 'Ye are the fruits of one tree, and the leaves of one branch.' 'Bend your minds and wills to the education of the peoples and kindreds of the earth, that haply . . . all mankind may become the upholders of one order, and the inhabitants of one city . . . Ye dwell in one world, and have been created through the operation of one Will.' 'Beware lest the desires of the flesh and of a corrupt inclination provoke divisions among you. Be ye as the fingers of one hand, the members of one body.' And yet again: 'All the saplings of the world have appeared from one Tree, and all the drops from one Ocean, and all beings owe their existence to one Being.' And furthermore: 'That one indeed is a man who today dedicateth himself to the service of the entire human race.'[19]

Many souls who managed to break the strangle-hold held by the clergy on the hearts and minds of people to the point that they could think for themselves, recognized Bahá'u'lláh and His Revelation as God's latest intervention in human affairs. Not only were they inspired by a deep love for Bahá'u'lláh, but their hearts were aflame, through His teachings, with a divine love for all humanity. Regarding the diversity of the human family as a rich blessing from God, they worked fearlessly for 'every child of God' to realize 'that they are leaves of one tree, flowers in one garden, drops in one ocean, and sons and daughters of one Father, whose name is love!'[20] They spread His teachings far and wide, continuing the process of 'intervention', and in the early days, for the most part, were persecuted, tortured and mowed down for doing so. In some countries this is still happening. Humanity must become aware of their sacrifices that demonstrate, with their life's blood, that God's intervention continues.

Of singular importance is the luminous person of 'Abdu'l-Bahá, the eldest son of Bahá'u'lláh, His appointed successor, the interpreter of His works and the exemplar of every Bahá'í ideal. Sharing in His Father's exile, imprisonment and privations from the age of nine, He arose in the twilight of his life to offer the divine remedy to the peoples of the West. Between 1911 and 1913 He visited several European countries and more extensively many cities and centres in North America. In his first ever public address in London, He declared the essence of His Father's teachings: 'The gift of God to this enlightened age is the knowledge of the oneness of mankind and the fundamental oneness of religion.'[21] His talks and interviews received wide media attention and His magnetic personality attracted thousands of souls. His purpose in taking the arduous journey to Europe and America, while suffering a variety of maladies brought on by a life of sacrifice and privation, was not only to make His Father's teachings known in the West, but to alert everyone that a 'great war' was impending:

'All Europe is an armed camp. These warlike preparations will necessarily culminate in a great war. The very armaments themselves are productive of war. This great arsenal must go ablaze. There is nothing of the nature of prophecy about such a view,' said 'Abdu'l-Bahá; 'it is based on reasoning solely.'[22]

Some souls were moved to the depths of their being after coming into contact with 'Abdu'l-Bahá and committed the rest of their lives to taking the knowledge that God had sent Bahá'u'lláh, as the Promised One of all religions, and His teachings on the unity of mankind, to as many people as possible. Although 'Abdu'l-Bahá won the respect and admiration of many leaders of thought and those in authority, sadly, they and the mass of people who met Him did not respond in a way that could have secured a more peaceful future for the world. This is another example of the 'intervention of God' in human affairs in the person of 'Abdu'l-Bahá, an intervention that went unheeded, and plunged the remainder of the twentieth century into catastrophes the like of which no other century in the history of mankind has experienced!

We could consider the destruction of Jerusalem and the Jewish diaspora as a preliminary lesson for the rejection and persecution of a Manifestation of God, and view what follows in the same light. But there is a difference. What happened through the advent of Christ was limited to a small section of the earth's peoples. Now, through the advent of Bahá'u'lláh, one of His titles being 'the unifier of the children of men', we can expect the consequences to be world-wide. A brief review of some of the major consequences humanity has experienced as a result of dismissing the Divine Physician and the divine remedy for this day and age now follows.

Bahá'u'lláh, appearing in the middle of the nineteenth century, came at a time when colonialization by European countries was rampant; it continued well into the twentieth century. Millions of the earth's inhabitants were denied basic freedoms and self-determination, and terrible indeed were the injustices against them. In Congo in Africa, for instance, the most heinous atrocities were between 1877 and 1908:

> It has been estimated that during the first decade of the twentieth century over a million people in the Congo perished – starved, beaten, worked literally to death for the profit of their distant masters, a preview of the fate that was to engulf well over one hundred million of their fellow human beings across Europe and Asia before the century reached its end.[23]

Before, during and after the days of Bahá'u'lláh a militant and arrogant nationalism, a veritable deification of the state, fell upon the earth like a plague. Its devastating effect defied estimation then, and still does. The First World War alone bankrupted Europe. It is thought that the 1918 flu pandemic, because of the malnutrition and disease caused by the war, weakened and enfeebled peoples to the extent that up to 40 million died.[24] Over 16 million died in the war itself, with military and civilian casualties exceeding 37 million.[25] From this conflict the seeds were sown for the Second World War.

The rise of Hitler after the First World War stands as an object lesson in the evils of racism. Advocating a cancerous theory that the 'Arians' were the world's 'Master Race', he mobilized this deadly disease in the body of mankind with horrendous consequences. World War Two, the deadliest military conflict in history, left, it is estimated, over 60 million dead – 2.5% of the world's population; these included over 22 million military dead and over 38 million civilians, with about 15 million of these as a result of war-related disease and famine.[26] Within this pit of human suffering, and on a scale unprecedented in the organization of genocide, over six million Jews were systematically exterminated in an attempt to purge the human race of the Jewish peoples. The Holocaust extended to millions of other peoples, greater in number than the Jewish pogrom, peoples not considered fit to be in the human race according to Nazi ideology. Russians, Ukrainians, Belarusians, Roma Gypsies, the handicapped and black people, for instance, if not killed outright, died pitifully either from starvation, disease, forced labour, medical experimentation or brutality.[27] It's also important to remember that the war against Japan ended with America dropping atomic bombs on the cities of Nagasaki and Hiroshima, thereby taking humanity into the nightmare of the Cold War and possible nuclear annihilation.

Communism, an ideology that since 1917 through a bloody revolution in Russia, was spread by trampling on basic human rights, terror, torture, massacres, executions, and the exile of millions to the gulag system of slave labour camps. It claimed nearly 100 million lives worldwide, Soviet Russia and China bearing the greater burden of atrocities. Shoghi Effendi, writing about the Communist system in 1941, described:

> . . . the swift and sudden rise of that 'religious irreligion', that bold, conscious, and organized assault launched in Soviet Russia against the Greek Orthodox Church, that precipitated the disestablishment of the state religion, that massacred a vast number of its members originally numbering above a hundred million souls, that pulled down, closed, or converted into museums, theatres and warehouses, thousands upon thousands of churches, monasteries, synagogues and mosques, that stripped the church of its six and a half million acres of property, and sought, through its League of Militant Atheists and the promulgation of a 'five-year plan of godlessness', to loosen from its foundations the religious life of the masses . . .[28]

The ideologies of colonialism, nationalism, racism and communism are diametrically opposed to the teachings of Bahá'u'lláh, who not only advocated world unity based upon the consciousness of the oneness of mankind but stipulated that justice is the guiding principle for a united and harmonious world. Shoghi

Effendi passionately declared that 'God Himself has indeed been dethroned from the hearts of men' and 'an idolatrous world' has put in its place 'false gods which its own idle fancies have fatuously created, and its misguided hands so impiously exalted'. Highlighting what these false gods are, he writes:

> The chief idols in the desecrated temple of mankind are none other than the triple gods of Nationalism, Racialism and Communism, at whose altars governments and peoples, whether democratic or totalitarian, at peace or at war, of the East or of the West, Christian or Islamic, are, in various forms and in different degrees, now worshipping. Their high priests are the politicians and the worldly-wise, the so-called sages of the age; their sacrifice, the flesh and blood of the slaughtered multitudes; their incantations, outworn shibboleths and insidious and irreverent formulas; their incense, the smoke of anguish that ascends from the lacerated hearts of the bereaved, the maimed, and the homeless.[29]

Just like Christ, Bahá'u'lláh could foresee the consequences of not taking the divine remedy. Writing mostly from his place of incarceration in the penal colony of 'Akká from 1868 on, He laments that the human race is weighed down with injustice and recounts how a sick and diseased humanity will suffer even more as a result of the divine remedy being withheld. Here is a selection of Bahá'u'lláh's statements on this point:

> Justice is, in this day, bewailing its plight, and Equity groaneth beneath the yoke of oppression. The thick clouds of tyranny have darkened the face of the earth, and enveloped its peoples.[30]

> How long will humanity persist in its waywardness? How long will injustice continue? How long is chaos and confusion to reign amongst men? How long will discord agitate the face

of society? . . . The winds of despair are, alas, blowing from every direction, and the strife that divideth and afflicteth the human race is daily increasing. The signs of impending convulsions and chaos can now be discerned, inasmuch as the prevailing order appeareth to be lamentably defective. I beseech God, exalted be His glory, that He may graciously awaken the peoples of the earth, may grant that the end of their conduct may be profitable unto them, and aid them to accomplish that which beseemeth their station.[31]

Soon will the present-day order be rolled up, and a new one spread out in its stead. Verily, thy Lord speaketh the truth, and is the Knower of things unseen.[32]

After a time, all the governments on earth will change. Oppression will envelop the world. And following a universal convulsion, the sun of justice will rise from the horizon of the unseen realm.[33]

O ye peoples of the world! Know, verily, that an unforeseen calamity is following you, and that grievous retribution awaiteth you. Think not the deeds ye have committed have been blotted from My sight. By My beauty! All your doings hath My Pen graven with open characters upon tablets of chrysolite.[34]

The day is approaching when its [civilization's] flame will devour the cities, when the Tongue of Grandeur will proclaim: 'The Kingdom is God's, the Almighty, the All-Praised!'[35]

The world is in travail, and its agitation waxeth day by day. Its face is turned towards waywardness and unbelief. Such shall be its plight, that to disclose it now would not be meet and seemly. Its perversity will long continue. And when the appointed hour is come, there shall suddenly appear that which shall cause the limbs of mankind to quake. Then, and only then, will the Divine Standard be unfurled, and the Nightingale of Paradise warble its melody.[36]

A last thought on the subject of divine intervention needs to be mentioned. In a sense this point could be considered as countering the argument made earlier, that God should remove tyrants and oppressors and prove that He exists. If we cast our gaze over history, we are forced to conclude that God has indeed, removed every single tyrant and oppressor. Where, we may ask, are Nimrod, Pharaoh and Herod? Where are Caligula, Genghis Khan, Ivan the Terrible? And more recently, where are Hitler, Stalin, or Pol Pot? All of them are dead, all have been removed. In fact, the removal of tyrants is woven into the very fabric of man's existence. Yes, they have a time, a period when they wreak havoc and destruction, but they do not continue doing so forever. When Bahá'u'lláh wrote to the tyrants of His day, such as the Sultan of Turkey and the Shah of Persia, He reminded them that they were mortal and that their end would come, and they would be in manifest loss. Here is a succinct but pithy pronouncement written by Bahá'u'lláh, warning Napoleon III about the end result of his tyranny:

> Exultest thou over the treasures thou dost possess, knowing they shall perish? Rejoicest thou in that thou rulest a span of earth, when the whole world, in the estimation of the people of Bahá, is worth as much as the black in the eye of a dead ant? Abandon it unto such as have set their affections upon it, and turn thou unto Him Who is the Desire of the world. Whither are gone the proud and their palaces? Gaze thou into their tombs, that thou mayest profit by this example, inasmuch as We made it a lesson unto every beholder.[37]

For those who reject the divine remedy and are not involved with actively supporting aspects of it, there are consequences personal and social, as everything we do has consequences. Individuals who do so put themselves outside the flow of divine assistance and tend to sink deeper into a materialistic view of life, becoming entangled in its affairs. As they have rejected or ignored the divine remedy, they contribute to environments, albeit unconsciously, that produce tyrants and oppressive regimes – the very condition for which they would welcome a divine intervention. Bahá'u'lláh is quite emphatic here. Referring to the well-being, peace and security of mankind He writes: 'This unity can never be achieved so long as the counsels which the Pen of the Most High hath revealed are suffered to pass unheeded.'[38] In the last analysis, all tyrants and oppressors have been removed, as they have all died. Those still alive will sooner or later join the 'family' of oppressors in the grave. This process of warning and removal should also be seen as divine intervention, as the Messengers of God try to awaken wrongdoers, without removing their free will, to the fact that:

> Erelong shall your days pass away, as shall pass away the days of those who now, with flagrant pride, vaunt themselves over their neighbour. Soon shall ye be gathered together in the presence of God, and shall be asked of your doings, and shall be repaid for what your hands have wrought, and wretched is the abode of the wicked doers![39]

Yet again we must appeal to a sense of fairness. If there is little response to the intervention of God through Bahá'u'lláh, God's latest Messenger, and little response to continued intervention through His followers who take the remedy world-wide, is it fair to say that divine intervention does not exist? Here, then, is a last thought to ponder on this subject:

> Without this intervention from the world of God human nature remains the captive of instinct, as well as of unconscious assumptions and patterns of behaviour that have been culturally determined.[40]

21

GOD IS ALWAYS INVOLVED IN HIS CREATION

Another minefield that I needed to navigate pertained to the materialistic view of the universe. The universe seems to function quite independently with no involvement of a Higher Power. Everything in it seems to work perfectly well on its own. The planets orbit the sun, the moon orbits the earth. The stars in the Milky Way galaxy twinkle away as do all the other stars in all the other galaxies. Here on planet Earth, the seasons come and go, the sun shines, rain clouds form and water the plants; animals are born, complete their life cycle and die and human beings bring their intelligence to bear on all manner of things and then cease to physically exist. No involvement can be seen from a Higher Power in all these processes; therefore, this adds fuel to the non-believer's view that there is no God.

Yet again we come to the concept of perception; if we just look through a physical lens our perception of the universe will be that it is just physical, nothing more, nothing less. Ironically, animals come to this conclusion without using an ounce of thought on the subject. To them the only things that exist are physical, they have no other means to view the world other than through a material lens – the lens of their senses, as 'Abdu'l-Bahá humorously remarked:

Strange indeed that after twenty years training in colleges and universities man should reach such a station wherein he will

deny the existence of the ideal or that which is not percep-
tible to the senses. Have you ever stopped to think that the
animal already has graduated from such a university? Have
you ever realized that the cow is already a professor emeritus
of that university? For the cow without hard labor and study
is already a philosopher of the superlative degree in the school
of nature. The cow denies everything that is not tangible,
saying, 'I can see! I can eat! Therefore, I believe only in that
which is tangible!'

Then why should we go to the colleges? Let us go to the
cow.[1]

Human beings, however, have intelligence that can perceive
non-physical things. It is only by looking through the lens of
our intellect that humans have progressed to be the most developed species on earth. Based on this premise, the following is put
forward as a logical explanation that God is always involved with
His creation, sustaining it and providing everything necessary for
its continued existence.

'Abdu'l-Bahá explains that there are two types of realities – one
physical or material and the other non-physical or intelligible.
The material realities are known by the physical senses – sight,
hearing, taste, touch and smell. Material realities are sensible
objects, such as a tree that can be seen, a bird that can be heard,
a tomato that can be tasted, heat and cold that can be felt and a
flower that can be smelled. The intelligible realities exist but they
have no material form. They are invisible and cannot be detected
by the senses. For instance, every human being has thoughts, but
if you were able to collect all the thoughts from billions of human
beings, they would not occupy the space on a pin head; thoughts
are non-sensible realities. Similarly, love is an intelligible reality,
it exists but is not sensible. Our imagination is an intelligible
reality, so are all the virtues such as wisdom, patience, justice,
compassion and hope. Now if you were to meet someone for
the first time and there was no communication with that person,

you would not know what he is thinking, what is in his imagination, whether he is wise or patient, whether he is intelligent or not. However, you would know how tall he is, what clothes he wears, and the colour of his hair and eyes and so on – all the physical characteristics. The fact that you cannot detect by the senses any of the intelligible realities associated with that person is not a proof they do not exist. Yet most people would declare that a human being's intellectual capabilities and virtues are just as important as physical abilities – perhaps even more important.

Awareness of the difference between the physical and the intelligible, non-physical realities is essential when investigating everything God created. For, according to Bahá'í teachings, every material thing not only has its physical existence, which is sensible, but also an intelligible reality which is not picked up by the senses. Elaborating on this, 'Abdu'l-Bahá states that, 'The greatest power in the realm and range of human existence is spirit – the divine breath which animates and pervades all things.'[2] This spirit is an emanation from God similar to a song which emanates from a singer, or words that flow from a speaker. 'The spirit is the power of life.'[3] He further adds, 'the phenomena of the universe find realization through the one power animating and dominating all things, and all things are but manifestations of its energy and bounty. The virtue of being and existence is through no other agency.'[4] However, this spirit 'is manifested throughout creation in different degrees or kingdoms'.[5] In other words, the same 'spirit' is present in the mineral degree or kingdom, in the vegetable degree, in the animal degree and in the human degree.

So, within everything that is created throughout the universe, God uses the 'one power' called 'spirit', and this 'spirit' or 'power' is an intelligible reality which is not discernible to the senses. Spirit is an 'agency' emanating continuously from God to give 'life' or animation in varying 'degrees'. This one spirit guides all things, pervades all things and sustains all things. From these insights it is manifestly clear, to those who choose to see all created things with spiritual eyes, that the work of God, His care and power are ever present and active in everything He has created. One of the names of God is that He is the 'Sustainer'; and it is through the energy and bounty of the 'spirit' continually emanating from God, even as the rays emanate from the sun, that all things exist and are sustained. Another of the names of God, pertaining to this theme, Bahá'u'lláh reveals, is that He is the 'All-Pervading'. He states, 'that when the light of My Name, the All-Pervading, hath shed its radiance upon the universe, each and every created thing hath, according to a fixed decree, been endowed with the capacity to exercise a particular influence, and been made to possess a distinct virtue.'[6] It therefore becomes clear that God is far from just a 'winder up' of his creation and then returning to 'wind it up' again when it appears to be 'wound down', but is ever involved with it, sustaining and also guiding it to conform to His will.

Perhaps an analogy may make this clearer. If we think of the many machines and devices that use electricity: hairdryers, washing machines, vacuum cleaners, TVs, computers and so on, we notice that each of these is made to perform specific functions very different from each other. Yet, all are powered by the one power or energy of electricity and the moment the supply of electricity is cut off the machine or device ceases to function. Similarly, it is the power of 'one spirit' that activates, energizes and pervades all the variety of created things. You could take this analogy further by grading all the various appliances into those that perform simple tasks, such as a hair dryer, to those that perform complicated tasks, such as computers. However, all are still activated and energized and perform their functions through the one power of electricity. So, we find the one spirit causing and sustaining the power of attraction in the mineral kingdom (i.e. atomic attraction), the power of growth in the vegetable kingdom, the power of sense perception and instinct in the animal kingdom, and the power of intelligence (rational faculties) in the human kingdom.

We are further informed that it is this spirit, inherent in

everything, which causes everything in creation to make progress or grow or, in the words of science, to evolve. For instance:

> Every seed has, from the beginning, all the perfections of the plant. For example, all the vegetable perfections existed in this seed at the outset but were invisible and appeared only gradually. So it is the shoot which first appears from the seed, then the branches, leaves, and blossoms, and finally the fruit. But from the beginning of its formation, all of these existed potentially, albeit invisibly, in the seed.[7]

This process of gradual growth, or evolution from potential, can also be seen in the life of the terrestrial globe when some 4.5 billion years ago it started as a combination of elements and gradually evolved to produce all its wonderful life forms now present.

Similarly, in the life of the observable universe,[8] a 'hypothetical starting point of everything was an infinite concentration of energy referred to as a singularity'.[9] The veracity of the concept of a tiny singularity being the inherent condition of the Big Bang before it released its unimaginable energies causing, through a process of 'inflation', the cosmos as we know it today, is widely debated. Nonetheless, to avoid argumentation on this point, we may take it that the latent potential in the Big Bang was the 'seed' from which the universe grew. The concept of 'latent potential' itself is an intelligible reality which took billions of years to gradually develop into a material universe of galaxies, stars and planets. The same process occurs in all seeds, but in the case of, say, a poppy seed it happens over a short time. However, if those who hold a materialistic view of the universe were around at the time of the latent potential in the Big Bang, they would, with one voice, deny the fact that it would eventually develop into the universe we know today. Why? Because they would have no experience or knowledge of the intellectual reality called 'latent potential'. This process of growth, from potential to emergence, can be discerned as inherent, from the smallest created thing to the largest, hence

'Abdu'l-Bahá stated that progress 'is the expression of spirit in the world of matter'.[10] He elaborates on this process to the purpose of specifying that compositions in nature, whether large or small, come from one source and obey one universal law:

> But it is clear that this terrestrial globe in its present form did not come into existence all at once, but that this universal existent gradually traversed different phases until it appeared in its present completeness. Universal existences can be likened and compared to particular ones, for both are subjected to one natural order, one universal law, and one divine arrangement. For instance, you will find the smallest atoms to be similar in their general structure to the greatest entities in the universe, and it is clear that they have proceeded from one laboratory of might according to one natural order and one universal law, and can therefore be compared to one another.[11]

The idea of the smallest created thing corresponding to the greatest entities of the universe (as above so below), as touched on in a previous chapter, echoes the ancient teaching attributed to Hermes Trismegistus (Thrice Great). It has also been called 'the microcosm and the macrocosm'.

Another aspect of existence is that everything in nature can only exist and progress within the environment specific for its development. On this point 'Abdu'l-Bahá states: 'According to science, all forms of creation are endowed with life; this element of life and energy depending on environment and adaptations.'[12] So, we find that a baby grows in the environment of the womb, fish live in the environment of the sea, and mammals, for the most part, live in the environment of air. Interestingly, a creature called the Devil Worm can survive 'crippling pressure, lack of oxygen, high temperature' and 'has been found living up to 2.2 miles below the surface of the Earth . . . These worms spend their lives in total darkness, drinking 12,000-year-old water and eating simple bacteria.'[13]

Similarly, the potential universe may have existed in its own environment, which, as the planets, stars and galaxies do, may be space. If the potential universe did not exist in space or any other physical environment, then its existence is an intelligible existence, having its potential in an intelligible environment. This may be like thoughts, which have no physical existence but inhabit the environment of the mind – the mind also being an intelligible reality.

For those who view all existing things from a spiritual perspective, environments are also an aspect of creation, provided by God for the growth of all things. And because it is an aspect of the creative providence of God, we can say that these environments are expressions of His love. It is easy to understand that when a child grows in the womb of its mother, the womb itself is a perfect environment of love, protection and providence for the foetus. Perhaps we can go further and say that all created things exist in the ocean of God's love. Science, of course, will make more inroads into the physical details of these different environments, which should excite all of us, as it will no doubt expose much more of God's creative genius and the excellence of His foreknowledge of what He willed for creation. There are many indications and insights in the Bahá'í teachings that understanding physical and intelligible reality will enhance, even accelerate, our knowledge of the material and spiritual worlds.

When science and religion, faith and reason, join hands, as in this example, then we can appreciate the statement of 'Abdu'l-Bahá that: 'The sciences of today are bridges to reality', but if these sciences 'lead not to reality, naught remains but fruitless illusion. By the one true God! If learning be not a means of access to Him, the Most Manifest, it is nothing but evident loss.'[14] Unfortunately, materialistic perceptions of the nature of reality are leading humanity down the road to 'evident loss'. However, spiritual perceptions, focused on material and intelligible realities, will allow the mind to unchain itself from the limitations of materialism, a necessary requirement of modern cosmology and physics if it is to progress beyond 'fruitless illusion'.

22

DISBELIEF IN GOD LINKED WITH EXALTING ONE PROPHET ABOVE ANOTHER

One of the chief reasons why I called myself an atheist in my youth was that most followers of a religion believed that through their Prophet/Educator they were 'saved' and the rest were destined for 'damnation'. I remember arrogantly proclaiming to a sincere 'born again' Christian, who was trying to make me aware of a moral way of living (something that held no attraction for me at the time), that 'I would rather go to hell with my friends than to heaven with people like you!' Evidently, I had a lot of work to do on myself. This was greatly helped by understanding one of the major teachings of Bahá'u'lláh – that religion, in essence, is one. It cleared up the alienating 'saved/damned' mindset I had of religion and opened the door to a belief in God, a healthier lifestyle physically and mentally, and a kinder, wiser way of responding to others.

Initially I found one of the most attractive teachings of Bahá'u'lláh to be His emphasis on the oneness of mankind. From the start of Bahá'u'lláh's ministry in 1863 He proclaimed that mankind, with all its diversity, is 'one'. 'Abdu'l-Bahá explained that this teaching is a gift from God to humanity 'in this enlightened age'.[1] Unfortunately, humanity either refused this gift or gave scant attention to it. The world at that time – from the late nineteenth century and during most of the twentieth century – still held centuries-old prejudices exalting one part of the human race over another. In fact, racial prejudice was so entrenched that many believed that some sections of humanity, such as the native inhabitants of Australia, were actually not human beings, while in other parts, such as Africa, the black people were considered sub-human. In particular, but not exclusively, it was the white members of the human race that held these superiorist attitudes.

Consider what happened during the twentieth century to bring about the change of thinking leading to accepting that mankind is, indeed, one. The whole world was visited with unimaginable horrors, giving rise to immense suffering on a scale heretofore unencountered by the human race! Ongoing colonialism was still rampant at the beginning of that century; nationalism found a new outlet in the first of the World Wars; nationalism and racist ideologies swept the planet into the Second World War; and a host of other conflicts continued to bleed the human race dry as a consequence of these and other evils. But, for the most part, chastened and purified, the human race learnt it is one. All this terrifying suffering could have been avoided if a hearing ear had earlier been given to Bahá'u'lláh's teachings.

Just five years into the twenty-first century, a front-page head-line appeared in the media: 'The day the world became one'. Reporting on a string of concerts to 'Make Poverty History' organized by Bob Geldof, a rock musician, an estimated two billion people, a third of the earth's population, watched the Live 8 concerts held in ten different countries. The concerts 'were broadcast on 182 television networks and 2,000 radio networks' worldwide. The 'masses of mankind had become aware that they are indeed "planetary citizens".'[2]

However, is not history repeating itself at the start of the twenty-first century? Instead of the general belief held at the beginning of the twentieth century, that mankind is not one, there is the general belief that religion is not one. At the same time as Bahá'u'lláh presented the gift of God to our age that humanity is one, He also offered another gift – that religion is also fundamentally one, even if it has developed diverse traditions and creeds. Now we must ask ourselves, will it take the whole of the twenty-first century, or even longer, for humanity to realize the fundamental oneness of religion? And will this realization come about after more unimaginable horrors are visited upon the human race, or will it come from heeding the words of God's latest Manifestation?

What then, is stopping people from accepting that religion is essentially one? Many would argue that there are so many religions in the world that it would be impossible for them to unite around the idea that religion is one. Ignorance is so rife regarding the possibility of only one God that it is commonly asked, 'what God do you worship?' When there is strife and dissension between members of different religions and when there is conflict even among those of the same beliefs, it does not inspire confidence that God exists. Inter-religious wars throughout the ages, alongside bloody sectarian conflicts, have drained the cup of love proffered by all the great Manifestations of God.

In the modern world, where peoples of all faiths, beliefs and traditions rub shoulders with each other, an opportunity is created for them to exemplify their core teaching of love for their neighbour. In a minority of cases, we find this is so, but generally, communities of the same religion segregate themselves from others, preferring not to mix with communities of a different persuasion. Fear of being contaminated by peoples of different beliefs is still ubiquitous even in the twenty-first century. Religious fanaticism in the form of terrorism has now surfaced as a planetary evil to the extent that, yet again, the world could experience another conflagration. In a letter to the world's religious leaders appealing to them to 'face honestly and without further evasion the implications of the truth that God is one and that, beyond all diversity of cultural expression and human interpretation, religion is likewise one',[3] the Universal House of Justice (the governing body of the Bahá'í Faith) stated: 'With every day that passes, danger grows that the rising fires of religious prejudice will ignite a worldwide conflagration the consequences of which are unthinkable.'[4]

For many, then, religion is viewed as a significant cause of many problems in the world. So, to understand how so much hatred, strife and conflict has been generated by the followers of the world's religions, who all claim to worship God or a Higher Authority, is fundamental to reclaiming a belief in God by those who have moved into agnosticism or atheism. In an age where religion is increasingly losing its sway over the hearts and minds of people, this is perhaps the most difficult minefield to navigate. It is interesting, however, to note that this process of turning away from God during these times was actually foretold by Christ over 2,000 years ago, when speaking of future events associated with His return, He said, 'because iniquity shall abound, the love of many shall wax cold'.[5]

At the root of religious fanaticism and hatred is the insistence by many followers of religion that only their Manifestation of God is right or is superior to others. These claims of exclusivity and finality compel increasing numbers from each new genera-tion to turn away from belief in God. Such claims have resulted in 'winding their roots around the life of the spirit', and has 'been the greatest single factor in suffocating impulses to unity and in promoting hatred and violence'.[6] Yet, when we examine the sacred scriptures of all the great Faiths, not one of them has claimed exclusivity or finality for itself. On the contrary, they proclaimed the coming of future Prophets or Manifestations of God and that revelation, through these Manifestations, would be continuous. So the Jews expect the 'Everlasting Father', the 'Lord of Hosts'; Christians look forward to Christ returned 'in the glory of the Father'; followers of Shi'ih Islam await the return of the 'Imam Husayn', while those following Sunni Islam expect the descent of the 'Spirit of God' (Jesus); Zoroastrians are promised their 'Shah-Bahram'; Hindus, 'the reincarnation of Krishna'; and Buddhists, the 'fifth Buddha (Maitreya)'.[7] Emphasizing the profound fact that the revelations of God are inexhaustible, and by implication not final, Muhammad, the Messenger of God, stated:

> If all the trees that are upon the earth were to become pens, and if God should after that swell the sea into seven seas of ink, His words would not be exhausted: for God is Mighty, Wise.[8]

Notwithstanding the overwhelming evidence from the sacred scriptures of the world's religions that no one religion is final or exclusive, we find throughout history the majority of their followers, led by their religious leaders, vehemently denying the validity of every new Manifestation of God. So, for instance, history records that the Jews denied Christ as the Messiah, the Jews and Christians denied Muhammad as being the Apostle of God, and the Jews, Christians and Muslims, for the most part, deny Bahá'u'lláh as the Promised One of all religions. It must be said, however, that for a number of souls who believe in the existence of God, there is an intuitive awareness that it is the same One God that is worshipped by the members of the world's faiths. Unfortunately, stubborn and bigoted denial of this fact has done its harm over the centuries. Today, this has shattered into a thousand pieces confidence in the existence of God.

Let us now examine a passage from the Writings of Bahá'u'lláh which clearly states that the revelations given to the human race come from one source, from the One God:

> There can be no doubt whatever that the peoples of the world, of whatever race or religion, derive their inspiration from one heavenly Source, and are the subjects of one God. The difference between the ordinances under which they abide should be attributed to the varying requirements and exigencies of the age in which they were revealed. All of them, except a few which are the outcome of human perversity, were ordained of God, and are a reflection of His Will and Purpose. Arise and, armed with the power of faith, shatter to pieces the gods of your vain imaginings, the sowers of dissension amongst you. Cleave unto that which draweth you together and uniteth

you. This, verily, is the most exalted Word which the Mother Book hath sent down and revealed unto you. To this beareth witness the Tongue of Grandeur from His habitation of glory.[9]

In this passage, Bahá'u'lláh does not deny that there are differences of religious decrees and ordinances between the religions but advances the point that this is because different ages have different needs and require different solutions. In another place Bahá'u'lláh likens the world to the human body which falls prey to varying diseases over the eons of time. He further states that the Manifestations of God, as discussed in a previous chapter, can be seen as divine physicians who prescribe the remedy for the affliction of the age in which they appear. It would be manifestly illogical to prescribe the same remedy for every disease. Further information on this key teaching of the Bahá'í Faith can be found under the heading 'progressive revelation' in many Bahá'í introductory books, and the subject will be developed a little further later on in this chapter; but at present I wish to focus on the insight given by Bahá'u'lláh that those followers of the ancient religions who do not accept that religion is essentially one are actually not worshipping God at all. When we look closely at the passage above, we find that those who cling to one Manifestation of God above others worship 'gods of your [their] vain imaginings' which are 'sowers of dissension amongst you'.

Let me write clearly on this issue. The Jewish believer who does not accept that the revelation of Krishna is from the same Source as the revelation of Moses does not actually believe in God. A Christian who believes that Muslims worship a different God to the Source of Christ's Message does not believe in God. A Zoroastrian who does not believe that Buddha taught about the same God as spoken about by Zoroaster does not believe in God. Those who deny this assertion are only worshipping the idols of their own imagination. Bahá'u'lláh appeals to them to 'Cleave unto that which draweth you together and uniteth you.' For it is these souls who keep mankind divided into contending beliefs and, albeit unconsciously, make their contribution to the environment of religious fanaticism.

When we look upon the Manifestations of God with an unbiased mind, we will find that their spirit is one and that they are all united in service to the One God. So definite is this point that Bahá'u'lláh writes very strongly:

> Whoso recognizeth them hath recognized God. Whoso hearkeneth to their call, hath hearkened to the Voice of God . . . Whoso turneth away from them, hath turned away from God, and whoso disbelieveth in them, hath disbelieved in God. Every one of them is the Way of God that connecteth this world with the realms above, and the Standard of His Truth unto everyone in the kingdoms of earth and heaven. They are the Manifestations of God amidst men, the evidences of His Truth, and the signs of His glory.[10]

Who is it then, that have turned the people away from the Holy Scriptures and the Messengers of God of other religions? There has been a long-standing tendency for too many religious leaders to arrogate to themselves a spurious authority, and channel their unsuspecting followers into theologies, rites and dogmas that are the very negation of the teachings they claim to protect. In a very real sense, the worship of God has been replaced by the worship of religious leaders and their pronouncements; the love of God has been usurped by the fear of hell expounded by these self-same leaders. Consequently, these 'gate-keepers' to the way to truth have barred the way to unity, while at the same time opening a door to all the religious conflict humanity has experienced in the past and is still experiencing today. Like the Siren voices in Homer's tale of Odysseus, they have bewitched the souls of their erstwhile followers, smashed them on the rocks of idolatry and devoured their spirits, leaving them as spiritually dead.

Of course, their followers also must take responsibility, for they have been endowed with an individual mind and are expected to use it to think for themselves. Only in this age, however, do we find masses of people doing this, as they disconnect from superstitious religious teachings and claims to finality and exclusivity, indignant that so many generations have been duped by so few, over such a long period of time. Perhaps such observations as these can be mitigated by the fact that the mass of humanity in past ages had no education, living in a time that was not scientifically developed as now.

The intellectuals of the Age of Enlightenment, following on from the application of the scientific method by such illustrious thinkers as Copernicus and Galileo, were the first to lead many away from superstitious religion into anti-clericalism. But instead of leaving a belief in God firmly intact, a belief that thinkers such as Voltaire in France, Benjamin Franklin and Thomas Jefferson in America rigidly maintained, an increasing number of people are turning to atheistic views contained in the emerging new pseudo-religion of 'scientism', whose 'Enlightenment thinkers had hoped that science could replace religion as a basis for moral values, and thus provide the foundation for a new culture, a modern civilization.'[11] Many now believe that all of humanity's problems are solvable through the application of science!

It stands to reason that if, as Bahá'u'lláh states, all the Manifestations of God are the revealers of God's Will to mankind, then to exalt one above another is grossly unjust. This would be like saying that different teachers who educate children according to their growing capacity are not equal in their work. The Grade 1 teacher is as necessary as the Grade 4 teacher, and so on. This point is clearly made by Bahá'u'lláh in the following passage, ending with startling consequences:

> Beware, O believers in the Unity of God, lest ye be tempted to make any distinction between any of the Manifestations of His Cause, or to discriminate against the signs that have accompanied and proclaimed their Revelation. This indeed is the true meaning of Divine Unity, if ye be of them that

apprehend and believe this truth. Be ye assured, moreover, that the works and acts of each and every one of these Manifestations of God, nay whatever pertaineth unto them, and whatsoever they may manifest in the future, are all ordained by God, and are a reflection of His Will and Purpose. Whoso maketh the slightest possible difference between their persons, their words, their messages, their acts and manners, hath indeed disbelieved in God, hath repudiated His signs, and betrayed the Cause of His Messengers.[12]

Let us look into this passage a little closer. When Bahá'u'lláh uses the word 'beware' He means it in the strongest possible sense. A sign saying, 'Beware, bull in field' or 'Beware, radiation, do not enter', gives some feeling of the possible dangers that could be encountered should we ignore the sign. Whoever installs these signs is fully aware of the grave danger that will ensue from trespassing. The 'beware' sign is therefore a signal coming from a wise, caring and knowledgeable person to protect others from harm. Similarly, God, through Bahá'u'lláh, protects us from harm by alerting us to the dangers ahead – that are hidden, but intimated in the signal 'beware'. Before the dangers are disclosed Bahá'u'lláh informs us, in the above passage, that all the works, every act, and whatever pertains to every Manifestation of God in the past and in the future are all ordained by God and reflect His Will and Purpose. Applying this to the names of some of the Manifestations of God that we know of, He is saying that we should not make any distinction whatsoever between the Persons of Abraham, Moses, Krishna, Buddha, Zoroaster, Jesus, Muhammad, the Báb and Bahá'u'lláh Himself, as well as other Manifestations of God not mentioned. This means, in basic terms, that if a follower of a specific Manifestation of God, for instance, Jesus, holds the slightest feeling that Jesus is superior to any of the other Manifestations of God then he has entered the 'beware' zone.

So, what happens if the 'beware' zone is entered when a person is tempted to believe that his or her Manifestation of God is greater than any other? Well, there are three dangers. The first is that such a person may be adhering to a damagingly limited concept of God. The second is that he has 'repudiated' the signs of God, which means he has refused to recognize and obey the authority of God. Third, he has 'betrayed' the Cause of God, which means he has been disloyal to God and acted treacherously towards Him. Now, these three consequences of entering the 'beware' zone are diametrically opposite to the expectations held by a loyal follower of a specific Messenger of God, for he believes he is the essence of loyalty as he holds his Messenger of God to be greater than others.

We cannot, however, leave these three statements of Bahá'u'lláh without giving some rational explanation as to their reasons or some possible meanings. So, let's start with the first statement: that if a person thinks his Messenger of God is greater than any other Messenger he does not believe in God. The analogy mentioned above about the equality of all teachers, even though they teach different grades, can be helpful here. It is a fact that children require different levels of teaching at their different stages of development. As their capacity increases, a teacher appears who will respond to their growing capacity to understand and increase their knowledge. This process of teaching children a little at a time through different teachers, we call 'education'. Similarly, as the human race has been growing up, its capacities have increased – this we know as an evolutionary process. To meet the needs of humanity's growing capacities our Creator sends His Teachers, His Messengers or Manifestations. This process Bahá'ís call 'religion' even though some Messengers of God reveal more than others, and all have unique personal histories. However, this does not mean that any one of them is higher in station than others. Bahá'u'lláh states that:

> It is clear and evident to thee that all the Prophets are the Temples of the Cause of God, Who have appeared clothed in divers attire. If thou wilt observe with discriminating eyes,

thou wilt behold Them all abiding in the same tabernacle, soaring in the same heaven, seated upon the same throne, uttering the same speech, and proclaiming the same Faith.[13]

The Bearers of the Trust of God are made manifest unto the peoples of the earth as the Exponents of a new Cause and the Revealers of a new Message. Inasmuch as these Birds of the celestial Throne are all sent down from the heaven of the Will of God, and as they all arise to proclaim His irresistible Faith, they, therefore, are regarded as one soul and the same person. For they all drink from the one Cup of the love of God, and all partake of the fruit of the same Tree of Oneness.[14]

'Abdu'l-Bahá offers another way of understanding that religion is essentially one and that the Revealers thereof are to be regarded as one. He states, 'Be seekers of light, no matter from which lantern it shines forth. Be not lovers of the lantern.'[15] And in another place He states:

Light is good in whatsoever lamp it is burning! A rose is beautiful in whatsoever garden it may bloom! A star has the same radiance if it shines from the East or from the West. Be free from prejudice, so will you love the Sun of Truth from whatsoever point in the horizon it may arise! You will realize that if the Divine light of truth shone in Jesus Christ it also shone in Moses and in Buddha. The earnest seeker will arrive at this truth.[16]

Reflection on this passage reveals that we must be 'seekers of light', and light in this instance is a metaphor for a special power sent by God that flows through the Manifestations of God, commonly known as the Holy Spirit. Also, 'light' represents their teachings. If we see a light in a number of different lamps, we recognize that the light has the same qualities – in this case heat and rays that emanate from it. Similarly, if a special soul possesses the power of the Holy Spirit, as do the Manifestations of God, then it is the same power they share. Our challenge as human beings is to recognize the qualities of the light of the Holy Spirit emanating from the Messengers of God. If we truly recognize the light in one of them, then it follows that we will be able to recognize the light in all of them. If, however, we assume we have seen the light in one specific Manifestation but cannot see it in others, then it is questionable as to whether we have seen a light at all. Light is light; we should recognize its qualities anywhere it shines. We must ask, if a person cannot see light, the power of the Holy Spirit, in all the Messengers of God what is he mistaking for light in the particular Messenger he is following? Spurious interpretations, ecclesiastical formed rites and rituals, the splendour and pomp of his specific religion, attachment to centuries-old cultural and traditional practices may all combine to veil such a person from the light. So, when such souls consider whether another Messenger of God possesses the power of the Holy Spirit, he is not looking for the 'light' but only what he thinks is the light, in this case, the 'veils'. That is why it has been mentioned that such souls follow the idols of their own fancies which are veils that obscure them from the light.

'Abdu'l-Bahá in the passage above uses other metaphors, such as if we recognize a rose in one garden, we should be able to recognize a rose in a different garden, as it has the same qualities of fragrance and beauty. If we don't, we are either blind or veiled from it. To only see veils that obscure the light or the beauty of the rose in other gardens is to understand that such a person is blinded to this truth. Although he claims to be a believer in God – he is a believer in his own imagination!

A careful reading of the Holy Scriptures of past religions reveals that this problem, of people being veiled from the new Messenger of God, was always encountered. As mentioned before, it was the religious leaders who, for the most part, were the ones drawing the veils preventing the people from recognizing the new Manifestation. Actually, Bahá'u'lláh calls these religious leaders 'veils of glory':

Among these 'veils of glory' are the divines and doctors living in the days of the Manifestation of God, who, because of their want of discernment and their love and eagerness for leadership, have failed to submit to the Cause of God, nay, have even refused to incline their ears unto the divine Melody. 'They have thrust their fingers into their ears' [Qur'án 2:19]. And the people also, utterly ignoring God and taking them for their masters, have placed themselves unreservedly under the authority of these pompous and hypocritical leaders, for they have no sight, no hearing, no heart, of their own to distinguish truth from falsehood.[17]

To pierce these veils of glory, enabling one to see the beauty of the new Messenger of God with one's own eyes is a great deed

The second assertion is that those who think their Manifestation of God is superior to other Manifestations have 'repudiated' the signs of God, which means they have refused to recognize and obey the authority of God deposited in these signs. Again, to the believer who tenaciously clings to his specific Messenger, denying equality with all the Messengers of God, this assertion will not sit easy. In his mind he has been one of the most loyal and uncompromising believers of his faith and will consider that those who accept equality of the Messengers of God are at best misguided, at worst heretics – worthy of disdain or even persecution.

What then are the 'signs of God' that are repudiated? First, let us examine what is meant by a 'sign'. According to the *Concise Oxford Dictionary* there can be many meanings to the word 'sign'. The meaning which seems appropriate for this purpose is 'a thing indicating or suggesting a quality or state'. Applying this meaning to 'signs of God', it must mean that a 'sign of God' indicates or suggests a quality or state of God. The Bahá'í Writings are replete with evidence of these qualities of God which are plain to see, providing we have spiritual eyes to see them. On this point 'Abdu'l-Bahá states:

The favours of God are all-surrounding, but should the conscious eye of the soul of man remain veiled and darkened, he will be led to deny these universal signs and remain deprived of these manifestations of divine bounty. Therefore, we must endeavour with heart and soul in order that the veil covering the eye of inner vision may be removed, that we may behold the manifestations of the signs of God, discern His mysterious graces and realize that material blessings as compared with spiritual bounties are as nothing.[18]

If someone behaves in an exemplary spiritual way, he will 'manifest clearly the signs of the one true God'.[19] Unfortunately, because the masses of humanity are 'out of touch with the world of God . . . we do not see the signs of God in the hearts of men'.[20] Therefore, because we only rarely, perhaps never, come into contact with souls who manifest these signs, we believe they do not exist. Such souls who manifest the signs of God will be detached from all earthly things, will commit their lives to drawing people together in bonds of love and fellowship, will be willing to sacrifice for the benefit of others, love others unconditionally, overlook their faults, be forgiving and forbearing, promote the development of arts, crafts and sciences, and a host of other wholesome things. All these qualities can be summed up as making a good character. In a reference to this Bahá'u'lláh writes:

> The light of a good character surpasseth the light of the sun and the radiance thereof . . . A goodly character is a means whereby men are guided to the Straight Path and are led to the Great Announcement. Well is it with him who is adorned with the saintly attributes and character of the Concourse on High.[21]

Sadly, those who exalt one Manifestation of God above another only inadequately 'discern His [God's] mysterious graces' and therefore do not have a fuller realization, as mentioned above, 'that material blessings as compared with spiritual bounties are as nothing'. These souls are inclined to look at outward evidences which they feel proves God's existence, such as the pomp and pageantry of religious leaders and their institutions, or the physical fulfilment of prophecies in their Holy Scriptures that are meant to be taken symbolically. Consequently, when a new Manifestation of God appears, and does not come according to their expectations, they repudiate such a glorious Soul. For instance, when Jesus came, the Jews were expecting a king as their Messiah; Jesus was of the poor and lowly with no place to lay His head – yet He was a spiritual king, if they had the spiritual eyes to see.

'Abdu'l-Bahá states that 'the Holy Manifestations are the focal centres of the heavenly bounties, signs, and perfections (of God). Blessed are those who receive the light of divine bounties from those luminous Daysprings!'[22] Those who are alive at the time of any Manifestation of God and attain their presence have the inestimable privilege of experiencing from them obvious signs indicating the existence of God. Bahá'u'lláh relates that every Manifestation of God reflects the qualities of God in the world of creation. In reference to humanity, they are those qualities. In a prayer praising God He writes, 'Glory be to Thee, O My God, for Thy Manifestation of love to mankind. O thou Who art our Life and Light . . .'[23]

The Manifestations of God, then, are not just human beings who try to be loving, wise, compassionate, just and the like. They are those qualities of love, wisdom, compassion and justice. Meeting any one of them is to meet with all the qualities of God perfectly expressed, for humanity to relate to, in such a powerful way. For those who seek the 'light' and not that which covers it (the veils), their belief in the existence of God is enkindled and takes on new and thrilling dimensions. These souls are overwhelmed by the Manifestation's majesty, perfect love, divine power and authority. When every new Manifestation of God appears, it is these souls who are the first to accept Him, the first to recognize the signs of God in their person, the first to sacrifice their all in the path of God, the first to lay the foundations of a new civilization in advance of that which preceded it.

The third assertion of Bahá'u'lláh is that those who believe their particular Manifestation of God is superior to others have 'betrayed the Cause of His Messengers'.[24] How then, for instance, has a Christian betrayed the Cause of Christ if he does not accept Muhammad as a Messenger of God? Or how has a Buddhist betrayed the Cause of Buddha if He does not accept Moses as a Messenger of God? Betrayal is a very strong word and implies that one has not been faithful to a pledge one has made. For instance, if a person commits adultery, which is an act of treachery, he or she has not been loyal to their marriage vows to remain faithful. If you said to a Christian that he has betrayed the Cause of Christ by not accepting Muhammad as a Messenger of God, he would be most affronted. If you further pressed this point and stated that he had committed a treacherous act of infidelity by not doing so, then it is likely that, at the very least, he may never speak to you again.

To be faithful to the Cause of God implies that one has made a pledge, a commitment to follow faithfully the teachings of a Messenger of God. A careful examination of all the Holy Scriptures of the past religions reveals that each Founder has left a promise that another Messenger of God would be sent by the Almighty in the future. The purpose of the Messengers of God is to reinvigorate the spiritual life of humanity and bring guidance to meet the needs of a new age. This point has been made earlier. However, we must ask: to what extent do the followers of a specific Messenger of God take their guidance seriously? And if they take it seriously, have they abdicated their responsibility to be watchful for the coming of the Promised One mentioned in their Holy Scriptures and placed it in the hands of a minister of religion? It is the duty, therefore, of every follower of a Messenger of God to apprise himself of these teachings and prepare himself for the coming of that Expected One.

In the Bahá'í Writings there is great emphasis on being faithful to the Covenant of God; further reading of these Writings reveals that there are two types of Covenant. The one overarching Covenant is called the Greater Covenant, which refers to the process mentioned above with an emphasis on following the latest of God's Manifestations. The other is called the Lesser Covenant, which can be discussed another time. In each and every Holy Scripture there are teachings which refer the followers to expect within the one religion of God another Manifestation in the future, Who will come with more guidance for mankind. Moses did not start a new religion from Abraham Who preceded Him. Christ did not start a new religion to that of Moses; Muhammad did not start a new religion to Christ, Moses and Abraham. Bahá'u'lláh did not start a new religion to Muhammad, Christ, Moses, or Abraham. All of them linked their works with the Messengers that preceded them and referred their followers to see their works as one process, educating the human race a little at a time. 'This is the changeless Faith of God, eternal in the past, eternal in the future,'[25] declares Bahá'u'lláh. It is the religious leaders and their unthinking followers who have divided religion into separate religions competing for adherents. How egregious a work that is! However, this is not a static situation but just another barrier that will be overcome when more and more people understand the process of 'progressive revelation'. Sadly, for this to happen it seems that more suffering is in store for humanity:

We are moving from a fixed place of belief in just one Messenger of God, which, although far from ideal, was understandable in an unintegrated world, to an integrated world that has exposed us to the followers of many Messengers of God. To insist that only one Manifestation of God is right, or superior to others is to spread religious fanaticism and hatred which Bahá'u'lláh describes as 'a world-devouring fire, whose violence none can quench. The Hand of Divine power can, alone, deliver mankind from this desolating affliction . . .'[26]

Suffice it to say that those followers of the ancient religions who do not accept the latest Manifestation, Bahá'u'lláh, have actually broken their pledge to do so, or, put another way, broken the Greater Covenant that all the Manifestations of God established to guarantee the progress of humanity. In the last analysis, those who have betrayed the Cause of God by exalting one Messenger above another, have actually seriously impeded the development of a world civilization based upon spiritual values, and make their contribution to the horrific misery the world has experienced over so long a period of time.

23

HELL – JUSTICE AND FORGIVENESS

The subject of heaven and hell is of interest to many people, even if only a cursory one. For me it was all-consuming after the sudden death of my brother, Peter. Reading the Bahá'í Writings on life after death has been very illuminating and reassuring; in comparison to the ancient Faiths, these Writings are quite extensive. One of the life-influencing concepts embedded in all religious scripture is that of making progress spiritually. For those who made spiritual progress, 'heaven' was promised, while to those who neglected or spurned spiritual progress, 'hell' was the consequence. So, let's turn our intention firstly to the subject of 'hell'.

The traditional concept of hell is that it is a place. This misconception has done much to damage the relationship between the soul of man and God and has gone a long way to producing the materialistic age in which we now find ourselves. My wife, as a young girl and an active member of the Catholic Church, was told by her priest that hell was being put inside a steel box and roasted over a fire forever. Such superstitious teachings still abound, having originated from some influential Christian philosophers down the ages. St Augustine, for example, writing in the 5th century CE, was committed to a retributive theory of hell as punishment for wrongdoing. To him:

> the primary purpose of punishment is to satisfy the demands of justice or, as some might say, to balance the scales of justice.

And the Augustinian commitment to such a theory is hardly surprising. For based upon his interpretation of various New Testament texts, Augustine insisted that hell is a literal lake of fire in which the damned will experience the horror of ever-lasting torment; they will experience, that is, the unbearable physical pain of literally being burned forever. The primary purpose of such unending torment, according to Augustine, is not correction, or deterrence, or even the protection of the innocent; nor did he make any claim for it except that it is fully deserved and therefore just. As for how such torment could be even physically possible, Augustine insisted further that 'by a miracle of their most omnipotent Creator, they [living creatures who are damned] can burn without being consumed, and suffer without dying' (City of God, Book 21, ch 9). Such is the metaphysics of hell, as Augustine understood it.[1]

Why there has been such an emphasis on the nature of hell as some form of eternal torment may be due to the control it offered the clergy over church members over the centuries. Such control did little to stimulate personal responsibility for one's spiritual development, which was instead arrogated to ministers of religion who acted as intermediaries between God and their congregation. It must be remembered that for nearly the entire time of Christianity its followers were the illiterate, uneducated masses, easily manipulated by superstitious doctrines, and often oppressed by hierarchies of church and state. They were kept in their place by a double tyranny – fear of temporal punishment and fear of eternal damnation. Yet the teachings of Christ are full of the promise of forgiveness by God for sins and waywardness. Indeed, in the Lord's Prayer, the only prayer Christ left to humanity, there is an emphasis on developing a forgiving nature, with clear admonition in another place not to make judgements about others: 'For with what judgment ye judge, ye shall be judged: and with what measure ye mete, it shall be measured to you again.'[2] But those who wish to hold to a concept of eternal damnation have only one text of the Gospels to call on and it is this:

> Verily I say unto you, All sins shall be forgiven unto the sons of men, and blasphemies wherewith soever they shall blaspheme: But he that shall blaspheme against the Holy Ghost hath never forgiveness, but is in danger of eternal damnation.[3]

Even this text of Christ does not categorically state that someone will be eternally damned but is in 'danger' of being so. 'Abdu'l-Bahá gives an interpretation of this text without which it is most difficult to understand. Christ is not referring to souls who have committed terrible crimes, even heinous crimes. It is a reference to that rare number of individuals who are fully aware of the light of love, compassion, forgiveness, and the like, emanating from a Manifestation of God, but have an aversion to it and loathe 'divine perfections themselves'.[4] One such soul in Christian history was Judas Iscariot, a leading disciple of Christ who opposed the spiritual power of Christ, referred to as the Holy Ghost.

However, we have to square the concept of 'eternal damnation' with such statements of Bahá'u'lláh related to the greatness of God's mercy:

> The greatness of His mercy surpasseth the fury of His wrath, and His grace encompasseth all who have been called into being and been clothed with the robe of life, be they of the past or of the future.[5]

Shoghi Effendi, the Guardian of the Bahá'í Faith, also points out that others can also be involved in bringing God's forgiveness to wrongdoers and that they can make spiritual progress in the world beyond:

> . . . we believe that God's Mercy exceeds His Justice, and that through the repentance of a soul, the prayers and supplications

of other souls, and the goodness of God, even a person who has passed away in great spiritual darkness can be forgiven, educated spiritually in the next world and progress.[6]

Further, how do we understand concepts of God being 'All-Forgiving' and 'Ever-Forgiving'? Surely, we must conclude that no matter what sins are committed there must come a time, in this world or the next, that God's forgiveness, or perhaps His pardon, is visited upon transgressors. A statement of Christ bears out this possibility, when an offender, after wrongdoing, is promised that: 'Verily I say unto thee, Thou shalt by no means come out thence, till thou hast paid the uttermost farthing.'[7] This a clear statement of redemption if put another way. Christ is basically saying that when a wrongdoer has paid his time in prison in relation to the seriousness of his crime, exacted to the last moment decreed by justice, he will then be set free. In other words, the application of justice does not decree that a soul will for the rest of its existence, which is for eternity, receive eternal damnation.

Having been commissioned by God to act on His behalf in this world as perfect examples of 'right living', the Manifestations bring down to earth applications of the forgiveness of God. We could do no better than to survey the lives of the Manifestations of God for an understanding of His mercy and forgiveness. Here is a moving example from Christ, at the time He was on the cross, suffering a most painful end to His earthly life. For those that persecuted Him and secured His martyrdom, He pleaded with God: 'Father, forgive them; for they know not what they do.'[8]

Some may object to this assessment of the working out of justice in this way. They may feel that the crimes of a small number of human beings have been so great, so heinous, that they do not deserve any forgiveness or pardon from God, ever! But supposing such forgiveness was given in the world beyond after the equivalent of the passing of millions of years in this world, as the working of justice – surely this would appear as an eternity of damnation to that tyrannical oppressor? Even so, we must reflect on the attribute of God, the All-Forgiving. As the word clearly states, God forgives all, with no exceptions. Also, God is ready to forgive any wrongdoing great or small even before it is committed, which is what the act of 'forgiving' means – 'inclined readily to forgive'.[9] Further, because God is 'Ever-Forgiving' He forgives every human being that has ever lived, every human being that is alive now and every human being that will live in the future. When contemplating God's forgiveness, it would not be unreasonable to conclude that if, for example, God does not forgive someone spiritually malignant, He would cease to be God. But forgiveness does not necessarily imply that a wrongdoer remains unpunished for his sins; the justice of God must also be in operation. Even if the most heinous tyrant is forgiven, the fact should not be overlooked that his soul will have to carry, throughout eternity, the memory of his tyranny. Bahá'u'lláh assures us that, 'By My beauty! All your doings hath My pen graven with open characters upon tablets of chrysolite.'[10] How does one escape from such guilt and shame as are bound to follow?

Another consideration is that God can pardon a soul for his sins, which means that an offender will not receive the full sentence he deserves – he is 'let off' his punishment, so to speak. In the last analysis we must admit that when God applies any of His attributes, such as forgiveness, pardon, justice, mercy, compassion and the like, to specific individual cases, then we cannot dogmatically state what the All-Knowing, All-Wise Creator should do. Indeed, all these considerations reveal the complexity of making any categorical human statement on the subject. The best we humans can do is to be conscious that any attempt at so doing is like trying to walk a tightrope. However, Bahá'u'lláh has revealed an insight into the prerogative of God and His Manifestations that builds confidence in the decrees, understandings and teaching that flow to humanity from them. For we are informed:

He ordaineth as He pleaseth, by virtue of His sovereignty, and doeth whatsoever He willeth at His own behest. He shall not be asked of the things it pleaseth Him to ordain. He, in truth, is the Unrestrained, the All-Powerful, the All-Wise.[11]

This said, we may ask: what is the reason for the punishment of God? Is it to totally annihilate souls, to wipe them out such that there is no positive reason for bringing them into existence in the first place? Surely this cannot be correct, as it would also be incorrect to assume that God brings some souls into being just to be evil. Surely there is a deeper rationale for punishment other than retribution? As all humanity are children of our heavenly Father, we could do well to ask why we punish our children whom we love unreservedly. Wise parents' answers are – not for retribution. Parents sanction their children as a means of correcting their behaviour, to raise their awareness of wrongdoing, to evoke a contrite spirit, to stimulate the spirit of atonement for wrongdoing, and the like. If parents are wise and loving when training their children, can we not expect an even greater, perfect wisdom and love from our heavenly Father as He trains us? Sanctions for wrongdoing are aimed at encouraging wrongdoers to realize that they are damaging not only others, but their own selves, by placing obstacles in the way of releasing God-given potential. Interesting statements from most of those who undertake a review of their life during a 'near death experience' supports this. They report that for every hurt they inflicted on someone else, they experience that hurt returned to them with greater intensity. So, in fact, to hurt another is really to impede spiritual progress and hurt oneself.

An interesting interpretation of the meaning of 'hell' and 'heaven' is given by the philosopher Ralph Waldo Trine in his book *In Tune with the Infinite*. He writes:

> The word heaven means harmony. The word hell is from the Old English hell, meaning to build a wall around, to separate; to be helled was to be shut off from. Now if there is such a thing as harmony there must be that something one can be in

right relations with; for to be in right relations with anything is to be in harmony with it. Again, if there is such a thing as being helled, shut off, separated from, there must be that something from which one is helled, shut off, or separated.[12]

Hell is an internal condition, which has been described symbolically in the past as being consumed by fire, falling into a pit or deep abyss, as a bad or ill journey, a prison, a dark raging world, a place of torture, eaten by worms that don't die, grievous punishment and so on. An analogy given by Buddha seems to sum up the condition of being in hell, whether in this world or the next. He states: 'Just as the rust which develops on iron, derives from it but then proceeds to eat it away, so a person of unrestrained behaviour is drawn to hell by his own actions.'[13] So we can observe that a person is in 'hell' if overcome by the 'fire' of self – which could be extreme anger or jealousy, or has fallen into a 'deep abyss' through alcohol or drug abuse or addictive gambling; or set out on an 'ill journey' planning revenge or dissension; or is so grief-stricken and sorrowful they have put themselves in an internal 'prison'; or have made so many unwise choices that they have lost all hope and remain in 'darkness'; or experience the 'torture' of shame when aware of the cruel acts they have committed; or constant regret, remorse or disillusionment eats into their soul like 'worms' eat into a body because of sins of omission or commission. And so it continues, that the negative consequences experienced in the soul in varying degrees for wrongdoing, that have been described symbolically, are carried over into the next world if not remedied. And this is achieved, sooner or later, through awareness of, and taking responsibility for, wrongdoing, and seeking God's forgiveness or pardon. Indeed, if the wrongdoing is not acknowledged and atoned for in this life there are even more severe consequences in the world beyond. In all religions there is emphasis on the fact that what we do in this life greatly affects the soul in the world beyond. Bahá'u'lláh also dwells on this theme in several Tablets, one of which gives the insightful analogy of a soul who escapes punishment in this world but not the application of justice:

> Bahá'u'lláh . . . uses the example of a man who steals a seed of a tree from someone in the spring season. If he returns it to its owner in that same season, he has cleared his debt and does not owe him anything else. But if he fails to give it back in the spring, what does he owe him in the summer? He owes him a tree and its fruits, because to give back the seed in the summer is useless. This analogy explains that if the individual pays for his misdeeds in this life by receiving the punishment which is ordained in the Holy Writings, his burden of sin will be far lighter in the next life. Otherwise, who knows how heavily his soul will have to pay if he somehow avoids punishment in this world.[14]

The Bahá'í understanding of 'hell' is to be far away from God, to be 'helled up' from moving closer to God because of one's wrongdoing. Sinners have been held back 'by reason of what their hands have wrought', states Bahá'u'lláh.[15] One can clearly see that the following statement of 'Abdu'l-Bahá places the real meaning of hell to be related to those who 'possess a character that is evil and unsound':

> Good character must be taught. Light must be spread afar, so that, in the school of humanity, all may acquire the heavenly characteristics of the spirit, and see for themselves beyond any doubt that there is no fiercer hell, no more fiery abyss, than to possess a character that is evil and unsound; no more darksome pit nor loathsome torment than to show forth qualities which deserve to be condemned.[16]

Over and above a general understanding of the operation of the law of justice and forgiveness is an element on which Bahá'u'lláh places great significance. It falls under the general prerogative of God, as discussed above, that He can do whatever He wants, whenever He wants, and it is not for those whom He has created to question His authority. As an example of this, Shoghi Effendi writes that on the first day of Riḍván, 21 April 1863, Bahá'u'lláh characterized it:

> as the Day whereon 'all created things were immersed in the sea of purification,' whilst in one of His specific Tablets, He has referred to it as the Day whereon 'the breezes of forgiveness were wafted over the entire creation'.[17]

Yet another soul-stirring statement from Bahá'u'lláh is in similar vein:

> The celestial Youth, hidden ere now within the inviolable treasuries of God, hath appeared, even as the Sun of Reality and the Eternal Spirit, from the Dawning-Place of changeless splendour, adorned with the ornament of the Almighty and the beauty of the All-Praised. He hath rescued all who are in heaven and on earth from the perils of death and extinction, clothed them in the garment of true and everlasting existence, and bestowed upon them a new life.[18]

These are astounding statements that fully exemplify this prerogative of God. Consider, not only were all created things totally purified and forgiven by God on the first day of Riḍván, but we are also informed that everyone, whether in this world or the next, has been rescued from death and extinction and given a new life. As the soul cannot die, I take such a statement to mean that souls are rescued from spiritual death and extinction. I understand this wondrous decree of God to point in the direction of a completely new, fresh beginning for humanity upon planet Earth and in the world beyond.

It may be somewhat trite to say this is a unique spiritual 'amnesty' for all peoples of the past, but this is the closest I can come to understanding this decree. We may ask why such a date as 21 April 1863, which Bahá'ís know as the first day of a special twelve-day period called 'Riḍván', is such an important date. The answer is quite simple but may be quite difficult to accept by materialistically minded people. This period was the specific time Bahá'u'lláh made his first declaration as to His most majestic station as the Promised One of all religions and peoples. Put analogously, this is the date Bahá'u'lláh publicly proclaimed He was the 'Divine Physician' that had been sent by God to effect the total transformation of humanity in a global remedy of divine healing for all the world's ills. To those having difficulty with this concept I would ask, what other act of grace and forgiveness bestowed upon humanity by an Ever-Forgiving Creator matches, indeed warrants, such a proclamation, should that proclamation be true?

There is a parallel here in terms of the promise of redemption for the followers of the Messengers of God in the ancient religions – for Christians, through the crucifixion of Christ. But this is not a 'one time' affair located in just one Messenger. In different ways and in different words they have all offered souls the gift of redemption should such souls heed their call. And part of heeding their call is to accept, heart and soul, the latest Manifestation of God.

Be that as it may, in no way does Bahá'u'lláh's decree of purification and forgiveness imply that the human race, after the revelation of these words, can commit unseemly acts with impunity. Put in an analogous way, all humanity, on the first Day of Riḍván, was bathed clean, after this it still has its responsibility to remain clean. Unfortunately, this fresh start, this new beginning for the human race, this grace, this magnanimity, this outpouring of love and forgiveness of our Maker was totally ignored, except by Bahá'u'lláh's ardent followers. The path of horror humanity has chosen since the decree of purification was pronounced has been heart-breaking. Humanity has committed many atrocities – perhaps more than the sum total of the whole of history prior to this time. What a shame for this age, a shame never before experienced by humanity on such a scale.

In everything to do with progress towards God or remoteness from Him, there are degrees, there is no state of absolute closeness or remoteness. One could say the further away from God we are, the more tormenting our experience of the hell-like condition, whereas the closer we are to God the more we are wrapped in a sense of security, well-being, ecstasy and joy.

24

HEAVEN – INNER CONDITION OR DESTINATION?

Just as the ancient descriptions of hell were symbolic, suited to humanity's child-like phase of development and not to be taken literally, so too are the ancient texts related to 'heaven'.

One thing we note from the scriptures of the Old and the New Testament is that heaven is where God lives.[1] Then there are the many parables of Christ describing in symbolic language what the kingdom of heaven is like. Christ also describes Himself as 'the bread of life …which cometh down from heaven, and giveth life unto the world.'[2] He also promised that God's kingdom and His will 'be done in earth, as it is in heaven'.[3] Of all the words of Christ on this subject one statement is not an allegory but infers that the kingdom of God and heaven are synonymous. He said, 'the kingdom of God is within you'.[4]

When Muhammad came to the idolatrous, barbaric tribes of Arabia some 600 years after Christ, He adapted His knowledge of heaven to meet the educational and spiritual limitations of a very 'literal' people. Hence, Muhammad's description of heaven was couched in solid, concrete terms that would appeal to their level of spiritual development. The Qur'án, for instance, describes heaven as a 'Garden which the righteous are promised',[5] the 'meadows of Paradise',[6] 'storied pavilions beneath which . . . the rivers flow'.[7]

Marzieh Gail writes that Muhammad

speaks of the gardens of delight, and the cup that shall not oppress the sense, of the houris with faces fair as ostrich eggs, of the ever-blooming youths going roundabout with goblets, of lote-trees and acacias, of soft green cushions and delicate carpets. (Qurán 55,56, 37). He says of the believers in Paradise, 'No vain discourse shall they hear therein, nor any falsehood, but only the cry, "Peace! Peace!" (56:24–25).[8]

Each of these symbols in the above statements has a spiritual meaning which can be interpreted correctly only by the Manifestations of God or His Chosen Ones. The gift of authoritative interpretation is not given to any individual that falls outside the station of these exalted Souls. Christ makes clear, for instance, that the 'bread of heaven' is the Word of God, revealed at that time through Himself. Perhaps the most misunderstood symbolism in the above references is that pertaining to 'houris'. Many Muslims understand houris to be literally beautiful maidens 'who are the companions of the faithful in paradise' even if the more enlightened realize that the term signifies 'spiritual qualities or powers'.[9]

Much of what has been written about heaven in the past has focused on it as a place one goes after physical death. So we find dictionary definitions such as heaven 'in some religions, (is) the place, sometimes imagined to be in the sky, where God or the gods live and where good people are believed to go after they die, so that they can enjoy perfect happiness'.[10] Another definition states heaven is a 'place regarded in various religions as the abode of God (or the gods) and the angels, and of the good after death, often traditionally depicted as being above the sky'.[11] Such definitions fall seriously short of what a mature, intelligent person, these days, can accept!

Of course, we can still think of heaven as a destination, but a more mature way is to regard heaven as a state of 'being'. 'The best way to get to heaven is to take it with you,' wrote Henry Drummond, the Scottish evangelist, biologist, writer and lecturer (1851–97). The concept of heaven as an inner condition of 'being', approximates more with the words of Christ that 'the kingdom of God is within you'.[12]

Also, the traditional view of heaven holds that heaven is what you experience if you are a good person, after death. From what has been written above there is a big implication. If, as Christ states, 'the kingdom of God is within' and, as Drummond writes, that it is a state that can be taken with you, then we do not have to wait to experience heaven after death — we can be in heaven while here, in this physical world. 'Abdu'l-Bahá has made a profound statement on this point. He declares, 'Existential paradise and hell are to be found in all the worlds of God, whether in this world or in the heavenly realms of the spirit . . .'[13]

So, let's look into this point a little to advance a possible understanding of it. Supposing we divide humanity into those who are profoundly spiritually mature and those who are just about as evil as you can get. In between these extremes there are varying degrees of spiritual maturity, the number of spiritually mature and evil people being very small, with the mass of humanity somewhere between the two extremes. In statistical terms, we could see this represented by the bell-like shape of a normal curve of distribution. So, to get some handle on what is meant by spiritual maturity we can refer to the beautiful words of 'Abdu'l-Bahá, who writes:

> As for you, O ye lovers of God, make firm your steps in His Cause, with such resolve that ye shall not be shaken though the direst of calamities assail the world. By nothing, under no conditions, be ye perturbed. Be ye anchored fast as the high mountains, be stars that dawn over the horizon of life, be bright lamps in the gatherings of unity, be souls humble and lowly in the presence of the friends, be innocent in heart. Be ye symbols of guidance and lights of godliness, severed from the world, clinging to the handhold that is sure and strong, spreading abroad the spirit of life, riding the Ark of salvation. Be ye daysprings of generosity, dawning-points of

the mysteries of existence, sites where inspiration alighteth, rising-places of splendours, souls that are sustained by the Holy Spirit, enamoured of the Lord, detached from all save Him, holy above the characteristics of humankind, clothed in the attributes of the angels of heaven, that ye may win for yourselves the highest bestowal of all, in this new time, this wondrous age.[14]

As can be seen from this statement, spiritual maturity is not just a matter of being friendly and kind, supporting charity, caring for the family, attending church, mosque or temple, reciting a few prayers daily and the like, as important as these can be. It is something much, much higher and is directly connected to recognizing Bahá'u'lláh as the Manifestation of God for this 'wondrous age' and following what He says – that is why the statement above opens with the encouragement to 'make firm your steps in His Cause', which is the Cause of God for this day.

Conversely, let us receive an indication of the characteristics of an evil person by looking at another statement by 'Abdu'l-Bahá:

. . . when man does not open his mind and heart to the blessing of the spirit, but turns his soul towards the material side, towards the bodily part of his nature, then is he fallen from his high place and he becomes inferior to the inhabitants of the lower animal kingdom. In this case the man is in a sorry plight! For if the spiritual qualities of the soul, open to the breath of the Divine Spirit, are never used, they become atrophied, enfeebled, and at last incapable; whilst the soul's material qualities alone being exercised, they become terribly powerful – and the unhappy, misguided man, becomes more savage, more unjust, more vile, more cruel, more malevolent than the lower animals themselves. All his aspirations and desires being strengthened by the lower side of the soul's nature, he becomes more and more brutal, until his whole being is in no way superior to that of the beasts that perish.

Men such as this plan to work evil, to hurt and to destroy; they are entirely without the spirit of Divine compassion, for the celestial quality of the soul has been dominated by that of the material.[15]

All people on planet Earth, whether spiritually mature or evil and all those in between, occupy the same planet – they co-exist. There is not one specific place for evil people, nor is there a specific place where the spiritually mature live. It becomes obvious that if a person's inner condition is good and pure, as that described above by 'Abdu'l-Bahá, then that soul is already in heaven while still on earth. On the other hand, an evil person, with all those evil characteristics mentioned, is in hell while still on earth. In the words of 'Abdu'l-Bahá: 'there is no fiercer hell, no more fiery abyss, than to possess a character that is evil and unsound; no more darksome pit nor loathsome torment than to show forth qualities which deserve to be condemned.'[16]

Another major difference between the spiritually mature person and an evil person is that of consciousness or awareness. The spiritually mature are fully aware they are in heaven while still on earth, whereas an evil person, for the most part, is totally ignorant of his low position which has placed him in the condition of hell. 'The root cause of wrongdoing is ignorance, and we must therefore hold fast to the tools of perception and knowledge,' writes 'Abdu'l-Bahá.[17] From this insightful statement we can conclude that if a wrongdoer becomes aware that he is ignorant and is perceptive of bad consequences to be visited upon him in this world or the next, it is an inducement for a change of heart and the powerful quality of contrition to take hold of his soul. That moment is the start of a wayward soul's journey back to God. To begin this journey all he has to do, metaphorically, is turn on the spot so that he no longer has his back to the light, even if he has not taken one step towards it. Spiritual progress through attraction to the light can then be made, even if the first steps are faltering.

If we now approximate varying degrees of spiritual progress, or the lack of it, in symbolic terms, we could say that the lowest level humans occupy in the inner condition is that of the mineral, a higher stage is that of the vegetable, higher still is that of the animal and yet higher is that of a human and even higher is that of a human possessing the 'spirit of faith'. All these categories, symbolically represented, are occupied by humans who exist side by side on planet Earth. When the veils of the physical body no longer exist after death, differences or degrees of spiritual stations, as mentioned above, carry on. There is 'life' in all these stages but in varying degrees; the highest degree has life in abundance. All these stages not only exist side by side in the physical world, but also in the spiritual world beyond, indeed, in all the infinite worlds of God. Also implied by this analogy is that spiritual awareness and development can progress through each of these stages; no one is stuck (held back) forever at any specific stage. In each of these worlds, whether physical or one of the infinite levels of spiritual worlds created by our Creator, there are lower and higher stages. The lower stage in comparison to a higher stage is compared to 'hell' and the higher stage is compared to 'heaven'. It may be for these reasons that 'Abdu'l-Bahá stated that 'paradise and hell are to be found in all the worlds of God, whether in this world or in the heavenly realms of the spirit . . .'[18]

In fact, some differing categories or levels are mentioned in the long obligatory prayer revealed by Bahá'u'lláh. There He refers to four levels of being, the first is that of 'all created things', then the level of 'the Concourse on high,' next comes the level of 'the all-highest Paradise', and beyond them 'the Tongue of Grandeur itself from the all-glorious Horizon'.[19] It is within this framework that the following mysterious statement, quoted by 'Abdu'l-Bahá, seems to fit: 'The good deeds of the righteous are the sins of the near ones.'[20]

Bahá'u'lláh points to a principle of how souls separate themselves into varying levels of spiritual development and reveals a law of God that none can break, avoid or overpass. It revolves around what company we feel comfortable in coupled with what activities we engage in. Those who have little control over their sexual appetites, for instance, will seek similar company. Conversely, these souls will not feel comfortable when associating with those who lead a chaste and holy life. Those who are immersed in a materialistic lifestyle, to give another example, will find undesirable the company of those who have renounced the world and have developed spiritual lifestyles. Hence, we can find all manner of different communities on planet Earth, bound together by the pleasure they receive from association with those who seek the same things. So it is in the next world – without, of course, any physical ability to gratify one's earthly desires. Regarding this general principle of separation, Bahá'u'lláh writes:

> O Son of Desire! Give ear unto this: Never shall mortal eye recognize the everlasting Beauty, nor the lifeless heart delight in aught but in the withered bloom. For like seeketh like, and taketh pleasure in the company of its kind.[21]

We need to take our investigation into some of the important aspects of heaven, and by association, the subject of hell, a little further. We have considered heaven or hell as a condition we carry within us here on earth, that when we physically die, we enter the very first spiritual world that is considered heaven, if we have prepared for it, and hell if we have not. Another Bahá'í analogy can help us understand how important it is to prepare for the next world. This is like a healthy baby just born, who has all its bodily parts and faculties perfectly developed in the womb, wherein he was prepared and ready to take advantage of all the wonderful things God has created in this physical world. This could be considered physical heaven. Similarly, if a bodily part or function is not developed in the womb of its mother, say eyesight, then that child will not be able to see all the beauty God has created in this physical world when born. This could be considered physical hell. Preparation for the next life involves acquiring spiritual faculties and powers; for those who neglect preparation or ignore what needs to be developed, then the absence of spiritual faculties and powers is essentially hell.

We have also considered that there are different levels of spiritual progress in all the infinite worlds of God, with the implication that we humans are destined to travel through these worlds on the way back to our Maker. But the rate of progress along this route is different according to our actions in this life, and what God wills for us related to His beneficence, grace, mercy, compassion, bounty, justice, forgiveness, pardon and the like. Along this journey we will associate and feel comfortable with those on the same level of spiritual development and conversely feel uncomfortable, not prepared or not worthy, outside this comfort zone, in relation to those on a higher level, until, that is, we are ready to move higher. Then the assistance of God to progress is invoked. Bahá'u'lláh offers an insight into the different levels that separate human beings from each other:

> They that are of the same grade and station are fully aware of one another's capacity, character, accomplishments and merits. They that are of a lower grade, however, are incapable of comprehending adequately the station, or of estimating the merits, of those that rank above them.[22]

Let us now consider something which is at the very heart of an understanding about spiritual progress. What prompts us in the first place, we may ask, to look higher than the material world in which we are deeply embedded? What is the source, the motive power for all transformation from a lower condition to a higher one? We may look to our own selves and think, 'I can do it, I'm my own source of moving from a base condition (hell) to an exalted station (heaven).' We may look at others and take a lesson from some as how not to behave, and from others as an inspiration of heavenly conduct. We may even read sacred scriptures from the great spiritual teachers of mankind and regard these as our source. We may even think: 'All I have to do is make a direct link between myself and God, then I don't need anything else, as I've gone directly to the highest source for all transformation.'

May I suggest that there are flaws in each of these approaches? Let's take the first two – looking only to ourselves or to others for the source of transformation. Let us consider that each soul is like a seed with all its wonderful potential stored inside, and let us then ask, is it possible for that seed by itself or by close proximity to other seeds to release all its potential without the sunshine? Of course not. Similarly, it is obvious that for the soul's spiritual development it needs a power outside itself, a power that, analogously, is as the sunshine for our souls. Bahá'u'lláh states that all man's potential is 'latent within him, even as the flame is hidden within the candle and the rays of light are potentially present in the lamp,' and further: 'Neither the candle nor the lamp can be lighted through their own unaided efforts . . .'[23]

We may think that transformation or growth is achieved solely by reading the sacred scriptures of the great world Educators. This of course is necessary, extremely necessary, but it is not by itself the source of our spiritual progress. If we say that God is the source of our growth, even as the sun is the source of its rays, it would not be incorrect – but it would, however, be incorrect to assume that we can have a direct relationship with the Source (God), just as the seed cannot have a direct relationship with the sun. By a direct relationship, I mean such that we do not need the Manifestations of God to help us move from a lower, hell-like condition to a higher heavenly one. Any attempt to make redundant the Manifestations of God in our lives results in what could be termed the 'most great unemployment'. God has employed His Manifestations specifically to bring us back to Himself and has made them as His representatives. Our wise Creator has commissioned them to act on His behalf, to be as God to humanity. Please note: I have not said the Manifestations are God, I have said they are as God to us. So Bahá'u'lláh states that the Manifestations of God are essential intermediaries between God and man. These are His words:

And since there can be no tie of direct intercourse to bind the one true God with His creation, and no resemblance whatever can exist between the transient and the Eternal, the contingent and the Absolute, He hath ordained that in every age and dispensation a pure and stainless Soul be made manifest in the kingdoms of earth and heaven. Unto this subtle, this mysterious and ethereal Being He hath assigned a twofold nature; the physical, pertaining to the world of matter, and the spiritual, which is born of the substance of God Himself.[24]

Humanity's source of progress, spiritual transformation, is the 'pure and stainless Souls,' the Manifestations of God. They are the source of 'spiritual sunshine' in our lives, the ones that ignite the candle of our hearts. Past Manifestations such as Krishna, Abraham, Moses, Buddha, Christ and Muhammad, through close contact with their early followers, transformed them from earthly beings grounded in materialistic assumptions, attitudes and lifestyles, into heavenly beings. Their followers allowed themselves to be transformed by these Great Souls through a compelling attraction, as a hummingbird is attracted to a rose or a moth to a flame. When other souls, receptive to spiritual forces, came into contact with the followers of the Manifestations, they too were changed for the better by attraction to the Manifestation of God. However, they recognized that the followers, no matter how influential in their spiritual development, were not the source of this attraction and influence. What these followers ostensibly did was to bring others into contact with the Manifestation for their age when He was physically alive or, after His ascension, through stories of His being, personal testimonies of His person and the example of heavenly characteristics. When the 'candle of the heart' was 'lit' by the Manifestation, their journey on the one and only path of transformation began. The implication here must be stated explicitly – the Source of all transformation is the Manifestation of God in whichever age one lives. For this day and age our Source is Bahá'u'lláh.

Even as a flower turns to the sun for its growth, we are able to turn to Bahá'u'lláh for our transformation. Fundamental to our spiritual development are His thought-provoking insights on heaven and hell. Bahá'u'lláh states:

> They say: 'Where is Paradise, and where is Hell?' Say: 'The one is reunion with Me; the other thine own self.[25]

Paradise, then, or heaven, is a specific condition of the soul when it is in union with or reunited with the Manifestation of God for this age, Bahá'u'lláh. Hell is one's own lower nature that has trapped the higher nature in selfish desires, prejudices, ignorant views and opinions, materialistic assumptions, passions and life-styles. In extreme cases, to have all those hellish characteristics mentioned above is the dark side of our dual nature in this world. These souls will dismiss out of hand giving even a few seconds contemplation to the idea that a Great Soul has recently come from the heavenly world to enable them to grow all their wonderful, latent potential. Others will rise up, as has been experienced, in opposition and even do harm to those who have responded positively to Bahá'u'lláh as God's latest Manifestation.

It is no exaggeration to say that those who came into the presence of Bahá'u'lláh felt they had entered heaven, providing their hearts were not closed to the intimations of the spirit. Stories abound about how these souls were magnetized by His presence, could not stay away from Him, were consumed in the joy and ecstasy of intense love emanating from Him, returning to their daily life with longing desire to sacrifice their all in efforts to please Him.

The distinguished Orientalist E. G. Browne of Cambridge University, who, two years before Bahá'u'lláh passed away in 1892, came into His presence on four different occasions, writes:

> The face of him on whom I gazed I can never forget, though I cannot describe it. Those piercing eyes seemed to read one's very soul; power and authority sat on that ample brow . . . No need to ask in whose presence I stood, as I bowed myself

before one who is the object of a devotion and love which kings might envy and emperors sigh for in vain.[26]

Unlike the history of the past religions of God, there is a wealth of reliable stories documented in the Bahá'í texts exemplifying the love, devotion and attachment to Bahá'u'lláh, described by Professor Browne. Bahá'u'lláh's followers were prepared to follow Him anywhere, even, metaphorically, to the gates of hell and beyond. We could describe the last place of exile Bahá'u'lláh experienced as 'hell on earth' – the penal colony, the prison city of 'Akká. He entered that filthy, foul-smelling city in 1868 to join the worst criminals of the Ottoman Empire. Many of His followers chose to accompany Him in exile rather than experience the soul-searing grief of being separated from Him. They were fully aware that the explicit orders of Sultan Abdul-Aziz condemned Bahá'u'lláh and His fellow exiles to 'perpetual banishment,' and 'stipulated their strict incarceration', forbidding them 'to associate either with each other or with the local inhabitants'.[27] By such means it was expected that the exiles would be exterminated.

In past ages heaven was to be in union with Muhammad or Christ or Moses or Buddha or any of the Manifestations of God for the age in which people lived associated with these Great Beings. If you research the history of the times of these heavenly Teachers, you will find that their followers sacrificed their all to be in their presence. As an iron nail cannot be but attracted by a magnet, so too were those souls magnetized by the person of the Manifestation for their age, and when joined with them were in paradise. For them, paradise was irrespective of the environment or general conditions prevailing at the time, whether in the deathly desert of Arabia, the oppressive atmosphere of Roman occupation, the wanderings in the unyielding wildernesses of the freed slaves of the Pharaohs or in the harrowing experience of the Black Pit dungeon of Tehran with Bahá'u'lláh.

This attraction continued after the passing of each of these Great Beings through a special Spirit released by them that uplifted, inspired, guided and comforted. These believers had given their hearts to the Great Being and through steadfastness in their allegiance to Him, they experienced what Christ promised: 'I am with you always, even unto the end of the world.'[28] In this way souls had, and still do have, access to heaven in every age, which is closeness to the Person of the Manifestation of God. 'He hath made everything beautiful in his time,'[29] we are informed in the Old Testament. It follows then, that we can experience heaven, which, in this day, is being close to Bahá'u'lláh, who promises us: 'We shall always be with you; if We inhale the perfume of your fellowship, Our heart will assuredly rejoice, for naught else can satisfy Us.'[30] In another place Bahá'u'lláh, in soul-entrancing words, underlines the fact that paradise is experienced through Him today, as the Manifestation of God for this age:

> As to Paradise: It is a reality and there can be no doubt about it, and now in this world it is realized through love of Me and My good-pleasure. Whosoever attaineth unto it God will aid him in this world below, and after death He will enable him to gain admittance into Paradise whose vastness is as that of heaven and earth. Therein the Maids of glory and holiness will wait upon him in the daytime and in the night season, while the day-star of the unfading beauty of his Lord will at all times shed its radiance upon him and he will shine so brightly that no one shall bear to gaze at him.[31]

And 'Abdu'l-Bahá writes:

> Therefore do the lovers of the Abhá Beauty [Bahá'u'lláh] wish for no other recompense but to reach that station where they may gaze upon Him in the Realm of Glory, and they walk no other path save over desert sands of longing for those exalted heights. They seek that ease and solace which will abide forever, and those bestowals that are sanctified beyond the understanding of the worldly mind.[32]

25

MATERIAL AND SPIRITUAL PROGRESS SHOULD GO HAND IN HAND

It must be admitted, it is very difficult to prove the existence of God. Conversely, it is also very difficult to prove the non-existence of God. So, we seem to be trapped in a vacuum of our own inabilities. In today's sceptical, cynical, disbelieving, hard-hearted, secular world a growing mass of people have rejected belief, and for many reasons, which have been examined in previous chapters. Just as in past ages there was the herd mentality to believe in God without examining rationally their beliefs, so today have the unbelievers herded themselves together, confident that their disgust, amongst other reasons, for all the ignorance of superstitious, fanatical beliefs of the past is incontrovertible evidence that God does not exist. Who can blame them for such a stance, when there is no doubt that all the ancient religions have descended into modes of thinking and functioning that are incapable of meeting the needs of modernity?

The gap of centuries since Islam, the last major religion prior to the Bahá'í Faith, is over 1,200 years. A huge amount of change has taken place during this time, especially in science and technology. What we today understand to be science was not known at the time of Muhammad. However, a host of His followers over the centuries, building on the knowledge of the ancient world, developed the foundation upon which modern science and technology was built. Hence there came a need in the dispensation of Bahá'u'lláh to address the disconnect between religion and science. 'Abdu'l-Bahá stated that humanity is to see religion and science as the two wings of a bird – both essential for flight: 'Religion and science are inter-twined with each other and cannot be separated. These are the two wings with which humanity must fly. One wing is not enough.'[1]

This principle is at the heart of material and spiritual progress. Unfortunately, because most of the human race is not aware of it, views of religion have degenerated, even to the point of regarding religion as archaic, a phase humanity has had to pass through.

To avoid the indictment of prejudice, however, we would be wise to acknowledge that the regenerative spirit of each of the ancient religions was the primary civilizing power in society. These religions have now lost their power, even as the sunshine of last year has done its work and is incapable of causing things to grow this year. This is not at all to disparage the historic religions, but a simple statement of fact upheld by science. Why, we may ask, as an example of this, after 2,000 years of Christianity, did Christian nations fight each other to the death in two world wars in complete neglect of all the directives of Christ to love each other – even one's enemies. The recreative, regenerating influence of the ancient religions, depleted and exhausted, has now been eclipsed by materialism, a negative force in the absence of true religion. Materialism's cancerous growth is eating into the souls of an unsuspecting humanity, robbing it of those distinctly human qualities of unconditional love, wisdom, self-effacement, humility, altruism, service and duty. And what does materialism put in its place? Personal ambition, status, acquisition, disconnection from the life to come and the exaltation of men's rational faculties over their spiritual faculties.

The choice is ours; we can join the materialistic herd confident that religion has no role to play in the progress of humanity, or we can look for spiritual answers to personal and collective problems that morally guide, complement and encourage the sound use of science and technology, whilst meeting the needs of a world shrunk to the size of a global village. But there is grave difficulty here. Answers to today's problems will not be found in the ancient religions, as they do not give guidance on how to relate to massive material progress. Answers to today's problems will not be found by taking spiritual understandings from here, there and everywhere, to construct a personally invented spirituality which may be individually satisfying but incapable of being a uniting agency for the human race, a necessity if progress is to be made. Answers to today's problems are not found by roaming through a plethora of pseudo-religious beliefs promising personal salvation and quick fixes for unhappiness.

Seekers of 'happiness' will never find it unless and until they be earnest truth-seekers or reality-seekers, even if 'truth' or 'reality' does not agree with some personally held views or opinions. To seek truth is to investigate 'reality', but in the domain of what gives light, love, illumination and tranquillity to our hearts and souls, plus the inspiration to sacrifice one's own desire to the will of a Higher Power and serve the purpose of helping humanity, in this radically different age to that of the historic religions. The reality that is sought is, for the most part, non-physical, above nature. We may ask, for instance, where, in all the wonderful discoveries of science, can solace be found for a mother whose son has been killed in a war; or where, in the realm of human invention, is there assurance that peace will be established on earth? We may further ask, where can we find answers to such existential questions as, what is the purpose of life, is there any meaning to suffering, and am I a creation of a Higher Power or just the result of chance physical occurrences within a materialistically defined evolutionary process?

Do we expect to find answers to these questions by, for instance, investigating all the wonders of the natural world? Will they be answered by being overwhelmed with awe at new cosmological theories? or, perhaps we can find some comfort in examining fossils of creatures that existed millions of years ago? Yet, in a sense, this is how modern materialistic man goes about investigating reality – to him the only reality worth investigating is what exists physically. To be facetious, our addiction to materialism has lowered the spiritual sight of man to the extent that he would prefer to ask a carrot these existential questions rather than seek enlightenment from a Higher World! 'Abdu'l-Bahá has a word to say on this point:

> But man's ambition should soar above this – he should ever look higher than himself, ever upward and onward, until through the Mercy of God he may come to the Kingdom of Heaven. Again, there are men whose eyes are only open to physical progress and to the evolution in the world of matter. These men prefer to study the resemblance between their own physical body and that of the ape, rather than to contemplate the glorious affiliation between their spirit and that of God. This is indeed strange, for it is only physically that man resembles the lower creation, with regard to his intellect he is totally unlike it.[2]

The human heart is not satisfied or tranquillized with materialistic assumptions, views and opinions of reality. Yet it is important that we live in the physical world from which we receive our sustenance and physical comfort. Of course, we need to have enough food to live, shelter to keep warm, health to carry out work in life and so on. But who can rest content while these necessities of life are not available to the whole of humanity? All the staggering advances in our material well-being, especially since the Industrial Revolution, have been wonderful. No one advocating a spiritual interpretation of reality would want to neglect the physical benefits that have come from scientific, technological developments and social reform during this time. Who, in their right mind, would not be moved to the core when learning about the squalid and unhealthy conditions of the poor in past centuries, conditions conducive to infectious diseases which spread in the form of epidemics like smallpox, typhoid or cholera? I am reminded of accounts of the terrible conditions for many families at this time; here is one of them reported in 1838:

> I visited eighty three dwellings, all without furniture, old boxes for tables, stools or large stones for chairs, beds of straw, sometimes covered by torn pieces of carpet, sometimes with no covering. Food was oatmeal for breakfast; flour and water and skimmed milk for dinner; oatmeal and water again for those who had three meals a day. I saw children eating rotting vegetables in the market.[3]

Those who acted for public health reform in Britain during the 18th, 19th and 20th centuries were, no doubt, motivated by spiritual feelings of altruism and deserve our gratitude, praise and to be honoured. Much has been written about these souls who helped reform the ugly conditions of the time. These have been recorded as historical events that students of social, economic and environmental history can study elsewhere.

Yet, coupled with the welcomed material improvements of this time, all the horrors of modernity crashed into our lives. Along with material development came problems – problems so dangerous and so incomprehensible to previous generations, problems that threaten to annihilate the whole human race. Weapons of mass annihilation, unheard of in past ages, slaughtered millions upon millions; the Chernobyl nuclear disaster, benign in its origin, along with the nuclear horrors of Hiroshima and Nagasaki have sent shock-waves throughout the world; now we are warned of the dangers of climate change from global warming. These are just a few examples of material developments being out of control. On this point 'Abdu'l-Bahá states:

> Until the heavenly civilization is founded, no result will be forthcoming from material civilization, even as you observe. See what catastrophes overwhelm mankind. Consider the wars which disturb the world. Consider the enmity and

hatred. The existence of these wars and conditions indicates and proves that the heavenly civilization has not yet been established. If the civilization of the Kingdom be spread to all the nations, this dust of disagreement will be dispelled, these clouds will pass away and the Sun of Reality in its greatest effulgence and glory will shine upon mankind.[4]

It is becoming increasingly evident that although the wealthy countries have access to more and more material resources, happiness, contentment and tranquillity, along with international peace, have eluded their populations. It must be remembered that it was the affluent, scientifically and technologically developed nations that plunged humanity into two world wars. In fact, more and more people have come to realize that it is an illusion to expect that material, physical things can prevent us from such dreadful evils as war, terrorism, economic collapse, alcoholism, drug addiction, suicide, depression, self-harming, divorce and the consequent deadly damage it does to children, etc. We are left with the general feeling that major problems, individual and collective, seem to be unsolvable, leaving a toxic social atmosphere of dread for the future – a dread with which we contaminate every new-born child. But these are not new observations. There have been those whose spiritual awareness during these centuries realized that material advances, without spiritual development, would give birth to a host of insidious, nefarious problems. Shoghi Effendi, writing in the 1930s, eloquently expressed the demise in which society now finds itself:

The recrudescence of religious intolerance, of racial animosity, and of patriotic arrogance; the increasing evidences of selfishness, of suspicion, of fear and of fraud; the spread of terrorism, of lawlessness, of drunkenness and of crime; the unquenchable thirst for, and the feverish pursuit after, earthly vanities, riches and pleasures; the weakening of family solidarity; the laxity in parental control; the lapse into luxurious indulgence; the irresponsible attitude towards marriage and the consequent rising tide of divorce; the degeneracy of art and music, the infection of literature, and the corruption of the press; the extension of the influence and activities of those 'prophets of decadence' who advocate companionate marriage, who preach the philosophy of nudism, who call modesty an intellectual fiction, who refuse to regard the procreation of children as the sacred and primary purpose of marriage, who denounce religion as an opiate of the people, who would, if given free rein, lead back the human race to barbarism, chaos, and ultimate extinction – these appear as the outstanding characteristics of a decadent society, a society that must either be reborn or perish.[5]

Surely, these are challenges enough to act as a spur for us to free ourselves of 'worshipping' the false god of materialism? Surely, we must be moved to the depths of our being, at least to give some attention to the possible existence of a spiritual domain to which we can aspire? Surely, we can realize that we need to rise to a higher level of awareness than that which engulfs us in problems, for not to do so is to become part of the problem we so urgently need to solve?

No one would deny that the physical, material world is real and necessary, but what is being questioned is our relationship with it. All the above observations are clearly the consequences of our being ignorant about the spiritual nature of human beings and the means to meet the requirements and exigencies of this age, all of which can be found in the Revelation of Bahá'u'lláh. Take, for instance, the words of Bahá'u'lláh, claiming to speak from the realities that exist in the spiritual domain, warning mankind about the futility of excessive attachment to physical things:

The generations that have gone on before you – whither are they fled? And those round whom in life circled the fairest and the loveliest of the land, where now are they? Profit by their example, O people, and be not of them that are gone astray.

Others ere long will lay hands on what ye possess, and enter into your habitations. Incline your ears to My words, and be not numbered among the foolish.[6]

And in another place He makes it clear that if our life is spent solely in materialistic pursuits then we have wasted the precious purpose of our lives on that which decays and perishes. And in the end we also will decay and perish, unable to carry the things of this world into the next.

Say: If ye be seekers after this life and the vanities thereof, ye should have sought them while ye were still enclosed in your mothers' wombs, for at that time ye were continually approaching them, could ye but perceive it. Ye have, on the other hand, ever since ye were born and attained maturity, been all the while receding from the world and drawing closer to dust. Why, then, exhibit such greed in amassing the treasures of the earth, when your days are numbered and your chance is well-nigh lost? Will ye not, then, O heedless ones, shake off your slumber?[7]

From His exalted spiritual domain, Bahá'u'lláh not only warns of that which will harm us, He also points out that which is helpful, that which brings tranquillity, security, love and understanding to our hearts and peace, harmony and progress to humanity – all spiritual conditions that enable us to live in a proper relationship with the physical world:

For every one of you his paramount duty is to choose for himself that on which no other may infringe and none usurp from him. Such a thing – and to this the Almighty is My witness – is the love of God, could ye but perceive it.[8]

The future of humanity outlined by Bahá'u'lláh is a balanced relationship between the physical and spiritual aspects of living. Progress is not considered in economic and material terms only. A statement from the Bahá'í International Community reads:

> . . . unprecedented economic crisis, together with the social breakdown it has helped to engender, reflects a profound error of conception about human nature itself . . . We are being shown that, unless the development of society finds a purpose beyond the mere amelioration of material conditions, it will fail of attaining even these goals. That purpose must be sought in spiritual dimensions of life and motivation that transcend a constantly changing economic landscape and an artificially imposed division of human societies into 'developed' and 'developing'.[9]

The human race is summoned to maturity wherein and whereby material and spiritual progress will be understood as real progress. At this time a minority of humanity in the affluent countries reap the benefits of a materialistic civilization unaware that their souls, laden with unimagined spiritual potential, are being 'consumed', even as fire consumes.

Striking an optimistic note, however, it will be increasingly understood that the development of the spiritual nature of man, as outlined by Bahá'u'lláh, along with His God-inspired Revelation of just governance at the local, national and international levels, is necessary for global well-being. All people, everywhere, have been created by a loving God for unity whereby material and spiritual progress is assured. Either we take this route to prosperity or, recalling the words of Shoghi Effendi quoted above, we degenerate further into 'a decadent society, a society that must either be reborn or perish'.

26

THE PROOF OF THE SUN IS THE SUN ITSELF

A man searching for the sun found a path leading to it. Here he met a friend walking away from the sun and asked, 'Why are you walking away from the source of all light?'

'I've always walked this way,' was the reply.

'But if you just turn around, you'll see the sun, which is the source of all our light,' exclaimed the man walking towards the sun.

'I've heard others speak of what you're talking about, but I've ample light to see where I'm going and don't want to waste my time looking for a sun I do not believe exists. Besides, even if the sun exists and is the source of all light, what benefit is that to me?' was the blunt reply.

'But don't you understand, my friend, that if you just turn around you will have proof of the existence of the sun?'

'I did it once,' was the quick reply, 'and all I saw were clouds. I have no desire to change my mind.'

'Why not try it again on a clear day, then you are bound to see the sun', returned the man who was walking toward the sun.

'No chance, my path is set, and I will not listen any longer to what is clearly a product of your imagination!'

The man who was walking toward the sun, out of concern for his friend, asked him to consider what happens further away from the light source.

'Nothing will happen, the light is there, and I can see my chosen path.

And look,' he added, 'I'm in the company of thousands upon thousands who are walking my way, yet I can see only a handful walking in your direction,' was the assured reply.

The man walking toward the sun did not press the point, but realized, deep in his heart, that by degrees and over the years his friend's path would become darker and darker the further he travelled away from the light source.

For life is lived either walking towards the Light or away from it and the stories we tell of this journey make up the history of the human race!

* * * *

Previously I said that it is difficult for our intellectual faculties to prove or disprove the existence of a Higher Power. That is why there is so much confusion about the subject, for were it possible to do so then all the gifted intellectuals throughout the world would have proved conclusively, by now, the case for or against God's existence. We must admit that our rational faculties are severely limited; no matter how acute they are, they are incapable of being all-knowing. We examined the possibility of material things being the source of spiritual realities such as love, justice, compassion and the like, and concluded that science discovers the secrets of physical things, and religion uses examples in nature as a means of education about spiritual reality.

The material world exists and is open to our physical senses. The spiritual world also exists, just waiting to be discovered when man has acquired the spiritual capacity to make such investigations. Related to this there is a growing feeling amongst many that material things on their own do not satisfy the deeper needs of man who, prompted by dissatisfaction, feels the urge to reach out to the non-physical world, the world of the spirit. Another point mentioned earlier is that material progress without spiritual development creates a dangerous imbalance for humanity's progress. Under these circumstance, true progress requires a balance of the material and spiritual aspects of existence. If this does not happen then the life of man becomes like a bird, with one strong wing and the other so weak that the bird is incapable of flying. In fact, that is exactly what is happening – the stronger the materialistic wing develops the more the bird goes around in circles, revisiting points on the earth it is trying to rise above. Flight is impossible under these conditions!

Guidance to the spiritual domain, to develop a higher consciousness, comes from the Great Souls throughout history such as Buddha, Moses, Christ and Muhammad, who have been the source of enlightenment for humanity during its immature phases of evolution. For today, during humanity's burgeoning powers of maturity, Bahá'u'lláh is the source of illumination, bringing understandings of reality suited for this 'never before experienced' age.

It is to these Great Souls, founders of the historic religions, and more recently the Báb and Bahá'u'lláh, that mankind has not only been safely guided on its journey back to the Creator but who have been the closest we can get to God. To the Jews, God's existence is proved by Moses. Similarly, for all Christians there is total proof of God's existence as manifest in Christ. The theme does not change with the followers of Muhammad, who have come to firmly believe that the proof of God's existence can be seen in the life and works of Muhammad. The proof of the sun is the sun itself – the proof of the existence of God are the Manifestations of God, for they mirror all His qualities. They are as the 'sun' to the world of the heart and mind of man. It is through these Great Souls, and others not mentioned, that humanity has had access to the presence of God and the divine realm from whence they have all come.

The difficulty is that the founders of the historic religions are now obscured in antiquity, and the fragmentary accounts of their lives are shrouded in many misunderstandings. Added to this is the prevailing materialistic atmosphere that tends to disable any soul from making an unbiased, independent investigation of their lives. People's thoughts have been so contaminated against religion that the mere mention of the names of the Messengers of God tends to switch off interest in taking investigation any further.

If, by some marvellous demonstration of equanimity, we can look unencumbered past all these stumbling blocks to reality, it may be possible to put effort into examining the life and teachings of Bahá'u'lláh, who claimed to be modernity's Great Teacher/ Educator or Manifestation of God. The reason for this is central to the theme of there being a source of spiritual awareness and progress coupled with reasonable evidence that a Higher Power does exist. Throughout the Writings of Bahá'u'lláh, written between 1852 and 1892, there are myriads of insights, encouragement and truths for the release of every individual's immense potential, mysterious powers available to enable the happiness of every heart, spiritual disciplines for the soul's development, guidance to construct a global civilization that embodies the will of God, and warnings against ignoring His health-giving, life-saving spiritual teachings. For those who search for reality these are readily accessible, right now, in the wealth of information available not only on Bahá'u'lláh but on the Báb, His Herald, and 'Abdu'l-Bahá, His eldest son, the three Central Figures of the Bahá'í Faith.

One of the key insights frequently mentioned in the Bahá'í Writings and touched upon in previous chapters is that because there are different degrees or levels of existence, 'the inferior degree cannot comprehend the superior'. 'Abdu'l-Bahá takes this one step further and asks, how can we, mere limited and finite human beings, comprehend God, Who, by definition, must be on a level of existence far, far above human limitations? [1]

Here then is our human problem: we do not possess any ability, faculty or function to comprehend what to us is the highest level of existence – God Himself, in the realm of unknowability. This can be quite disturbing for some who, because they refuse to admit that human intellect cannot grasp something non-physical existing at a higher level, dismiss the idea that God exists at all.

But for those who have acquired a spiritual perspective of

reality, the concept of the unknowability of God is not at all off-putting, but uplifting, as it indicates that God is absolute perfection, purity, love, power and majesty – qualities of perfection entirely beyond the reach of even the most developed human being. On this point Bahá'u'lláh states: 'let the tidings of the revelation of Thine incorruptible Essence bring me joy, O Thou Who art the most manifest of the manifest and the most hidden of the hidden!'[2] The assurance that such a Being of absolute grace and loving-kindness exists enables the human heart to confidently rest in the bosom of affection, peace and tranquillity – a condition that prevents any soul from falling into the materialistic pit of anxiety, worry, fear, low self-esteem, hubris or self-aggrandisement. Throughout the Bahá'í Writings we are assured that because God is the Highest Power to which we can turn, He will never let us down. Here is one of the many heart-warming, uplifting assurances on this subject:

> If the heart turns away from the blessings God offers how can it hope for happiness? If it does not put its hope and trust in God's Mercy, where can it find rest? Oh, trust in God! for His Bounty is everlasting, and in His Blessings, for they are superb. Oh! put your faith in the Almighty, for He faileth not and His goodness endureth for ever! His Sun giveth Light continually, and the Clouds of His Mercy are full of the Waters of Compassion with which He waters the hearts of all who trust in Him. His refreshing Breeze ever carries healing in its wings to the parched souls of men! Is it wise to turn away from such a loving Father, Who showers His blessings upon us, and to choose rather to be slaves of matter?[3]

Inculcated in the Writings of Bahá'u'lláh is the theme that the fundamental nature of God, which is termed His Essence, is Unknowable. This fits the mature stage of humanity's development, as it now has the capacity to understand this concept. If we search the Old and New Testaments, we will not find God mentioned as an 'Essence' although John states: 'No man hath seen God at any time.'[4] Previous, child-like, phases of humanity's growth could only partially absorb this point, and so God was mostly depicted in physical terms such as Lord, Judge or Father. The leftover of this way of thinking is that God is somewhat like a magisterial, white-bearded Zeus living in the clouds. Not only did immature minds of that age reduce God to terms that their child-ish minds could fathom, but they created three distinct 'crude and fantastic' theories of the Almighty.[5] The one mostly adopted by Christians is that God is incarnate in Christ; another, having its influence mainly throughout the far eastern world, is the pan-theistic view of God, whilst the last one – an anthropomorphic conception of God – pervades social thinking about God and providing arguments for and against His existence,

It is made plain in Bahá'u'lláh's Writings that God is:

'. . . the unknowable Essence, the Divine Being, . . . immeasur-ably exalted beyond every human attribute such as corporeal existence, ascent and descent, egress and regress . . . He is, and hath ever been, veiled in the ancient eternity of His Essence, and will remain in His Reality everlastingly hidden from the sight of men . . . He standeth exalted beyond and above all separation and union, all proximity and remoteness . . . "God was alone; there was none else beside Him" is a sure testimony of this truth.

'From time immemorial,' Bahá'u'lláh, speaking of God, explains, 'He, the Divine Being, hath been veiled in the inef-fable sanctity of His exalted Self, and will everlasting continue to be wrapped in the impenetrable mystery of His unknow-able Essence . . . Ten thousand Prophets, each a Moses, are thunderstruck upon the Sinai of their search at God's forbid-ding voice, "Thou shalt never behold Me"; whilst a myriad Messengers, each as great as Jesus, stand dismayed upon their heavenly thrones by the interdiction "Mine Essence thou shalt never apprehend!"'[6]

Meditation about the 'unknowable Essence' will free the mind and heart of reducing the Infinite within a finite body (as in Christ) as incarnation; imagining that everything in creation makes up God, as in pantheism; and foolishly believing that God has human characteristics as in anthropomorphisms.

To thinking, mature people in this age of gathering maturity, it has been one or other of these 'crude and fantastic' theories, propounded by spiritually immature religious leaders and theologians of all the ancient religions, that tends to put them off giving any credence to the possible existence of a Higher Power. Certainly, when, as an atheist, I read in the Bahá'í Writings that the unknowable God is called the 'innermost Spirit of Spirits' an' 'eternal Essence of Essences' and that His 'all-embracing Reality' is 'incorruptible',[7] it struck a chord in me that, if God exists, this is how to refer to Him.

It may come as a surprise to learn from Bahá'u'lláh, after reading the above passages from Him, that even those Great Souls, the Manifestations of God, who speak by His leave and in His Name, have no knowledge whatever of the unfathomable essence of God. For in reality, they too are His handiwork, although created to be at a higher level of existence than the combined characteristics and qualities of humanity.

If we apply the principle stated earlier, that a lower level of existence can have no understanding or experience whatever of a higher level of existence, then it becomes reasonable to accept that man, created at a lower level than the Manifestations of God, is totally dependent on such Beings for his progress and well-being. One of the many analogies used in the Bahá'í Writings, touched on earlier to explain this dependency, is that God is likened to the sun and the Manifestations of God likened to the reflection of the sun and its rays in a mirror: 'Consider the rays of the sun', Bahá'u'lláh writes, 'whose light hath encompassed the world. The rays emanate from the sun and reveal its nature, but are not the sun itself.'[8] The rays are sent to earth by the power of the sun, causing all things on earth to exist, grow and develop. The sun, in its exalted domain, does not come to earth to enable growth – if it did, then all things on earth would be instantly destroyed. Similarly, the Manifestations of God have been created by the Almighty to be the intermediaries between God and humanity, causing the human spirit to reveal its hidden potential, just as the rays of the sun are the intermediaries between the sun and the earth. Writing on this point, Bahá'u'lláh states:

> The door of the knowledge of the Ancient Being hath ever been, and will continue for ever to be, closed in the face of men. No man's understanding shall ever gain access unto His holy court. As a token of His mercy, however, and as a proof of His loving-kindness, He hath manifested unto men the Day Stars of His divine guidance [Manifestations of God], the Symbols of His divine unity, and hath ordained the knowledge of these sanctified Beings to be identical with the knowledge of His own Self. Whoso recognizeth them hath recognized God. Whoso hearkeneth to their call, hath hearkened to the Voice of God, and whoso testifieth to the truth of their Revelation, hath testified to the truth of God Himself. Whoso turneth away from them, hath turned away from God, and whoso disbelieveth in them, hath disbelieved in God. Every one of them is the Way of God that connecteth this world with the realms above, and the Standard of His Truth unto every one in the kingdoms of earth and heaven. They are the Manifestations of God amidst men, the evidences of His Truth, and the signs of His glory.[9]

A concept mentioned earlier is that God does not 'incarnate His infinite, His unknowable, His incorruptible and all-embracing Reality in the concrete and limited frame of a mortal being . . .'[10] However, the concept of 'incarnation' is not totally without validity – it is just what is incarnated that needs to be identified. Shoghi Effendi states that it is the 'names and attributes of God' that are incarnate in the Manifestations of God.[11] Just as the rays of the sun incarnate the heat and illumination of the sun, similarly, do the Manifestations of God incarnate the knowledge, love, wisdom, majesty and power of God.

Although the 'pre-existent Reality',[12] God, is incomprehensible to man, nonetheless 'Knowing God . . . means the comprehension and the knowledge of His attributes, and not of His Reality.'[13]

My yearning for 'truth' or 'reality' in the spiritual domain brought me to its Source. Just as light is the rays emanating from the sun as its source, so too do all the wonderful qualities and attributes emanate from God through the Manifestations of God. Every single Manifestation of God is therefore the source of spirituality, living embodiments of love, justice, compassion, mercy, sacredness, holiness and the like. This is the closest we can get to prove the existence of God, as has been written above – 'Whoso recognizeth them hath recognized God.'[14]

With these thoughts in mind, I would next like to focus on Bahá'u'lláh, the most recent Manifestation of God, for proof of the existence of God.

27

A FOCUS ON BAHÁ'U'LLÁH

In the previous chapter I mentioned that it is very difficult to get an accurate picture of the historic Manifestations of God. Over time, they have become enshrouded in all manner of imagined and man-made interpretations of their reality. However, Bahá'u'lláh, who to His followers is the latest of God's Manifestations, does not fall into this category. He appeared in Persia in the nineteenth century and His ministry lasted for 40 years, after which He passed away in 1892. Extensive historical accounts of His life have been written about Him, all available to the sincere soul who is truly seeking an understanding of the Source of spiritual reality and proof of the existence of God. On this point Bahá'u'lláh writes:

> If it be your wish, O people, to know God and to discover the greatness of His might, look, then, upon Me with Mine own eyes, and not with the eyes of any one besides Me. Ye will, otherwise, be never capable of recognizing Me, though ye ponder My Cause as long as My Kingdom endureth, and meditate upon all created things throughout the eternity of God, the Sovereign Lord of all, the Omnipotent, the Ever-Abiding, the All-Wise. Thus have We manifested the truth of Our Revelation, that haply the people may be roused from their heedlessness, and be of them that understand. [1]

It has been well documented that the unconditional love Bahá'u'lláh had for everyone, even those that became His bitterest enemies, radiated from Him so intensely that all could not help but be attracted to His person. This power of attraction was noted even when He was a child. 'Abdu'l-Bahá speaks of this time:

> From childhood He was extremely kind and generous. He was a great lover of outdoor life, most of His time being spent in the garden or the fields. He had an extraordinary power of attraction, which was felt by all. People always crowded around Him. Ministers and people of the Court would surround Him, and the children also were devoted to Him.[2]

In numerous cases, this love so penetrated the mind, heart and soul that the recipient was consumed as in a conflagration of heavenly fire. In Bahá'u'lláh's presence they entirely forgot self, were overcome with feelings of 'nothingness', and were uplifted to the spiritual domain that awaits all who sincerely make efforts to attain it. They were attracted like a moth to a flame and revelled in such ecstasy that a moment's separation from this all-consuming joy felt like death. These souls had come in contact with the Source of unconditional love in this day and age. Perhaps no person in recorded history has had, during His lifetime, such a magnetizing effect upon the souls of so many. It was not just a handful of His apostles who were thus affected – thousands of souls became His followers in His day, many of whom willingly gave their lives as martyrs in His path. Throughout His life He continually attracted to His person eminent religious, political and aristocratic people in the areas to which he was banished – although, it must be said, that it is also from these ranks of people, most of whom were blind to His station, that he received opposition and cruel treatment. Even those who were his jailers in the places he experienced incarceration were won over by His loving kindness, majesty and perfect humility. Here is an account of the stupendous effect Bahá'u'lláh's unconditional love had upon the people of Baghdad over His ten-year exile in that area:

Numerous and striking are the anecdotes which have been recounted by those whom duty, accident, or inclination had, in the course of these poignant years, brought into direct contact with Bahá'u'lláh. Many and moving are the testimonies of bystanders who were privileged to gaze on His countenance, observe His gait, or overhear His remarks, as He moved through the lanes and streets of the city, or paced the banks of the river; of the worshippers who watched Him pray in their mosques; of the mendicant, the sick, the aged, and the unfortunate whom He succoured, healed, supported and comforted; of the visitors, from the haughtiest prince to the meanest beggar, who crossed His threshold and sat at His feet; of the merchant, the artisan, and the shopkeeper who waited upon Him and supplied His daily needs; of His devotees who had perceived the signs of His hidden glory; of His adversaries who were confounded or disarmed by the power of His utterance and the warmth of His love; of the priests and laymen, the noble and learned, who besought Him with the intention of either challenging His authority, or testing His knowledge, or investigating His claims, or confessing their shortcomings, or declaring their conversion to the Cause He had espoused.[3]

At the end of Bahá'u'lláh's ten-year sojourn in Baghdad, there came a time when His enemies had secured a further banishment. Bahá'u'lláh's freedom amongst the population had given Him access to thousands from the Muslim community. His unconditional love for them attracted so many that the authorities deemed this to be a threat to Islam. The sudden news that Bahá'u'lláh was to be further exiled, this time to Istanbul (Constantinople), crushed the life out of the colony of fellow exiles. They could not bear to be separated from Him and many regarded death, rather than life, as their means of assuaging their broken hearts. It was at this time, however, that the first declaration of His station as the One promised of all past sacred scriptures, was transmitted to some of His followers.

Later on, and of particular interest to the Christian world, Bahá'u'lláh proclaimed He was 'Christ returned in the Glory of the Father' (it is the return of the Holy Spirit of Christ, not His body, that is meant).

The general population of Baghdad came to hear of Bahá'u-'lláh's impending forced departure from them. They were shaken to the core and could not imagine life without Him. Shoghi Effendi describes that as Bahá'u'lláh was leaving His house for the last time to enter the Riḍván Garden, where He made His great announcement, He did so 'amidst weeping and lamentation' of the population.[4] An account of this time is given by Adib Taherzadeh:

> Outside the house, the lamentation and weeping of those who did not confess to be His followers were no less spectacular and heartrending. Everyone in the crowded street sought to approach Him. Some prostrated themselves at His feet, others waited to hear a few words and yet others were content with a touch of His hands or a glance at His face. A Persian lady of noble birth, who was not herself a believer, pushed her way into the crowd and with a gesture of sacrifice threw her child at the feet of Bahá'u'lláh. These demonstrations continued all the way to the riverbank.[5]

Bahá'u'lláh's departure from the Riḍván Garden some twelve days later, just prior to the journey to His next place of exile, again witnessed the grief-stricken lamentations of His followers and those of the general population. Of this time, according to an eye-witness:

> Believers and unbelievers alike sobbed and lamented. The chiefs and notables who had congregated were struck with wonder. Emotions were stirred to such depths as no tongue can describe, nor could any observer escape their contagion.[6]

These events occurred over a brief period of less than two weeks. Imagine then the extent of the influence of Bahá'u'lláh's unconditional love and compassion over a forty-year period and bestowed on all with whom He came into contact, not from a life of comfort and luxury, but through the most heart-breaking, agonizing tribulations, privations and afflictions. Yet, so, so sadly, there are few who have made efforts to read about His life. On the other hand, Bahá'u'lláh knew people would be slow to respond to His person and His Message but assured us that 'erelong God will raise up a people who will recount His troubles and demand the restitution of His rights from His oppressors'.[7]

Although it may be possible for a human being to acquire the ability of 'unconditional love', there is, however, a huge difference between this ability and that which is held by a Manifestation of God. The Manifestations of God are the embodiment of not only unconditional love, but of all the qualities and attributes of God. They are compassion, wisdom, justice, sacredness and the like. These qualities are an inherent part of their reality as a function of the one Spirit from God operating at a very high level. This, as stated before, sets them apart from us limited, finite beings who have been created at a lower level of abilities and functions.

This is a major characteristic of being a Manifestation of God as distinct from human beings. Just as humans are a higher level of creation than the animals, the Manifestations of God are a higher level of creation in relation to man. As stated before, it is the one Spirit that functions at different levels of creation from the mineral up to the vegetable to the animal, and then in man as the human spirit. At the level of the Manifestation of God, the one Spirit is called the Holy Spirit, which sheds its illumination over the heart and soul of man, empowering it to make spiritual, moral, intellectual and social progress.

The word we use for such an ability is 'innate', as distinct from 'acquired'. Perhaps we can get an insight into 'innateness' by reflecting on some of man's innate abilities. He has, for instance, the ability to think, imagine and memorize, abilities with which he is born. Man does not acquire these abilities from any other person, nor does he have to attend school or university to do so. Of course, education can enhance these abilities, but the teacher does not put these functions into his students. Another, perhaps simpler, example comes to mind; if a person suffers toothache, he knows this without anyone placing the knowledge of that ache inside him. He does not have to acquire the realization he has toothache by an educational process – it is an innate knowledge. In fact, no one would know he had toothache unless he spoke about his pain.

So, another huge difference between human beings and the Manifestations of God is that the former acquire knowledge through learning, whilst the latter have an innate ability to 'know' whatever God directly desires they should know for the betterment of the individual and society. On this point 'Abdu'l-Bahá stated:

> The divine teacher does not come to acquire knowledge, for this tree of life is a fruit tree by birth and not through graft-ing. Behold the sacred tree which spreads its shade over the whole world! This is the mission of Bahá'u'lláh – for under this tree all questions are solved![8]

And speaking further on this topic:

> . . . these holy, divine Manifestations are and must always be distinguished above all other beings in every attribute of glory and perfection, in order that it may be proven that the Manifestation is the true Teacher and real Trainer; that He is the Sun of Truth, endowed with a supreme splendour and reflecting the beauty of God. Otherwise, it is not possible for us to train one human individual and then after training him, believe in him and accept him as the holy Manifesta-tion of Divinity. The real Manifestation of God must be endowed with divine knowledge and not dependent upon

learning acquired in schools. He must be the Educator, not the educated; His standard, intuition instead of tuition. He must be perfect and not imperfect, great and glorious instead of being weak and impotent . . . In a word, the holy divine Manifestation of God must be distinguished above all others of mankind in every aspect and qualification, in order that He may be able to train effectively the human body politic, eliminate the darkness enshrouding the human world, uplift humanity from a lower to a higher kingdom, be able through the penetrative power of His Word to promote and spread broadcast the beneficent message of universal peace among men, bring about the unification of mankind in religious belief through a manifest divine power, harmonize all sects and denominations and convert all nativities and nationalities into one nativity and fatherland.[9]

There are so many examples of the innate knowledge of Bahá'u'lláh that the bounds of brevity would be exceeded if they were all mentioned. We can, nonetheless, ponder a few examples.

Bahá'u'lláh was a master of both the Persian and Arabic languages, yet He never attended school. He did receive a few years of elementary education under a home tutor as a child in Tehran, but because He was of the nobility this education was very limited to 'calligraphy, the study of the Qur'án and the works of the Persian poets'.[10] This would not account for His mastery of Persian and Arabic which, to the Western ear, would appear very similar but are as distinct as English is from Russian. In fact, Persian and Arabic are from two different families of languages – Persian is Indo-European while Arabic is Semitic. But there is more to this than on first hearing. There is also a huge difference in Arabic between 'the written or classical form and the spoken or colloquial':

Arabic is not widely used or spoken in Persia; nor was it so used or spoken in Bahá'u'lláh's lifetime. Neither the nobility nor the peasantry, as a rule, knew anything of the language. The one class for which knowledge of Arabic was considered important was the Islamic community, who used it in their study of the Qur'án. These Muslim divines laboured for years to master the subtleties of Arabic grammar and terminology, as well as its complex literary conventions.[11]

'Abdu'l-Bahá writes about Bahá'u'lláh's mastery of Arabic even though He did not receive one lesson in it, as Persians are passionately proud of the independent status of their language:

> Bahá'u'lláh never studied Arabic, had a teacher or tutor, or entered a school. Nevertheless His eloquence and fluency in spoken Arabic, as well as in His Arabic Tablets, would astonish the most articulate and accomplished among the Arab men of letters, and all acknowledged that in this His attainments were without peer or equal.[12]

We would do well to reflect on this ability of Bahá'u'lláh's. No one in the entire range of human history has been born with the ability to speak with such mastery and eloquence a language totally foreign to their mother tongue. Is this not an indication that Bahá'u'lláh's knowledge is innate?

We may be tempted to dismiss this ability of Bahá'u'lláh, as we have no personal experience of it. To those around Him, nonetheless, He appeared to them, at the very least, a prodigy. Even as a child He could answer the most abstruse questions troubling the great and learned men of His country, and in such a way that they were completely won over by His humble but majestic way of doing so.

As a child, Bahá'u'lláh was aware that He was 'different' from other souls. Knowledge of all manner of various branches of knowledge just emanated from Him even as the rays of the sun pour out from that source of illumination. Although the station of Bahá'u'lláh as the Manifestation of God for this day and age was veiled to those around Him during the early days of His life, He, Himself, was fully aware of it. It must be emphasized that at no point in Bahá'u'lláh's life, whether in the terrible dungeon of the Black Pit or when he disclosed His station to a handful of followers in the Riḍván Garden, did He suddenly 'become' a Manifestation of God. No, indeed, He was born into this station with all the divine attributes, and only years later proclaimed His office as a Manifestation of God. On this point we may consider that no human being suddenly becomes a human being at a certain time in their life but is actually born one. Even as a child he is aware that he is a human being.

At a very early age Bahá'u'lláh experienced a condition such that only a Chosen One of God could experience:

> In one of His Tablets Bahá'u'lláh gives us a glimpse of the stirrings of God's Revelation within Him in His early life. Although we shall never be able to understand fully the reality and all the implications of what took place, nevertheless the story is awe-inspiring. Bahá'u'lláh states that once during His childhood, He read the story of the bloodshed which resulted from the massacre of the tribe of Qurayzah [during the days of Muhammad] . . . He relates how He was overtaken by feelings of intense sadness and grief as a result of reading this episode. At that time He beheld the limitless ocean of God's forgiveness and mercy surging before Him. Then he beseeched God to vouchsafe unto all the peoples of the world that which would establish unity and love among them. He then describes how suddenly on a certain day before dawn, He was overcome by a condition which completely affected His manners, His thoughts and His words. It was a transfiguration which gave Him the tidings of ascendancy and exaltation, and which continued for twelve days. After this He testifies that the ocean of His utterance began to surge, and the Sun of Assurance shone forth and He continued in this state until He manifested Himself to man. He further

testifies in the same Tablet that in this Dispensation, He has, on the one hand, removed from religion anything which could become the cause of suffering and disunity and, on the other, ordained those teachings which would bring about the unity of the human race.[13]

The direction of Bahá'u'lláh's Revelation, as can be seen from the above, was set long before He proclaimed His station in 1863. He foresaw a united world community with a population that had been so transformed that love and harmony would be their sincerest aspirations. The power of God was deeply stirring His soul, creating a potent force to bring mankind together in bonds of love, cooperation and reciprocity.

During Bahá'u'lláh's forty-year ministry, and prior to it, His innate knowledge poured through Him from God overwhelming and stunning thousands of souls. Such a demonstration of immense abilities could not fail to attract the attention of scholars, high-ranking religious leaders, holy men and even that of princes who followed His daily activities. It should attract our attention now, even as the scientific genius of Einstein bewildered and excited the scientific community at the beginning of the 20th century. Sadly, this is not the case. We must ask, why? The answers, of course, can be as various as the number of human beings. But perhaps one answer that surfaces is because so much damage has been done to the good name of religion that people have no appetite, no inclination, to investigate the life of Bahá'u'lláh, Who arose with all His stupendous powers in the religious domain.

At this point it is instructive to look at an example, out of the huge range and magnitude of Bahá'u'lláh's innate knowledge, of His innate ability related to the task of transforming humanity through the Word of God. The year was 1862, a handful of months before His declaration in the Garden of Riḍván. Siyyid Muhammad, one of the three maternal uncles of the Báb, visited Bahá'u'lláh in Baghdad. He was unconvinced about the station of his nephew being the Qá'im, the Promised One, especially of

Shí'ih Islam, as well as the precursor of Bahá'u'lláh and a Manifestation of God in His own right. He had been troubled by two
major concerns. The first had been answered on a previous occasion; he wondered how his nephew, of all people, could be the
Promised Qá'im and had received a straightforward and penetrat-
ing answer from a follower of the Báb. He was told that Hamza,
one of the uncles of Muhammad, had the same perplexity to overcome and managed to do so, becoming one of the greatest heroes
in Islamic history. This may give us an insight into the mindset of
people at the time as, from their understanding of the prophecies
in the Qur'án, a more mystical, magical or physically apocalyptic
fulfilment of prophecies was expected. In Siyyid Muhammad's
case it had seemed too down to earth, too mundane, that he
could be the uncle of a Messenger of God!

During his meeting with Bahá'u'lláh, Siyyid Muhammad was
asked what stood in his way of recognizing the Báb as the long-
awaited Promised One. He told Bahá'u'lláh that he had many
questions that needed to be answered before he could accept that
his nephew was a Messenger of God. He was advised by Bahá'u'lláh
to write down his questions. It is recorded that Siyyid Muhammad worded his questions under four headings, as follows:

1. The Day of Resurrection. Is there to be corporeal resurrection? The world is replete with injustice. How are the just to
   be requited and the unjust, punished?
2. The twelfth Imám was born at a certain time and lives on.
   There are traditions, all supporting the belief. How can this
   be explained?
3. Interpretation of holy texts. This Cause does not seem to
   conform to beliefs held throughout the years. One cannot
   ignore the literal meaning of holy texts and scripture. How
   can this be explained?
4. Certain events, according to the traditions that have come
   down from the Imáms, must occur at the advent of the
   Qá'im. Some of these are mentioned. But none of these has
   happened. How can this be explained?[14]

What happened next was so extraordinary that nothing throughout the history of humanity, except in the Báb's case, has ever recorded its like. Bahá'u'lláh, in the space of just two days and two nights, wrote a two-hundred-page book in answer to all Siyyid Muhammad's questions. These answers covered themes of immense significance and import, not just for Siyyid Muhammad himself, but for the whole of mankind. For in these pages Bahá'u'lláh not only interpreted such abstruse topics as the day of resurrection, signs of the return of Christ and the spiritual meaning of 'life' and 'death', but also, brilliantly, gave proofs that all the major religions have come from the one God, with teachings pertinent to their times, in a great unfolding of God's redemptive plan for all humanity. From then on, Siyyid Muhammad was illumined with the light of faith, became a devoted follower and eventually gave his life as a martyr, rather than recant his belief in Bahá'u'lláh and His herald, the Báb. These answers to Siyyid Muhammad's questions have now been spread around the world in a book called Kitáb-i-Íqán (The Book of Certitude) and is accessible to all people.

But let us look more closely at this phenomenon. At no time was Bahá'u'lláh's response to Siyyid Muhammad's questions premeditated. He did not visit any library to take notes for a possible reply, nor did He discuss a possible response with anyone, nor did He correct any part of the script when writing it (as not a single mistake was made or alteration needed) – all known means whereby a writer will construct a book over a length of time requiring much longer than two days and nights. The answers just flowed through Him without the slightest hesitation. And these Words were not just any old words that any competent writer could have written, but were of such profound import that millions of souls, since the revelation of the Kitáb-i-Íqán, have found to satisfy their hearts and minds that religion is essentially one. This profound work, written by someone who never attended school, has been described as 'a model of Persian prose, of a style at once original, chaste and vigorous, and remarkably lucid, both cogent in argument and matchless in its irresistible eloquence . . .'[15]

The Kitáb-i-Íqán is one amongst a profusion of proofs of Bahá'u'lláh's innate knowledge at work. It enables all peoples to unite in bonds of love and affection, even as one family. It is the flow of the Word of God through the Bearer of His Message, totally independent of all acquired knowledge. It is the major impetus for the progress of humanity as its influence gathers momentum eventually to encompass the whole of mankind.

On a personal note: my mother, a Welsh woman totally alien to the world in which Bahá'u'lláh lived, and after years of searching for 'truth', was given the Kitáb-i-Íqán to read, which she did over a three-week period. Her heart, mind and soul were completely convinced of the veracity of Bahá'u'lláh's teachings, whereupon she did not hesitate in identifying herself as one of His followers. Such is the powerful influence of this tremendous work of Bahá'u'lláh!

Although written in 1862, surely, today, we are in need of such a unifying spirit when the forces of religious fanaticism are wreaking havoc throughout the world? 'Well may it be claimed', Shoghi Effendi writes,

> that of all the books revealed by the Author of the Bahá'í Revelation, this Book alone, by sweeping away the age-long barriers that have so insurmountably separated the great religions of the world, has laid down a broad and unassailable foundation for the complete and permanent reconciliation of their followers.[16]

Yet another facet of Bahá'u'lláh's innate ability has to be mentioned. Time and again we read of accounts of souls who, while in the presence of Bahá'u'lláh, became aware that He knew their innermost thoughts. Nothing was hidden from Him, and in many cases, this came as a complete surprise to those who entered His presence for the first time. On this point, one of the believers recounts that while he and a few others were in the presence of Bahá'u'lláh he was

> immersed in the ocean of His grace and bounties. After some time He arose to depart. We accompanied Him to the door and as He went out, He signalled to us not to accompany Him further. I watched from behind His graceful stature and the majesty of His walk, until He disappeared from my sight. I was so carried away, and in that state I said to myself: What a pity! If only the kings of the world could recognize Him and arise to serve Him, both the Cause and the believers would be exalted in this day.
>
> The following day when we attained His presence, He turned His face to me and addressed the following words to me with infinite charm and loving kindness. He said: 'If the kings and rulers of the world had embraced the Faith in this day, you people could never have found an entry into this exalted Court. You could never have had the opportunity to attain Our presence, nor could you ever have acquired the privilege of hearing the words of the Lord of Mankind. Of course the time will come when the kings and rulers of the world will become believers, and the Cause of God will be glorified outwardly. But this will happen after the meek and the lowly ones of the earth have won this inestimable bounty.'[17]

Summing up this particular facility of Bahá'u'lláh, 'Abdu'l-Bahá writes:

> Since those sanctified realities, the universal Manifestations of God, encompass all created things both in their essence and in their attributes, since They transcend and discover all existing realities, and since They are cognizant of all things, it follows that Their knowledge is divine and not acquired — that is, it is a heavenly grace and a divine discovery.[18]

One of the greatest proofs of the authenticity of the Manifestations of God I have left to last; it is the revelation of the Word of God. This has never been fully understood by the followers of past Manifestations of God. Indeed, a dominant facet of religious expectation of past generations concerning a Promised One is that a Prophet of God should perform miracles. This would be, to them, a key factor as to whether or not such a person, claiming to be a Prophet, was true or false. Yet to put such emphasis on this expectation exposes ignorance and spiritual immaturity, for it misjudges the true work of God's Chosen Ones. On this point, we may ask that if a doctor, when visiting a sick patient, does not prescribe any remedy but flies around the room, can we consider the doctor to be proficient in his work? Evidently flying around the room is a miracle, but it does not in the least help the patient. It is not that the Prophets of God do not perform miracles, but the emphasis put on miracles diverts attention from their main work. The true miracle is that the holy Words of God flow through God's Chosen Ones to release human potential and knit the hearts together of disparate peoples and populations, even uniting those that previously hated each other, in bonds of love and affection. This is the true miracle and has been touched on in a previous chapter.

There are many metaphors for the Word of God – Bread of Heaven, Water of Life, the choice Wine, the Divine Elixir, to name a few. The Word of God streaming from Bahá'u'lláh has been likened to 'copious rain' which has fallen, in this day, on the parched ground of the human heart, and from it, 'Abdu'l-Bahá states: 'The ground of existence shall surely be developed into myrtles of the wisdom of God, for the fragrances of holiness have encompassed the earth, east and west . . .'[19]

In conversations I have had with atheists, they have been at pains to point out that we cannot rely on the authenticity of the Word of God in past sacred scriptures, as they were written years after their revelation (some, centuries later) and are subject to the corruption inherent in handing down oral accounts of scripture to future generations. We know this corruption as 'Chinese whispers'. I have, with reservations, agreed with them. Nonetheless, although ancient scriptures were not recorded exactly word for word, the spiritual potency they contained still provided the main impetus for the progress of civilization at those times. But some people may not be aware that there are three sacred scriptures that pass the test of authenticity – the Holy Qur'án, the Writings of the Báb and the Revelation of Bahá'u'lláh.

Authenticity of Bahá'u'lláh's Writings was of no small concern to Bahá'u'lláh Himself. Although Bahá'u'lláh did write with His own hand some of His voluminous works, the vast majority were dictated by Him to one or more of His secretaries. These were checked for accuracy by Bahá'u'lláh, transcribed and then sealed with one of His ten seals

Bahá'u'lláh's Revelation may be compared to an ocean revealed over a forty-year period. God's Words of love, power and majesty streamed through Him to produce this ocean. Never has so much loving knowledge and guidance been given to humanity from God – it stands unique in the annals of history. Indeed, Bahá'u'lláh Himself declares that if all His Writings were to be compiled, they would make up no less than one hundred volumes of sacred scripture. This is necessary because the human race has never before attained the age of maturity. It is not that past Manifestations of God could not have revealed the equivalent in their days, but they were constrained by the fact that humanity's child-like phases of development would not be able to grasp it. In regard to this, Christ stated that He had many things that He would have imparted to His followers but held back from doing so as they would be incapable of understanding – they would not be able to 'bear them now'.[20]

Bahá'ís often speak about the volume of revelation flowing through the Manifestations of God in terms of 'verses'. For instance, the total number of verses in the Gospels amount to 3,779 and this amount would be greatly reduced if repetition is considered. The holy Qur'án, revealed by Muhammad during a

23-year period, amounted to just over 6,300 verses.

It is important to know this, as the extent of the Revelations of the Báb and Bahá'u'lláh are not only measured by their books and Tablets but also by the number of verses they revealed. During the six-year ministry of the Báb, for instance, He revealed over 500,000 verses, a veritable torrent streaming through Him from God. These verses totally upset the corrupt equilibrium of Persia at that time. Thousands of souls flocked into His Cause, including highly educated Islamic scholars. To the existing upholders of the social order this constituted 'heresy' and all who supported the Báb were guilty of causing mischief in the 'umma' (religious community), a fate punishable by death. Indeed, thousands of the Báb's followers were brutally tortured and slaughtered rather than recant their faith in the new Manifestation of God and His Revelation. From this it can be surmised that the 500,000 verses of the Báb were not just a hotchpotch of man-made ramblings but a potent elixir that transformed the souls of all who 'drank from this cup' of His Revelation.

We must ask ourselves how it is possible for 500,000 verses to flow from the Báb over six years, when it took 23 years for just over 6,300 verses to be recorded in the Qur'án? The difference of volume is immense and the pressure on the Báb as pure conduit for revelation must have been all-consuming, occupying the greatest effort of His Ministry. In consideration of this question, we would do well to reflect, once again, on the station of a Manifestation of God. They are not just more advanced, highly intelligent human beings, nor can their station be understood as that of 'genius'. No, their reality is as different from us mere finite beings as we are different from animals – they are, in fact, of a species created by God for His grace and comfort to flow to us through perfections that no human being can attain.

The torrent of divine verses that burst through the Báb continued to do so through Bahá'u'lláh over a 40-year period. Surprisingly, thousands of these verses were wiped clean of ink and Bahá'u'lláh instructed his secretary to throw the pages into the river. The secretary was reluctant to carry out Bahá'u'lláh's orders, but was reassured by Him that, 'None is to be found at this time worthy to hear these melodies.' 'Not once or twice,', said the secretary, 'but innumerable times, was I commanded to repeat this act.'[21]

Another believer, who had experienced the flow of divine revelation from the Báb, was privileged to be in the presence of Bahá'u'lláh on occasions when He was revealing the divine verses. It had a profound effect upon him to such an extent that he declared Bahá'u'lláh's verses

> superior, in the rapidity with which they were penned, in the ease with which they flowed, in their lucidity, their profundity and sweetness to those which I, myself saw pour from the pen of the Báb when in His presence. Had Bahá'u'lláh no other claim to greatness, this were sufficient, in the eyes of the world and its people, that He produced such Verses as have streamed this day from His pen.[22]

When I was a young believer in the 1960s I attended a conference where the guest speaker was a most loved and distinguished older Bahá'í from Iran. Tarazu'lláh Samandari was, I believe, was the last person alive at that time to have been in the presence of Bahá'u'lláh. How honoured and humbled I felt to be in this great soul's company and to shake the hand of one who had actually experienced the joy and life-changing power of the presence of the Manifestation of God for this day. Mr Samandari had attained the presence of Bahá'u'lláh when he was just a youth, sixteen years of age. He was present on two occasions when Bahá'u'lláh was in the process of revealing the Word of God. Here is his account of this process:

> In those days Mírzá Áqá Ján [the secretary], as instructed by Bahá'u'lláh, would first read the letters to Him and then, as Bahá'u'lláh dictated, write the Tablets in answer to them. The

verses of God were revealed with great rapidity and without prior contemplation or meditation. By reason of the speed with which these were written, the recorded words were mostly illegible. Some of them no one was able to read; even Mírzá Áqá Ján himself at times had difficulty in deciphering his own writing and had to seek the help of Bahá'u'lláh for clarification. Thus the Word of God was revealed. The greatest proof of the authenticity of the Manifestations of God is the revelation of the words of God. No one else is capable of doing this. The holy Word revealed from the heaven of the Will of the All-Merciful first descends upon the pure and radiant heart of the Manifestation of God and then is spoken by Him. In His Tablet to Násiri'd-Dín Sháh [the King of Persia], Bahá'u'lláh confirms this in these words: 'This thing is not from Me, but from One Who is Almighty and All-Knowing'. . . I had the great privilege of being present on two occasions when Tablets were being revealed . . . The holy words were flowing from His lips as He paced up and down the room, and His amanuensis was recording them . . . It is not easy to describe the manner in which revelation came to Bahá'u'lláh.[23]

The torrent of revelation continued throughout Bahá'u'lláh's ministry. He Himself makes reference to this:

'Such are the outpourings . . . from the clouds of Divine Bounty that within the space of an hour the equivalent of a thousand verses hath been revealed.' 'So great is the grace vouchsafed in this day that in a single day and night, were an amanuensis capable of accomplishing it to be found, the equivalent of the Persian Bayán [the Báb's major work] would be sent down from the heaven of Divine holiness.' 'I swear by God!' He, in another connection has affirmed, 'In those days the equivalent of all that hath been sent down aforetime unto the Prophets hath been revealed.' 'That which hath already been revealed in this land (Adrianople),' He, furthermore, referring to the copiousness of His writings, has declared, 'secretaries are incapable of transcribing. It has, therefore, remained for the most part untranscribed.'[24]

An interesting observation from the above is that just as Christ was constrained from giving a fuller Revelation to a population not mentally, spiritually and socially ready for it, so, indeed, has Bahá'u'lláh declared that a vast portion of His Revelation, which was thrown into the river, is in advance of humanity's ability to comprehend it. Reflection on this makes it clear that we finite human beings have no faculty to understand the Word of God in its entirety – it is limitless, and we are limited. Muhammad made us aware of this when he declared:

> And if all the trees on earth were pens and the Ocean (were ink), with seven Oceans behind it to add to its (supply), yet would not the Words of Allah be exhausted (in the writing): for Allah is Exalted in power, Full of Wisdom.[25]

More revelation is to come, but this is for a future time when the next Manifestation of God will appear, as specified by Bahá'u'lláh, in a thousand years or more. During the period between now and then, everything revealed by Bahá'u'lláh for this day and age will be accomplished, as it is the command of God invested with indescribable power. All mankind, whether or not it knows it, is experiencing transforming spiritual forces released from the Revelation of Bahá'u'lláh. These forces spiritualize humanity and sweep aside the lamentably defective systems of governance that hinder the emergence of just local, national and global institutions, for it is the will of God for this age that all humanity will unite as citizens of 'one country' called planet Earth. Nothing can stop this process, no obstacle, however great, can derail this general direction in which the world is headed. Terrible suffering has been prophesied by Bahá'u'lláh for all peoples that impede this process – those that cling to ancient or outworn institutions, assumptions and immature behaviour. The old world of ingrained prejudice, divisions, estrangements, conflict and moral decay is disintegrating in front of our eyes. It will continue to do so until the mass of the people wake to the fact that the grace and loving care of our heavenly Father has been deposited in Bahá'u'lláh, as the Healer of all our ills. The world is being shaken to its core with calamities and portentous happenings daily, producing a sharp contrast between those who hold a confident vision of the future and those who do not. The difference between the two has been expressed in the following terms:

> . . . the contrast between the confident vision that propels the constructive endeavours of an illumined community and the tangled fears seizing the millions upon millions who are as yet unaware of the Day in which they are living. Bereft of authentic guidance, they dwell on the horrors of the century, despairing over what these could imply for the future, hardly appreciating that this very century contains a light that will be shed on centuries to come. Ill-equipped to interpret the social commotion at play throughout the planet, they listen to the pundits of error and sink deeper into a slough of despond. Troubled by forecasts of doom, they do battle with the phantoms of a wrongly informed imagination. Knowing nothing of the transformative vision vouchsafed by the Lord of the Age, they stumble ahead, blind to the peerlessness of the new Day of God.[26]

28

SOME CONCLUDING THOUGHTS FOR ALL WHO WISH TO NAVIGATE THE MATERIALISTIC MINEFIELDS OF THIS AGE

To end this book, I would like to speak directly to anyone who continues to hold a materialistic assumption of reality over that of a spiritual one. Such a view is nothing more than the dying remnants of an immature age. Its time is limited before the dangers and confusions they bring, and have brought, are washed away through wave after wave of spiritual forces which are, even now, creating an entirely new world – a just global civilization, embodying the will of God for this age.

I deeply believe, however, that most people are spiritual in nature and manifest their spirituality in many different ways – from the love and sacrifices they make for their children and parents to the work they do for the running of the community. Yet all this is undertaken within the most difficult and precarious of circumstances. All of humanity has been born into this rising swamp of materialism and is influenced by the normalizing of materialistic lifestyles. Many experience a deep void in their innermost being which they seek to fill with the things that eventually turn to dust, and copy behaviours that bring to their door bitter regret. Sometime during the process of spiritual progress, we become dissatisfied with 'tinsel and gold' and yearn for wisdom and inner calm, rejecting behaviours that experience shows destroy any sense of tranquillity. Perhaps further down the road of spiritual development we begin to question our mental processes that can be distorted by materialistic assumptions that lead us away from true happiness. At this time the human spirit may be in a state of receptivity that longs for a relationship with a Higher Power as experienced through the spiritual forces of transformation released by the Divine Spirit through the Manifestations of God.

Materialistic philosophy offers no proof of the existence of anything above physical reality, yet the human spirit declares otherwise, if one would only give some attention to it. Since the coming of the Báb and Bahá'u'lláh materialism has, like a pandemic virus, spread to become the dominant force in society, the symptoms of which are severe indeed, a form of 'spiritual malnutrition', that includes the following: gnawing anxieties and worries; engagement in feverish pursuits and frenetic activities; distorted and disturbing mental reasoning bringing frustration and discontent; escapist and hedonistic lifestyles that are completely addictive; an inability to know what will truly help or harm ourselves and others in the long run. The animal rule of 'survival of the fittest' and the struggle for existence has entered the human world, seeping into all thought processes. Sadly, the end of life 'reward' of such a struggle is regret, disillusionment and possibly great bitterness.

We are advised by 'Abdu'l-Bahá to look at the physical world with true insight and come to realize that:

> the world is even as a mirage rising over the sands that the thirsty mistaketh for water. The wine of this world is but a vapour in the desert, its pity and compassion but toil and trouble, the repose it proffereth only weariness and sorrow. Abandon it to those who belong to it . . .[1]

Further, 'Shall we pursue the phantom of a mortal happiness which does not exist', 'Abdu'l-Bahá asks, 'or turn toward the tree of life and the joys of its eternal fruits?'[2]

Acknowledging that there is a huge range of spiritual awareness (or lack of it) in humanity's present condition, the Manifestations of God have led us to an inflection point. With the coming of Bahá'u'lláh a new paradigm for a world is outlined, anticipated by Him, that is considered to be a 'global village' and has encouraged all to turn 'toward the tree of life, and the joys of its eternal fruits' This paradigm attracts those to a higher vision of spiritual and social progress: work is to be undertaken, not for selfish ends but in a spirit of service to humanity; and homes are to be spiritual environments in which children can begin to grow their immense potential; the habit of reading the soul-stirring, transforming Words of Bahá'u'lláh daily is developed in the home, when the family can become fully conscious that just as the body needs physical food to be healthy, so too does the soul need nourishment from the Word of God. Within this environment human beings realize, deep in their souls, that they are powerless to effect any personal transformation without calling on God in humble supplication for His aid and assistance. Hence prayer becomes a natural, constant activity and can be likened to a seed willing to put itself under the influence of the sun for growth to take place.

This paradigm shift involves joining with others, no matter what beliefs (or none) they profess, to be involved in community building at the grass roots, realizing that everyone has been created to make their unique contribution for a materially and spiritually prosperous society. Through the dawning of the need for unity comes a desire to reach out to others, for they are aware that without coming together in bonds of love and affection, there is disintegration of the fabric of society. In this regard they are aware that the conversations they have with family, friends, colleagues and neighbours should not be exclusively determined by materialistically minded people. Such conversations portray the addictive, worldly characteristics of souls who can only speak about physical things – holidays, work, fashion, TV programmes, food, clothes, etc.

Learning how to free oneself from prejudice and engage

others in conversations about spiritual concepts is a significant feature in this paradigm shift. For much depends upon higher-level thought, expressed in conversations that lead to sharing a common beatific vision of 'oneness'. It is by the power of wise utterance and a sound character that those on this spiritual path hope to attract the hearts of others to a spiritual lifestyle, a life of humble dedication to the Almighty as outlined in the Revelation of Bahá'u'lláh.

Those committed to this new paradigm, this new way of viewing reality, like all peoples, are beset by many of the problems and ugliness of a materialistic society. Nonetheless, spiritual souls are challenged to recast the tests and trials of life not in terms of obstacles to well-being but the means to develop further their 'gems of inestimable value',[3] and are even to be 'thankful in adversity', as Bahá'u'lláh advises.[4] Progress along the path of spiritual, moral, social and intellectual well-being is not easy; most do so, not in huge leaps forward but 'little by little, day by day'. It is known that all effort made to live by His counsel to: 'Let deeds, not words, be your adorning,'[5] wins the good-pleasure of God. Those on the path to following these precepts, although few in number, are responsible for the 'light' of spiritual progress in the world, which is needed to keep material progress within the bounds of that which will be of benefit to humanity. Spiritually minded souls become aware that 'human happiness is founded upon spiritual behaviour'.[6] Metaphorically, they are happy to be walking towards the Sun, as described in the opening story of the last chapter. 'Man is a spiritual being,' we are informed by 'Abdu'l-Bahá, although he has a material body with its legitimate needs, but 'only when he lives in the spirit is he truly happy.'[7]

A supreme necessity at this time when religious fanaticism would take us back to hatred and barbarism is to follow the directives of Bahá'u'lláh to 'Consort with all men' and the 'followers of all religions in a spirit of friendliness and fellowship'.[8] Love for and understanding of the interconnectedness of all the major religions as one divine process is now gathering momentum through the interfaith movement. This adds spiritual empowerment to those who are willing to form a distinctive, open to all, community of people that can commit to and amplify endeavours for the betterment of society. Realization is growing that constant association with materialistic and worldly-wise people increases sorrow, that the lifestyles they endorse tend to cover the soul with 'rust'. Rust, in this sense, is a corrosion that eats into the vitals of the human spirit, disintegrating all virtues and higher aspirations.

For spiritually minded people, contemplation of the next life is extremely important, not so as all one's attention is given to it, but to orient the soul to tread 'the mystical way with practical feet'.[9] Unfortunately, materialistically minded people are unaware that we are developing the condition of our soul in preparation for the world to come, even as a child in the womb is preparing for life after it is born. As mentioned in a previous chapter, 'Abdu'l-Bahá states that one of the factors that degrade one's inherent nobility is the belief that at death we no longer exist. We are reminded that He also states that the concept of 'annihilation' is 'a cause of human debasement and lowliness, a source of human fear and abjection. It has been conducive to the dispersion and weakening of human thought . . .'[10] If all our associations are with people who deny the continued existence of the soul after the physical body dies and are unaware that we will be called to an account for our earthly life, we risk being debased. This may involve being entangled in shameful, degenerate conversations and behaviours, and even criminality in extreme cases. Further, the thought of death and the belief that there is no afterlife contributes to fear and tends to predispose people to act in non-virtuous and selfish ways. For them there is no accounting for wrongdoing if they can get away with it in this world. And because priority is given to physical things, intellectual faculties are constrained within the physical world preventing intelligence from attaining the power of flight into the non-physical worlds – such limitations lead, as stated above, to 'the dispersion and weakening of human thought.'

In a powerful but succinct statement, Bahá'u'lláh warns

mankind that 'mortal eyes' will never 'recognize the everlasting Beauty, nor the lifeless heart delight in aught but in the withered bloom'.[11] His plea to every soul is to rise above the perilous sea of materialism, which Christ did when He walked upon the waters, and to follow the spiritual life outlined by all the Manifestations of God. The alternative is to be swallowed up and eventually drown in this 'sea'. What does it mean to 'drown' in this sea? It means that one's perfectly created human soul is immersed in thoughts, attitudes, assumptions, aspirations and lifestyles where there is no 'breath of life'. Bahá'u'lláh also provides us with a yardstick whereby we can measure whether our lives are more materialistically or spiritually inclined. We are to look at the company we choose to keep. Are they souls whose lifestyles are immersed in the material world or are they of those who have higher aspirations and are willing to selflessly serve humanity? 'For like seeketh like,' states Bahá'u'lláh, 'and taketh pleasure in the company of its kind.'[12]

Finally, more souls are aware that a major reason for uniting with others is to apply the healing remedy of Bahá'u'lláh's teachings. By so doing the unique identity of everyone is preserved, protected and developed. A simple example from nature informs us of the importance of this: consider that each soul is like a drop of water which has fallen from heaven upon various places. If left by itself, (an aspect of 'individualism') it is likely to be evaporated by the sun or wind. However, if it merges with other drops in a trickle and the trickle merges with other trickles to become a stream, and if streams merge to become a river, and if the river finds its way to the ocean, then we can be confident that the identity of each drop is preserved in the 'sea of oneness'.[13] 'Strive then,' Bahá'u'lláh writes:

> that thou mayest forsake the path of illusion and imitation and gain admittance into the realm of inner vision and the kingdom of spiritual discoveries. For in these days all are bewildered in the drunkenness of ignorance, save those whom thy

Lord hath willed to spare. Some consider the fading mirage to be the billowing ocean and reckon the impenetrable darkness as the radiant morn. Others, having forsaken the river of eternal life, content themselves with a vanishing drop. Such is the state and condition of the people . . .[14]

I hope it's not too late at this juncture to return to the dream I mentioned in the second chapter of this book. If you recall, some interpretations became apparent quite soon after the dream, others took some time to surface. I became aware that it was significant that I was a child in the dream, which seemed to relate to the words of Christ when He said, 'Verily I say unto you, Whosoever shall not receive the kingdom of God as a little child, he shall not enter therein.'[15] It became obvious to me, when reflecting on the significance of being in a condition of a child, that the baggage of scepticism, cynicism and prejudice had not yet accumulated. A child is innocent, open to things that the regrets, hurts, shameful lifestyles, and disillusionments – all aspects of a materialistic society – have not, as yet, encumbered the soul. Since that dream of many years ago I have become a parent and realized that parents must be vigilant when nurturing their offspring, as there are all manner of harmful beliefs out there, some preying on the naiveté of children. However, this fact should not blind us to the wonderful 'openness' of children but encourage adults to be much more knowledgeable and wiser in their role as parents.

Let us now focus on an interpretation of the majestic, kindly looking man in the booth, who manipulated objects on the counter such that they floated above the counter surface. You will recall that in the dream he said, 'This is what you can do if you believe.' My understanding of this is not that I should develop the powers of telekinesis, but if I truly 'believed' I would be able to control the material things of life. In other words, I would not be controlled, manipulated, overcome or enthralled with a materialistic perspective of living but would be able to use the physical things of life in subordination to spiritual principles – I would control my material world, it would not control me! In a practical sense, my wife and I from our first days of marriage decided to try our utmost to serve the Cause of Bahá'u'lláh as a life priority, rather than 'feathering our own nest' first and then applying ourselves to service.

Lastly, you will recall, the majestic, dignified man in the dream changed from one shape to another and very fast – as fast as the flicker in the old black and white movies. He went through many animal shapes and many human shapes but all the time his eyes stayed the same, very kind, loving and focused on my response. Then he stopped changing, came back to his original form and stated: 'This is what you can do if you love.' It was suggested to me that the frequent occurrence of the changing shapes from animal to human is an indication of the many Manifestations of God that have come to the human race at all stages of its development. The only unchanging feature with each form were the 'eyes', which could represent the 'Holy Spirit' being the one, never changing special power expressed through different forms/manifestations throughout humanity's development. You may recall the analogy mentioned earlier in the book that underpins this truth: 'Light is good in whatsoever lamp it is burning!'[16]

However, this understanding presented a difficulty for me, as it seemed to imply that all I have to do is 'love' and I would become a Manifestation of God. For Bahá'ís, I have learnt, this is a 'no go' area! And there is a good reason for this. Alluded to in this book several times is the understanding that a lower category of existence, no matter how far developed, will never jump into a higher category. So, for example, a radish, no matter how well cultivated, will never progress to become a rabbit. Similarly, no matter how far a human being develops he will never become a Manifestation of God. This being the case, I had to understand the dream in a different way. The interpretation that now makes most sense is as follows. If I love God and His Manifestations, I will be able to progress through many processes of transformation in this world and continue doing so in the next. I will evolve spiritually but always as a human being, realizing that because my soul is something that the Creator has created, He will never uncreate it. This process of spiritual evolution requires eternity, hence the creation of each of the infinite worlds of God to enable progress to happen. None of us knows the immense potential stored within the human soul which Bahá'u'lláh explicitly states 'is a sign of God, a heavenly gem whose reality the most learned of men hath failed to grasp, and whose mystery no mind, however acute, can ever hope to unravel'.[17]

Whether we know it or not, we are involved in a never-ending journey of 'transformation' back to God, the knowledge of which brings great joy and happiness to the spiritually minded person. Supporting spiritual happiness is the insight that the soul, beginning at the time of physical conception, is created to obey the will of God after volunteering, through one's own free will, to do so. It is ignorance that prevents us from gaining insight into the soul's mode of healthy functioning. This is why we need the Manifestations of God, Who, functioning on a much higher plain than human beings, educate us about what they perceive in every single soul. Eventually, it is adamantly stated in the Bahá'í Writings, humanity will evolve and 'appear in the utmost beauty' as is expressed in this loving prayer, a prayer that an increasing number of souls offer for children:

> O God! Educate these children. These children are the plants of Thine orchard, the flowers of Thy meadow, the roses of Thy garden. Let Thy rain fall upon them; let the Sun of Reality shine upon them with Thy love. Let Thy breeze refresh them in order that they may be trained, grow and develop, and appear in the utmost beauty. Thou art the Giver. Thou art the Compassionate.[18]

For that potential to have the best possible environment for its flourishing, many teachings are given in Bahá'í scripture. Hence

Bahá'u'lláh writes that every new-born child is to be encouraged and trained to make their unique contribution to 'an ever-advancing civilization', and that all 'have been created' for this purpose.[19] How humanity carries forward an ever-advancing civilization has been a main concern of every Manifestation of God. Today, serious consideration must be given to the words of Bahá'u'lláh, Who specifies how civilization can advance in this global age:

> That which the Lord hath ordained as the sovereign remedy and mightiest instrument for the healing of all the world is the union of all its peoples in one universal Cause, one common Faith. This can in no wise be achieved except through the power of a skilled, an all-powerful and inspired Physician.[20]

A significant ingredient of this objective, dwelt on in previous chapters, is the principle of the essential harmony of religion and science. The interaction of these two knowledge systems is at the heart of material and spiritual progress necessary for advancing civilization. Where are we now in this delicate but profoundly necessary balance?

'Early in the 20th century a materialistic interpretation of reality had consolidated itself so completely as to become the dominant world faith insofar as the direction of society was concerned', writes the Universal House of Justice.[21] Sadly, true religion was mixed with so many literal interpretations of symbolic references in holy scriptures that it proved untenable to an increasing number of people, especially in the West, who were gradually becoming literate and educated. Coupled with this were theologies and doctrines developed over centuries by the various religious authorities of all faiths that were incomprehensible to the growing army of educated people. Disappointment with immoral, materialistic and arrogant behaviours of ecclesiastics contributed to the birth of the 'Age of Enlightenment' in the eighteenth century. Its influence spread over the next few centuries producing wave after wave of anti-clericalism. All this combined with other factors to move an ever-growing number of people away from religion and many into atheism – and it still does. The 'wing' of superstitious religion was strong – it had to be challenged. This could be a significant reason why 'Abdu'l-Bahá, early in the twentieth century, spoke in many places throughout Europe and North America about the importance of science in the process of investigating truth. Religion would be shorn of superstition by the application of scientific knowledge, and rightly so. True religion and science never contradict each other. However, it would not be untrue to state that the influence of true religion has now degenerated so much that a condition, antithetical to promoting an ever-advancing civilization, has developed. In the first decades of the twenty-first century, things radically changed. In a sense 'the baby has been thrown out with the bathwater'. Not only has superstition been thrown out, but religion too.

We are now living in a time that could be viewed as the de-Christianization of the West and a gradual return to paganism. By now, several generations have had no contact with Holy Scriptures at all. Unfortunately, the wing of materialistic science has since grown strong and replaced superstitious religion. The pendulum has swung to an opposite extreme, just as damaging to personal well-being and harmony as is priestly domination and superstitious religion. We are now living with the fruits of materialism, fruits that do not nourish the soul of anyone. Several times have the terrifying results of materialism in the ascendancy been expressed throughout this book. And let it be understood that just as it is wrong to reject science, because it has been used to underpin materialistic perspectives of reality, it is equally wrong to reject religion, which has been obfuscated through materialistic assumptions. The following passage, partly quoted previously, is full of insights for our happiness and progress:

All things are beneficial if joined with the love of God; and without His love all things are harmful, and act as a veil between man and the Lord of the Kingdom. When His love is there, every bitterness turneth sweet, and every bounty rendereth a wholesome pleasure. For example, a melody, sweet to the ear, bringeth the very spirit of life to a heart in love with God, yet staineth with lust a soul engrossed in sensual desires. And every branch of learning, conjoined with the love of God, is approved and worthy of praise; but bereft of His love, learning is barren – indeed, it bringeth on madness. Every kind of knowledge, every science, is as a tree: if the fruit of it be the love of God, then is it a blessed tree, but if not, that tree is but dried-up wood, and shall only feed the fire.[22]

It is interesting that Srinivas Ramanujan, a deeply religious Hindu and a great mathematical genius mentioned in an earlier chapter, declared: 'An equation for me has no meaning, unless it expresses a thought of <u>God</u>.'[23]

The choice between a spiritual perspective of reality or a material perspective is ever-present, and it is a daily personal choice. Hopefully what has been written here may stimulate a worldview and access to a spiritual lifestyle, based upon the Writings of Bahá'u'lláh and His son 'Abdu'l-Bahá. No soul who chooses to investigate their works and their lives will be disappointed. However, Bahá'u'lláh declares that any attempt to make sense out of life, to gain meaning that satisfies the soul, to realize our unique purpose for living, and to make our contribution to an 'ever-advancing civilisation' depends on our own efforts. He writes:

Success or failure, gain or loss, must, therefore, depend upon man's own exertions. The more he striveth, the greater will be his progress. We fain would hope that the vernal showers of the bounty of God may cause the flowers of true understanding to spring from the soil of men's hearts, and may wash them from all earthly defilements.[24]

BIBLIOGRAPHY

'Abdu'l-Bahá. *'Abdu'l-Bahá in London* (1912, 1921). London: Bahá'í Publishing Trust, 1982.

— *Abdul Baha on Divine Philosophy.* Comp. I. F. Chamberlain. Boston: The Tudor Press, 1918.

— *Paris Talks: Addresses given by 'Abdu'l-Bahá in 1911* (1912). London: Bahá'í Publishing Trust, 12th ed. 1995.

— *The Promulgation of Universal Peace: Talks Delivered by 'Abdu'l-Baha During His Visit to the United States and Canada in 1912* (1922, 1925). Comp. H. MacNutt. Wilmette, IL: Bahá'í Publishing Trust, 2nd ed. 1982.

— *The Secret of Divine Civilization.* Trans. M. Gail. Wilmette, IL: Bahá'í Publishing Trust, 1957.

— *Selections from the Writings of 'Abdu'l-Bahá.* Comp. Research Department of the Universal House of Justice. Haifa: Bahá'í World Centre, 1978.

— *Some Answered Questions* (1908). Comp. and trans. Laura Clifford Barney. Haifa: Bahá'í World Centre, rev. ed. 2014.

— *Tablets of 'Abdu'l-Bahá* (etext in the Ocean search engine; originally published as *Tablets of Abdul-Baha Abbas.* 3 vols. Chicago: Bahá'í Publishing Society, 1909–1916). Wilmette, IL: National Spiritual Assembly of the Bahá'ís of the United States, 1980.

— 'Tablet to Dr. Auguste Henri Forel', in *The Bahá'í World 1968–1973*, vol. XV, pp. 37–43.

— *Will and Testament of 'Abdu'l-Bahá.* Wilmette, IL: National Spiritual Assembly of the Bahá'ís of the United States, 1944.

Al-Khalili, Jim. *The Golden Age of Science.* London: Penguin, 2012.

American Heritage Dictionary of the English Language. New York: Houghton Mifflin, 5th ed. 2016.

An-Nawawi. *Forty Hadith of an-Nawawi.* http://www.unification.net/ws/themeo15.htm.

Anushasana Parva. http://www.unification.net/ws/themeo15.htm.

Atwater, P. M. H. 'The out-of-body aspect of near death experience', online article, 1998, at: http://meta-religion.com/Paranormale/NDE/obe_aspect_of_nde.htm#.Uh.

Bahá'í International Community. *Bahá'u'lláh*. New York: Bahá'í International Community Office of Public Information, 1992.

— *The Prosperity of Humankind.* New York: Bahá'í International Community Office of Public Information, 1995.

— *Who is Writing the Future? Reflections on the Twentieth Century* (1999). Wilmette, IL: Bahá'í Publishing Trust, 2000.

Bahá'í Prayers: A Selection. London: Bahá'í Publishing Trust, 1975.

Bahá'u'lláh. *The Call of the Divine Beloved: Selected Mystical Works of Bahá'u'lláh.* Haifa: Bahá'í World Centre, 2018.

— *Days of Remembrance: Selections from the Writings of Bahá'u'lláh for Bahá'í Holy Days.* New York: Bahá'í International Community, online at Bahá'í Reference Library.

— *Epistle to the Son of the Wolf.* Trans. Shoghi Effendi. Wilmette, IL: Bahá'í Publishing Trust, rev. ed. 1976.

— *Gems of Divine Mysteries: Javáhiru'l-Asrár.* Haifa: Bahá'í World Centre, 2002.

— *Gleanings from the Writings of Bahá'u'lláh.* Trans. Shoghi Effendi. Wilmette, IL: Bahá'í Publishing Trust, 2nd ed. 1976.

— *The Hidden Words of Bahá'u'lláh.* Trans. Shoghi Effendi. Wilmette, IL: Bahá'í Publishing Trust, 1970; New Delhi: Bahá'í Publishing Trust, 1987.

— *The Kitáb-i-Aqdas: The Most Holy Book.* Haifa: Bahá'í World Centre, 1992.

— *Kitáb-i-Íqán: The Book of Certitude.* Trans. Shoghi Effendi. Wilmette, IL: Bahá'í Publishing Trust, 2nd ed. 1950, 1981; London: Bahá'í Publishing Trust, 1961.

— *Prayers and Meditations by Bahá'u'lláh.* Trans. Shoghi Effendi. Wilmette, IL: Bahá'í Publishing Trust, 1938, 1987.

— 'The Seven Valleys', and 'The Four Valleys' in *The Call of the Divine Beloved: Selected Mystical Works of Bahá'u'lláh.* Haifa: Bahá'í World Centre, 2018.

— *The Summons of the Lord of Hosts: Tablets of Bahá'u'lláh.* Haifa: Bahá'í World Centre, 2002.

— *Tablets of Bahá'u'lláh Revealed after the Kitáb-i-Aqdas.* Comp. Research Department of the Universal House of Justice. Haifa: Bahá'í World Centre, 1978.

Balyuzi, H. M. *Bahá'u'lláh, the King of Glory.* Oxford, George Ronald, 1980.

Bartlett, Viv. *Finding the Real You.* Oxford: George Ronald, 1988, 2011.

— *Nurturing a Healthy Human Spirit in the Young.* Oxford: George Ronald, 2014.

Beauregard, Mario. *Brain Wars: The Scientific Battle Over the Existence of the Mind and the Proof That Will Change the Way We Live Our Lives.* New York: Harper One, 2013.

Bible. *Holy Bible.* King James version. London: Eyre and Spottiswoode, various dates.

Bigger, Stephen. *Report on the Work and Effectiveness of the Swindon Youth Empowerment Programme, 2001–2008.* University of Worcester, March 2008. Eprints.worc.ac.uk

Brain, Marshall. 'How sleep works', online article, at: https://science.howstuffworks.com/life/inside-the-mind/human-brain/sleep1.htm.

Branch, Raymus. *Harry Edwards: The Life Story of the Great Healer.* Guildford: Healer Publishing, 1991.

Buddha. Dhammapadha. Trans. J. Richards, *Sayings of Buddha*, at: http://www.edepot.com/dhamma2.html.

— The Eightfold Path, Majjhima-Nikaya, No. 21.

Byrne, John A. 'The greatest entrepreneurs of our time – and what you can learn from them', in *Fortune*, 9 April 2012.

Cain, Fraser. 'The end of everything', online article in *Universe Today*, 25 July 2007. http://www.universetoday.com/11430/the-end-of-everything/.

— 'How long will life survive on planet Earth?', online article in *Universe Today*, 30 September 2013. http://www.universetoday.com/25367/how-long-will-life-survive-on-earth/#ixzz2ZbMnzaRf.

Catholic Encyclopedia. http://www.newadvent.org/cathen/06259a.htm.

Chalmers, Sarah. 'Yes, we do have a sixth sense: The in-depth study of our intriguing dreams that convinced one doctor', in *Daily Mail Online*, 6 October 2009.

Cherry, Kendra. 'The sensorimotor stage of cognitive development', online article at: http://psychology.about.com/od/piagetstheory/p/sensorimotor.htm.

Clarkson, Josie. 'Animal brains v. human brains: Let the Battle of the Brains commence!', in *BBC Science Focus Magazine*, 20 October 2017.

Concise Oxford Dictionary. Oxford: Oxford University Press, 12th ed. 2011.

The Compilation of Compilations. Prepared by the Universal House of Justice 1963–1990. 2 vols. Sydney: Bahá'í Publications Australia, 1991.

Cooke-Taylor, William. *Tour in Manufacturing Districts of Lancashire* (1838). Palala Press, 2016.

Dossey, Larry. *The Power of Premonitions: How Knowing the Future Can Shape Our Lives*. New York: Hay House, 2009.

Esslemont, J. E. *Bahá'u'lláh and the New Era* (1923). Wilmette IL: Bahá'í Publishing Trust, rev. ed. 1980.

Faizi, Abu'l-Qasim Faizi, 'A flame of fire', in *Penned by A. Q. Faizí* (Oxford: George Ronald, 2021), pp. 45–60. Also on the Ocean search engine.

Fitzgerald, Andrew. '10 terrible famines in history', online article, 10 April 2013. http://listverse.com/2013/04/10/10-terrible-famines-in-history/.

Frankl, Viktor. *Man's Search for Ultimate Meaning*. Cambridge, Mass: Perseus Publishing, 2000.

Franklin, Benjamin. *The Art of Virtue: His Formula for Successful Living*. New York: Simon & Schuster, 2011.

Gail, Marzieh. *Six Lessons on Islám*. Wilmette, IL: Bahá'í Publishing Trust, 1953.

Greenfield, Susan. 'How to think about the brain,' in *Guide to Brain Health* (Washington: Dana Press, 2002), pp. 5–16.

Haisch, Bernard. *The God Theory: Universes, Zero-Point Fields, and What's Behind it All*. San Francisco: Weiser Books, 2009.

Hall, Stuart; Gieben, Bram (eds). *Formations of Modernity*. London: Polity Press in Association with the Open University, 1992.

Handwerk, Brian. '"Bird flu" similar to deadly 1918 flu, gene study finds', in *National Geographic News*, 5 October 2005.

Herculano-Houzel, Suzana. 'What's so special about the human brain? ', TED talk, August 2015.

Holder, Rodney. *Big Bang, Big God*. London: Lion Hudson, 2013.

Ives, Howard Colby. *Portals to Freedom*. Oxford: George Ronald, 1943.

Kanigel, Robert. *The Man Who Knew Infinity: A Life of the Genius Ramanujan*. New York: Scribner's, 1991.

Keith, Fritha. '10 cases of feral children', online article in *Listverse*, 7 March 2008. http://listverse.com/2008/03/07/10-modern-cases-of-feral-children/

Kisslinger, Tanja. 'Reports from the field: Inside a Romanian orphanage: Reflections by a volunteer caregiver', in *Human Rights Tribune*, vol. 8, no. 3 (Winter 2002). See her update on a return visit, 'Inside a Romanian orphanage', 2 February 2020, at http://areweconnecting.com/inside-a-romanian-orphanage/.

Kurzius, Brian (comp.). *Fire and Gold*. Oxford: George Ronald, 1995.

'Ladysmith Black Mambazo', at *Encyclopedia.com*, 11 June 2018.

Lights of Guidance: A Bahá'í Reference File. Comp. H. Hornby. New Delhi: Bahá'í Publishing Trust, 5th ed. 1997.

Loehle, Craig. *On the Shoulders of Giants*. Oxford: George Ronald, 1994.

Long, Jeffrey; Perry, Paul. *God and the Afterlife*. New York: Harper One. 2016.

—; —; Dunsworth, *Evidence of the Afterlife*. New York: Harper Collins, 2010.

Longaker, Christine. *Facing Death and Finding Hope: A Guide to the Emotional and Spiritual Care of the Dying*. New York: Doubleday, 1997.

Matthews, Gary L. *The Challenge of Bahá'u'lláh*. Oxford: George Ronald, 1993.

Matson, Floyd. *The Idea of Man*. New York: Delacorte Press, 1976.

McLeod, Saul. 'Concrete operational stage', updated 2021, online article at: http://www.simplypsychology.org/concrete-operational.html.

Milman, Henry Hart. *The History of the Jews, from the Earliest Period down to Modern Times*. London, 1829.

Nietzsche, Friedrich. *Thus Spake Zarathustra* (1883). Various modern editions.

Obringer, Lee Ann. 'How dreams work', online article at: http://science. howstuffworks.com/life/inside-the-mind/human-brain/dream9.htm.

Pace, Eric. 'Arthur Koestler and wife suicides in London', in *The New York Times*, 4 March 1983.

Qur'án. *The Holy Qur'an*. Trans. Abdullah Yusuf Ali. 1934. Rev. ed. 2009/10 available at sacred-texts.com.

Rutter, Michael. 'Romanian orphans adopted early overcome deprivation', Brown University, Child and Adolescent Behavior Letter, June 1996.

Sabet, Huschmand. *The Heavens Are Cleft Asunder*. Oxford: George Ronald, 1976.

Saifullah, Khaled. 'Causes of flooding in Bangladesh', online article, 27 March 2009. http://freshclick.wordpress. com/2009/03/27/causes-of-the-flooding-in-bangladesh/.

Sample, Ian. 'NASA has figured out how the world will end', in *The Guardian,* 22 October 2015.

Savi, Julio. *The Eternal Quest for God*. Oxford: George Ronald, 1989.

Shoghi Effendi. *The Advent of Divine Justice* (1939). Wilmette, IL: Bahá'í Publishing Trust, 1984.

— *God Passes By* (1944). Wilmette, IL: Bahá'í Publishing Trust, rev. ed. 1974.

— *Unfolding Destiny: The Messages from the Guardian of the Bahá'í Faith to the Bahá'í Community of the British Isles*. London: Bahá'í Publishing Trust, 1981.

— *The World Order of Bahá'u'lláh: Selected Letters by Shoghi Effendi* (1938). Wilmette, IL: Bahá'í Publishing Trust, 2nd rev. ed. 1974.

Stanford Encyclopaedia of Philosophy. https://plato.stanford.edu/.

Stewart, Anita L.; Ware, John E. 'Sleep measures', ch. 14 in *Measuring Functioning and Well-Being: The Medical Outcomes Study Approach*. Durham, N.C.: Duke University Press, 1992.

Stibich, Mark. 'What is the Somatic Mutation Theory of aging? A look at one of the many theories of aging', online article, 19 March 2017. https://www.verywell.com/the-somatic-mutation-theory-of-aging.

Taherzadeh, Adib. *The Child of the Covenant: A Study Guide to the Will and Testament of 'Abdu'l-Bahá*. Oxford: George Ronald, 2000.

— *The Revelation of Bahá'u'lláh*. 4 vols. Oxford: George Ronald, 1974–1987.

Teichman, Jenny; Evans, Katherine C. *Philosophy A Beginners Guide*. Oxford: Blackwell, 2nd ed. 1996.

Thomas, Rachel. 'Ramanujan: Dream of the possible', quoting Ken Ono, in *Plus* magazine, 20 December 2018, https://plus.maths.org/content/celebrating-ramanujan.

Thomson, Helen. 'Near-death experiences are overwhelmingly peaceful', in *New Scientist*, 26 June 2014.

Talmud. http://www.unification.net/ws/theme015.htm.

Townshend, George. *The Heart of the Gospel*. Oxford: George Ronald, 1960.

Trine, Ralph Waldo. *In Tune with the Infinite* (1897). Richmond: The Oaklea Press, 2002. See also http://ralphwaldotrine.wwwhubs.com.

UK Bahá'í. No. 24 (December 2017).

The Universal House of Justice. *Century of Light*. New Delhi: Bahá'í Publishing Trust, 2001.

— 'Child abuse, psychology and knowledge of self', 2 December 1985. Available on the Ocean search engine.

— Letter to the World's Religious Leaders, April 2002. Available at Bahá'í Reference Library.

— Message to the Bahá'ís of the World, Riḍván 156, 1999. Available at Bahá'í Reference Library.

— *One Common Faith*. Haifa: Bahá'í World Centre, 2005; Wilmette, IL: Bahá'í Publishing Trust, 2005.

— *The Promise of World Peace* (1985). Many editions.

Vitelli, Romeo. 'Storming into adulthood: Are adolescents really emotional volcanoes waiting to explode?' (blog), in *Media Spotlight*, 30 September 2013. http://www.psychologytoday.com/blog/media-spotlight/201309/storming-adulthood.

Vivancos, Valérie. 'Ocean Viva Silver' (blog). http://oceanvivasilver.com/5-namakkals-infinity-dream-srinivasa-ramanuja.

Walker, Graham. 'Science and morality', in *The Bahá'í World 2004–2005* (Haifa: Bahá'í World Centre, 2006).

Webster's Collegiate Dictionary. New York: Random House Kernerman, 2010.

World Health Organization (WHO). *Global Status Report on Alcohol and Health 2018.* Geneva: WHO, 2018.

Wikipedia. www.wikipedia.org.

Woolson, Gayle. *The Divine Symphony.* Buenos Aires: Ebila, Bahá'í Publishing Trust, 1992. New Delhi, Baha'i Publishing Trust India.

NOTES AND REFERENCES

1 Days of Search

1 John 14:2.
2 Branch, *Harry Edwards: The Life Story of the Great Healer*, p. 174.
3 See http://en.wikipedia.org/wiki/Robert_James_Lees.
4 Matt. 7: 7–8.
5 Trine, *In Tune with the Infinite*, Preface to the First Edition.
6 ibid. Ch. 13: 'The Basic Principle of All Religions – The Universal Religion'.
7 https://www.britannica.com/topic/materialism-philosophy.
8 *American Heritage Dictionary of the English Language*, Fifth Edition (2016).
9 See https://en.wikipedia.org/wiki/Spiritual_but_not_religious.
10 *Webster's Collegiate Dictionary* (2010).
11 Frankl, *Man's Search for Ultimate Meaning*, p. 28.

2 Becoming Aware

1 Frankl, *Man's Search for Ultimate Meaning*, p. 134.
2 ibid.
3 Franklin, *The Art of Virtue: His Formula for Successful Living.*
4 The Universal House of Justice, *One Common Faith*, para. 11.
5 The Universal House of Justice, *Century of Light*, p. 89.
6 ibid. pp. 89–90.
7 Bahá'í International Community, *Who Is Writing the Future?*
8 Bahá'u'lláh, *Kitáb-i-Íqán*, para. 1, p. 3.
9 ibid. para. 2, p. 4.
10 ibid. para. 2, p. 3.
11 ibid.
12 Bahá'u'lláh, *Tablets of Bahá'u'lláh Revealed after the Kitáb-i-Aqdas*, p. 188.
13 ibid. p. 41.
14 ibid. p. 51.
15 Bahá'í International Community, *Who Is Writing the Future?*

3 Materialistic Assumption 1: There is a Beginning of the Universe, which Occurred by Chance

1 See https://www.reference.com/science/evidence-support-big-bang-theory. There are several YouTube videos on the Big Bang theory.

2 Baháʼuʼlláh, quoted by Shoghi Effendi in *The Advent of Divine Justice*, p. 80.

3 See https://www.sciencefocus.com/space/what-caused-the-big-bang/. Several YouTube videos explore different theories.

4 ʼAbduʼl-Baha, *Some Answered Questions*, no. 7, pp. 28–9:

> . . . as you know, before the observations of the renowned astronomer of later times [Copernicus], that is, from the first centuries down to the fifteenth century of the Christian era, all the mathematicians of the world were unanimous in upholding the centrality of the earth and the movement of the sun. This modern astronomer was the source of the new theory that postulated the movement of the earth and the fixity of the sun. Until his time, all the mathematicians and philosophers of the world held to the Ptolemaic system, and whosoever uttered a word against it was considered ignorant. It is true that Pythagoras, and Plato during the latter part of his life, conceived that the sun's annual movement around the zodiac did not proceed from the sun itself but from the earth's movement around it, but this theory was entirely forgotten and the Ptolemaic theory was universally accepted by all mathematicians. But in the Qurʼán a number of verses were revealed which contradicted the Ptolemaic system. One of them, 'The sun moves in a fixed place of its own' (36:37), alludes to the fixity of the sun and its movement around an axis. Likewise, in another verse, 'And each swims in its own heaven' (36:38), the movement of the sun, the moon, the earth, and the other celestial bodies is specified. When the Qurʼán was spread abroad, all the mathematicians scoffed and attributed this view to ignorance. Even the Muslim divines, finding these verses contrary to the Ptolemaic system, were obliged to interpret them figuratively, for the latter was accepted as incontrovertible fact and yet was explicitly contradicted by the Qurʼán.
>
> It was not before the fifteenth century of the Christian era, nearly nine hundred years after Muḥammad, that new observations were made by a famous mathematician [Galileo], that the telescope was invented, that important discoveries were made, that the rotation of the earth and the fixity of the sun were proven, and that the latter's movement about an axis was likewise discovered. Then it became evident that the explicit text of the Qurʼán was in full agreement with reality and that the Ptolemaic system was sheer imagination.

See also: 'Heliocentric concepts in the Quran', at https://lampofislam. wordpress.com/2014/08/08/heliocentric-concepts-in-the-quran/.

5 'Abdu'l-Bahá, *Some Answered Questions*, no. 47, p. 207.
6 Bahá'u'lláh, *Gleanings from the Writings of Bahá'u'lláh*, pp. 60–61.
7 Bahá'u'lláh, *Tablets of Bahá'u'lláh Revealed after the Kitáb-i-Aqdas*, p. 140.
8 Stibich, 'What is the Somatic Mutation Theory of aging?' This theory states that an important part of aging is determined by what happens to our genes after we inherit them. From the time of conception, our body's cells are continually reproducing. Each time a cell divides, there is a chance that some of the genes will be copied incorrectly. This is called mutation. Additionally, exposures to toxins, radiation or ultraviolet light can cause mutations in your body's genes. The body can correct or destroy most of the mutations, but not all of them. Eventually, the mutated cells accumulate, copy themselves and cause problems in the body's functioning related to aging.
9 'Abdu'l-Bahá, *Some Answered Questions*, no. 53, p. 236.
10 Rev. 3:16.
11 'Abdu'l-Bahá, 'Tablet to Dr Auguste Henri Forel'.
12 Loehle, *On the Shoulders of Giants*, p. 146.
13 'Abdu'l-Bahá, quoted in the Introduction to Bahá'u'lláh, *The Kitáb-i-Aqdas*, p. 5.
14 Buddha, The Eightfold Path.
15 'Abdu'l-Bahá, *Some Answered Questions*, no. 53, p. 234.
16 Savi, *The Eternal Quest for God*, pp. 69–70.
17 Murchie, *The Seven Mysteries of Life*, p. 611, quoted ibid. pp. 69–70.
18 'Abdu'l-Bahá, 'Tablet to Dr Auguste Henri Forel'.
19 Bahá'u'lláh, *Gleanings from the Writings of Bahá'u'lláh*, XCIII, pp. 187–8.
20 ibid. LXXXII, p. 163.
21 ibid. LXXIX, p. 152.

4 Materialistic Assumption 2: Man is No More than an Intelligent Animal

1 'Abdu'l-Bahá, *The Promulgation of Universal Peace*, pp. 50–51.
2 ibid. p. 51.

5 Materialistic Assumption 3: Man's Rational Faculties are the Product of His Brain

1 https://www.bna.org.uk/about-neuroscience/.
2 'Abdu'l-Bahá, *The Promulgation of Universal Peace*, p. 357.
3 Clarkson, 'Animal brains v. human brains: Let the Battle of the Brains commence!', in *BBC Science Focus Magazine*, 20 October 2017.
4 ibid.

5   https://www.learning-mind.com/animal-intelligence/.

6   'Abdu'l-Bahá, *The Promulgation of Universal Peace*, p. 77.

7   Savi, *The Eternal Quest for God*, p. 80.

8   'Abdu'l-Bahá, *Paris Talks*, no. 23, p. 68.

9   The Universal House of Justice, *The Promise of World Peace*, October 1985.

10   https://www.apa.org/action/science/brain-science/.

11   https://phys.org/news/2019-09-dogs-brains-mri-scans-reveal.html#.

12   https://royalsociety.org/people/raymond-dolan-11345/.

13   https://medicalxpress.com/news/2018-06-scientists-intelligence-brain-scans.html#.

14   Walker. 'Science and morality', in *The Bahá'í World 2004–2005*, pp. 189–90. For the experiment, see Greenfield, 'How to think about the brain', in *Guide to Brain Health*, pp. 5–16.

15   ibid.

16   The Encephalization Quotient (EQ) is 'the ratio between brain weight to the entire body weight. Humans have a ratio of about 1-50, whereas most other mammals are closer to 1-180. This means that the brain takes up more weight in a person than it does in other animals...For example, humans have an EQ of about 7.5, which means that our brains are seven and a half times larger than what you would expect from an animal of our size. A squirrel, on the other hand, has an EQ of 1.1. This is pretty average for an animal of its size' (https://max-brainfunction.com/major-differences-human-animal-brains/).

17   Herculano-Houzel, 'What's so special about the human brain?', TED talk, available on YouTube.

18   'Abdu'l-Bahá, *Some Answered Questions*, no. 48, para. 2, p. 213.

19   'Abdu'l-Bahá, *Paris Talks*, no. 28, p. 82.

20   'Abdu'l-Bahá, *The Promulgation of Universal Peace*, p. 177.

21   'Abdu'l-Bahá, *Paris Talks*, no. 29, p. 91.

22   'Abdu'l-Bahá, *Abdul Baha on Divine Philosophy*, p. 128.

23   Bahá'u'lláh, *Gleanings*, LXXX, p. 154.

24   'Abdu'l-Bahá, *Some Answered Questions*, no. 67. p. 281.

25   'Abdu'l-Bahá, 'Tablet to Dr Auguste Henri Forel'.

26   'Abdu'l-Bahá, *Some Answered Questions*, no. 55, p. 242.

27   'Abdu'l-Bahá, 'Tablet to Dr Auguste Henri Forel'.

28   Bahá'u'lláh, *Gleanings*, LXXXI, p. 157.

6 Materialistic Assumption 4: It is Impossible to Change Human Nature Because Humans are Selfish and Aggressive

1   The Universal House of Justice, *The Promise of World Peace*, p. 1.

2   Bahá'u'lláh, *Tablets of Bahá'u'lláh*, p. 156.

3   'Abdu'l-Bahá, *Selections from the Writings of 'Abdu'l-Bahá*, no. 111, p. 136.

4   The interpretation of the Adam and Eve story in the Bible is regarded by Bahá'ís as being symbolic in nature and not to be taken literally. Science has proven that mankind has been around a lot longer than the 6,000 plus years, originally thought by Christian theologians to be the age of the human race.

5   Gen. 2:9.

6   The Universal House of Justice, *The Promise of World Peace*, p. 1.

7   ibid.

8   ibid.

9   ibid.

10 'Abdu'l-Bahá, *Selections from the Writings of 'Abdu'l-Bahá*, no. 159, p. 190.

11 Bahá'u'lláh, *Hidden Words*, Arabic no. 11.

12 ibid. no. 12.

13 ibid. no. 13.

14 Bahá'u'lláh, *Gleanings from the Writings of Bahá'u'lláh*, CXXII, p. 260.

15 ibid. p. 259.

16 'Abdu'l-Bahá, *Some Answered Questions*, ch. 3, p. 9.

17 'Abdu'l-Bahá, *The Promulgation of Universal Peace*, p. 288.

18 'Abdu'l-Bahá, *Some Answered Questions*, ch. 3, pp. 9–10.

19 Bahá'u'lláh, *Gleanings from the Writings of Bahá'u'lláh*, CXXXII, p. 287.

20 'Abdu'l-Bahá, *The Promulgation of Universal Peace,*, p. 465.

21 'Abdu'l-Bahá, *Selections from the Writings of 'Abdu'l-Bahá*, no. 103, p. 130.

22 'Abdu'l-Bahá, *Paris Talks*, no. 18, p. 55.

23 ibid.

24 'Abdu'l-Bahá, *The Promulgation of Universal Peace*, pp. 465–6.

25 Bahá'u'lláh, *Tablets of Bahá'u'lláh*, p. 36.

26 Bahá'u'lláh, *Gleanings from the Writings of Bahá'u'lláh*, CXXII, p. 259.

27 From a letter written on behalf of Shoghi Effendi to an individual believer, 24 November 1956, in *Lights of Guidance*, p. 600.

28 John 10:10.

29 'Abdu'l-Bahá, in *Baha'i Prayers*, p. 86.

30 For more information about SYEP, see Bartlett, *Nurturing a Healthy Human Spirit in the Young*.

31 Bahá'u'lláh, *Gleanings from the Writings of Bahá'u'lláh*, CXXII, p. 260.

32 'Abdu'l-Bahá, *Selections from the Writings of 'Abdu'l-Bahá*, no. 103, p. 130.

33 Along with a variety of funding streams over the years, SYEP was granted £80,000 for two years from Swindon's Trustees of the Local Authorities Education budget. After the economic crash of 2008, funding streams to pay the coordinator her wages and a part-time administrator were not forthcoming. However, SYEP is still ongoing

in Swindon and has since started in a primary school in Wales (2021).

34 Bigger, *Report on the Work and Effectiveness of the Swindon Youth Empowerment Programme, 2001–2008*, Executive Summary.

7 Materialistic Assumption 5: An Innate Sense of Human Dignity Will Prevent Man from Committing Evil Actions

1   'Abdu'l-Bahá, *The Secret of Divine Civilization*, p. 97.

2   https://en.wikipedia.org/wiki/Humanism.

3   www.bbc.co.uk/religion/religions/atheism/types/humanism.shtm.

4   'Abdu'l-Bahá, *The Secret of Divine Civilization*, p. 97.

5   Nietzsche, *Thus Spake Zarathustra*, quoted from https://www.goodreads.com/quotes/22827-god-is-dead-god-remains-dead-and-we-have-killed.

6   ibid.

7   Kisslinger, 'Reports from the field: Inside a Romanian orphanage: Reflections by a volunteer caregiver', in *Human Rights Tribune*, vol. 8, no. 3 (Winter 2002). See, by contrast, her update on a return visit, 'Inside a Romanian orphanage', 2 February 2020, at http://areweconnecting.com/inside-a-romanian-orphanage/.

8   Rutter, 'Romanian orphans adopted early overcome deprivation', Brown University, Child and Adolescent Behavior Letter, June 1996.

9   'Abdu'l-Bahá, *The Secret of Divine Civilization*, pp. 97–8.

10 Keith, '10 cases of feral children', in *Listverse*, 7 March 2008.

11 ibid.

12 ibid.

13 ibid.

14 'Abdu'l-Bahá, *Some Answered Questions*, ch. 3, p. 9.

15 'Abdu'l-Bahá, *The Secret of Divine Civilization*, p. 97.

16 Qur'án 16:38.

17 Bahá'u'lláh, *Gleanings from the Writings of Bahá'u'lláh*, LXXXVII, p. 174.

18 ibid. p. 172.

19 Bahá'u'lláh, quoted in Shoghi Effendi, *The Advent of Divine Justice*, p. 67.

20 Bahá'u'lláh, *Tablets of Bahá'u'lláh*, p. 127.

21 Letter written on behalf of Shoghi Effendi to an individual, 14 July 1943, in *Lights of Guidance*, p. 491.

22 'Abdu'l-Bahá, *The Secret of Divine Civilization*, p. 97.

23 ibid.

24 Bahá'u'lláh, *Gems of Divine Mysteries*, p. 14.

25 'Abdu'l-Bahá, *The Promulgation of Universal Peace*, p. 466.

26 Luke 6:27–28.

27 ibid.

28 Buddha, The Eightfold Path, in *Majjhima-Nikaya*, no. 21.

29   'Abdu'l-Bahá, *The Promulgation of Universal Peace*, pp. 362–3.
30   ibid. p. 363.
31   Matson, *The Idea of Man*, pp. 11–12.

8 Materialistic Assumption 6: There Should Be No Limit to Personal Liberty Providing One's Freedom Does No Harm to Others

1   'Abdu'l-Bahá, *Some Answered Questions*, ch. 40, p. 181.
2   ibid. ch. 20, p. 105.
3   'Abdu'l-Bahá, *Selections from the Writings of 'Abdu'l-Bahá*, no. 21, p. 50.
4   'Abdu'l-Bahá, *Some Answered Questions*, ch. 45, p. 196.
5   Bahá'u'lláh, *Prayers and Meditations*, CLXIII, p. 257.
6   'Abdu'l-Bahá, *Paris Talks*, no. 39, p. 124.
7   'Abdu'l-Bahá, *The Promulgation of Universal Peace*, p. 221.
8   Bahá'u'lláh, *Gleanings from the Writings of Bahá'u'lláh*, CX, p. 216.
9   ibid.
10   Bahá'u'lláh, *Tablets of Bahá'u'lláh*, p. 219.
11   Bahá'u'lláh, *Hidden Words*, Arabic no. 56.
12   'Abdu'l-Bahá, *Selections from the Writings of 'Abdu'l-Bahá*, no. 100, p. 127.
13   'Abdu'l-Bahá, *Some Answered Questions*, ch. 40, p. 181.
14   'Abdu'l-Bahá, *Will and Testament*, p. 13.
15   Bahá'u'lláh, *The Kitáb-i-Aqdas*, paras. 122–125, pp. 63–4.
16   'Abdu'l-Bahá, *Some Answered Questions*, ch. 40, p. 181.

9 Evidence of the Human Spirit and a Spiritual World

1   Ibn Sina, quoted in al-Khalili, *The Golden Age of Science*, p. 180.
2   'Abdu'l-Bahá, *Some Answered Questions*, ch. 61, p. 261.
3   ibid. pp. 261–2.
4   'Abdu'l-Bahá, *The Promulgation of Universal Peace*, p. 242.
5   'Abdu'l-Bahá, *Paris Talks*, no. 57, p. 192.
6   'Abdu'l-Bahá, *The Promulgation of Universal Peace*, p. 464.
7   ibid. p. 243.
8   'Sleep measures', in Stewart and Ware (eds): *Measuring Functioning and Well-Being: The Medical Outcomes Study Approach*, pp. 235–59.
9   Brain, 'How sleep works':

     If you attach an **electroencephalograph** to a person's head, you can record the person's brainwave activity. An awake and relaxed person generates **alpha waves**, which are consistent oscillations at about 10 cycles per second. An alert person generates **beta waves**, which are about twice as fast.

     During sleep, two slower patterns called **theta waves** and **delta waves** take over. Theta waves have oscillations in the range of 3.5 to 7 cycles per second, and delta waves have oscillations of less than 3.5 cycles per second. As a person falls asleep and sleep deepens, the brainwave patterns slow down. The slower the brain-wave patterns, the deeper the sleep -- a person deep in delta wave sleep is hardest to wake up.

At several points during the night, something unexpected happens – **rapid eye movement** (REM) sleep occurs. Most people experience three to five intervals of REM sleep per night, and brainwaves during this period speed up to awake levels. . .

REM sleep is when you dream. If you wake up a person during REM sleep, the person can vividly recall dreams. If you wake up a person during NREM (non REM) sleep, generally the person will not be dreaming.

You must have both REM and NREM sleep to get a good night's sleep. A normal person will spend about 25 percent of the night in REM sleep, and the rest in NREM. A REM session – a dream – lasts five to 30 minutes.

10 'Abdu'l-Bahá, *Some Answered Questions*, ch. 61, p. 261.

11 Byrne, 'The greatest entrepreneurs of our time – and what you can learn from them', in *Fortune*, 9 April 2012.

12 http://dreamtraining.blogspot.co.uk /2010/12/inventions-that-came-in-dreams-largest.html.

13 ibid.

14 See Kanigel, *The Man Who Knew Infinity: A Life of the Genius Ramanujan*.

15 Vivancos, 'Ocean Viva Silver' (blog). Information from Kanigel, *The Man Who Knew Infinity.*

16 Thomas, 'Ramanujan: Dream of the possible', quoting Ken Ono, in *Plus* magazine, 20 December 2018.

17 Vivancos, 'Ocean Viva Silver' (blog).

18 http://en.wikipedia.org/wiki/Sleep_and_creativity#Anecdotal_accounts_of_sleep_and_creativity.

19 'Ladysmith Black Mambazo', at Encyclopedia.com, 11 June 2018.

20 Chalmers, 'Yes, we do have a sixth sense: The in-depth study of our intriguing dreams that convinced one doctor', in *Daily Mail Online*, 6 October 2009. Information in her article is from Dossey, *The Power Of Premonitions: How Knowing The Future Can Shape Our Lives.*

21 ibid.

22 ibid.

23 'Abdu'l-Bahá, *Some Answered Questions*, ch. 61, p. 261.

24 Quoted by Obringer, 'How dreams work'.

25 'The Seven Valleys', in Bahá'u'lláh, *The Call of the Divine Beloved*, p. 42.

26 Bahá'u'lláh, *Gleanings from the Writings of Bahá'u'lláh*, LXXIX, p. 152.

27 'The Seven Valleys', in Bahá'u'lláh, *The Call of the Divine Beloved*, p. 43.

28 ibid.

29 Beauregard, *Brain Wars: The Scientific Battle Over the Existence of the Mind and the Proof That Will Change the Way We Live Our Lives*, Ch. 7.

30 Thomson, 'Near-death experiences are overwhelmingly peaceful', in *New Scientist*, 26 June 2014.

31 Atwater, 'The out-of-body aspect of near death experience', online article, 1998.

32 Beauregard, *Brain Wars: The Scientific Battle Over the Existence of the Mind and the Proof That Will Change the Way We Live Our Lives*, Ch. 7.

33 ibid.

34 ibid.

35 Longaker, *Facing Death and Finding Hope: A Guide to the Emotional and Spiritual Care of the Dying*, p. 188.

36 Haisch, *The God Theory*, citing an article in *The Journal of Near Death Studies* (September 2002), p. 61.

37 'Abdu'l-Bahá, *Paris Talks*, no. 23, p. 68.

10 The Extent of Suffering

1 Letter on behalf of Shoghi Effendi to an individual, 9 December 1931, in *Lights of Guidance*, no. 678.

2 Letter on behalf of Shoghi Effendi to an individual, 29 May 1935, in Shoghi Effendi, *Unfolding Destiny*, p. 434; also in *The Compilation of Compilations*, vol. I, p. 477.

3 Bahá'u'lláh, Tablet to a Physician, cited by Esslemont, *Bahá'u'lláh and the New Era*, p. 107.

4 See http://www.oddee.com/item_90608.aspx#dybqsKrhvpishdfo.99.

5 See https://www.who.int/health-topics/cancer#tab=tab_1.

6 Wikipedia: 'List of wars by death toll'.

7 ibid: 'Taiping Rebellion'.

8 ibid: 'List of famines'.

9 Fitzgerald, '10 terrible famines in History', online article, 10 April 2013.

10 WHO, *Global Status Report on Alcohol and Health 2018*, p. xv.

11 Suffering: Responsibility and Detachment

1 Sample, 'NASA has figured out how the world will end', in *The Guardian*, 22 October 2015.

2 Cain, 'How long will life survive on planet Earth?', online article in *Universe Today*, 30 September 2013.

3 Cain, 'The end of everything', online article in *Universe Today*, 25 July 2007.

4 Quoted by Bahá'u'lláh in 'The Seven Valleys', in Bahá'u'lláh, *The Call of the Divine Beloved*, p. 44.

5   Matt. 6:19–21.
6   'Abdu'l-Bahá, *Paris Talks*, no. 35, p. 110.
7   'Abdu'l-Bahá, *The Promulgation of Universal Peace*, p. 90.
8   'Abdu'l-Bahá, *Abdul Baha on Divine Philosophy*, p. 134.
9   'Abdu'l-Bahá, *The Promulgation of Universal Peace*, p. 236.
10 Bahá'u'lláh, *The Kitáb-i-Aqdas*, para. 148, p. 73.
11 Bahá'u'lláh, *Tablets of Bahá'u'lláh*, p. 71.
12 For a discussion of the Golden Rule in different cultures see, for example, http://en.wikipedia.org/wiki/Golden_Rule.
13 Talmud, Shabbat 31a.
14 Matt 7:12.
15 ibid. 22:39.
16 *Forty Hadith of an-Nawawi*, no. 13.
17 Anusasana Parva 113.8.
18 Quoted in Woolson, *Divine Symphony*, p. 3.
19 ibid. p. 2.
20 Yoruba proverb, Nigeria.
21 https://www.rgs.org/schools/teaching-resources/.
22 Saifullah, 'Causes of flooding in Bangladesh', 27 March 2009.
23 Bahá'u'lláh, *Hidden Words*, Arabic no. 51.
24 'Abdu'l-Bahá, *Abdul Baha on Divine Philosophy*, p. 118.
25 Bahá'u'lláh, *Gleanings from the Writings of Bahá'u'lláh*, CIX, p. 215.
26 ibid. CVI, p. 213.
27 Frankl, *Man's Search for Ultimate Meaning*, p. 32.
28 Information on cystic fibrosis available at: http://www.medicinenet.com/cystic_fibrosis/page4.htm.
29 'Abdu'l-Bahá, *Paris Talks*, no. 35, p. 110.
30 ibid.
31 ibid. pp. 110–11.
32 ibid. p. 11.
33 ibid.
34 Buddha, The Eightfold Path.
35 'Abdu'l-Bahá, *'Abdu'l-Bahá in London*, pp. 119–20 (in an interview with Isabel Fraser).
36 ibid. p. 121.
37 Bahá'u'lláh, *Gleanings from the Writings of Bahá'u'lláh*, CIX, p. 215.
38 Abdu'l-Bahá, *Abdul Baha on Divine Philosophy*, p. 136.
39 ibid. pp. 136–7.
40 Bahá'u'lláh, *Gleanings from the Writings of Bahá'u'lláh*, LXXXV, p. 169.
41 Bahá'u'lláh, *Bahá'í Prayers*, p. 52.
42 Bahá'u'lláh, *Hidden Words*, Arabic no. 51.
43 'Abdu'l-Bahá, *Selections from the Writings of 'Abdu'l-Bahá*, no. 197, p. 239.

12 Oppressors and the Suffering of the Innocent

1   Shoghi Effendi, *The World Order of Bahá'u'lláh*, pp. 193–4.
2   Bahá'u'lláh, quoted in Shoghi Effendi, *The Advent of Divine Justice*, p. 23.
3   Bahá'u'lláh, *Gleanings from the Writings of Bahá'u'lláh*, XII, p. 17.
4   Bahá'u'lláh, *Hidden Words*, Persian no. 64.
5   Bahá'u'lláh, *The Summons of the Lord of Hosts*, pp. 206–7.
6   ibid. p. 226.
7   The Universal House of Justice, 'Child abuse, psychology and knowledge of self', 2 December 1985.
8   ibid.
9   'Abdu'l-Bahá, quoted ibid.
10 'Abdu'l-Bahá, *The Promulgation of Universal Peace*, p. 89.
11 Bahá'u'lláh, *Gleanings from the Writings of Bahá'u'lláh*, CXIV, p. 236.
12 Bahá'u'lláh, *Hidden Words*, Arabic no. 31.
13 Bahá'u'lláh, in *The Call of the Divine Beloved*, p. 95.
14 Bahá'u'lláh, quoted in Shoghi Effendi, *The Advent of Divine Justice*, p. 64.
15 ibid. p. 71.
16 'Abdu'l-Bahá, *The Promulgation of Universal Peace*, p. 89.
17 Bahá'u'lláh, *Gleanings from the Writings of Bahá'u'lláh*, LXXXI, pp. 156–7.

13 Free Will

1   'Abdu'l-Bahá, *Some Answered Questions*, ch. 70, p. 287.
2   ibid.
3   'Free will', in *Catholic Encyclopedia*, online at: http://www.newadvent.org/cathen/06259a.htm.
4   ibid.
5   'Abdu'l-Bahá, *Some Answered Questions*, ch. 70, p. 287.
6   Shoghi Effendi, *God Passes By*, p. 201; information from Taherzadeh, *The Revelation of Bahá'u'lláh*, vol. 4, p. 387.
7   Esslemont, *Bahá'u'lláh and the New Era*, p. 131.
8   'In the Ghetto', words and music by Scott Davis.
9   Teichman and Evans, *Philosophy: A Beginners Guide*, p. 44.
10 Matt. 7:1–2.
11 Bahá'u'lláh, *Hidden Words*, Persian no. 40.
12 'Abdu'l-Bahá, Tablet to the Hague, in *Selections from the Writings of 'Abdu'l-Bahá*, no. 227, p. 302.

14 Free Will and the Power of the Manifestations of God

1   Bahá'u'lláh, *Tablets of Bahá'u'lláh*, p. 197.
2   ibid. pp. 108–9.
3   The Báb, *Selections from the Writings of the Báb*, p. 68.

4   Gen. 1:28.

5   Bahá'u'lláh, quoted in Shoghi Effendi, 'The Dispensation of Bahá'u'lláh', in *The World Order of Bahá'u'lláh*, p. 116.

6   Bahá'u'lláh, *The Summons of the Lord of Hosts*, p. 142.

7   Quoted in Taherzadeh, *The Revelation of Bahá'u'lláh*, vol. 3, p. 303.

8   ibid. vol. 2, p. 9.

9   Bahá'u'lláh, 'The Seven Valleys', in Bahá'u'lláh, *The Call of the Divine Beloved*, p. 46.

10 *UK Bahá'í*, no. 24 (December 2017), pp. 8–9.

11 Shoghi Effendi, *God Passes By*, p. 136.

12 Taherzadeh, *The Revelation of Bahá'u'lláh*, vol. 1, p. 102.

13 ibid.

14 Shoghi Effendi, *God Passes By*, p. 136.

15 ibid. p. 135.

16 Faizi, 'A flame of fire'.

17 Bahá'u'lláh, *Kitáb-i-Íqán*, para. 144, p. 133.

18 John 19:10–11.

19 'Abdu'l-Bahá, *Some Answered Questions*, ch. 70, pp. 288–9.

20 ibid. p. 289.

15 Evil and How to Counter It

1   'Abdu'l-Bahá, *Paris Talks*, no. 56, p. 190.

2   'Abdu'l-Bahá, *Some Answered Questions*, pp. 303–4.

3   **'Light** or **visible light** is electromagnetic radiation within the portion of the electromagnetic spectrum that is perceived by the human eye . . . In physics, the term "light" sometimes refers to electromagnetic radiation of any wavelength, whether visible or not . . . Like all types of electromagnetic radiation, visible light propagates as waves. However, the energy imparted by the waves is absorbed at single locations the way particles are absorbed. The absorbed energy of the electromagnetic waves is called a photon and represents the quanta of light. When a wave of light is transformed and absorbed as a photon, the energy of the wave instantly collapses to a single location and this location is where the photon «arrives». This is what is called the wave function collapse. This dual wave-like and particle-like nature of light is known as the wave–particle duality' (Wikipedia: 'Light').

4   https://www.newscientist.com/article/mg21128274-700-photons-made . . .

5   'Abdu'l-Bahá, *Some Answered Questions*, pp. 303–4.

6   'Abdu'l-Bahá, *Selections from the Writings of 'Abdu'l-Bahá*, pp. 130–31.

7   Bahá'u'lláh, *The Kitáb-i-Aqdas*, para. 138, p. 69.

8   Letter written on behalf of Shoghi Effendi to an individual, 4 October 1950, in *Lights of Guidance*, no. 1341, p. 404.

9   The Universal House of Justice, *One Common Faith*.

10   ibid.
11   ibid.
12   'Abdu'l-Bahá, *Paris Talks*, no. 39, p. 123.

16 Does God Allow Evil? A More Involved Answer

1   Bahá'u'lláh, *Gleanings from the Writings of Bahá'u'lláh*, XXVII, p. 65.
2   Bahá'u'lláh, *Tablets of Bahá'u'lláh*, p. 140.
3   'Abdu'l-Bahá, *Paris Talks*, no. 23, p. 68.
4   'Abdu'l-Bahá, *The Promulgation of Universal Peace*, p. 378.
5   'Abdu'l-Bahá, *Paris Talks*, no. 36, p. 114.
6   'Abdu'l-Bahá, *The Promulgation of Universal Peace*, p. 352.
7   Bahá'u'lláh, *Gleanings from the Writings of Bahá'u'lláh*, XXVII, p. 65.
8   ibid. LXXVII, p. 149.
9   Quoted in Bahá'u'lláh, *Days of Remembrance*, no. 9, para. 1.
10   Bahá'u'lláh, *Tablets of Bahá'u'lláh*, p. 21.
11   Bahá'u'lláh, *The Summons of the Lord of Hosts*, p. 23.
12   Bahá'u'lláh, *Tablets of Bahá'u'lláh*, p. 23.
13   http://www.thefreedictionary.com/holy+war.
14   http://www.bbc.co.uk/religion/religions/buddhism/buddhistethics/war.shtml.
15   Bahá'u'lláh, *Epistle to the Son of the Wolf*, para. 18, p. 14.

17 No Imperfections in Creation

1   Bahá'u'lláh, *Gleanings from the Writings of Bahá'u'lláh*, LXXVII, p. 150.
2   'Abdu'l-Bahá, *The Promulgation of Universal Peace*, p. 93.
3   Qur'án 67.
4   'Abdu'l-Bahá, *Some Answered Questions*, ch. 46, pp. 203–4.
5   'Abdu'l-Bahá, *The Promulgation of Universal Peace*, p. 79.
6   'Abdu'l-Bahá, *Selections from the Writings of 'Abdu'l-Bahá*, no. 103, p. 130.
7   'Abdu'l-Bahá, *Paris Talks*, no. 55, pp. 189–90.
8   ibid.
9   ibid.

18 Gradual Emergence of Maturity

1   See http://en.wikipedia.org/wiki/Human_evolution.
2   ibid.
3   ibid.
4   'Abdu'l-Bahá, *The Promulgation of Universal Peace*, pp. 69–70.
5   'Abdu'l-Bahá, quoted in Shoghi Effendi, *The World Order of Bahá'u'lláh*, p. 164.
6   Shoghi Effendi, ibid. pp. 163–4.
7   Vitelli, 'Storming into adulthood: Are adolescents really emotional

volcanoes waiting to explode?', in *Media Spotlight*, 30 September 2013.

8   'Abdu'l-Bahá, *The Promulgation of Universal Peace*, p. 295.

9   Shoghi Effendi, *The World Order of Bahá'u'lláh*, p. 202.

10 For a brief description of Piaget's work see www.simplypsychology. org/piaget.htm; among the various web sites outlining support and criticism of Piaget's Theory, see https://www.verywellmind.com/ support-and-criticism-of-piagets-stage-theory-2795460.

11 Cherry, 'The sensorimotor stage of cognitive development'.

12 ibid.

13 McLeod, 'Concrete operational stage'.

14 ibid.

15 Cherry, 'The sensorimotor stage of cognitive development'.

16 ibid.

17 The Universal House of Justice, *One Common Faith*.

18 Cherry, 'The sensorimotor stage of cognitive development'.

19 'Abdu'l-Bahá, *The Promulgation of Universal Peace*, p. 288.

20 'Abdu'l-Bahá, *'Abdu'l-Bahá in London*, p. 89.

21 Bahá'u'lláh, *Gleanings from the Writings of Bahá'u'lláh*, LXXXVII, p. 172.

22 Letter on behalf of Shoghi Effendi to an individual, 4 October 1950, in *Lights of Guidance*, no. 1696, p. 504.

23 'Abdu'l-Bahá, *The Promulgation of Universal Peace*, p. 463.

24 Shoghi Effendi, *The World Order of Bahá'u'lláh*, p. 58.

25 Bahá'u'lláh, *Gems of Divine Mysteries*, p. 15.

26 Matt. 25:30.

27 Qur'án 47:15.

28 Bahá'u'lláh, *Gleanings from the Writings of Bahá'u'lláh*, LXXXI, p. 156.

19 Interpreting History in Terms of an Evolutionary Process

1   Bahá'u'lláh, *Kitáb-i-Íqán*, para. 183, p. 171.

2   Bahá'u'lláh, *Gleanings from the Writings of Bahá'u'lláh*, CXX, p. 255.

3   ibid. CXVII, p. 250.

4   Bahá'u'lláh, *Tablets of Bahá'u'lláh*, p. 138.

5   Sabet, *The Heavens Are Cleft Asunder*, p. 42.

6   ibid. pp. 40–41.

7   Deut. 5:17.

8   Luke 6:27.

9   Matt. 18:22.

10 Qur'án 2: 256.

11 The Universal House of Justice, *Century of Light*, p. 90.

12 Townshend, *The Heart of the Gospel*, p. 43.

20 Divine Intervention or Not?

1   See http://www.buddhistchannel.tv/parami/buddhistanswers/what_about_miracles.htm.
2   ibid.
3   Matt. 12:38–39.
4   Matt. 6:33.
5   Bahá'u'lláh, *Gleanings from the Writings of Bahá'u'lláh*, XXXIV, p. 80.
6   ibid. CVI, p. 213.
7   ibid, CXXXI, p. 286.
8   Shoghi Effendi, *The Promised Day Is Come*, p. 88.
9   http://judaism.about.com/od/jewishhistory/a/greatrevolt.htm.
10 https://en.wikipedia.org/wiki/Siege_of_Jerusalem_(70).
11 ibid. quoting Milman, *The History of the Jews*, Book 16.
12 Matt. 22:17–21.
13 Matt. 26:51–52.
14 Luke 6:27.
15 Luke 6:28–32.
16 Luke 19: 42–44.
17 Shoghi Effendi, *The Promised Day Is Come*, pp. 5–6.
18 ibid. p. 118.
19 ibid.
20 'Abdu'l-Bahá, *Paris Talks*, no. 6, p. 20.
21 'Abdu'l-Bahá, *'Abdu'l-Bahá in London*, p. 19.
22 The Universal House of Justice, *Century of Light*, p. 28.
23 ibid. p. 3.
24 Handwerk, '"Bird flu" similar to deadly 1918 flu, gene study finds', in *National Geographic News*, 5 October 2005.
25 See http://en.wikipedia.org/wikiWorld_War_1casualties.
26 See http://en.wikipedia.org/wiki/World_War_II_casualties.
27 ibid.
28 Shoghi Effendi, *The Promised Day Is Come*, p. 108.
29 ibid. pp. 117–18.
30 Bahá'u'lláh, *Gleanings from the Writings of Bahá'u'lláh*, XLIII, p. 92.
31 ibid. CX, pp. 216—17.
32 Ibid. IV, p. 7.
33 Bahá'u'lláh, quoted by Shoghi Effendi, *The Promised Day Is Come*, p. 121.
34 Bahá'u'lláh, *Gleanings from the Writings of Bahá'u'lláh*, CIV, pp. 209–10.
35 Bahá'u'lláh, quoted by Shoghi Effendi, *The Promised Day Is Come*, p. 1.
36 Bahá'u'lláh, *Gleanings from the Writings of Bahá'u'lláh*, LXI, pp. 118–19.
37 Bahá'u'lláh, *The Summons of the Lord of Hosts*, p. 82.
38 Bahá'u'lláh, *Gleanings from the Writings of Bahá'u'lláh*, CXXXI, p. 286.

39 Bahá'u'lláh, *The Summons of the Lord of Hosts*, p. 226.
40 Bahá'í International Community statement, *Bahá'u'lláh*.

21 God Is Always Involved in His Creation

1   'Abdu'l-Bahá, *The Promulgation of Universal Peace*, p. 361.
2   ibid. p. 58.
3   'Abdu'l-Bahá, *Tablets of Abdul-Baha Abbas*, vol. III, p. 611.
4   'Abdu'l-Bahá, *The Promulgation of Universal Peace*, p. 286.
5   ibid. p. 58.
6   Bahá'u'lláh, *Gleanings from the Writings of Bahá'u'lláh*, XCIII, p. 189.
7   'Abdu'l-Bahá, *Some Answered Questions*, ch. 51, p. 229.
8   I have used the term 'observable universe' as presently accepted by a great number of cosmologists. There are many diverse theories concerning the universe and its possible creation. One in-depth study of these theories is set forth by the Christian cosmologist the Revd Dr Rodney Holder in *Big Bang, Big God* (2013). Dr Holder is a former Course Director of the Faraday Institute for Science and Religion, Cambridge. There are also many videos available on this subject that present complex cosmological subjects in a digestible way (see, for example, YouTube).
9   https://www.sciencealert.com/big-bang.
10 'Abdu'l-Bahá, *Paris Talks*, no. 29, p. 88.
11 'Abdu'l-Bahá, *Some Answered Questions*, ch. 47, pp. 209–10.
12 'Abdu'l-Bahá, *Abdul Baha on Divine Philosophy*, p. 165.
13 www.realclear.com/science/2013/07/09/extreme_animals.
14 'Abdu'l-Bahá, *Selections from the Writings of 'Abdu'l-Bahá*, no. 72, p. 110.

22 Disbelief in God Linked with Exalting One Messenger Above Another

1   'Abdu'l-Bahá, *'Abdu'l-Bahá in London*, p. 19.
2   See Bartlett, *Finding the Real You*, p. 178.
3   The Universal House of Justice, Foreword to *One Common Faith* (2005).
4   The Universal House of Justice, Letter to the World's Religious Leaders, p. 7.
5   Matt. 24:12.
6   The Universal House of Justice, Letter to the World's Religious Leaders, p. 4.
7   See Shoghi Effendi, *God Passes By*, pp. 94–5.
8   Qur'án 31:27.
9   Bahá'u'lláh, *Gleanings from the Writings of Bahá'u'lláh*, CXI, p. 217.
10 ibid. XXI, p. 50.
11 Hall and Gieben (eds), *Formations of Modernity*, pp. 258–9.

12 Bahá'u'lláh, *Gleanings from the Writings of Bahá'u'lláh*, XXIV, pp. 59–60.
13 ibid. XXII, p. 52.
14 ibid. p. 50.
15 'Abdu'l-Bahá, *The Promulgation of Universal Peace*, p. 248.
16 'Abdu'l-Bahá, *Paris Talks*, no. 41, p. 40.
17 Bahá'u'lláh, *Kitáb-i-Íqán*, para. 175, p. 164.
18 'Abdu'l-Bahá, *The Promulgation of Universal Peace*, p. 90.
19 Bahá'u'lláh, *Gleanings from the Writings of Bahá'u'lláh*, CXLVII, pp. 316–17.
20 'Abdu'l-Bahá, *The Promulgation of Universal Peace*, p. 305.
21 Bahá'u'lláh, *Tablets of Bahá'u'lláh*, p. 36.
22 'Abdu'l-Bahá, *Some Answered Questions*, ch. 59, p. 256.
23 *Bahá'í Prayers*, no. 57, p. 60.
24 Bahá'u'lláh, *Gleanings from the Writings of Bahá'u'lláh*, XXIV, p. 60.
25 ibid. LXX, p. 136.
26 ibid. CXXXII, p. 288.

23 Hell – Justice and Forgiveness

1   'The Augustinian Understanding of Hell', in *Stanford Encyclopaedia of Philosophy*.
2   Matt. 7:2.
3   Mark 3:28–29.
4   'Abdu'l-Bahá, *Some Answered Questions*, ch. 31, p. 144.
5   Bahá'u'lláh, *Gleanings from the Writings of Bahá'u'lláh*, LXVI, p. 130.
6   Letter written on behalf of Shoghi Effendi, to an individual, 7 February 1947, in *Lights of Guidance*, no. 615. p. 187.
7   Matt. 5:26.
8   Luke 23:34.
9   As defined in the *Concise Oxford Dictionary*.
10 Bahá'u'lláh, *Hidden Words*, Persian no. 63.
11 Bahá'u'lláh, *Gleanings from the Writings of Bahá'u'lláh*, CXXIX, p. 284.
12 Trine, 'Prelude' to *In Tune with the Infinite*.
13 Dhammapada (R. J. Richards translation).
14 Taherzadeh, *The Revelation of Bahá'u'lláh*, vol. 3, p. 296, describing a Tablet of Bahá'u'lláh in Ishráq Khávarí (comp.), *Má'idiy-i-Ásamání*, vol. 7, pp. 119–25.
15 Bahá'u'lláh, *Bahá'í Prayers*, no 22, p. 29.
16 'Abdu'l-Bahá, *Selection from the Writings of 'Abdu'l-Bahá*, no. 111, p. 136.
17 Shoghi Effendi, *God Passes By*, p. 154.
18 Bahá'u'lláh, Tablet of the Immortal Youth, para. 36, in *Days of Remembrance*.

24 Heaven – Inner Condition or Destination?

1 I Kings 8:43; Mark 11:25–26.
2 John 6: 32–33.
3 Matt. 6:10.
4 Luke 17:21.
5 Qur'án 13:35.
6 ibid. 42:21.
7 ibid. 39:21.
8 Gail, *Six Lessons on Islám*, p. 15.
9 Glossary in the UK edition of Bahá'u'lláh, *Kitáb-i-Íqán*, p. 165.
10 See http://dictionary.cambridge.org/dictionary/english/heaven.
11 See https://en.oxforddictionaries.com/definition/heaven.
12 Luke 17:21.
13 'Abdu'l-Bahá, *Some Answered Questions*, ch. 60, p. 257.
14 'Abdu'l-Bahá, *Selections from the Writings of 'Abdu'l-Bahá*, no. 199, p. 242.
15 'Abdu'l-Bahá, *Paris Talks*, no. 31, p. 96.
16 'Abdu'l-Bahá, *Selections from the Writings of 'Abdu'l-Bahá*, no. 111, p. 136.
17 ibid.
18 'Abdu'l-Bahá, *Some Answered Questions*, ch. 60, p. 257.
19 Bahá'u'lláh, Long Obligatory Prayer, in most Bahá'í prayer books.
20 'Abdu'l-Bahá, *Some Answered Questions*, ch. 30, p. 142.
21 Bahá'u'lláh, *Hidden Words*, Persian no. 10.
22 Bahá'u'lláh, *Gleanings from the Writings of Bahá'u'lláh*, LXXXVI, p. 170.
23 ibid. XXVII, pp. 65–6.
24 ibid. p. 66.
25 Bahá'u'lláh, *Epistle to the Son of the Wolf*, p. 132.
26 Quoted in Shoghi Effendi, *God Passes By*, p. 194.
27 ibid. p. 186.
28 Matt. 28:20.
29 Eccl. 3:11.
30 Bahá'u'lláh, *Gleanings from the Writings of Bahá'u'lláh*, CXLVI, p. 316.
31 Bahá'u'lláh, *Tablets of Bahá'u'lláh*, p. 189.
32 'Abdu'l-Bahá, *Selections from the Writings of 'Abdu'l-Bahá*, no. 156, p. 184.

25 Material and Spiritual Progress Should Go Hand in Hand

1 'Abdu'l-Bahá, *'Abdu'l-Bahá in London*, pp. 28–9.
2 'Abdu'l-Bahá, *Paris Talks*, no. 23, p. 67.
3 Cooke-Taylor, *Tour in Manufacturing Districts of Lancashire*.
4 'Abdu'l-Bahá, *The Promulgation of Universal Peace*, p. 96.
5 Shoghi Effendi, *The World Order of Bahá'u'lláh*, pp. 187–8.

6 Bahá'u'lláh, *Gleanings from the Writings of Bahá'u'lláh*, CXXIII, p. 261.
7 ibid. LXVI, p. 127.
8 ibid. CXXIII, p. 261.
9 Baha'i International Community, *The Prosperity of Humankind.*

26 The Proof of the Sun is the Sun Itself

1 'Abdu'l-Bahá, *Some Answered Questions*, ch. 59, p. 254.
2 Bahá'u'lláh, in *Bahá'í Prayers*, p. 165, and in many other Bahá'í prayer books.
3 'Abdu'l-Bahá, *Paris Talks*, no. 34, pp. 108–9.
4 I John 4:12.
5 Shoghi Effendi, *The World Order of Bahá'u'lláh*, p. 112.
6 ibid. p. 113, quoting the words of Bahá'u'lláh.
7 ibid. p. 112.
8 Bahá'u'lláh, *Tablets of Bahá'u'lláh*, p. 61.
9 Bahá'u'lláh, *Gleanings from the Writings of Bahá'u'lláh*, XXI, pp. 49–50.
10 Shoghi Effendi, *The World Order of Bahá'u'lláh*, p. 112.
11 ibid.
12 'Abdu'l-Bahá, *Selections from the Writings of 'Abdu'l-Bahá*, no. 21, p. 50.
13 'Abdu'l-Bahá, *Some Answered Questions*, ch. 59, p. 254.
14 Bahá'u'lláh, *Gleanings from the Writings of Bahá'u'lláh*, XXI, p. 50.

27 A Focus on Bahá'u'lláh

1 Bahá'u'lláh, *Gleanings from the Writings of Bahá'u'lláh*, CXXVII, pp. 272–3.
2 'Abdu'l-Bahá, quoted in Esslemont, *Bahá'u'lláh and the New Era*, pp. 29–30.
3 Shoghi Effendi, *God Passes By*, pp. 135–6.
4 ibid. p. 149.
5 Taherzadeh, *The Child of the Covenant*, p. 70.
6 Quoted in Shoghi Effendi, *God Passes By*, p. 155.
7 ibid. p. 175.
8 'Abdu'l-Bahá, *Abdul Baha on Divine Philosophy*, p. 54.
9 'Abdu'l-Bahá, *The Promulgation of Universal Peace*, p. 467.
10 Taherzadeh, *The Child of the Covenant*, p. 19.
11 Matthews, *The Challenge of Bahá'u'lláh*, pp. 172–3.
12 'Abdu'l-Bahá, *Some Answered Questions*, ch. 9, p. 40.
13 Taherzadeh, *The Revelation of Bahá'u'lláh*, vol. 2, pp. 348–9.
14 Balyuzi, *Bahá'u'lláh, the King of Glory*, pp. 164–5.
15 Shoghi Effendi, *God Passes By*, p. 138.
16 ibid. p. 139.
17 Quoted in Taherzadeh, *The Revelation of Bahá'u'lláh*, vol. 3, p. 161. Taherzadeh comments: 'These are not to be taken as the exact words which Bahá'u'lláh spoke on that occasion.

18 'Abdu'l-Bahá, *Some Answered Questions*, ch. 40, p. 180.
19 'Abdu'l-Bahá, *Tablets of Abdul Baha Abbas*, vol. III, p. 713.
20 John 16:12.
21 Shoghi Effendi, *God Passes By*, p. 138.
22 ibid.
23 Quoted in Taherzadeh, *The Revelation of Bahá'u'lláh*, vol. 1, pp. 36–7.
24 Bahá'u'lláh, quoted in Shoghi Effendi, *God Passes By*, p. 171.
25 Qur'án 31:27.
26 The Universal House of Justice, Message to the Bahá'ís of the World, Riḍván 156, 1999, p. 4.

28 Some Concluding Thoughts for All Who Wish to Navigate the Materialistic Minefields of this Age

1 'Abdu'l-Bahá, *Selections from the Writings of 'Abdu'l-Bahá*, no. 157, p. 186.
2 'Abdu'l-Bahá, *The Promulgation of Universal Peace*, p. 186.
3 Bahá'u'lláh, *Gleanings from the Writings of Bahá'u'lláh*, CXXII, p. 260.
4 ibid. CXXX, p. 285.
5 Bahá'u'lláh, *Hidden Words*, Persian no. 5.
6 'Abdu'l-Bahá, *Selections from the Writings of 'Abdu'l-Bahá*, no. 100, p. 127.
7 'Abdu'l-Bahá, *Paris Talks*, no. 23, p. 68.
8 Bahá'u'lláh, *Gleanings from the Writings of Bahá'u'lláh*, CXXXII, p. 289, and XLIII, p. 95.
9 Ives, *Portals to Freedom*, p. 242.
10 'Abdu'l-Bahá, *The Promulgation of Universal Peace*, p. 89.
11 Bahá'u'lláh, *Hidden Words*, Persian no. 10.
12 ibid.
13 'Abdu'l-Bahá, *Selections from the Writings of 'Abdu'l-Bahá*, no. 7, p. 20.
14 Bahá'u'lláh, in *Days of Remembrance*, p. 151.
15 Mark 10:15.
16 'Abdu'l-Bahá, *Paris Talks*, no. 41, p. 140.
17 Bahá'u'lláh, *Gleanings from the Writings of Bahá'u'lláh*, LXXXII, p. 158.
18 'Abdu'l-Bahá, in most Bahá'í prayer books.
19 Bahá'u'lláh, *Gleanings from the Writings of Bahá'u'lláh*, CIX, p. 215.
20 Bahá'u'lláh, *The Summons of the Lord of Hosts*, p. 91.
21 The Universal House of Justice, *One Common Faith*.
22 'Abdu'l-Bahá, *Selections from the Writings of 'Abdu'l-Bahá*, no. 154, p. 181.
23 https://en.wikipedia.org/wiki/Srinivasa_Ramanujan.
24 Bahá'u'lláh, *Gleanings from the Writings of Bahá'u'lláh*, XXXIV, pp. 81–2.

ABOUT THE AUTHOR

Born and brought up in Cardiff, Viv Bartlett left school at 15 with no qualifications and entered the world of work as an apprentice in an engineering firm, playing guitar in a rock group in his spare time. At 20 he became a Bahá'í and shortly after qualified as a tradesman, joining the Merchant Navy as a Junior Engineer Officer. After travelling the world for two years he came home to South Wales, married and had children, and decided to become a teacher. Attending night school three evenings a week after work brought him the qualifications to go to college and by the age of 30 he had a B. Ed Hons degree and started teaching Design and Technology in a large secondary school in Newport. Later on in life he and his wife, Rita, became foster-carers.

Viv served on several national Bahá'í committees, including the Welsh Teaching Committee until 1976. As an Auxiliary Board Member for Wales and Southwest England for over 20 years he had an educational and pastoral role in the community with a special interest in the development of young people. Between 1999 and 2004 he served on the Bahá'í Training Institute for Wales and then on the first elected Bahá'í Council for Wales. He has travelled extensively lecturing on the Bahá'í Faith.

He is a founder member of the Interfaith Council for Wales and served as a Bahá'í representative from 2003 until recently. In parallel, he served as a member of the Interfaith Forum of Wales (a separate body to the Council) which meets regularly in consultation with the Wales Assembly Government's First Minister, other Ministers, and government agencies.

Viv's book *Nurturing a Healthy Human Spirit in the Young* (2014) documents the endeavours of the Swindon Young People's Empowerment Programme (SYEP), established in 2000, of which Viv is a founder member. Based on Bahá'í teachings, this programme was welcomed into over 20 primary and secondary schools in Swindon; Viv is now introducing it into schools in Wales. He has also written a chapter on the history of the Bahá'í Faith in Wales for the Welsh Academic Press publication (2014) titled *The Religious History of Wales*. More recently he and a Bahá'í colleague have worked with educational writers to include information on the Bahá'í Faith for teachers of the new Welsh Curriculum focused on 'Religion, Values and Ethics' in primary and secondary schools.